Times of Trouble

This book was published with the support of

THE UNIVERSITY OF SOUTHERN CALIFORNIA

THE UNIVERSITY OF ILLINOIS AT URBANA-CHAMPAIGN

THE UNIVERSITY OF CALIFORNIA, DAVIS
DEPARTMENT OF HISTORY

WASHINGTON AND LEE UNIVERSITY

THE UNIVERSITY OF NEW HAMPSHIRE
CENTER FOR THE HUMANITIES and
THE COLLEGE OF LIBERAL ARTS

THE DEPARTMENT OF RUSSIAN AND SLAVIC STUDIES,
UNIVERSITY OF ARIZONA

THE DIVISION OF ARTS AND SCIENCES,
BRANDEIS UNIVERSITY

ANONYMOUS DONORS

Times of Trouble

Violence in Russian Literature and Culture

Edited by

MARCUS C. LEVITT

and

TATYANA NOVIKOV

THE UNIVERSITY OF WISCONSIN PRESS

The University of Wisconsin Press
1930 Monroe Street
Madison, Wisconsin 53711

www.wisc.edu/wisconsinpress/

3 Henrietta Street
London WC2E 8LU, England

5 4 3 2 1

Library of Congress Cataloging-in-Publication Data
Times of trouble : violence in Russian literature and culture /
edited by Marcus C. Levitt and Tatyana Novikov.
p. cm.
Includes bibliographical references and index.
ISBN 0-299-22430-9 (cloth: alk. paper)
1. Russian literature—Themes, motives. 2. Violence in literature.
3. Violence—Russia—History. 4. Violence—Soviet Union—History
I. Levitt, Marcus C., 1954- II. Novikov, Tatyana, 1952-
PG2986.T56 2007
891.709´3552—dc22 2007011822

Contents

Preface

The escalating violence of the modern world has increasingly begun to dominate the national consciousness and is causing a dramatic shift in the American view of the world. The premise underlying the discussions in this book is that much can be learned from investigating violence in literature and culture, a process that can foster a better grasp of the phenomenon. The book represents one of the first studies dedicated to the problem of violence in Russia. While Russia surely has no exclusive claim to violence, the problem of violence has been a constant concern throughout its history, as the essays in the volume show. Nevertheless it is hard to gainsay the fact that the Russian twentieth century was arguably the bloodiest epoch in world history (second only in numbers to the Black Plague of the fourteenth century, although that was a natural rather than human-made catastrophe as in Russia); this was the age that contributed such terms as "pogrom," "purges," and "Gulag" to our everyday discourse, and there are those who argue that the problems of ideological violence and terrorism today have their roots in the Russian (and especially Soviet) experience.

This volume offers a spectrum of analyses of violence in Russian history, literature, and culture. Topics include capital punishment and violence in war; in government conflicts and revolutions; against ethnic groups—Jews and Chechens; in concentration camps; and against women; as well as violence as an ingrained problem in human society and culture. The works of fiction and art analyzed by the authors of this volume exhibit a rich diversity, and include historical narratives, classical, absurdist, postmodern, and feminist fiction, Web-posted memoirs, as well as painting and art criticism. Historical essays explore specific periods of Russian history that have been particularly marked with violence, starting with the impact of Mongol invasion on Russian culture and especially focused on tracing the tradition of modern political violence in Russia from nineteenth-century "nihilism" through the present day. In the process, the articles explore national identity and raise matters of responsibility, effect, and redemption on personal, communal, and national levels.

Arranged chronologically, the articles by prominent American and European scholars cover a wide range of historical periods, writers, materials, and issues, recognizing and stressing the thematic centrality of violence in Russian literature and culture. The volume is designed to address the ongoing need for college-level materials on the topic of violence, and is to some degree a synthesis of current scholarship, but it is hoped that it may also find an audience among enthusiasts of Russian history and culture and stimulate the work of specialists. We hope that the volume will find a niche in courses on Russian literature, history, culture, as well as for those on more specialized courses on topics such as violence in Russian culture, terrorism in Russia, women in Russian culture, and others.

Transliteration from the Cyrillic to the Latin alphabet is a perennial problem. The editors have used a modification of the Library of Congress system in the text, substituting standardized American spelling for well-known names (e.g., Dostoevsky instead of Dostoevskii, Archangel instead of Arkhangel'sk).

The editors would like to thank the reviewers of the University of Wisconsin Press for their comments and helpful suggestions on an earlier draft of this book. We would also like to thank all the participants for their contributions to the current volume. Our special thanks go to the University of Southern California, the University of California at Davis, Washington and Lee University, Brandeis University, University of Arizona, University of Pennsylvania, University of Illinois at Urbana-Champaign, University of New Hampshire Center for the Humanities and the College of Liberal Arts, and many anonymous donors for generous financial support in the preparation and production of this volume. Lastly, the editors note with sadness the loss of our colleague Daniel Brower, who passed away during the preparation of this volume.

Times of Trouble

Introduction

The Consciousness of Violence in Russian History and Culture

MARCUS C. LEVITT

There is something in our blood that resists all real progress. In a word, we have lived, and live now merely to furnish some great lesson to a remote posterity.

Peter Chaadaev, *First Letter on the Philosophy of History*

Of course you are right when you say that it is not new . . . but what is *really* original in it . . . is that you uphold bloodshed as *a matter of conscience* . . .

Razumikhin on Raskolnikov's theory of the superman, in Dostoevsky's *Crime and Punishment*

Russia offers a most favorable soil for the experiments and fantasies of the artist, though his lot as a human being is sometimes terrible indeed.

Andrei Siniavskii, *A Voice from the Chorus*

Human beings are remarkably brutal creatures, but Russian culture, it seems, has been particularly and emphatically marked by violence. Russians and non-Russians have long debated the reasons for the country's endemic violence and the factors that shaped what Vladimir Nabokov called "a country famous for its misfortunes."[1] Some have cited Russia's unforgiving climate as something that determined the national character and destiny, while others have pointed to the country's huge size and exposed geographical position as things that made invasion easy and keeping order difficult. Some have tried to fix the blame on particular rulers or unfortunate episodes in the nation's history, and others on broader patterns of cultural development. In the latter category, for example, there have been those who trace Russia's alleged lack of legal consciousness to the legacy of Byzantium, from which the early rulers of Kievan Rus' received Christianity, literacy, and their political and cultural identity. Others have regarded Kievan Rus' as a lost golden age and have held the devastating Mongol invasion of the mid-thirteenth century responsible both for demolishing Kievan civilization and for retarding Russia's progress vis à vis the rest of Europe. Still others have implicated the first "tsar," Ivan IV (the Terrible, 1533–84), for his extension of Russian autocratic rule and for the disastrous wars of the later sixteenth century. These shaped Russia's traumatic contact with the West and led to the infamous "Time of Troubles" of 1603–13, a period of interregnum and foreign invasion.[2] A common debate since Peter I (the Great, 1685–1725) has been the questionable legacy of his forcible, top-down westernization—what a recent Russian history of his reign calls an unfortunate pattern of "progress through coercion."[3] Last but certainly not least in this catalogue of explanations, many, especially since the collapse of the USSR, point to the Revolution of 1917 (and some to Stalin's bloody rule), as Russia's greatest "tragedy," and even as "history's turning point."[4] The French historian Hélène Carrère d'Encausse has even attempted to generalize violence as the overriding theme and "malady" of Russian history in her book *The Russian Syndrome: One Thousand Years of Political Murder*.[5]

Whether or not political murder is a specifically *Russian* syndrome is debatable, and almost all of the above-mentioned diagnoses of violence in Russian history remain a matter of opinion, subject to a greater or lesser degree of verifiability. In the opening chapter of our collection, Charles Halperin effectively challenges one of them—the widespread truism encapsulated in the proverb "Scratch a Russian, find a Tatar"—often attributed to Napoleon Bonaparte—suggesting that the Mongol invasion and rule bequeathed a legacy of violence and barbarism to the Russian body politic. What is perhaps equally striking as the debunking of this myth is its longevity, despite the dearth of hard evidence as Halperin demonstrates. Perhaps we should speak here about the Russian cultural imperative to mythologize violence, Russians' preoccupation with making sense of it and coming up with narratives within which to interpret national traumas and dislocations. Along with Peter Chaadaev, cited in the first epigraph to this introduction, many Russians have sought "some great lesson" in Russia's hard-luck history, whether it be good or bad. For the cultural historian, what seems most conspicuous about political violence in Russia is not so much its existence or scale as the fact that throughout Russian history violence has been acknowledged and articulated as a central problem, whether in the realm of theology, ethics, or politics. A major example from the modern period is the espousal of revolutionary terrorism—the first reasoned apologia for political violence as a purposeful tool, and for some even an entire political program. In their articles in this volume Daniel Brower and J. Frank Goodwin discuss the genesis and development of this phenomenon. From the very beginning of its written history, however, the Russian theological tradition placed the problem of violence front and center, valorizing humility and Christ-like self-sacrifice in the face of violence as fundamental to the Orthodox notion of selfhood and national definition. This idea, which the belligerently atheist revolutionary tradition self-consciously turned on its head, was championed in the modern period in Leo Tolstoy's works and his doctrine of Nonviolent Resistance (which left its mark on Gandhi and indirectly on Martin Luther King Jr.).[6]

As the essays in this book show, Russian writers have persistently turned violence into an imaginative resource, expressing harsh truths about the Russian character and its intersections with larger political, social, religious, economic, cultural, and gender systems. In the latter part of this introduction, I will survey the contributions to this volume, which examine the problem of violence over the course of the last two centuries of Russian history and culture.[7] First, however, I will make a brief excursion into earlier Russian cultural history and offer some speculation on the roots of this phenomenon—the *yin* and *yang* of violence and nonviolence in Russia.

As the subtitle to d'Encausse's book—*One Thousand Years of Political Murder*—suggests, she identifies violence as lying at the very origin of Russian historical consciousness. She sees this even in Grand Prince Vladimir's very decision to convert his people to Christianity in the year 988. She writes: "Vladimir the conqueror devoted all of his violence to the service of God. He unleashed it on the multiple [pagan] gods revered only yesterday: all the idols were smashed and the huge statue of Perun publicly whipped before being thrown into the Dnieper. The same violence was used to baptize his people. . . . Entering Christianity as a soldier, Vladimir was to become the soldier of God."[8] The symbolic act of overthrowing false gods and erecting new ones resounds strongly in Russian culture—one might recall the dismantling of the huge statue of Alexander III that opens Eisenstein's film *Ten Days That Shook the World* (a.k.a. *October*, 1927); the toppling of the statue of Felix Dzerzhinskii, founder of the Soviet secret police, on Lubianka Square in Moscow, which marked the end of the USSR in 1991; or the equally symbolic replicating of Moscow's Cathedral of Christ the Savior, demolished by Stalin in 1933, to mark the city's 850th anniversary in 1997. (Stalin's plan had been to erect a gigantic "Palace of Soviets" in its place, but this proved impossible due to the site, which was used for a huge, heated outdoor swimming pool instead.)

The best analysis of this archetypal moment of violent change was made by the Russian semioticians Iurii Lotman and Boris Uspenskii in their seminal article "The Role of Dual Models in the Dynamics of Russian Culture (Up to the End of the Eighteenth Century)."[9] According to Lotman and Uspenskii, medieval Russian culture functioned according to an extreme dualistic ("bipolar") system of values that, in contrast to the Roman Catholic West, did not develop a "neutral axiological zone" to mediate between them. In terms of theology, where the West believed in an afterlife divided into three zones—Hell, Purgatory, and Heaven—in Russia there was no mediating middle realm. In earthly life this third region created room for secular values to develop; that is, it offered a field of action not sharply marked as either divine or demonic, but allowing for more complex combinations. In diachronic, historical terms, this "neutral zone" permits gradual change, whereas in the bipolar scheme the choice stands between total stasis and—as in the case of Vladimir's overthrowing of the idols—complete transformation. In a bipolar system, any change, however minor, threatens to undermine the entire system, insofar as it casts doubt on its holiness. Lotman and Uspenskii isolate two mechanisms for change in such a system: either the name is kept but the value is reversed (a former god—for example, a Perun or a Dzerzhinskii—becomes a Devil) or the name is changed but the assessment is retained (Stalin's plan to replace the Christian Cathedral of Christ the Savior with an atheist Palace of Soviets). In either case, however, despite radical change and dislocation, the underlying system of values preserves a fundamental continuity, as older, seemingly discarded values are actually preserved, albeit in inverted or renamed form. The bipolar scheme suggests an essentially ahistorical perception of history, the striving to overcome history. In the realm of social psychology, it outlines a dynamics of selfhood, seen as a sharp opposition between a good and a bad self. Thus Russian cultural oppositions are typically cast as oppositions between Self and Other, with the "Other" assuming the role of either Ideal to be attained or evil to be shunned; so both poles (such as "Russia" and the "West") in great measure represent imaginative projections. Part of the brilliance of Lotman and Uspenskii's analysis is that it exposes the underlying mechanism of cultural values as a *system*, on which *both* poles depend. It also makes us aware of the dangerous tendency to confuse cultural mythology and ideological projection with objective reality and—as several of our contributors point out—tends to blur the boundaries between art and life.

We should keep in mind that it would be wrong to apply the bipolar scheme to all aspects of Russian culture indiscriminately.[10] Nonetheless, bipolar systems are especially relevant for understanding the psychology of and philosophical justification for violence, which is typically the product of maximalist "yes or no" thinking. In general, the salient feature of violence in the Judeo-Christian and Islamic traditions may be described as not their penchant for violence per se—which they share with the family of man—but the wedding of violence and its ideological justification.[11] This is the "truly original" discovery Razumikhin sees in Raskolnikov's theory (cited as one of our epigraphs), and is what has allowed readers (like Daniel Brower in this volume) to connect Raskolnikov's philosophical experiment with political murder, nihilism with terrorism. From this perspective, the problem of political violence in the modern world may be said to have its roots in monotheism—a totalizing value system based on absolute right and wrong—and Russia simply offers one dramatic example of it.[12] Insofar as the bipolar model is framed in terms of absolute, ultimate truths, it may be said to be fundamentally "religious," even when it serves secular purposes. It lies at the root of all extremist, totalizing systems that attempt to establish utopia on earth, whether divine or artificial. As many commentators have pointed out, the many revolutionary "isms," from nihilism to Stalinism and Maoism, may be seen as kinds of "religious" belief systems.[13]

But it would also be a mistake to conclude that all monotheistic religious value systems, or the Russian bipolar model in particular, necessarily dictate violent action. As noted, another dualistic inversion marked in the Russian cultural tradition is that of nonviolence. If

Vladimir's Christianization of Russia offered the prototype of earthly revolutionary violence, the deaths of his sons, the first Russian saints, Boris and Gleb, at the hand of their elder brother Grand Prince Sviatopolk helped define Eastern Orthodoxy in Russia as the religion of "kenosis," the humble imitation of Christ.[14] While some scholars have taken a negative view of such martyrdom in the Russian religious tradition, considering it in psychoanalytic terms as a kind of "moral masochism," violence directed at the self,[15] others make a fundamental distinction between asceticism of the religious and of the revolutionary kind.[16] In any case, the image of Boris-Abel struck down by Sviatopolk-Cain provided Russian culture not only with a political legacy stemming from "an age of fratricide" (as d'Encausse terms it) but also a Biblical frame of moral reference that continues to reverberate in Russian culture. This is clearly evident, for example, in Alexander Yakovlev's recent call to Russian repentance in *A Century of Violence in Soviet Russia.* Yakovlev, a member of Gorbachev's politburo who has headed a commission for the rehabilitation of victims of communist repression, offers a painful review of the events he refers to as "neo-Cainism," taking place in "the century of Cain, the century that saw Russia ruined."[17]

The remaining authors in this volume trace various ways in which Russians have grappled with the problem of violence in the last two centuries, from the reign of Nicholas I (1825–55) to the present day. The Nikolayevan era marks a useful starting point insofar as it was this repressive monarch who tightened the censorship and established the Third Section (secret police), an era when the public sphere began to struggle for recognition. This struggle was manifested in such things as the "birth of the intelligentsia," the development of revolutionary doctrine, as well as the canonization of a modern "Russian Literature" as defined by socially conscious literary critics. In his article David Powelstock shows how violence in various forms was at the center of the life and works of Mikhail Lermontov (1814–41), whose own life and literary heroes expressed a zenith of Romantic alienation. Powelstock describes Lermontov's "wickedly ironic novel" *A Hero of Our Time* as "the seminal literary examination of violence in the Russian language." He sees the novel as a not-so-covert attack on "elements of coercive social ideology that enslave" its readers. At the same time, Powelstock mentions the paradox—registered by many other contributors—that despite the fact that Lermontov's works lay bare "the mechanisms by which violence propagates itself," the critique of violence that is offered is "in itself . . . quite violent." Nevertheless, even while Lermontov destroys illusions and poses "insoluble questions," his efforts are still "in the service of moral discovery," suggesting that responses and outcomes other than violence may at least be imagined.

In their articles, Ludmilla Trigos and Ilya Vinitsky consider the problem of public executions under Nicholas I. Vinitsky analyzes the poet Vasilii Zhukovskii's argument, shocking to his contemporaries, that ritualized public violence is needed as a means of communicating a religious ideal of community. In contrast, Trigos demonstrates how the tsar's desire to set a "fearsome example" by having the five Decembrist rebel leaders hanged in 1825 was undermined by the failure to stage a public "spectacle of the scaffold." Where Zhukovskii later argued for forceful, public, ritualized executions, Nicholas enforced a virtual press blackout, which, according to Trigos, completely backfired, turning the Decembrists into martyrs whose example helped inspire the formation of organized revolutionism. In both of these cases, the parties involved were acutely aware of violence's great potential as a means of communication, yet both are also prime examples of how easy it is for violence to convey the wrong message. This is surely a problem even in the best-controlled situations, but especially so in cases where a fragile public sphere cannot serve as "neutral zone" for the peaceful exchange of opinion but is driven to escalating extremes by both left and right.

Many of the articles in this volume suggest that the ways in which Fyodor Dostoevsky (1821–81) framed the problem of violence were exceedingly important not just for understanding his own works but for understanding how violence was conceptualized in nineteenth-century Russia in general. Elena Krasnostchekova addresses the problem of violence's effects on human psychology in her reappraisal of Dostoevsky's early novel *Netochka Nezvanova* (1849). She argues that the revised post-exile version of 1861 should not be considered unfinished, as it usually is, but that it should be read as a new genre, as a bildungsroman, a "novel of education." It should not be read as the narrative of a woman's liberation (like those of George Sand and Eugène Sue), which the early critics were disappointed in not receiving, but as the story of the heroine's long-term growth. According to Krasnotshchekova, the twist that Dostoevsky gives to the classical bildungsroman is that in his version violence plays the central role. We might pose the question this way: if the standard Enlightenment bildungsroman describes the formation of the personality, usually a male of noble or upwardly mobile social status, what happens when that process is chronicled for a woman from among the "insulted and injured" of Russia's urban poor?

In "Violence and the Word: Dostoevsky," Harriet Murav considers the problem of violence as "an effect of language" in the writer's later and more famous works. Her article continues the discussion of language as a weapon analyzed by Powelstock, and also returns to the issue of public execution, in this case discussing Nicholas I's role as author-figure in Dostoevsky's own mock execution in 1849, when his death sentence was commuted to hard labor and exile in Siberia. Even while "Dostoevsky blurs the boundaries between those who perpetrate the kinds of violent acts, those who describe the acts in verbal statements, and those who receive the statements," his goal is to overcome pain and to reassert a community of love. Of all the writers discussed in this volume, Dostoevsky arguably offers the most optimistic response to the "insoluble questions" raised not only by the violence of Russian society but implicit in language itself.

Daniel Brower chronicles "the emergence of terrorism as the principle tool of the revolutionaries" and traces the intellectual and institutional continuity between the radical "nihilist" subculture of the 1860s and later Populist terrorism. While debates over the ethics of using terror continued unresolved, revolutionary violence escalated, taking on "a dynamics of its own" that reflected the mentality of total war. But in theory, at least, for most of those Brower analyzes, terror served as a selective and pragmatic tool, a means rather than an end. This is in sharp contrast to the legacy of Mikhail Bakunin (1814–76), the "apostle" or "poet of violence," as described in J. Frank Goodwin's article. As Goodwin shows, "Bakuninism" represented one pole of a larger debate within the revolutionary movement, the "Jacobin" position—that any and all violent means were valid in the name of overthrowing the existing order. If one pole of Russia's utopian ideal was the total stasis of Holy Russia as embodiment of the Kingdom of God on earth, Bakuninist anarchism represents perhaps the closest thing to the principle of revolution for revolution's sake. Bakunin's position, which put him most famously at odds with Karl Marx, who assigned a major role to the revolutionary state, advocated instinctive, passionate, bloody, maximalist violence. To what extent Lenin should be seen as follower of Bakunin has been a subject of heated controversy, as Goodwin shows. Defining Bakunin's legacy for the Bolshevik Revolution of 1917 means defining the ideological role of violence in the revolution, and hence for the Soviet system in general. The relevance of this question for Anna Geifman's and J. Arch Getty's articles on revolutionary "Red Terror" and the character of Stalinist violence should be clear.

Kevin Platt's discussion of the public scandal that ensued when an allegedly deranged young man took a knife to Il'ia Repin's painting of Ivan IV ("Ivan the Terrible") in 1913 takes the discussion of the blurred boundaries between violence in works of art and in life to a new level: "There is a fascinating mirroring effect in this story, where an artistic response to political life is echoed by a political response to artistic life—a conflation of the murder of people with the murder of paintings, of real blood and horror with aesthetic violence and criticism." Furthermore, what was only a more or less implicit problem, as seen in Powelstock's analysis of Lermontov and Murav's of Dostoevsky, here became the subject of public debate. As Platt shows, the series of problems involving Repin's painting, from the "strangely distorting allegorical lens" of its violent subject matter to the attacks on it and on its author, also reflected a debate over the nature of the public sphere and over Russian identity. The episode suggested an opposition between Repin as a classic Russian artist, who was canonizing an important moment in national history, however difficult, and those aesthetic modernists or political rebels who would denigrate such things as Art, Nation, and civilized public discourse. However, Platt sees a paradox in Repin's painting similar to what Powelstock sees in Lermontov—a similar disturbing "tendency to use violence to overcome violence," thus perpetuating what they would eradicate. Platt sees this sad circularity working on the macro level of Russian culture in general: "Repin rejects Ivan's violence [depicted in his painting], but with such violence that Repin becomes conflated with the bloodshed he rejects, becoming a target for Balashev's and Voloshin's violent attacks, which repeat this same irony. The Bolsheviks reject the violence of the Imperial Russian state, yet they do so with such murderous zeal and fanaticism that they ultimately create a system of political repression that far outdoes anything the most reactionary tsar could have imagined."

In his article, Ronald LeBlanc surveys a variety of late-nineteenth- and twentieth-century ideological explanations for violence by examining images of violent eating ("alimentary violence") in Russian literature from Dostoevsky to the 1990s. As in many of the previous articles, Dostoevsky's works are seen both to grapple directly with the problem of violence and also to provide other writers and critics with a point of departure for their own positions. LeBlanc chronicles a moment when food imagery takes on a new character, disturbing both for the kind of violence these images depict and for the new ideological import they assume, as they serve as kind of shorthand or code for particular philosophical *isms*. In part this may follow from Dostoevsky's practice of "the ideological novel," and partly from reference to Darwin's "survival of the fittest" (which Dostoevsky interpreted to mean "dog-eat-dog," taken literally). As LeBlanc shows, eating as a "code of power" assumes mostly sinister ramifications in various ideological and literary formations (Nietzschean, Marxist, primitivist, etc.).

In the polarized ideological situation of late imperial Russia, the Jews were increasingly demonized as "agents of modernity"—either as rich capitalists (among which there were actually few Jews) or as revolutionaries (which Russia's discriminatory practices virtually created).[18] Characteristically, in a bipolar system all opponents become lumped together into a composite Other, however implausible. Brian Horowitz's examination of the ways in which Russian-Jewish writers (that is, Jewish authors writing in Russian) responded to pogroms offers a case study of one kind of violence that helped bring down the Old Regime, not from without by the actions of revolutionary discontents but from within, by violence that the state practiced or encouraged upon its own citizens.[19] Horowitz argues that by the very act of writing in Russian, authors like Simeon Frug, Sergei Iaroshevskii, David Aizman, and Rachel Khin were entering into dialogue with Russian culture. However, state-sanctioned pogrom violence rendered all such attempts at communication meaningless and "Russian-Jewish" literature oxymoronic. The literature responding to anti-Jewish violence that Horowitz surveys suggests a kind of minority report: a heartbreaking chronicle of the increasing desperation of the Jewish population, which was responding to the violence either by turning to national separatism, to revolutionary political activity, or by voting with its feet (three million Jews emigrated from the Russian empire between 1882 and 1914).[20]

Goodwin's article describes the revolutionaries' ambivalence about Bakunin's support for violence in theoretical debates, but Anna Geifman demonstrates that the Bolsheviks unequivocally, indeed enthusiastically, endorsed its use in practice—starting with the fact that they called their policy "Red Terror," admitting kinship to the French Revolution's notorious Reign of Terror. Geifman substantiates what many of the Soviet Union's harshest critics often charged: that state-sponsored violence was "the cardinal feature" of the new Soviet state. Terror was used purposefully and more or less indiscriminately to subjugate the entire population. Undoubtedly, Revolutionary and Civil War violence should be seen within the larger dehumanizing and apocalyptic context of the period. Russia's disastrous participation in World

War I was certainly a major factor in precipitating revolutionary upheavals and cheapening the value of life.[21] Yet as Geifman notes, even though the Red Terror was defended as a necessary, rational response to foreign invasion and counter-revolution, and despite the fact that the enemies of the Bolsheviks may have committed equivalent acts of atrocious violence, the principal motivation and implementation of this violence was doctrinal rather than pragmatic. This was ideological warfare on a scale never before seen.

Geifman's horrific picture of Civil War terror coupled with Horowitz's portrait of how the Old Regime alienated its Jews help highlight "The Problem of Revolutionary Violence in Babel''s Stories" as described by Victor Peppard. On the one hand, the stories of Isaac Babel''s *Red Cavalry* offer a hopeful, at times lyrical, view of Lenin's revolution and its humanist pathos (associated at some points with Jewish spirituality). On the other hand, Babel' offers unvarnished images of atrocities and grotesque sadism proudly committed in the name of the Revolution. If Lermontov's depiction of violence could, in Powelstock's formulation, enlist "the peculiar moral ambivalence born of insolubility in the service of moral discovery," with "moral discovery" implying some way to recoup a moral ideal (perhaps such as that promised in Krasnostchekova's reading of *Netochka Nezvanova*), Babel''s ambivalence is if anything more urgent and more intractable, demanding but refusing to give "moralizing guidance," as Peppard argues.

However shocking the revolutionary violence that inspired Babel''s perplexity, in retrospect Lenin's revolutionary reign of terror appears as but a rehearsal for what was to come under Stalin. According to R. J. Rummel's estimate, Soviet "democide" (defined as "the murder of any person or people by a government, including genocide, politicide [murder for political reasons], and [indiscriminate] mass murder") reached at least 61,911,000 victims, approximately fifty million of them under Stalin.[22] Rummel ranks this bloodletting as second in scale only to the Black Death, the pandemic plague that killed seventy-five million people in 1347–51—although the Soviet experiment in social engineering would jump to first place if we limited ourselves to human-made carnage. How can we wrap our minds around the extent of this horror or understand the reasons for how and why it could have happened? These questions are part of the Soviet legacy to humanity, and for all their insolubility, like the problem of human violence in general, they nevertheless demand our attention. Together with a catalogue of Stalinist violence, J. Arch Getty offers a spectrum of historians' opinions on the subject and suggests some new perspectives on the "how" of Stalinism, on the ways in which it functioned institutionally. Contrary to the notion of a monolithic, top-down "totalitarianism," systematically implementing its calculated designs, Getty sees "a wild, only loosely controlled campaign characterized by excess and improvisation more than tight control or planning." He likens Stalinist atrocities to "traditional," "primitive," even "primordial" forms of violence rather than as something more regimented and rational. He characterizes the Stalinist political leadership as "nervous little monsters" who no matter how secure in power felt themselves continually under siege and who "could think of no way of governing without resorting to massive force." This is a case where Russian bipolar extremism manifests itself as something approaching clinical bipolar disorder—what Getty refers to as "the political equivalent of a psychotic break," irrational and elemental in its power.

Stalin's evil genius, then, may have been in maintaining a manically insecure regime under a façade of total control. Maureen Perrie revisits one of the most notorious episodes of Stalin's manipulation of Russian art and scholarship—his rehabilitation of Ivan the Terrible. Stalin's "cultural revolution" overthrew the Marxist historical school of Mikhail Pokrovskii of the 1920s, which was militantly critical of Russia's past. This past now became a source of national pride and heroic role models, including that most tsarist of tsars, Ivan IV. Ironically, Stalin offered a cynically deliberate demonstration of Pokrovskii's dictum that "History is politics applied to the past." As Perrie notes, Stalin faulted the historical Ivan, as well as Aleksei Tolstoi's and Sergei Eisenstein's depictions, for being "insufficiently terrible" (!) and not enough "an analogue of his own [Stalin's] self-image as a heroic and farsighted ruler." In contrast to Repin, who had highlighted the problematic relationship of past and present, and posed a moral question about violence and its depiction, these state-sponsored Stalinist representations of Ivan IV—as Perrie shows—not merely offered history as an explicit justification for present actions (i.e., state terror) but forced the past into an allegory of the present with little pretense at historical accuracy. Such allegorization was not without its danger, as Stalin himself probably understood when he banned the second installment of Eisenstein's film: if part 1 could project the USSR's heroic present on the past, part 2's depiction of Ivan as (to borrow Getty's phrase) a "nervous little monster" may have offered a less-than-heroic projection of the past onto the present.

The work of Daniil Kharms (1906–42), who, like Babel', fell victim to the Stalinist Terror, is often described as an appropriately "absurdist" reaction to the reigning insanity. Mark Lipovetsky counters that view with a remarkable reading of Kharms's *Incidents* as a profound philosophical meditation on the nature of writing and as a systematic deconstruction of Modernist discourse, with its elevation of the author to the status of demiurge and divine creator. This is "writing in its pure, 'zero degree' form, supposedly cleansed from the traces of history and subjectivity." The "universal signifier" in this purified writing is violence. Violence not only serves (as Lipovetsky demonstrates) as an allegory of the process of artistic creation, it is shown to be fundamental to language itself, with every act of communication implying or signifying an act of violence. Kharms lays bare what is usually only implied, and thus "exposes the emptiness behind its own product"—emptiness because the ultimate logic of violence is death. Kharms's critique of language extends to the limits of authorship, as the writer's godlike privileged position—his presumed control over the world-text and thus his "safe haven" from the violence that overtakes his characters—is also undermined. The ordering principle that remains is not the reassuring force of individual creativity but the impersonal, unstoppable, primitive logic of ritualized violence. While the connections to Stalinism are suggestive, Kharms may also be seen as taking Lermontov's pessimistic critique of language as analyzed by Powelstock to a higher level, demonstrating the systemic impossibility of "moral discovery." Rather, Kharms systematically reveals the complete "insolubility" (the ultimate absurdity) of human existence.[23]

Nina Efimov and Natasha Kolchevska offer perspectives in their articles on how survivors and later Russian writers have tried to come to grips with Stalinism. Kolchevska examines memoirs by two women survivors of the Gulag, Evgeniia Ginzburg and Evfrosiniia Kersnovskaia, while Efimov examines the works of Vasilii Aksenov within the context of "Gulag" fiction. According to Kolchevska, Ginzburg and Kersnovskaia responded to the problem of bearing witness in very different ways. Ginzburg remained a true believer in communism and advocated its communal, nurturing, humanist side, while Kersnovskaia tenaciously held on to her identity as a fighter and outsider. Ginzburg—as Kolchevska argues—adopted a motherly, "female" role to survive, Kersnovskaia a "male" one. Ginzburg wove a traditional verbal narrative, while for Kersnovskaia drawing helped convey what words could not. In her analysis, Nina Efimov describes the life and works of Vasilii Aksenov, Ginzburg's son who grew up in the camps to become a major figure of the Russian dissident movement of the 1960s and 1970s, despite—or perhaps more accurately, because of—his apolitical stance. A popular "official" writer at the start of his career during the Thaw, Aksenov emigrated to the United States, like many talented writers forced out of the country during the Brezhnev period (among them Vladimir Voinovich, Sasha Sokolov, Sergei Dovlatov, and Alexander Solzhenitsyn). As Efimov shows, in his novels Aksenov struggles with the legacy of Stalinism, as violence permeates his writing. Resolutely nonideological, Aksenov depicts political propaganda and sloganeering as providing rationalization and outlet for sado-sexual aggression. According to Efimov, Aksenov refuses to "explain away" the crimes of Stalinism, and while he seems to advocate forgiveness for evildoers, the nonpunishing God that appears in his work hardly offers a satisfying or effectual counter to the violence. Efimov, like several of the authors who follow, sees the struggle with the legacy of Stalinism as a major factor in working out a new Russian national identity.

This can certainly be said for Viktor Astaf'ev (1924–2001), who in Julian Moss's reading offers a harsh critique of everyday life in the Soviet Union during glasnost and perestroika. At first Astaf'ev was grouped with "Village Prose" writers, fierce nationalists who advocated a return to the unspoiled values of the Russian countryside and who were among the leading figures of the "loyal opposition" under Gorbachev. But Moss shows how Astaf'ev's works—starting with his shockingly non-heroic trilogy about the Second World War (which had been a major positive theme in official "Socialist Realist" literature)—offer an unrelieved picture of futility. Astaf'ev's exposé of the appalling conditions within the army and especially the harsh, often deadly treatment of recruits reverberated loudly in the context of the war in Afghanistan and later the war in Chechnya. (One might compare this to American revisionist depictions of World War II, which echoed dissatisfaction with the war in Vietnam, like Kurt Vonnegut's *Slaughterhouse Five* or Joseph Heller's *Catch-22*.) As Moss argues, in some sense Astaf'ev seems to be offering a genuinely "socialist" critique (e.g., his depiction of the class conflict between officers and enlisted men in the army), although his ruthlessly bitter portrait of the mundane horrors of Soviet conditions, the corruption of village life, and destruction of the natural environment offers little or no room for hope—yet another catalogue of "insoluble problems."

Nadya Peterson's analysis of four works, including one by Astaf'ev, comes to similar conclusions about violence and futility in "fin-de-siècle" Soviet literature, centering on the way this plays out in individual psychology and through the prism of gender roles. As in Aksenov, images of women who are raped and murdered ("erasures of the feminine") seem to become a plot staple. For the male writers Peterson analyzes, violence against women serves as a symbolic recreation of Russia's modern dilemma and suggests the return to a "primordial past" in which female sacrifice is a ritual necessity. In the works by Svetlana Vasil'eva and Elena Tarasova, the "erasure of the feminine" is both less symbolic and less detached, as the female protagonists forge closer individual connections to, and take more personal responsibility for, the evil they confront. Nevertheless, here too "the punishment [that] is meted out by a woman author on her female character . . . is as unavoidable as it is futile."

The "Soviet experiment" has been characterized as an attempt to realize "Utopia in Power,"[24] so that, as Elena Vassileva and Boris Lanin show, contemporary interest in utopian and anti-utopian literature may be clearly seen as another struggle with its legacy. Because of the totalizing, ideological nature of the utopian project, violence also serves as one of its main literary features, or, in the case of anti-utopia, a test case for social justice that utopia fails. Vassileva and Lanin focus specifically on the topical issues of ethnic violence, the "dictatorship of law," and nostalgia for empire—each of which recur in utopian literature and may be seen as a litmus test for social attitudes toward violence.

Teresa Polowy's "The Female Face of Violence: Russian Culture and Violence against Women" helps to explain this sense of futility by looking at misogyny and violence against women in a long perspective. However endemic to traditional Russian society, anti-female exploitation and violence has increased exponentially since the end of the USSR, with a boom in pornography, prostitution, spousal abuse, and other gender-related evils. The advent of "democratic freedoms" has seemed to entail freedom *from* law, not freedom *under* law, and as in traditional Russian society, women often take the brunt of the pain of social change. Among other sources for Russia's ingrained misogynistic attitudes, Polowy indicts Russian Orthodoxy, although as she also notes—and as Elizabeth Skomp explores—Orthodox religious models (kenotic humility, martyrdom, holy foolishness) may offer uniquely Russian varieties of women's liberation (the concept of "feminism," as Skomp notes, is almost universally scorned by Russians).

The articles by Skomp and Tatyana Novikov analyze the problem of violence against women in contemporary Russia from the point of view of women writers who express deep outrage at their treatment. Novikov's analysis of "revenge fantasies" in stories by Nina Sadur suggests as strident and extreme a feminism as that of any Western radical of the last generation. While the desire to vent violent outrage on one's victimizer may be a necessary and even healthy impulse in the process of throwing off the yoke of oppression, the scenarios described in Sadur's stories merely seem to replace male chauvinist pigs with female chauvinist pigs, characters who exult in their newfound despotic power but who remain crippled by insecurity and rage. If women are now free to liberate their will to power, the power itself turns out to be corrupting and imprisoning, and the "mythologization of gender" remains intact. Nevertheless, the possibility arises that this moment of rage and role reversal may lead to new recognition—if not for the characters within the stories, then perhaps for Sadur's readers.

Skomp's analysis of two stories by Sadur and Svetlana Vasilenko suggests some of the unusual paths this new self-recognition may take. As Skomp describes it, the imaginative world constructed here is one in which the unconscious predominates—a world of grotesque violence, transgression, strangely logical madness. In Skomp's analysis, as in Novikov's, the writers describe "a world of extremes" in which "the excessive and hyperbolic become commonplace." Skomp experiments in applying various concepts from Western literary and gender theory to indigenous and particularly "Russian" behavioral patterns, such as the making of a pilgrimage, voluntary martyrdom, and holy foolishness. Some of these paths may be seen as a return to older Orthodox patterns of behavior that offer the promise of redemption, yet they take place at a strangely elemental, primordial, and rather depersonalized level. Here traditional "feminine" (and nonviolent) powers reemerge: giving spiritual birth, healing, and a motherly saintliness—significantly, connected with moving from silence to speech.

Anna Brodsky's analysis of Chechen War memoirs, which closes this collection, dramatically reemphasizes the ways in which language—especially after decades of being bled of meaning by communist doublespeak—may serve to sanction the banality of evil rather than bringing it to transcendent consciousness. Just as violence against women may be seen as a compensatory mechanism for low social and national self-esteem, in Brodsky's analysis racism and violence against the Chechens also "fills the vacuum left by ideology." This is not merely an official, top-down policy of ethnic cleansing, as may be argued in the case of Milosevic's Yugoslavia, but in Brodsky's view it is a disturbingly broad-based, grassroots phenomenon. According to Brodsky, Russia's failure to develop a satisfactory post-Stalinist or post-Soviet national identity has lead to the substitution of the logic of the blood-feud. Political rhetoric becomes patent apologia, with hardly any pretense of logic or truth. As Brodsky shows, the new identity—which boils down to a justification of ethnic violence—is "amorphous and opportunistic" and can just as easily employ American racial epithets as neo-Nazi fascist rhetoric or second-hand Soviet sloganeering. As in Kharms's stories, language seems to deteriorate into meaningless verbiage, whose deeper logic and universal signifier is violence.

Juxtaposing the idiosyncratic genius of Kharms and the mindless horror of ethnic cleansing may suggest some of the troubling paradoxes of violence in Russia, which—as the reader will see from this book—can be both dehumanizingly destructive and also lead to brilliantly sensitive and inspired creativity. Many differing conclusions may be drawn from this volume, depending on one's perspective; violence may be seen as source of profound philosophical and psychological insight as well as meaningless suffering and death. What seems significant, either for the historian or cultural observer, are the many rich and complex ways in which Russians have conceptualized violence as a fundamental problem of human existence and the ways they have tried to act upon it, for better or worse (mostly for worse!). However intractable human violence may be, the process of describing it as a problem, of bringing the conundrum of violence to consciousness, is certainly a necessary step, if not to a "solution," at least to a better understanding of our human nature and of the forces that define our world.

Notes

1. "Russian Writers, Censors, and Readers," in *Lectures on Russian Literature,* ed. Fredson Bowers (New York: Harcourt Brace Jovanovich, 1981), 2.

2. Alexander Yanov, *The Origins of Autocracy: Ivan the Terrible in Russian History,* trans. Stephen Dunn (Berkeley: University of California Press, 1981).

3. Evgenii V. Anisimov, *The Reforms of Peter the Great: Progress through Coercion in Russia,* trans. John T. Alexander (Armonk, N.Y.: M. E. Sharpe, 1993). The subtitle evidently belongs to the translator.

4. Prime minister of the ousted Provisional Government, Alexander Kerensky (1881–1970), for example, called his memoirs *Russia and History's Turning Point* (New York: Duell, Sloan and Pearce, 1965). His other books on the Revolution were no less eloquently entitled: *The Catastrophe* (1927); *The Crucifixion of*

Liberty (1934); and *The Road to the Tragedy* (on the murder of the Romanovs [1935]). Numerous other historians, Russian and non-Russian, have also looked at the revolutionary experience in similar apocalyptic terms. A score of Russian-authored histories of the Revolution (as well as of other episodes of Soviet history) include the word "tragedy" in their titles, including that of the anarchist Alexander Berkman (*The Russian Tragedy* [1922]). The term has made a comeback in a post-Soviet English-language survey of Russian history (Hugh Ragsdale, *The Russian Tragedy: The Burden of History* [Armonk, N.Y.: M. E. Sharpe, 1996]) and in a major analysis of the revolutionary experience (Orlando Figes, *A People's Tragedy: The Russian Revolution, 1891–1924* [New York: Penguin, 1998]).

5. Hélène Carrère d'Encausse, *The Russian Syndrome: One Thousand Years of Political Murder,* trans. Caroline Higgitt; foreword Adam B. Ulam (New York: Holmes & Meier, 1992). Ulam notes that the French title—"Le malheur russe"—means simply "Russia's Misfortune" (xii–xiii).

6. Tolstoy's doctrine ("Tolstoyanism") has often been referred to as "Non-Resistance to Evil" *(neprotivlenie zlu),* a paraphrase of Matthew 5:38–9 ("You have heard that it was said, An eye for an eye, and a tooth for a tooth: but I say unto you, resist not him that is evil"), but this seems a misnomer; "Nonviolent Resistance" more accurately reflects the idea that evil must in fact be resisted—but not by violent means. On Tolstoy's nonviolence, see Ronald Sampson, *Tolstoy: The Discovery of Peace* (London: Heinemann, 1973); on his rejection of war, *Lev Tolstoy and the Concept of Brotherhood,* ed. Andrew Donskov and John Woodsworth (New York: Legas, 1996), and Alexander Fodor, *A Quest for a Non-Violent Russia: The Partnership of Leo Tolstoy and Vladimir Chertkov* (Lanham, Md.: University Press of America, 1989). For a recent provocative discussion of the international influence of both terrorism and Tolstoyanism, see Steven Marks, *How Russia Shaped the Modern World: From Art to Anti-Semitism, Ballet to Bolshevism* (Princeton, N.J.: Princeton University Press, 2003), chapters 1 and 4.

7. Halperin's article is the exception, so I have discussed his arguments in this early part of the introduction.

8. D'Encausse, *The Russian Syndrome,* 9–10. D'Encausse is referring primarily to the description of the conversion given in *The Russian Primary Chronicle: Laurentian Text,* trans. and ed. Samuel Hazzard Cross and Olgerd P. Sherbowitz-Wetzor (Cambridge, Mass.: Mediaeval Academy of America, 1953), 110–19.

9. In Ju. M. Lotman, B. A. Uspenskii, *The Semiotics of Russian Culture,* ed. Ann Shukman (Ann Arbor: Department of Slavic Languages and Literatures, University of Michigan, 1984), 3–35.

10. Lotman, who died in 1993, himself continually sought ways to give priority to the values of "culture" (defined in terms of a neutral zone) over "explosion," as in one of his final works, the book *Kul'tura i vzryv* (1992).

11. According to Maurice Cranston's definition of ideology (which follows that of A.-L.-C. Destutt de Tracy, who coined the term at the time of the French Revolution), among other things "it contains an explanatory theory of a more or less comprehensive kind about human experience"; "it sets out a program . . . of social and political organization"; and "it conceives the realization of this program as entailing a struggle"—one which commonly involves a greater or lesser degree of violence. "Ideology," *Encyclopædia Britannica Online.* Accessed 9

Aug. 2007, http://search.eb.com/eb/article-9106294. Many critics of communism and its atrocities have seen ideology as the big villain. See for example Aleksandr Solzhenitsyn, *The Gulag Archipelago, 1918–1956: An Experiment in Literary Investigation*, trans. Thomas P. Whitney (parts 1–4) and Harry Willetts (parts 5–7); abridged by Edward E. Erickson Jr. (New York: Harper & Row, 1985), 77–78 (part 1, chap. 4).

12. On monotheism and ideological violence see Rodney Stark, *One True God: Historical Consequences of Monotheism* (Princeton, N.J.: Princeton University Press, 2001), chap. 3 and passim; and Mark Juergensmeyer, *Terror in the Mind of God: The Global Rise of Religious Violence* (Berkeley: University of California Press, 2000).

13. They have also struggled to define the essential differences between them.

14. See George P. Fedotov, *The Russian Religious Mind*, vol. 1 (Cambridge, Mass.: Harvard University Press, 1946). For a useful introduction to the Eastern Orthodox tradition see Kallistos Ware, *The Orthodox Church*, 2nd ed. (New York: Penguin Books, 1993). Jostein Børtnes debates the appropriateness of the term "kenosis" for Russian Orthodoxy in Iustin Bertnes, "Russkii kenotism: K pereotsenke odnogo poniatiia," in *Evangel'skii tekst v russkoi literature XVIII–XX vekov: Tsitata, reministsentsiia, motiv, siuzhet, zhanr. Sbornik nauchnykh trudov*, ed. V. N. Zakharov (Petrozavodsk: Izd-vo Petrozavodskogo univ., 1994), 61–65.

15. Daniel Rancour-Laferriere, *The Slave Soul of Russia: Moral Masochism and the Cult of Suffering* (New York: New York University Press, 1995). Analogous critiques have been made of revolutionary psychology, e.g., Victor E. Wolfenstein, *The Revolutionary Personality: Lenin, Trotsky, Gandhi* (Princeton, N.J.: Princeton University Press, 1967); Bruce Mazlish, *The Revolutionary Ascetic: Evolution of a Political Type* (New York: McGraw-Hill, 1976); and William H. Blanchard, *Revolutionary Morality: A Psychosexual Analysis of Twelve Revolutionists* (Santa Barbara, Calif.: ABC-Clio Information Services, 1984).

16. See especially Sergei Bulgakov's classic essay "Heroism and Asceticism: Reflections on the Religious Nature of the Russian Intelligentsia," in *Landmarks: A Collection of Essays on the Russian Intelligentsia, 1909*, ed. Boris Shragin and Albert Todd, trans. Marian Schwartz (New York: Karz Howard, 1977), 23–63.

17. Alexander N. Yakovlev, *A Century of Violence in Soviet Russia* (New Haven, Conn.: Yale University Press, 2002), 22. Contrary to d'Encausse, Yakovlev sees 1917 as the defining moment when Russia's "thousand-year-old model of development [was] cast aside" (ibid.).

18. See Marks, *How Russia Shaped the Modern World*, chap. 5.

19. The issue of responsibility for the pogroms and their scope has been recently raised by Solzhenitsyn's *Two Hundred Years Together (1795–1995) [Dvesti let vmeste]*, 2 vols. (Moscow: Russkii put', 2001–3). Solzhenitsyn's work downplays the government's role in the pogroms and that may be taken as an overall apologia for Russia's treatment of the Jews. In any case, the controversy over this work indicates that the drama of "Russian-Jewish" identity remains a sore issue in contemporary Russia.

20. Marks, *How Russia Shaped the Modern World*, 146. See also the works cited in Brian Horowitz's article.

21. According to the *Encyclopædia Brittanica,* the First World War claimed over nine million Russian casualties, including dead, wounded, missing—76.3 percent of all soldiers mobilized. "Table 4: Armed Forces Mobilized and Casualties in World War I," *Encyclopædia Britannica Online.* Accessed 10 March 2003, http://search.eb.com/eb/article?eu=126556.

22. This does not include those killed in World War II, but does include those killed by famine (natural and human-made), deportations, concentration camps, and mass killing ("terror"). See R. J. Rummel, *Lethal Politics: Soviet Genocides and Mass Murders 1917–1987* (New Brunswick, N.J.: Transaction Publishers, 1990); *Death by Government: Genocide and Mass Murder in the Twentieth Century* (New Brunswick, N.J.: Transaction Publishers, 1994); and his Web site at http://www.hawaii.edu/powerkills/, accessed 21 July 2003, from which this figure is taken. See also J. Arch Getty's discussion of the statistics in this volume.

23. Language and artistic creation belong to the fallen, earthly world, sunk in the inescapable chains of suffering and death, and some have argued that this "absurdist" position is fully compatible with a religious, even fully Russian Orthodox, conception of another, divine, transcendent reality. This opposition between earthly and heavenly realms accords with the idealist logic of the bipolar model. On Kharms and "the theology of the absurd," see for example Sarah Pratt, *Nikolai Zabolotsky: Enigma and Cultural Paradigm* (Evanston, Ill.: Northwestern University Press, 2000), 77–86.

24. Mikhail Heller and Aleksandr Nekrich, *Utopia in Power: The History of the Soviet Union from 1917 to the Present,* trans. Phyllis B. Carlos (New York: Summit Books, 1986).

The Scourge of God

The Mongols and Violence in Russian History

CHARLES J. HALPERIN

Russian historians have blamed the Mongols for everything that anyone has ever thought "wrong" with Russian history, including political, economic, and cultural backwardness; authoritarianism; servility; xenophobia; messianism and imperial aggression; and isolationism. Certainly the Tatars, as the East Slavic sources called the Mongols, ruled Russia long enough to influence Russian life in many ways, from the conquest campaigns of 1237–38 and 1239–40 until 1480, a date that only acquired its symbolic significance later.[1] During the "Tatar Yoke," an anachronistic description of Mongol rule,[2] Russia was subservient to the "Golden Horde," the anachronistic name of the successor state of the world Mongol Empire centered on the lower Volga river. Historians, notably George Vernadsky, have often identified Mongol influence by contrasting Muscovite Russia with pre-Mongol Kievan (Kyivan) Rus'.[3] The role of the Mongols in Russian history remains very controversial. Specialists in Russian history in Russia remain strongly influenced by national and cultural prejudice against the notion that civilized, Christian Russians could have been influenced, except negatively, by uncivilized, barbarian, pagan or Muslim Tatars.[4]

Historians of the Mongol period have not previously addressed the subject of violence per se, but the concept is a very useful rubric under which several aspects of Russian life can be subsumed: 1) the destructiveness and economic impact of Mongol conquest and rule; 2) political morality; 3) social change; and 4) foreign expansion. Examination of these categories suggests that the Mongols neither significantly nor permanently increased the level of violence in Russian history, which was comparable at all times to that of other European states.

Although Mongol conquest and rule were extremely destructive, the Russian economy on the whole successfully recovered within a century without long-term detriment.[5] The East Slavic chronicles, of course, exaggerated the violence of the Mongol conquest of the East Slavic principalities and city-states, rhetorically depicting the merciless massacre of entire urban populations without regard to age, gender, or religious vocation.[6] The violence inflicted on cities that resisted was very real, however, and Kiev, for example, did not recover until the seventeenth century. Tatar raids against the forest-steppe border city of Riazan' inflicted so much damage that its inhabitants had to relocate to a nearby site to rebuild. Tatar punitive raids against disobedient princes or cities were violent indeed. Mongol governance cost the East Slavs a pretty penny in taxes, tribute, and conscripts. On the other hand, cities that surrendered, like Veliky Novgorod, were spared, and Russian cities that could benefit from Mongol patronage of foreign trade especially prospered.[7] Within a century of the Mongol conquest, stone construction, especially churches, had resumed, indicating a strong economic recovery.[8] The expense of defending against the steppe nomads, during and after Mongol rule, was very high, but not necessarily higher than Polish or Holy Roman Empire military expenditures against the Crimean Tatars and Ottomans. If Russian economic backwardness cannot be attributed to the level of destruction of the Mongol conquest and subsequent rule, then the level of violence in Russian life cannot be explained as a consequence of the impoverishment the Mongols inflicted on Russia.

From Karamzin on, Russian historians have wrongly blamed the Mongols for inculcating violence and political amorality among the East Slavic princes. It is true that under Mongol rule various princes exploited the military might of the Mongols to aggrandize their neighbors. For example, Ivan Kalita of Moscow employed Tatar punitive forces against Tver'. Riurikid princes employed every means of deceit and cunning to cultivate the favor of their Genghizid rulers. However, such interprincely violence was hardly absent during the Kievan period. In 1169 the armies of grand prince Andrei Bogoliubskii of Vladimir-Suzdal' looted Kiev as if it were alien enemy territory.[9] Chernigov

(Chernihiv) princes were no less violent in their treatment of the "mother of Rus' cities." In 1174 Sviatoslav Vsevolodovich led a twelve-day plunder of Kiev, and in 1203 Riurik Rostislavovich and his Polovtsy allies inflicted worse devastation on Kiev than in 1169.[10] Ivan Kalita was only following a Kievan precedent in using steppe nomads against his Rus' enemies. The most famous example of fraternal strife within the dynasty was Sviatopolk's eleventh-century assassination of his later canonized brothers Boris and Gleb. Prince Vasil'ko was blinded in Kiev in 1097. In 1170 Galich, to coerce Yaroslav Osmomysl to reconcile with his spurned wife, Olga, her supporters burned her husband's concubine at the stake and also killed the prince's henchmen.[11] Political violence, therefore, preceded the Mongol conquest, and princely political amorality hardly needed Mongol inspiration.[12]

Ironically, historians have criticized Russian princes for not reacting violently enough against Tatar oppression. Supposedly, Russian princely servility toward their Tatar overlords resulted from a lack of courage, patriotism, and self-sacrifice. Such accusations derive their ardor from injured national pride. In actuality, when the balance of power vis-à-vis the Mongols changed, or a prince thought it had, the Russians tried to take advantage, as in the battle of Kulikovo Field of 1380, and "the Russian people" never lost their willingness to revolt against the Tatars, as in Tver' in 1327.[13]

The level of violence in domestic Russian society may have increased during the Mongol and Muscovite periods, but not because of Mongol influence. Such violence may be analyzed in terms of capital punishment and torture, levels of crime, treatment of peasants, and the persecution of religious dissenters. Before the Mongols the East Slavs did not practice capital punishment, but the Russians could just as easily have imported capital punishment from the Germans or Byzantium as from the Mongols.[14] In the sixteenth century the Englishman Anthony Jenkinson criticized the Muscovites for not using capital punishment enough—for example, only on the third offence for theft.[15] Torture was ubiquitous in Europe during these centuries as a tool of criminal investigation. It would be misleading to attribute the atrocities perpetrated by Ivan IV "the Terrible" to "Mongol barbarism." The horrendous tortures and modes of execution Ivan IV employed were hardly more inhumane than those employed in England, where, after being tortured in the Tower of London, traitors were hung, drawn, and quartered. The Romans probably wrote the book on pre-modern torture by their imaginative methods of creating early Christian martyrs.

Sixteenth-century European visitors to Muscovy projected their own concerns onto it.[16] Giles Fletcher expressed horror at the level of crime, specifically rape, murder, and robbery, in Muscovy,[17] but the level of violent crimes in Russia was probably no higher than elsewhere. The streets of Moscow were no more dangerous at night than those of London, Paris, or Rome. Nor was banditry in the countryside more prevalent in Muscovy. Justice could be coerced in sixteenth-century Poland-Lithuania, where local powerbrokers employed armed entourages to terrorize neighbors, as the Muscovite émigré prince Andrei Kurbskii learned to his sorrow.[18] Kurbskii expended enormous effort in endless litigation with his neighbors over land, people, and revenue, from which violence, and even murder, were not absent. On the whole, European travel accounts, despite their obsession with Muscovite barbarity and cruelty, "did not report excessive levels of popular violence,"[19] probably because they so emphasized Russian servility.

Violent persecution of religious dissent in Muscovy cannot be traced to Russia's Mongol heritage. Although the Mongol executions of princes Mikhail of Chernigov in the thirteenth and Mikhail of Tver' in the fourteenth century were presented as Christian martyrdoms warranting sainthood, in fact they were political, and the Mongols, including the Golden Horde after its official conversion to Islam, practiced religious tolerance. Indeed, the Mongol khans granted extensive and lucrative privileges to the Russian Orthodox Church. Through the sixteenth century, religious violence in Russia was much less than elsewhere in Europe. True, the Muscovites did burn some heretics at the stake, but then, that was their fate throughout Europe during the Middle Ages and the Reformation. The medieval Crusades, the Albigensian Crusade, "Bloody Mary" Tudor, the St. Bartholomew's Day Massacre, the French Wars of Religion, and the Thirty Years War attest to a level of religious violence not achieved in Muscovy until the late-seventeenth-century persecution of the Old Believers. After capturing Polotsk (Polatsk) from Lithuania in 1563, Ivan IV ordered the execution of its Jews, but death was also the fate of Jews along the Rhine and in Jerusalem during the First Crusade. Violence against "heretics" and "unbelievers" was not Mongol in origin.

The "crisis of the seventeenth century" in Europe, with its endemic political, social, economic, and religious violence, included Muscovy. The aggregate level of societal violence in early modern Muscovy was comparable to that in other European states.[20] The treatment of peasants in Muscovy before and after enserfment in 1649 was no more violent than anywhere in East Central Europe at the time. Civil unrest was characteristic of early modern Europe, when nation-states increased the level of fiscal exploitation to finance gunpowder armies and bureaucracies. The level of violence in Muscovy during the sixteenth and seventeenth century—Ivan IV's sack of Novgorod, the Time of Troubles, the uprisings of Bolotnikov and Razin, urban riots like Moscow in 1648—was matched by that manifested in Habsburg campaigns against the rebellious Netherlands, the English Civil War, the German Peasants' Revolt, and the Khmelnytsky uprising in Ukraine.

Muscovy's aggressive foreign policy and imperial expansion were not violent expressions of its identity as a successor state of the Golden Horde. Muscovy did annex actual successor states of the Golden Horde, the khanates of Kazan' and Astrakhan' on the Volga River, because they were security threats and offered profit from the Volga River trade to Persia, Central Asia, and India. Ivan IV used Tatar troops in his Livonian War to conquer port cities on the Baltic,[21] but Poland-Lithuania had its own Lithuanian Tatar contingents, and Stefan Bathory's German and Hungarian mercenaries were hardly more fastidious about collateral damage than the Tatars. Some Tatar Nogai mirzas flattered Ivan IV as a descendant of Genghiz Khan (Mongolian: Chinggis Khan), but Ivan IV was not a descendant of Genghiz Khan and did not claim to be.[22] Muscovy did not conceive of itself as a successor state of the Golden Horde, nor did it try to recreate the boundaries of the Golden Horde. Rather, it pursued foreign policy goals—such as the conquest of Livonia—that had nothing to do with Golden Horde policies.[23] Genghiz Khan did not intend to conquer the "world," since his divine mandate from the Great Blue Sky was to rule only steppe nomads who lived in felt tents, even if in practice Mongol armies kept going until they were stopped; nor was Ivan IV imitating Genghiz Khan, since he did not aspire to conquer China, Central Asia, or Iran. Muscovy was not a violent "Oriental Despotism," in Karl Wittfogel's terminology, even if such a type of regime ever existed.[24] Muscovite imperial expansion should be compared to European imperialism and colonialism, not Mongol.[25]

Without question Ivan IV's Oprichnina—in which he divided the realm in two and ruled his private half through his black-robed "security police," the oprichniki—constituted the most violent use of political terror that Muscovy ever saw, although historians cannot agree against whom it was directed or even if it was rational. Genghiz Khan consciously employed terror as an instrument of conquest, to convince various peoples that resistance to Mongol conquest was futile. Nevertheless, Ivan IV was not imitating Genghiz Khan, and Ivan IV's experiment did not set a precedent for future Muscovite rulers.[26]

Violence pervaded medieval and early modern Russian history during the Mongol and Muscovite periods, but no more so than elsewhere in Europe. However, analysis of the supposed economic, social and political impact of the Mongols on Russian history demonstrates that the level of violence in Russia should not be blamed on the Mongols.

Notes

The author wishes to express his sincerest appreciation to Barbara Skinner for suggestions on improving an earlier draft of this essay. I remain solely responsible for any errors.

1. Charles J. Halperin, *The Tatar Yoke* (Columbus, Ohio: Slavica Publishers, 1985), 150–66.
2. Charles J. Halperin, "The Tatar Yoke and Tatar Oppression," *Russia Mediavalis* 5:1 (1984): 24–39; Donald Ostrowski, *Muscovy and the Mongols: Cross-Cultural Influences on the Steppe Frontier, 1304–1589* (Cambridge: Cambridge University Press, 1998), 244–45.
3. Charles J. Halperin, "George Vernadsky, Eurasianism, the Mongols and Russia," *Slavic Review* 41:3 (1982): 477–93; Charles J. Halperin, "Russia and the Steppe: George Vernadsky and Eurasianism," *Forschungen zur osteuropäischen Geschichte* 36 (1985): 55–194.
4. Charles J. Halperin, "Omissions of National Memory: Russian Historiography on the Golden Horde as Politics of Inclusion and Exclusion," *Ab Imperio* 3 (2004): 131–44.
5. Charles J. Halperin, *Russia and the Golden Horde: The Mongol Impact on Medieval Russian History* (Bloomington: Indiana University Press, 1985), 75–86.
6. Halperin, *The Tatar Yoke*, 29–63.
7. Ibid., 64–93.
8. David. B. Miller, "Monumental Building as an Indication of Economic Trends in Northern Rus' in the Late Kievan and Mongol Periods, 1138–1462," *American Historical Review* 94:2 (1989): 360–90; David B. Miller, "Monumental Building and Its Patrons as Indicators of Economic and Political Trends in Rus', 900–1262," *Jahrbücher für Geschichte Osteuropas* 38:3 (1990): 321–55; Ostrowski, *Muscovy and the Mongols*, 108–32.
9. Jaroslav Pelenski, "The Sack of Kiev of 1169: Its Significance for the Succession to Kievan Rus," *Harvard Ukrainian Studies* 11:3/4 (1987): 303–16, reprinted in Jaroslav Pelenski, *The Contest for the Legacy of Kievan Rus'* (Boulder, Colo.: East European Monographs, 1998), 45–60.
10. Martin Dimnik, *The Dynasty of Chernigov, 1146–1246* (Cambridge: Cambridge University Press, 2003), 129, 243–45.
11. Ibid., 121.

12. Halperin, *Russia and the Golden Horde,* 44–60.

13. "The Russian people" *(narod)* could not have been "traumatized" by the violence of the Mongol conquest since no such entity existed then. See ibid., 106–7.

14. Ibid., 93–94.

15. Lloyd E. Berry and Robert O. Crummey, eds., *Rude and Barbarous Kingdom: Russia in the Accounts of Sixteenth-Century English Voyagers* (Madison: University of Wisconsin Press, 1968), 35.

16. Charles J. Halperin, "Sixteenth-Century Foreign Travel Accounts to Muscovy: A Methodological Excursus," *The Sixteenth-Century Journal* 6:2 (1975): 89–111.

17. Berry and Crummey, *Rude and Barbarous Kingdom,* 245.

18. Inge Auerbach, *Andrej Michajlovič Kurbskij: Leben in osteuropäischen Adelsgesellschaften des 16. Jahrhunderts* (Munich: Otto Sagner, 1987).

19. Nancy Shields Kollman, *By Honor Bound: State and Society in Early Modern Russia* (Ithaca, N.Y.: Cornell University Press, 1999), 103.

20. Ibid., 180–83.

21. Janet Martin, "Multiethnicity in Muscovy: A Consideration of Christian and Muslim Tatars in the 1530s–1580s," *Journal of Early Modern History* 5:1 (2001): 1–23; Janet Martin, "Tatars in the Muscovite Army during the Livonian War," in *The Military and Society in Russia (1475–1977),* ed. Eric Lohr and Marshall Poe, 365–87 (Leiden: E. J. Brill, 2002).

22. Charles J. Halperin, "Ivan IV and Chinggis Khan," *Jahrbücher für Geschichte Osteuropas* 51:4 (1998): 481–97.

23. Charles J. Halperin, "Vymyshlennoe rodstvo: Moskovia ne byla naslednitsei Zolotoi Ordy," *Rodina* 12 (2003): 68–71.

24. Ostrowski, *Muscovy and the Mongols,* 85–107.

25. Michael Khodarkovsky, *Russia's Steppe Frontier: The Making of a Colonial Empire, 1500–1800* (Bloomington: Indiana University Press, 2002).

26. Ostrowski, *Muscovy and the Mongols,* 188, 192–93; Andrei Pavlov and Maureen Perrie, *Ivan the Terrible* (London: Pearson/Longman, 2003), 116, 173.

Violent Outcomes

Mikhail Lermontov and Romanticism's Insoluble Problems

DAVID POWELSTOCK

The worst of it is not that a certain number of people suffer patiently, but that an immense number suffer without realizing it.

M. Iu. Lermontov

Hermann Broch, the Austrian novelist whom I love above all, has said, "The only morality for a writer is knowledge." Only a literary work that reveals an unknown fragment of human existence has a reason for being. To be a writer does not mean to preach a truth; it means to discover a truth.

Milan Kundera

Violence permeates the works of Mikhail Iur'evich Lermontov (1814–41), Russia's greatest Romantic writer.[1] His earliest narratives were obsessed with warfare and blood vengeance, as well as notably lacking in any apparent preoccupation with the political or historical context for the violence portrayed.[2] Even in works depicting historical armed conflict, the emphasis is generally on individual revenge (as in the long narrative poem *Izmail-Bei*, 1832, and the unfinished novel *Vadim*, begun in 1832) or personal experience of bloody battle (as in his later masterpiece of war literature, "Valerik," Lermontov's most famous long lyric, 1840). Also typical are plots in which violence arises out of passionate love, such as the tragedy *The Masquerade* (in which the hero poisons his beloved wife, whom he wrongly suspects of infidelity, 1835–36) and the verse narratives *The Demon* (whose eponymous spirit falls in love with a human princess, only to kill her instantly with his first kiss, 1829–39) and *The Song of Tsar Ivan Vasil'evich, His Young Bodyguard, and the Bold Merchant Kalashnikov* (wherein Kalashnikov kills Ivan the Terrible's duplicitous bodyguard to avenge the latter's sexual assault on his wife and is subsequently executed, 1837).[3]

Nor was violence confined to the page in Lermontov's life. He fought two duels, dying in the second of these before his twenty-seventh birthday. By this time he had seen two separate tours of active duty in the Caucasus, exiled both times by Tsar Nicholas I: the first time for a ferociously angry poem written in response to Alexander Pushkin's death in 1837 and clandestinely circulated to wide acclaim;[4] the second time for dueling. Such exile was widely seen as a form of barely commuted death sentence, but Lermontov survived and even, in his second tour, distinguished himself in combat, although the tsar himself personally vetoed the poet's citation for a medal. It was during this tour of duty that he fought his second, fatal, duel in 1841. Although violent deaths were not rare among the writers of Lermontov's time, one is hard pressed to think of a nineteenth-century Russian author in whose life and works violence played so prominent a role.[5]

Violent themes remained pervasive in Lermontov's work throughout his short life, but the rhetorical and aesthetic aims served by this violence shifted over time. In the early works, Lermontov's obsession with violence may be attributed in large part to the confluence of rebellious temperament and Romantic fashion. Here violent plot action serves primarily as an objective correlative of the *Sturm und Drang* conflict between passionate individualism and the indifferent world. There is, too, a whiff of English Romantic social critique in Lermontov's tendency to implicate social injustice in his heroes' violent acts. It might be noted, though, that by comparison with English practice, the hero's justifying complaint is remarkably diffuse. It frequently invokes an oppressive force no more concrete than "fate," with vague undertones of intractable social, cosmic, or psychological forces, a fate against which the passionate Lermontovian protagonist is in perpetual rebellion, despite being committed to no discernible ideal. Lermontov's embrace of this struggle of the individual with a hostile world was central to a worldview more purely Romantic than that of most of his Russian contemporaries. It is typically Romantic to frame such a struggle as a "problem known to have no solution"—which is to say no rational or pragmatic solution.[6] Where they do not generate impotent despair, the insoluble problems of Romanticism—the individual's alienation from his fate, from humanity, from language, or from the cosmos itself—give rise to eternal conflicts of self against other. The Romantic positing of these conflicts as absolutely irresoluble renders violent outcomes inevitable. In Lermontov's early Romanticism, violence represents a prominent symptom of insolubility. Like the bottomless pathos of which it was the perverse twin, it was a conspicuous "non-solution" to the social and psychological conundrums with which the poet was obsessed.

Beginning with Pushkin's death in 1837, the rebelliousness of the Lermontovian hero rather quickly acquired a sharper focus. "The Poet's Death" and a number of lyrics that followed gave voice to a concerted critique of the society in which Lermontov lived:[7]

How often, encircled by the motley crowd,
When before me, as if in dream,
Amid the clamor of music and dance,
Amid the savage whispering of speeches learned by rote,
Flash by the soulless images of people,
Masks stretched taut with propriety . . . [8]

The response of the poet, thus surrounded, is the urge "to hurl in their faces an iron verse, / Dripping with bitterness and malice."[9] While it was largely the critical attitudes expressed in such poems that earned him the lasting enmity of Nicholas I, Lermontov's recalcitrant views, even those he expressed in private, contained little that was explicitly political. His greatest scorn was reserved for upper-class society and the superficial, slavish habits of thought it instilled in its participants. What infuriated Lermontov most was the "best" society's self-enforcing homogeneity, sustained by its obliviousness to its own constrictiveness, hypocrisy, and vacuity. (He was especially annoyed that this bastion of mediocrity had, prior to his sudden rise to fame, ignored him.) His critique was, above all, moral, rather than political.

Nevertheless, political factors contributed both to the moral character of court society and, more obliquely, to the vehemence with which Lermontov condemned it. It was a time of profound political and social repression. Nicholas I ascended the throne in the act of suppressing the Decembrist gentry rebellion of 1825. The new tsar's exceptionally severe response to the uprising—five of the conspirators were hanged and dozens more exiled—set the tone for his thirty-year reign. The threat of political repression hung diffusely in the atmosphere, adding cravenness to the insincerity and unthinking conventionality that Lermontov so despised. The eyes and ears of Nicholas's newly created secret police chancellery were everywhere, and every thinking person knew it. Lermontov lamented the suppression of dissenting voices, but what particularly galled him was that very few people seemed even inclined to dissent.

In the wake of the Decembrist catastrophe, overt political opposition was unthinkable. Moreover, the mood of those dissatisfied with the regime was understandably pessimistic. There is no evidence that Lermontov ever entertained the slightest hope for social or political reform on Russian soil. Nevertheless, everything Lermontov wrote, and even much of his everyday behavior, sounded an implicit challenge to the status quo. Twenty years after Lermontov's death, Russia's greatest nineteenth-century liberal, Alexander Herzen, wrote in exile that Lermontov was "equally as ardent and faithful in his friendships as he was vindictive and unrelenting in his hatreds . . . he never entered, like Pushkin, into a compromise with the society in which he was to live."[10] The provocative "iron verses" of Lermontov's fierce Romantic individualism, despite their political inchoateness, were drenched in the undeniable, albeit sublimated, political violence of the poet's milieu.[11]

Even as the poet's deepening art and thought eroded his interest in bloody mayhem for its own sake—or rather for its exclusively melodramatic function of underscoring insoluble conflict—the place of violence in his works and worldview did not so much diminish as undergo a transformation. Most importantly, violence became, in Lermontov's only completed novel, *A Hero of Our Time* (1840, second edition 1841),[12] the object of novelistic examination, rather than a mere literary effect. Lermontov's thematic treatment of violence correspondingly became much broader in range, with each of the novel's five chapters offering one or more different variations. For instance, along but one salient axis, we find in *Hero* an example of an elaborately premeditated conspiratorial murder plot—that of the Captain of Dragoons and his cronies to kill Pechorin in a rigged duel—alongside the seemingly random slaughter of Vulich by the drunken and inscrutable Cossack Efimych. Different cultural types of violence are juxtaposed, also—from the blood-vengeance of the native Circassians (Kazbich's kidnapping and stabbing of Bela and his murder of her father to avenge the theft of his horse by her brother) to the ritualized formality of the European duel (complete with Pechorin's cool literary allusion upon dispensing with Grushnitskii: "Finita la commedia!"). In yet another example of the novel's exhaustive cataloging of brutality, violence against a woman (Bela) is matched by a woman smuggler's attempt to drown Pechorin in the "Taman'" chapter.

Beyond the numerous overtly violent acts in the novel, however, it is the attention paid to subtler forms of violence and coercion that distinguishes *Hero* from its author's earlier works. Lermontov goes to great pains to portray often hidden forces of rhetorical and cognitive violence—"intelligence in the form of violence"[13]—and their impact. William Mills Todd III has identified the substratum of violence that motivates the characters' social performances in the "Princess Mary" chapter, which "reproduces [the] values and patterns" of polite society, but "transforms them radically, so that they become not forces of harmonization, but weapons in what must be seen as a competition, the goal of which is to ruin the performance, to penetrate the interlocutor's defenses, to discover his or her secrets."[14] Peter Scotto has aptly interpreted the "Bela" chapter as "an interrogation of the discourse and practice of Russian imperialism." Even in death, Scotto argues, Bela "remains trapped in the same discourses of power that held her captive in life," as Maksim Maksimych adorns her grave with "the instruments of her 'taming.'"[15] The violence of Russia's conquest of the Caucasus is shrouded behind claims of bringing "civilization" to the "savages." As Scotto notes, Maksim never tires of stereotyping the native tribes: "Terrible rogues, these Asiatics!" (205); "an utterly foolish people . . . incapable of any education" (207).[16]

Rhetorical and cognitive violence pervades the novel, sometimes hiding in surprising places. In the "Maksim Maksimych" chapter, for example, one's first impression is that Pechorin has been cruel in treating Maksim so coolly. But if one carefully examines Maksim's thoughts and words, he is revealed to be a less-than-innocent victim. At the end of "Bela" he explains why he restrains himself from bringing the episode up with Pechorin: "I saw that it would be unpleasant for him, so why do it?" (237) Several pages later, upon seeing Pechorin after several years, it is one of the first things he brings up, clearly having an unpleasant effect on Pechorin, who "paled slightly and turned away" (245). Maksim's friendship turns quickly to resentment. By the time Pechorin rides off, Maksim is prepared to have Pechorin's notes made into cartridges (247), symbolically completing his conversion of life experience into ammunition for further moralistic salvos. "Yes, I always knew he was a fickle person, on whom one couldn't depend" (246), Maksim says of Pechorin, to whom he had referred only hours earlier as his "bosom buddy" (*drug zakadychnyi,* 241). His tendency toward stereotypes emerges again, as he now lumps the blameless Traveling Editor together with Pechorin: "You are young men of society, you are haughty: here beneath the Circassian bullets you're more or less all right . . . but run into you later and you're ashamed even to shake your brother's hand" (247–48).[17]

The novel, then, takes on the task of revealing the violence behind the multiple decorous masks of civilization. Indeed, part of *Hero*'s unsettling effect is that the more one looks, the more violence one finds hidden in the world of the novel. Nevertheless, while *A Hero of Our Time* reveals various mechanisms by which violence propagates itself—social and imperial ideologies, mediated desire[18]—such revelation, strikingly, does not seem to suggest any solution, certainly none along the traditional lines of Christianity or humanism. No obvious antidote or alternative to violence emerges. Even Pechorin's arguably superior consciousness somehow falls short of the capacity to redeem or transform even his own life. Despite the long tradition of evaluating Pechorin morally as either a genuine (perhaps tragic) hero or a "truly satanic character,"[19] his character is fundamentally ambivalent—neither wholly savior nor entirely demon—and thus the novel's problems cannot be solved by either taking him as a model or identifying him as the problems' cause. The introduction that Lermontov added to the second edition indeed strongly implied the nonexistence of a solution: "It is sufficient that the disease has been pointed out; but as for how to cure it, only God knows!" (203) Violence itself, it would appear, had succumbed to Romantic treatment as an insoluble problem.

In place of a "cure," Lermontov offers "bitter medicines, caustic truths" (203), but what sort of medicine makes no claim to effect a cure? This paradox, together with the apposition of "medicines" to "truths," betrays the irony—perhaps even sarcasm—with which Lermontov invokes the then-commonplace trope of moral "disease" in the first place. The trope was first introduced not by the novel in its first edition, but by critics who blamed it for its unwillingness to "treat" *(vrachevat')* moral weaknesses in its readers[20] and even for glorifying, in the person of Pechorin, the "disease of the age," by which was meant a combination of "Western maladies": individualism ("pride of spirit") and hedonism ("the baseness that derives from satiated flesh").[21] In attacking these misreadings, Lermontov's introduction to the second edition suggests the inadequacy of the pathological metaphor for moral evils: diseases attack the body indiscriminately and independently of the mind and will; moral turpitude, on the other hand, pertains to the choices and attitudes of individuals. Morality concerns not the body, but the mind. Any potential cure therefore begins and ends with individual consciousness. As the precondition of any moral betterment, the problem must first be seen, the "caustic truths" revealed.[22] The novel undertakes this revelatory project, but because the choice to live without illusions is a matter of individual will, the next step belongs to the reader.

In place of medicine, the introduction prescribes an alternative metaphor for the novel's moral revelation: covert warfare aimed at the destruction of Russian society's self-serving illusions. *Hero* is motivated by the same impulse that drives the poet to "hurl iron verses" in the public's face, but its method is subtler. The "poorly brought up" Russian reader, "does not get a joke and does not sense irony" and "does not yet understand that in decent society and in a decent book there can be no place for overt hostility [*iavnaia bran'*]; that modern enlightenment [*obrazovannost'*] has discovered a weapon that is sharper, almost invisible, but nevertheless lethal, which under the guise of flattery delivers an inescapable and unerring blow" (202). This statement frames the novel doubly, as both violent in intention and surreptitious in method. To the extent that the novel aims at revealing and condemning society's hidden violence, it does so by violent means of its own, by fighting fire with fire. In the face of corrupting social influences, it proposes not an idyllic Rousseauean alternative, but a rhetorical duel.

The novel implies that both violence and stealth are necessitated by the threat of censorship, of course, but even more significantly by the specific character of the social illusions it combats. Society's delusions were more than mere "deceit[s] of the senses" or "error[s] of reason" that have been "mistake[n] for conviction[s]" (347). They constituted a highly developed, self-reinforcing and self-propagating system, whose individual parts worked unceasingly to sustain the whole: a moral ideology "composed of the vices of our entire generation, in full flower" (203). In the novel, as in Nicholas's Russia, challenges to the homogenizing ideology were met by a form of social coercion: the removal of the offending individual from society, through either expulsion or liquidation. The Captain of Dragoons, together with his posse of vigilantes, finds it necessary to destroy Mary's reputation for looking at him wrong (285) and to murder Pechorin for his "arrogant smile" (311). Grushnitskii's exclusion from better society parallels the cooling of Mary's interest in him and excites his hostility. Nicholas's enthusiastic use of exile—including his exile of Lermontov himself, twice—merely reflected social practice on the level of state policy. As any rebel or misfit in good society would soon discover, society was entirely capable of disgorging the heterodox without the tsar's help.[23] Any remaining hint of ideological dissonance was glossed over by rationalization: the commutation of the death sentence to exile displayed the tsar's "mercy"; and Peter Chaadaev's frank critique of Russian culture could not be explained otherwise than by his "insanity."[24] Compare the Captain of Dragoons' response to Pechorin's intention to reload his pistol, which the captain has left unloaded as part of the conspiracy: "But you do not have the right to reload . . . no right whatsoever . . . it is absolutely against the rules—I cannot allow it" (330). The captain's dogmatic repetition of the "rules," like Maksim's narrow-minded insistence on the savagery of the Caucasian natives, reflects "the violent mind's incapability of capturing what it should think about if it wanted to remain a mind."[25]

The novel's capacity to deliver a sneak attack that violently ruptures the complacent illusions of its readers is vividly illustrated by the response to it of Russian society's paterfamilias himself, Tsar Nicholas I: "The character of the captain [Maksim Maksimych] is prettily drawn. Beginning the story, I had hoped and rejoiced that he would probably be the hero of our time, for there are among this class of men [heroes] much more real than those upon whom this epithet is all too vulgarly conferred. Among the Corps in the Caucasus there are surely many such men—which one only learns too rarely to recognize. But this hope turns out to be unrealized in the work, and Monsieur Lermontov has proved unable to follow this noble and so simple a character, replacing this individual with despicable and very little interesting personages who, if they have annoyed, would have been better left unknown, in order not to provoke disgust."[26] The tsar's own violent annoyance and disgust suggest that the novel hit its mark. He responds characteristically, rhetorically consigning Pechorin to the literary exile of "very little interesting personages" and his author to actual exile in Caucasus, concluding with the envoy, "Bon voyage to M. Lermontov, he has only to purify his head in a milieu where he might manage to acquire the character of his captain, if he is indeed capable even of grasping and depicting it."

It is somewhat disturbing to realize that Lermontov's literary response to the violence of his age was in itself, in its own way, quite violent. One wants the most talented writers to provide positive alternatives to base reality, or at least a degree of redemption or transcendence.

Lermontov's wickedly ironic novel instead presents its readers with a mirror designed to leave no flaw unreflected. The novel's brutality may be excused in part by Lermontov's youthful lack of wisdom—the same lack, arguably, that got him killed in a duel little more than a year after the first appearance of his novel.[27] It might further be pointed out that Lermontov's strong Romanticism, and concomitant preoccupation with insoluble problems, was unlikely to produce any sort of stable redemptive vision. (Indeed, moral ambivalence and pessimism are the hallmarks of the Romantic narrative from *The Sorrows of Young Werther* to *Moby Dick.*) However, if we take seriously Milan Kundera's view that "knowledge is the novel's only morality,"[28] excuses of this sort are unnecessary. *A Hero of Our Time* is without question the seminal literary examination of violence in the Russian language. Even the violent attitude it assumed toward its reader was intended to be revelatory—to enable the reader to discover and extirpate the elements of coercive social ideology that enslave the individual conscience. The violence of Lermontov's society—especially in its rhetorical and cognitive manifestations as "intelligence in the form of violence"—was a pervasive problem with no pragmatic solution, but for Lermontov art found its necessary and sufficient raison d'être in bringing the suppressed problem to awareness. In this light, it is possible to see how Lermontov's Romantic art in *A Hero of Our Time* contributes to the tradition of the novel as an epistemological genre, as Broch and Kundera conceive it, enlisting the peculiar moral ambivalence born of insolubility in the service of moral discovery.

Notes

1. With the possible exception of Pushkin, if one considers Pushkin a Romantic. Some scholars, especially in the Soviet academy, have tendentiously emphasized Realist tendencies in Lermontov's later works. For a concise, yet moderately detailed recent summary of Lermontov's life and career, including some discussion of his works, see my "Mikhail Iur'evich Lermontov," in *The Age of Pushkin and Gogol: Poetry and Drama* (*Dictionary of Literary Biography*), vol. 206, ed. Christine Rydel (Detroit: Gale Research Publications, 1998), 179–205. Further general bibliography, including book-length biographies in English, may be found there.

2. One of Lermontov's first narrative poems, *The Prisoner of the Caucasus* (1828), is telling in this regard. Although it replicates the basic plot of Pushkin's seminal poem of the same name (1822), Lermontov ups the Romantic ante by providing a much bloodier climax. A valuable survey of Lermontov's narratives and plays can be found in William Edward Brown, *A History of Russian Literature of the Romantic Period*, 4 vols. (Ann Arbor, Mich.: Ardis, 1986), 4:175–261.

3. Romantic love is also connected to violence in "Valerik," which takes the form of an epistle addressed from the battlefield to a former lover in St. Petersburg. See my "Living into Language: Mikhail Lermontov and the Manufacturing of Intimacy," in *Russian Subjects: Empire, Nation, and the Culture of the Golden Age,* ed. Monika Greenleaf and Stephen Moeller-Sally (Evanston, Ill.: Northwestern University Press, 1998), 314–18.

4. It was the conclusion of this poem, "The Poet's Death," that gave offense by its vehement damnation of the courtiers whom Lermontov deemed responsible for conspiring to incite Pushkin's fatal duel. The tsar frequently punished officers like Lermontov by demoting them to the rank of soldier, transferring them from comfortable guard duty in Russia to active duty in the Caucasus—effectively a form of exile—or both.

5. Pushkin also died in a duel. Alexander Griboedov was torn to pieces by an angry anti-Russian mob in Teheran, where he was a diplomat. Alexander Bestuzhev-Marlinskii was killed under mysterious circumstances in a skirmish in the Caucasus. None of these writers was older than forty. All of them, including Lermontov, died within a dozen years of each other, between 1829 and 1841. Nevertheless, only the "ultra-Romantic" (Pushkin's phrase) Bestuzhev-Marlinskii—a career soldier, participant in the Decembrist rebellion, and author of popular adventure tales—authored an oeuvre and life that approaches Lermontov's in cumulative violence. The literary merits of Lermontov's works, however, are considerably greater. On Bestuzhev-Marlinskii, see Lewis Bagby, *Alexander Bestuzhev-Marlinsky and Russian Byronism* (University Park: Pennsylvania State University Press, 1995).

6. Lydia Ginzburg indirectly and offhandedly provides this rich definition of Romanticism in a study concerned with something entirely different, her *On Psychological Prose,* trans. and ed. Judson Rosengrant (Princeton, N.J.: Princeton University Press, 1991), 21.

7. Quoted here is "How often, circled by the motley crowd" ("Kak chasto, pestroiu tolpoiu okruzhen," 1840). See also "The Poet" ("Poet," 1838), "Meditation" ("Duma," 1838), "Trust Not Thyself" ("Ne ver' sebe," 1839), and "The Journalist, the Reader and the Writer" ("Zhurnalist, chitatel' i pisatel'," 1840).

8. "Kak chasto, pestroiu tolpoiu okruzhen, / Kogda peredo mnoi, kak budto by skvoz' son, / Pri shume muzyki i pliaski, / Pri dikom shepote zatverzhennykh rechei, / Mel'kaiut obrazy bezdushnye liudei, / Prilich'em stianutye maski."

9. "Brosit' im v glaza zheleznyi stikh, / Oblityi gorech'iu i zlost'iu!"

10. [Alexander Herzen and M. Meizenburg], "Russian Literature: Michael Lermontoff," *National Review,* London, 11 (1860): 334–5. Although published anonymously, the authorship of this article has been established by L. M. Arinshtein in his "Neizvestnaia stat'ia A. I. Gertsena i M. Meizenburg o Lermontove," in *M. Iu. Lermontov: Issledovaniia i materialy,* ed. M. P. Alekseev (Leningrad: Nauka, 1979), 283–308.

11. Two further factors contributed to lend Lermontov's general rebelliousness the air of political opposition. First, St. Petersburg society was Nicholas I's society; he was, as it were, the patriarch of this extended family. An affront to it was perceived as an affront to the throne. Second, the autocrat viewed any

strong personality, especially one as increasingly influential as Lermontov, as a threat in principle to his own absolute authority.

12. I assume basic familiarity with the novel. As a minimal crib for those who do not know it, I note that it is composed of two parts. Part 1 comprises the author's "Introduction" (added only in the second edition), and two stories narrated by a Traveling Editor: "Bela," much of which is occupied by Maksim Maksimych's narration, as related to the Editor; and "Maksim Maksimych." Part 2 consists of three excerpts from "Pechorin's Journal," obtained from Maksim Maksimych and prefaced by the Editor ("Preface"): "Taman'," "Princess Mary," and "The Fatalist." A detailed diagram of the novel's complex narrative structure can be found in my *Becoming Mikhail Lermontov: The Ironies of Romantic Individualism in Nicholas I's Russia* (Evanston, Ill.: Northwestern University Press, 2005), 338–39.

13. "The pure tautology, which propagates the concept while at the same time refusing to define that concept—and which instead mechanically repeats the concept—is intelligence in the form of violence." See Theodor W. Adorno, *The Jargon of Authenticity*, trans. Knut Tarnowski and Frederic Will (Evanston, Ill.: Northwestern University Press, 1973), 133.

14. William Mills Todd III, *Fiction and Society in the Age of Pushkin: Ideology, Institutions, and Narrative* (Cambridge, Mass.: Harvard University Press, 1986), 155.

15. Peter Scotto, "Prisoners of the Caucasus: Ideologies of Imperialism in Lermontov's 'Bela,'" *PMLA*, 107:2 (1992): 247.

16. All parenthetical page references are to *Geroi nashego vrementi*, in M. Iu. Lermontov, *Sochineniia v shesti tomakh*, ed. N. F. Bel'chikov et al. (Moscow-Leningrad: AN SSSR, 1954–57), vol. 6.

17. I discuss the cognitive and rhetorical violence of Maksim's stereotypical thinking and the novel's deflationary irony in greater detail in the chapter on *Hero* in *Becoming Mikhail Lermontov*.

18. Todd was the first to suggest the role of mediated desire in Pechorin's behavior. See his *Fiction and Society*, 157–58.

19. L. V. Brant, "'Geroi nashego vremeni' M. Lermontova," *Russkii invalid*, 17–18 (22 January 1841): 71–72. English translations of this review, the Burachok and Shevyrev reviews cited below, and several other notable contemporary reviews of the novel have been made available for the first time in *Lermontov's* A Hero of Our Time: *A Critical Companion*, ed. Lewis Bagby (Evanston, Ill.: Northwestern University Press, 2002).

20. S. A. Burachok, "'Geroi nashego vremeni' M. Lermontova," *Maiak* 1840, ch. 4, gl. 4, 210–19, and ch. 5, gl. 4, 1–22.

21. S. P. Shevyrev, "'Geroi nashego vremeni' M. Lermontova," *Moskvitianin* 1841, ch. 1, no. 2, 515–38.

22. As Vladimir Golstein argues, the novel "embodies a massive critique of expectations and illusions of any kind." See his *Lermontov's Narratives of Heroism* (Evanston, Ill.: Northwestern University Press, 1998), 129. In my opinion, Golstein elides somewhat the brutality of Lermontov's revelatory methods.

23. The seminal literary example is society's rejection of the gadfly Chatskii in Alexander Griboedov's *Woe from Wit* (*Gore ot uma*, 1824).

24. After Chaadaev's first "Philosophical Letter" was published in *Telescope* in 1836, the journal was suspended, its editor was exiled, and Chaadaev himself was officially declared insane and placed under house arrest. Interestingly, Nicholas's first response to Lermontov's "The Poet's Death" was to order an examination of its author to "ascertain whether he might not be insane." See the tsar's "Resolution," reproduced in *M. Iu. Lermontov v vospominaniiakh sovremennikov,* ed. V. E. Vatsuro et al. (Moscow: Khudozhestvennaia literatura, 1989), 486.

25. Adorno, *The Jargon of Authenticity,* 133.

26. Emma Gershtein, *Sud'ba Lermontova* (Moscow: Sovetskii pisatel', 1964), 467–68. The final phrases in the tsar's letter are even more convoluted and ungrammatical in the original French than in my English rendering: "misérables et fort peu intéressants personnages qui s'ils ont ennuyé [*sic*] auraient mieux fait de rester ignorés pour ne provoquer le dégoût."

27. According to most reports Lermontov's challenger in duel, Nicholas Martynov, was insulted by the poet's incessant public jibes regarding his foppish dress and manner. The two had known each other for years, and there had been previous instances of friction, including a possible romantic link between Lermontov and one of Martynov's sisters. See Powelstock, "Mikhail Iur'evich Lermontov," 201–2, and the various contemporary accounts of the duel and its causes in *M. Iu. Lermontov v vospominaniiakh sovremennikov.*

28. Milan Kundera, *The Art of the Novel* (New York: Harper and Row, 1988), 6.

The Spectacle of the Scaffold

Performance and Subversion in the Execution of the Decembrists

LUDMILLA A. TRIGOS

On December 14, 1825, a small group of military officers, noblemen, progressive civil servants, and civic-minded poets led approximately two thousand troops onto Senate Square to refuse to take an oath to the new tsar, Nicholas I, and to demand a change in the government. The rebellion, precipitated by Tsar Alexander I's death and the uncertainty surrounding the succession came at the end of a lengthy interregnum during which Constantine, the brother next in line for the throne, renounced his right but refused to return to the capital from his home in Warsaw to make his renunciation public. This demonstration—perpetrated by members of a secret society who desired the overthrow of the autocracy, the abolition of serfdom, and the establishment of some sort of constitution guaranteeing rights to all citizens—became known as the Decembrist uprising, and its participants as the Decembrists. The rebels rallied their troops under the banner, "Constantine and a constitution," playing upon the troops' sympathy to Constantine and their dislike of his younger brother, Nicholas, who became the heir to the throne after Constantine's renunciation. After several unsuccessful attempts to negotiate with the rebels, tsarist forces quickly quashed the revolt, imprisoned the survivors, and began to interrogate them to determine the scope of the dissention. After several months of reviewing the testimony, the authorities handed down the sentences: the five so-called leaders of the revolt were sentenced to death, and hundreds to penal servitude and exile. Nicholas celebrated his victory over the Decembrists with a memorial mass annually during his reign.

The Decembrists' revolt has been perceived in Russian history and culture as one of the central, cataclysmic events of the nineteenth century. Yet despite their failure the Decembrists attained a legendary status in the eyes of generations of Russians. Both Russian and Western historians have pointed to the importance of the Decembrist uprising as a legend, yet until recently few have speculated as to how and why this legend has held such long fascination.[1] Nicholas Riasanovsky points to a compelling reason when he notes that the execution of the movement's five leaders allowed for the perception of the Decembrists as martyrs. The valorization of suffering, an integral component of Russian Orthodox belief, further enhanced their sacrificial image and thus guaranteed their lofty status in the mid-nineteenth century among the members of the radical intelligentsia, who strove to construct a genealogy of revolutionaries as models for their own future course of action. This same perception of the Decembrists' martyrdom also facilitated their later entry into the Bolshevik revolutionary martyrology as part and parcel of the new regime's creation of its own saints.[2] The Decembrists eventually joined the ranks of the other heroes of the Revolution, sanctified by the Bolshevik (later Communist) Party along with the Populists, Marx, Engels, and Lenin.

The execution of the Decembrist leaders has survived as an iconic moment in the history of the Russian revolutionary movement. Moreover, the official suppression of the public spectacle of the execution served to enhance even further the sacred and legendary aura of the deceased Decembrists. In this article, my focus will be two-fold. First, my discussion of the public perception of the execution will illustrate the centrality of this moment to Russian cultural history.[3] To this end, I will examine the varied depictions of the execution in contemporary memoirs. Second, I will trace the subsequent transposition of the event in literary texts. The fact that the execution was a hidden spectacle—to coin an oxymoronic phrase—led to a paucity of sources as the small number of witnesses left few written representations of the events. Instead, the remaining Decembrists had to piece together the information from a variety of sources; they then attempted to construct their own narrative from that collected information.[4] In the memoirs of the Decembrists and their contemporaries we find a number of competing representations, further emphasizing the multiple and contested meanings of ritual events. When later authors were finally able to portray the Decembrists in literary works, they frequently referred to the memoirs for a sense of what happened, but they had no conclusive version of the truth. These works of literature confront the issue of how a writer imagines *(voobrazit')* an event when the image *(obraz)* itself—that is, an uncontested representation—does not exist.

A reconstruction of the basic facts of the execution follows. On July 13, 1826, Pavel Pestel', Kondratii Ryleev, Sergei Murav'ev-Apostol, Peter Kakhovskii, and Mikhail Bestuzhev-Riumin were hanged on the ramparts of Peter-Paul Fortress. Though scheduled for 3 a.m., the ceremony did not begin until 5:30 a.m. because of faulty construction of the scaffold. The five fettered men were led out: Kakhovskii walked alone first, behind him Murav'ev-Apostol with Bestuzhev, then Ryleev and Pestel'. After they heard their sentence read aloud, the men made their final obeisance to the Lord, and then they walked onto the scaffold. The executioners placed nooses and white hoods on them. On their chests hung black leather signs on which their names were written, along with the words "criminal, regicide."[5] When the command was given, the board on which they stood was removed and at that moment three bodies fell, their ropes having broken.[6] Ryleev, Murav'ev-Apostol and Kakhovskii, in varying stages of consciousness, were helped back up onto the scaffold and hanged a second time.[7] There the bodies remained until 6 a.m., when a doctor pronounced them dead and they were removed and disposed of in an unknown location.[8] The official news of the execution and exile of the remaining "state criminals" appeared in *The Northern Bee* and other newspapers days later (July 17), and religious services were held to cleanse symbolically the stain of rebellion from society and commemorate the tsarist victory over the rebels in Petersburg on Senate Square (July 14) and in Moscow (July 19) at the Kremlin.

None of the imperial family saw the execution, though they were told about its every aspect; a courier went back and forth between Tsarskoe Selo and Peter-Paul fortress every half hour with progress reports.[9] None of the remaining Decembrists witnessed the event themselves, but they were informed by the priest who presided at the execution as well as by officers and guards while they were still in the Peter-Paul Fortress. Nicholas suppressed as much information about the execution as possible out of fear of public disturbance. Despite the attempts made by the authorities to discourage attendance, a very small group did see the hanging in addition to the army troops and police officers who were involved in the execution.[10]

Prior to the execution, rumors circulated that Nicholas would annul the death penalty at the last minute as a result of the empress's intercession on behalf of the Decembrists. Given the severity of the crime against the state and the person of the tsar, the punishment of the five conspirators was legally justified and followed the precedent of execution set by earlier tsars.[11] Yet all the same, in this case public opinion deemed the sentence too harsh. In fact, the execution of the Decembrists instead "drew a sharp line between the reigns of Alexander and Nicholas."[12] Certainly, the notion that Russia was an enlightened nation was shattered by the execution of members of the elite. As Richard Wortman comments: "The execution of five of the leaders . . . and the exile of other young, attractive and talented aristocrats confounded and shocked even conservative members of the elite. It confuted the belief that the monarchy was becoming a milder, more humane institution that would utilize its powers to achieve the good that elsewhere had come from conflict and violence."[13] Instead Nicholas determined to follow the letter of the law, rather than to exercise his sovereign right to lessen judgment. Immediately after the uprising, Nicholas told the French envoy, Count de la Ferronays, "The law dictates punishment, and I will not use my right of clemency for them. I will be implacable. I am obliged to give this lesson to Russia and to Europe."[14] For Nicholas then, the task remained to provide a fearsome example of the harsh punishment that would meet anyone—no matter what his rank—conspiring against the tsar and state.

Nicholas's concern is apparent from his elaborate orchestration of the rituals of state: his numerous manifestos, his presentation of his son to imperial troops immediately after the uprising, and his attention to the trial, sentencing, and execution reveal an urge for self-legitimization through his role as defender of the Romanov dynasty and hence, the Russian state.[15] The lesson Nicholas I was determined to give to Russia and to Europe backfired in the long run; instead, the execution was subverted by denying witnesses the opportunity to experience and therefore to narrate it. Since it was not public, and it remained unseen by the people, it took on even more scandalous shades of illegality. No framework could be devised to interpret and thus make meaning of the event, since no definitive account of the execution could be accessed.

In his seminal work, *Discipline and Punish,* Michel Foucault points out that executions were considered socially useful and successful as means of control only when the onlookers were sufficiently impressed by the spectacle of the event: "public torture and execution must be spectacular, it must be seen by all almost as its triumph. The very excess of the violence employed is one of the elements of its glory."[16] In his discussion of the transition from public to private infliction of punishment beginning at the end of the eighteenth century, he focuses on the increasingly negative attitude toward capital and corporal punishment throughout Europe: "Punishment had gradually ceased to be a spectacle. . . . It was as if the punishment was thought to equal, if not to exceed, in savagery the crime itself . . . to make the executioner resemble a criminal, judges murderers, to reverse roles at the last moment, to make the tortured criminal an object of pity or admiration."[17] Thus Foucault emphasizes the fact that the negative association between the crime and the punisher provided a strong impetus for the veneration of the punished.[18]

The execution of the Decembrists occurs at just this juncture of history. Given both the changing mentalities and politics in Europe, it comes as no surprise that Western diplomats and educated Russian society viewed the execution for the most part negatively. In the case of the Russian nation, the level of legal development clashed with its citizens' moral evolution.[19] Once the edificatory aspect of the punishment had been withdrawn or undermined, the execution had little value as a means of mobilizing societal support or as a "ceremonial of power."[20] In this case, the rite orchestrated by Nicholas would be witnessed only by those officials and members of the military who did not need to be convinced of their loyalty to the state. The Decembrist A. Rozen pondered the unusual situation: "I don't know to what to attribute the reason that the execution was not performed before our eyes, in our presence. . . . Of course, they didn't want to suppress it; it must serve as an example and a deterrent."[21] In this case of hidden spectacle, the public did not witness the ceremonial enactment of the restoration of the sovereign's power. Perhaps more important, the people's vengeance could not become part of the sovereign's vengeance against those who would threaten his person and the state.[22]

Obviously, Nicholas I recognized both the ambivalent nature of the spectacle of punishment and the punishment itself. His decision to punish the conspirators severely could appeal only to the most zealous and conservative of patriots, given the Decembrists' class standing, somewhat ambiguous actions and, in many cases, total disavowal of revolutionary opinions after incarceration and questioning. With the exception of the official accounts, a sense of moral shock and outrage permeates many of the memoir accounts of the event. We need only recall the famous lines from Alexander Herzen's mythogenic memoir, *My Past and Thoughts:* "The accounts of the rising and of the trial of the leaders, and the horror in Moscow, made a deep impression on me; a new world was revealed to me which became more and more the center of my moral existence. . . . I felt I was not on the same side as the grapeshot and victory, prisons and chains. The execution of Pestel and his associates finally dissipated the childish dream of my soul."[23] The execution was seen by many as a sacrifice for the lofty ideals of freedom and equality rather than the punishment due to criminals. The executed men were referred to as "our five martyrs" *(nashi piat' muchenikov)* by the remaining Decembrists and their sympathizers.[24]

After the sentencing and execution, mention of the Decembrists in any public forum was forbidden; their names could not be mentioned in print, nor could the surviving Decembrists obtain permission to have their portraits painted even years later in exile. This censorship, the hiding of the Decembrists (remaining and deceased) from any kind of public view, was equivalent to the hiding of the spectacle of the execution. References to the execution of the Decembrists, and to the Decembrists in general, moved to more private genres, such as letters and memoirs. In their memoirs, the Decembrists take the first step toward meaningful interpretation of the execution. Yet beyond the most basic facts of the execution, the memoirists differ—in their description of which three men fell from the scaffold, on which men spoke last words, and what those last words were.[25] Ryleev's last words exist in more than six different versions[26] and Murav'ev-Apostol's in at least two variations.[27] In the memoirs penned by the remaining Decembrists and those sympathetic to their cause and fate, the transcribers perhaps not surprisingly tend to privilege words that testify to the courage of the Decembrists and their unflagging scorn of tyranny to the very end. The official account, on the other hand, suppresses the last words entirely. Some witnesses who attended in a military or police capacity attest to their admiration of the Decembrists and provide fitting last words, while others cite last words to illustrate what they believe was baseness in the Decembrists' characters, thereby implying they believed the death sentence to be justified.[28]

Yet in all cases, the sources attest to the strong impression the execution, especially the moment when the three fell from the gallows, made on the few who did witness it. The German historian J. H. Shnitzler calls it a "terrifying spectacle" in his account.[29] The writer N. Putiata comments: "Several nights after that I could not sleep peacefully. As soon as my eyes closed, the gallows and the victims *(zhertvy)* fallen from it appeared before my eyes."[30] Even imperial officers were struck by the scene. One policeman in attendance remarked that as the five Decembrists said their final prayers upon the scaffold, "it was difficult, brother, to look upon them!" The policeman highlighted his horror at having to witness the execution: "We could see their faces clearly. . . . They looked for the last time at the sky, brother, so mournfully, that our stomachs flip-flopped and we got shivers up our spines. . . . It was terrifying, brother, oh, terrifying! Our hair stood on end."[31] An unnamed official emphasized the harmful effect of the event: "The spectacle made a strong impression on those immediately present: the architect [of the scaffold] Gernei [Harney] died a month later from a fever. The police captain Posnikov suffered from illness for more than a year and died; he always said that it [the execution] was the cause of his illness."[32] Here the common superstitious belief manifests itself that those who participate in the actual execution somehow become tainted by association with the instruments of death, the location, and/or the hangmen themselves.[33] Hence the official need for cleansing ceremonies, performed ostensibly to purge the site of the original bloodshed of the uprising and to congratulate Nicholas I on preserving the Russian state.[34] Naturally, the services occurred immediately after the punishment, signifying the closure of the episode; yet they also stem from and illustrate a need to neutralize not only the revolt but also the punishment. According to a Third Section document, the tsarist government began to regain some of its lost support only after the purifying services were performed. Yet despite the various ceremonies accompanying his ascension to the throne, Nicholas was successful in galvanizing the support of some, but not all of the onlookers.[35]

Because of censorship restrictions, the portrayal of the execution of the Decembrists was left to later generations freed from the constraints of tsarist censorship. However, beginning immediately after their sentencing and exile and continuing into the twentieth century, the Decembrists became an important touchstone for generations of members of the Russian intelligentsia and revolutionaries. Alexander Pushkin, who espoused early in his career similar political views and counted among his closest friends several Decembrists, makes many veiled references in his poetry to the Decembrists, though he could not refer directly to them in his published work. His famous poem, "Deep in Siberian Mines" ("Vo glubine Sibirskikh rud," 1826), was delivered to the exiled

Decembrists by Alexandra Murav'eva (wife of the Decembrist Nikita Murav'ev), who followed her husband into exile.[36] As several scholars have suggested, the Decembrists continued to loom large in his imagination. His manuscripts are littered with portraits of Pavel Pestel', Kondratii Ryleev, Ivan Pushchin, Wilhelm Kiukhelbeker and others, but especially telling is his November 1826 drawing of a scaffold with five dangling bodies. This image is not unique to his work; drawings of hangings (of scaffolds and of the five Decembrists) reappear in his manuscripts of Poltava and of other works from 1828–29. These sketches and the frequent references to hanging in his works throughout the late 1820s illustrate Pushkin's obsession with the execution of the Decembrists. Though he imagined the scene, he could only represent it in a much refracted form.[37]

The Decembrists' first and most vocal proponents, Alexander Herzen and Nikolai Ogarev, participated in the mythmaking process, publishing the Decembrists' memoirs and their own tributes in the press abroad. It has been noted ad nauseam that Herzen featured the silhouettes of the five hanged Decembrists as the frontispiece to his journal *Polar Star (Poliarnaia Zvezda)*, named after the literary almanac published by Ryleev and Alexander Bestuzhev. Nikolai Nekrasov, among other socially engaged writers, depicted the lofty sacrifice of the Decembrists' wives in his renowned poem "Russian Women" ("Russkie zhenshchiny," 1877); this poem perpetuated a saintly image of the wives who followed their husbands into exile and by implicit association exalted the status of the Decembrists themselves. In such times when direct references to the Decembrists could not be made, the wives became an important part of their legend. Vera Figner, Georgii Plekhanov, and Vladimir Lenin all esteemed the Decembrists' noble sacrifice in the name of revolutionary change and frequently discussed them in their writings.[38]

The Decembrists' execution appears in literature only after the 1917 Revolution, and it figures prominently in the works produced for the 1925 centennial celebration of the Decembrist uprising. Without exception, the works that feature the execution draw upon the memoirs of the Decembrists—by then widely available—for their portrayals. In his novel, *Kiukhlia* (1925), Iurii Tynianov filters the unforgettable scene of the execution through the subjective consciousness of his protagonist, the Decembrist poet Wilhelm Kiukhelbeker (nicknamed Kiukhlia), whom he depicts as an eyewitness, selecting as Ryleev's putative last words the version that circulated among the aristocracy: "You may try to doze off—if only for a half hour or ten minutes—so as not to see the half-dead body in a sack fall from the gallows and cry with the voice of your friend, the lofty poet and friend, who sometime stroked your hand: 'You, General, probably came to see us die in torment.'" The execution reappears in Kiukhlia's dreams in a carnivalesque form: "He hadn't noticed there were actually five narrow, new swings. Ah, they are taking them to swing. The five of them. Five. Their hands are tied behind their backs with straps and straps bind their legs—they take teeny-tiny steps. . . . They are taking them to swing. Music. Children's swings."[39] The horrifying spectacle can only be imagined as a nightmare. Kiukhlia's inability or unwillingness to understand the meaning of the contraptions ("Children's swings") mirrors the destabilization and uncertainty felt in dreams. Tynianov thus captures the psychological impact of the spectacle in his portrayal.

Another novel written for the centennial, Mariia Marich's *Aurora Borealis (Severnoe siianie)*, provides the most elaborate and realistic depiction of the Decembrists' execution. Marich fully sets the scene: "The small crowd of people was ashamed to watch silently what would be perpetrated on the wooden scaffold. It was torturously shameful for the guards' regiments, who were brought to witness the execution. It was shameful, painfully shameful, for the musicians to play a military march. People were frightened to meet the gaze of the condemned men, and, shaken by what went on before their eyes, counted the terrible minutes."[40] Focusing on the visual impact of the event, Marich prepares the reader for the awful scene to come. After three bodies fall from the gallows, a "cry of horror" arises from the crowd, though it is drowned out by the beat of the drums. This vivid portrayal highlights the power of the spectacle as an indictment of the autocracy and its "shameful" deeds.

The film *The Decembrists* (*Dekabristy*, 1927, directed by Alexander Ivanovskii), begun during the centennial year but released in 1927, also draws heavily upon the memoirs in its depiction of the hanging of the Decembrists. The film, a blockbuster success at the box office,[41] provides a memorable, if melodramatic, final sequence that fully highlights the nature of the execution as a spectacle. In a rapid montage construction, the film alternates between a fireworks display in honor of Nicholas's coronation and the hanging of the Decembrists. The scaffold with five nooses dominates the screen; the shots shift from close-ups of the soldiers and the executioners to the Decembrists. Another rapid sequence of shots—of shrouds being pulled over the condemned men's heads—is intercut with close-ups of the drummers' hands, quickly tapping out the beat. Then the camera shifts back to the fireworks display, fading out slightly to superimpose onto the fireworks' backdrop the image of the gallows with five shrouded figures dangling from it. This superimposition draws attention to the connection between both spectacles as well as indicating their simultaneity. The fireworks fade out, and the scaffold with the hanging bodies, now seen at daylight, fills the screen, the spire of Peter-Paul fortress bisecting it. This stark image ends the filmic text. Though not a critical success, the film became a favorite of the masses, and ranked as fourth in a survey of the top ten most popular movies of the era.[42]

In addition to the centennial publications and the production of films on the Decembrists, stamps were issued to memorialize important moments in the Decembrist movement. The highest value, 14 kopeks, was assigned to the stamp with the image of the executed Decembrists, further impressing this iconic moment onto the popular consciousness. Accompanying the celebration of the uprising's centenary, events included a commemoration of the anniversary of the execution of the Decembrists in July 1926, when a monument to the five men was placed on the approximate location of their graves.[43] The ceremonial remembrance of the execution provided the Bolsheviks with an opportunity to redress the wrongs of the tsarist regime and to affirm their figurative kinship with the Decembrists. With their attempt to locate the Decembrists' graves and to provide a proper burial—though only a symbolic act—the Bolsheviks strove for the political, symbolic, and literal return of the Decembrists to their rightful place in the cosmic order as legitimating ancestors. Thus these rituals further emphasized the significance of the Decembrists' execution in the Soviet consciousness. In an inversion of the tsarist practice—of Nicholas's annual commemoration of his victory over the Decembrists—the Soviet Union celebrated the Decembrist revolt every year.[44]

A final testimonial to the power the execution of the Decembrists still holds over the cultural imagination can be seen in the continuing popularity of the theme in the post-Soviet era. A literary scandal ensued with the publication of an unauthorized sequel to Leo Tolstoy's renowned novel *War and Peace,* penned by a pseudonymous author (one Vasilii Staroi) and entitled *Pierre and Natasha* (1996). Panned by the critics and reviled by the intelligentsia as blasphemous, the sequel creatively, if sometimes absurdly, continues where *War and Peace* left off. The novel adopts a skeptical stance in its portrayal of the execution of the Decembrists, questioning the authenticity of the last words of the Decembrists and the version of events that passed down into history. This approach is echoed in Kama Ginkas's play *The Execution of the Decembrists (Kazn' dekabristov)*. The production was hailed as "a powerful and typically unorthodox presentation." Rather than realistically reenact the events, Ginkas has his actors "speak the language of interrogations, reports, or letters from which the text has been cut and pasted, while a figure called 'the Author' interrupts the flow of events, 'directing' the action and encouraging the spectators to remain skeptical about the characters' claims and confessions."[45] Ginkas demonstrates the symbolic value of the executed Decembrists by their unusual mode of representation; white nightshirts on hangers with nametags across their chests, they hang against the brick wall backdrop of the theater. The figures become important specifically as emblems of the repressive act of the tsarist government, rather than as characters speaking and acting upon the stage. Though a new postmodern approach has been taken toward the topic, these works continue to grapple with the execution and with the Decembrists' legacy to Russian culture.

Notes

1. For a more detailed discussion of the Decembrist movement, see Anatole Mazour, *The First Russian Revolution, 1825, the Decembrist Movement: Its Origins, Development and Significance* (Stanford, Calif.: Stanford University Press, 1937); Marc Raeff, *The Decembrist Movement* (Englewood Cliffs, N.J.: Prentice Hall, 1966); W. Bruce Lincoln, *Nicholas I: Emperor and Autocrat of All the Russias* (DeKalb: Northern Illinois University Press, 1989); and Nicholas V. Riasanovsky, *A Parting of the Ways: Government and the Educated Public in Russia 1801–1855* (Oxford: Clarendon Press, 1976). For a brief discussion of the Decembrist legend, see Ia. V. Leont'ev, "Legenda o dekabristakh," in *170 let spustia—: Dekabristskie chteniia* (Moscow: Gos. istoricheskii muzei, 1999), 172–76.

2. This entry was also facilitated by Vladimir Lenin's 1912 formulation of the three phases of revolutionary history, beginning with the Decembrists. See his article, "Pamiati Gertsena" (1912), in Vladimir Lenin, *Polnoe sobraniie sochinenii* (Moscow: Gosudarstvennoe izdatel'stvo politicheskoi literatury, 1958–65), 21:261.

3. Public opinion can be elusive and difficult to pinpoint. What I have in mind is to examine a variety of memoir and official accounts of the execution in order to see shifts in the way the Decembrists were perceived. The memoirs allow a look at the "apocrypha" concerning the execution since they document both eyewitness and received accounts of the event. As Irina Reyfman points out in her book *Vasilii Trediakovskii: The Fool of the "New" Russian Literature* (Stanford,

Calif.: Stanford University Press, 1990), anecdotes, rumors, and legends play an important role in the formation of collective consciousness (6).

4. In a recent article, K. G. Bolenko and N. V. Samover argue that the Decembrists also constructed their own version of the inquiry and court process the imperial authorities conducted against them. They also confirm my point that the sentence and execution facilitated the change in the public's perception of the Decembrists from criminals to martyrs. See their contribution, "Verkhovnyi ugolovnyi sud 1826 goda: dekabristskaia versiia v istoriograficheskoi traditsii" in *Pushkinskaia konferentsiia v Stenforde: Materialy i issledovaniia po istorii russkoi kul'tury* (Moscow: OGI, 2001), 7:143–70. My thanks to Ilya Vinitsky for calling my attention to this article.

5. Only one memoirist states that the leather boards had the words "zlodei, tsareubiets" written on them, though the police officer's account attests that their names and their crime were written on the boards ("Iz rasskaza politseiskogo," in *Pisateli-dekabristy v vospominaniakh sovremennikov v dvukh tomakh* [Moscow: Khudozhestvennaia literatura, 1980], 1:264).

6. The witnesses' accounts express uncertainty as to the identity of the three who fell. According to the official account of Golenishchev-Kutuzov, Ryleev, Murav'ev and Kakhovskii were the unfortunate ones. See "Vsepoddaneishee donesenie o kazni dekabristov (13 iiulia 1826)," *Byloe* 3 (1906), 232.

7. This action was contrary to the established European custom of pardoning a condemned man if the executioner failed. Michel Foucault discusses this tradition in his study of punishment practices. We should note here that most Russian memoirists censure the authorities for their nonobservance of this European custom. See Michel Foucault, *Discipline and Punish: The Birth of the Prison,* trans. Alan Sheridan (New York: Vintage Books, 1995), 52–53.

8. According to archival sources, Nicholas I himself arranged the event down to the smallest detail, despite the fact that he chose not to attend the execution. Nicholas provided a thorough timetable for the execution. See "Zapiski Nikolaia I o kazni dekabristov," *Novyi mir* 9 (1958): 277–78.

9. *Pisateli-dekabristy,* 1:418–19.

10. One accidental witness, the writer N. V. Putiata, after roaming the streets of Petersburg in search of news about the execution, went by boat across the Neva to the shore of the fortress, where, upon disembarking, he discovered the gallows still under construction. He found Baron A. Delvig and N. I. Grech among the crowd that had gathered, as well as an emissary of the French government, De La Rue, who happened to be a school friend of the Decembrist Sergei Muraviev-Apostol. (N. V. Putiata, "Rasskaz," first printed in *Russkii arkhiv* 2:2 (1881): 343–44, reprinted in *Pisateli-dekabristy,* 1:269.) According to J. H. Shnitzler, a German historian who lived in Petersburg from 1823 to 1828, people were drawn to the site by the faint beat of drums and the sound of a trumpet "to witness this mournful spectacle" (*Pisateli-dekabristy,* 1:267). The dowager empress Mariia Fedorovna writes in her diary that "the crowd was not large, but it grew larger as the execution came to a close" (*Pisateli-dekabristy,* 1:421).

11. For a discussion of the history of capital punishment in Russia, see Abby Schrader, *Languages of the Lash: Corporal Punishment and Identity in Imperial Russia*

(DeKalb: Northern Illinois University Press, 2002), 1–26; N. A. Shelkoplias, *Smertnaia kazn' v Rossii: istoriia stanovleniia i razvitiia* (Minsk: Amalfeia, 2002); Alan Wood, "Crime and Punishment in the House of the Dead," in *Civil Rights in Imperial Russia*, ed. Olga Crisp (Oxford: Oxford University Press, 1989), 215–33; and Cyril Bryner, "The Issue of Capital Punishment in the Reign of Elizaveta Petrovna," *Russian Review* 49:4 (Oct. 1990): 389–416.

12. Richard Wortman, *Scenarios of Power: Myth and Ritual in the Russian Monarchy* (Princeton, N.J.: Princeton University Press, 1995), 1:276.

13. Ibid.

14. N. K. Shilder, *Imperator Nikolai Pervyi, ego zhizn'i tsarstvovanie* (St. Petersburg: A. S. Suvorin, 1903), 1:453–54, cited in Wortman, *Scenarios of Power*, 275. The Decembrist N. P. Tsebrikov provides a similar anecdote, that Nicholas told the Duke of Wellington that he would "surprise Europe with his mercy" ("Vospominaniia o kronverskoi kurtine: Iz zapisok dekabrista," in *Pisateli-dekabristy*, 1:243).

15. Wortman, *Scenarios of Power*, 265. For a full discussion of Nicholas's creation of the official myth of the uprising and the ceremonies with which he confirmed his rule, see ibid., 264–78.

16. Foucault, *Discipline and Punish*, 34.

17. Ibid., 9.

18. "The great spectacle of physical punishment disappeared; the tortured body was avoided; the theatrical representation of pain was excluded from punishment" (Foucault, *Discipline and Punish*, 14).

19. See George L. Yaney, *The Systematization of Russian Government: Social Evolution in the Domestic Administration of Imperial Russia, 1711–1905* (Urbana: University of Illinois Press, 1973).

20. Foucault, *Discipline and Punish*, 49.

21. A. E. Rozen, "Iz zapisok dekabrista," in *Pisateli-dekabristy*, 1:166.

22. Foucault, *Discipline and Punish*, 57–59, 130.

23. Alexander Herzen, *My Past and Thoughts*, trans. Constance Garnett (Berkeley: University of California Press, 1973), 42.

24. For example, see N. P. Tsebrikov, "Vospominaniia," in *Pisateli-dekabristy*, 1:240–49.

25. Lydia Ginzburg notes that discrepancies from one memoir account to the next are common and inherent in the genre. Though in many cases memoirists insist that they have faithfully rendered events and transcribed exact words, their accuracy simply cannot be true, given the fact that a natural selection process must take place in determining which information to convey, not to mention the fact that memories may be compromised since many writers pen their accounts years after the events actually took place. Memoir accounts of the Decembrists' execution illustrate these very issues. See Lydia Ginzburg, *On Psychological Prose*, trans. Judson Rosengrant (Princeton, N.J.: Princeton University Press, 1991).

26. The Decembrist Nikolai Bestuzhev, a close friend of Ryleev, recounts Ryleev's last words as: "Our execution means little to them; they still need tyranny!" (N. A. Bestuzhev, "Vospominaniia o Ryleeve," in *Pisateli-dekabristy*, 2:89). The Decembrist Tsebrikov cites Ryleev's last words in verse form: "Ryleev

dies a criminal / Let Russia remember him!" (Tsebrikov, "Vospominaniia," in *Pisateli-dekabristy,* 1:246). The Decembrist Mikhail Bestuzhev, brother of Nikolai, provides the version of Ryleev's last words that circulated among aristocratic circles the day of the execution: "You, General, probably came to see us die. Gladden your tsar, that his wish is fulfilled: you see—we are dying in torment." After Petersburg Governor General Golenishchev-Kutuzov cried out for the executioners to hang the men a second time, Ryleev allegedly called out: "Base *oprichnik* of the tyrant! Give the executioner your aiguillettes so we do not have to die a third time!" ("Kazn' Ryleeva," in *Pisateli-dekabristy,* 1:252). However, an official witness recalls Ryleev's words differently; at the moment when this military man assisted him after his fall from the gallows, Ryleev supposedly said: "What misfortune!" ("So slov prisutstvovavshego po sluzhbe pri kazni," in *Pisateli-dekabristy,* 1:261).

27. One police witness attributes to Ryleev words allegedly uttered by Murav'ev-Apostol: "And they can't even properly hang someone!" though for the most part, in other accounts these words remain unique to Murav'ev-Apostol ("Iz rasskaza politseiskogo," in *Pisateli-dekabristy,* 1:267). According to the priest Myslovskii these words belonged to Murav'ev-Apostol and not Ryleev.

28. An anonymous eyewitness attributes the following comment to Murav'ev-Apostol: "What a shameful death! For us it doesn't matter, but it is a pity that this stain will lie upon our children.—And then, having fallen silent, he said:—Well, there's nothing to be done; Christ thus suffered having been less guilty than us. We have clear consciences and God will not abandon us." The narrator's gloss on these words follows: "These words show him to be an unrepentant sinner." He does, however, praise Ryleev and Pestel', who died as "good Christians"("Rasskaz samovidtsa o kazni, sovershennoi v Peterburge 1826 goda 13 iiulia," in *Pisateli-dekabristy,* 1:271).

29. J. H. Shnitzler, "Rasskaz," in *Pisateli-dekabristy,* 1:268.

30. N. V. Putiata, "Rasskaz," in *Pisateli-dekabristy,* 1:269.

31. "Iz rasskaza politseiskogo," in *Pisateli-dekabristy,* 1:264–65.

32. "So slov prisutstvovavshego po sluzhbe pri kazni," an anonymous account originally published in *Poliarnaia zvezda* 6 (1861): 72–75, quoted in *Pisateli-dekabristy,* 1:259.

33. Pieter Spierenburg, *The Spectacle of Suffering: Executions and the Evolution of Repression from a Preindustrial Metropolis to the European Experience* (Cambridge: Cambridge University Press, 1984), 42. Spierenburg's discussion posits several explanations for the association of infamy, from the survival of pagan popular beliefs to the subconscious rejection of a system of physical punishment that is transformed to a reaction of hatred to its active agent (21–23).

34. In his speech to the troops after the services, Nicholas himself emphasized the significance of the ceremony as "a purifying sacrifice for Russian blood shed for the faith, tsar and fatherland on this very spot" (Shilder, *Imperator Nikolai Pervyi,* 1:456–58, quoted in Wortman, *Scenarios of Power,* 270).

35. "Donesenie tainogo agenta o nastroenii umov v Peterburge posle kazni dekabristov," *Dekabristy: neizdannye materialy i stat'i* (Moscow: Vsesoiuznoe obshchestvo politkatorzhan i ssyl'no-poselentsev, 1925), 38–39. However, other

accounts attest that not all those who attended the purifying services were drawn back into the fold. Alexander Herzen points to the event as one of the first that awakened his revolutionary consciousness: "I was present at that service, a boy of fourteen lost in the crowd, and on the spot, before that altar defiled by bloody rites, I swore to avenge the murdered men, and dedicated myself to the struggle with that throne, with that altar, with those cannons. I have not avenged them: the Guards and throne, the altar and the cannons all remain, but for thirty years I have stood under that flag and have never once deserted it" (*The Polar Star*, 1855, as cited in Herzen, *My Past and Thoughts*, 44n13).

36. The poem remained unpublished until 1874. The topic of Pushkin and the Decembrists has become an entire industry; for a thorough and concise treatment, see Leonid Frizman, *Dekabristy i russkaia literatura* (Moscow: Khudozhestvennaia literatura, 1988), 89–112.

37. See Tatiana Tsiavlovskaia, *Risunki Pushkina* (Moscow: Iskusstvo, 1980), 160, 168–73, 178–87; Irina Reyfman, "Poetic Justice and Injustice: Autobiographical Echoes in Pushkin's *The Captain's Daughter*," *Slavic and East European Journal* 38:3 (1994): 463–78; and Anna Akhmatova, "Pushkin i Nevskoe vzmor'e," *Prometei* 10 (1975): 218–25.

38. See Vladimir Lenin's well-known periodization of the history of the Russian revolutionary movement—beginning with the Decembrists—in his article "Pamiati Gertsena" (1912), in *Polnoe sobranie sochinenii*, 21:261. For a more detailed discussion of the Decembrists and the revolutionary tradition, see M. Nechkina, *Dvizhenie dekabristov* (Moscow: Izdatel'stvo Akademii nauk, 1955); *14oe dekabria 1825 goda i ego istolkovateli: Gertsen i Ogarev protiv Barona Korfa* (Moscow: Nauka, 1994); and Ludmilla A. Trigos, "'Ardent Dreamers in the Land of Eternal Frost': Centennial Representations of the Decembrists (1825–1925)," (Ph.D. diss., Columbia University, 1998).

39. Iurii Tynianov, *Kiukhlia* (1925; repr. Voronezh: Izdatel'stvo Voronezhskogo Universiteta, 1987), 296, 304.

40. Mariia Marich, *Severnoe siianie* (Petrozavodsk: Izdatel'stvo Karelia, 1975), 2:132.

41. Denise J. Youngblood, *Movies for the Masses: Popular Cinema and Soviet Society in the 1920s* (Cambridge: Cambridge University Press, 1992), 19, 80–82.

42. The survey was published in 1927. Ibid., 60, 81.

43. For a more detailed discussion of the publications and events associated with the July 1926 commemoration, see Trigos, "Ardent Dreamers," 201–8.

44. Though the celebration would occur on the date of the uprising (new style), the memory of the execution remained a prominent one. The ritual commemoration would take place primarily among the intelligentsia, but in major anniversary years expanded union-wide to include the larger society.

45. For my summary of Ginkas's play, I am relying on John Freedman, "Big Names Keep Moscow Moving: The 1995–1996 Season," *Slavic and East European Performance* 16:3 (Fall 1996): 19–20.

The Invisible Scaffold

Execution and Imagination in Vasilii Zhukovskii's Works

ILYA VINITSKY

On January 4 (16), 1850, Vasilii Andreevich Zhukovskii (1783–1852), the founder of Russian Romanticism, the "poetic teacher" of Pushkin and the spiritual advisor to Gogol, wrote a letter to his former pupil and the future tsar, Grand Duke Alexander Nikolaevich (1818–81). A part of this long epistle served as the background for a brief article against disgusting spectacles of public executions in the West that discredited, according to the poet, the very idea of holy retribution. The article was banned by the Russian censors and published five years after Zhukovskii's death in a volume with a symbolic title—*Posthumous Works by Zhukovskii in Prose.*

In his article, Zhukovskii describes an ideal Christian "image of capital punishment" that, being forever concealed from public eyes, "will be a sublime act of human justice and a convincing sermon for public morality."[1] His attempt to "Christianize" the ritual of capital punishment was unanimously condemned by his contemporaries and friends as anti-Christian.[2] Moreover, it almost destroyed his reputation as a lofty Christian poet—"the only candidate for canonization from our Classic Literature" (Boris Zaitsev), who said at the end of his life: "Poesy is God in the holy dreams of Earth." The volume of paper used by critics far exceeded that for the work itself. It was branded blasphemous, barbaric, pharisaic, medieval, worthy of Nero and the Grand Inquisitor, bigoted, "foully moving," "basely solemn," and "incomparably abominable."

Leo Tolstoy indicated that an execution such as that described by Zhukovskii would have been a "more corrupting act than anything that all the devils could come up with in order to corrupt the human race."[3] Zinaida Hippius sarcastically wondered whether it was Christ himself who was being crucified behind closed doors to the accompaniment of moving hymns.[4] Fyodor Dostoevsky responded to Zhukovskii's article in his *Idiot* (1868). Nikolai Leskov ridiculed it in his *Rabbit's Warren* (1894), and Vladimir Nabokov made "deadly fun" of Zhukovskii's project in *The Gift* (1937–38) and *Invitation to a Beheading* (1938).[5]

In the present paper I endeavor to consider Zhukovskii's infamous article as both the Russian poet's passionate response to a contemporary European "penal crisis" and as the "crown" of his grandiose project of a Russian Christian poetry centered on the ideas of crucifixion and redemption. I view this article as a peculiar Romantic manifesto synthesizing in a single "image of execution" the poet's artistic, social, political, historical, and mystical views and aspirations.

Characteristic of the 1840s was the "crisis of capital punishment" as a political and ideological institution in the West. Zhukovskii's article is a response to this major controversy in European polemics. However, his response is addressed to a Russian audience that had not seen public executions for several decades.[6] In other words, in the age of Zhukovskii, the spectacles of the scaffold in Russia were associated either with the old Russian practice (rejected by Elizabeth I and Catherine II in the eighteenth century), or with modern European practice.[7] Executions were more a matter of historical recollection and imagination rather than of social experience. Why then did Zhukovskii decide to familiarize the Russian public with this pressing Western issue? To whom was his project addressed? What was its goal?

The work represents the Russian writer's immediate response to the recent (November 13, 1849) execution in London of the murderers Frederick and Maria Manning, who had killed a friend for his money and buried him under the kitchen floor. The event attracted a crowd of more than thirty thousand people. The unrepentant Maria Manning enjoyed public admiration for her graceful defiance. Following the execution, the mob went into a frenzy.[8] This initiated the "active agitation against public executions" pioneered by Charles Dickens, who condemned them as corrupting, diabolic spectacles in his powerful letters to *The Times* of January 13 and January 17, 1849.[9] According to Dickens, a scaffold should be concealed from public sight, with capital punishment being inflicted in "a private solemnity within the prison walls."[10] Dickens' penal reform project was condemned both by supporters of public spectacles and by abolitionists. The discussion found an immediate resonance in Western Europe, for it touched on one of the most controversial questions of the time.

Zhukovskii may also have "been inspired" by the "mock execution" of the Petrashevskii circle (a group of Russian socialists with Dostoevsky among them) on December 22, 1849.[11] Unlike the English "bourgeois-democratic" execution of the Mannings, the Russian spectacle, designed by the Emperor Nicholas I himself, was addressed not to the public (although a crowd of three thousand people "happened" to witness the execution) but to the state military machine (the tsar had intentionally selected as spectators his officers from the regiments in which some of the offenders had served—in a sort of state-sponsored moral lesson). The criminals could not be the heroes of the spectacle and therefore could not attract sympathy. There were no excesses, no brutality, and no carnivalesque blasphemies. Instead of the English crowd's chaos, stable Russian state order reigned. But the most important part of the Russian execution was its finale—the act of royal clemency. The emperor's goal was threefold: to punish the offenders by inflicting the fear of imminent death, to grant them their lives with an incomparable act of imperial mercy, and to show post-revolutionary Europe how Russia resolved the Western crisis of capital punishment, that is, the collision of traditional (feudal and symbolic) severity and modern (liberal and utilitarian) humanity.[12]

It is very likely that Zhukovskii had the St. Petersburg execution in mind as he was writing his letter to Grand Duke Alexander Nikolaevich, who had been in charge of the entire procedure. Characteristically, Zhukovskii's letter was written the day after the information regarding the execution had been published in German and French newspapers. It is evident that Zhukovskii's religious project was ideologically opposed not only to the "bourgeois-democratic" way of punishment, but also to the Russian feudal-military rite. Of course, the Russian model, which "neutralized" the element of public spectacle,[13] is closer to his heart, since it is more ceremonial and appropriate to the spirit of the event. But Zhukovskii understands capital punishment to be the most important event not only in the life of a state, but also in the life of a

Christian community. In place of the repulsive, bloody English spectacle and the ceremonial but heartless Russian military parade, Zhukovskii proposes a religious spectacle, the only spectacle capable of expressing the great and holy idea of retribution. The death penalty should not call forth thoughts of a satanic orgy ("the theater of hell," as Foucault puts it[14]), nor should it remind the public of a severe earthly sovereign and his manifestation of force; its moral goal is to disclose the pious image of the Savior in the soul of the offender and bystander alike. The act must evoke in the hearts of onlookers neither sinful curiosity nor morbid terror, but rather spark religious imagination.

Zhukovskii wrote his article in Germany, when the dispute over the subject had reached its culmination. Two radical positions concerning capital punishment collided in the late 1840s: that of the pietists and that of the liberals. The pietists advocated "outdoor" executions emphasizing the public repentance and confession of the malefactor at the decisive moment. The liberals demanded the abolition of capital punishment, which they believed incompatible with modern humanism and the progress of civilization.[15] Zhukovskii may also have been familiar with contemporary theoretical debates over the issue (Reidel, Messerschmidt, and, especially, Diestel, who stated in his *Das Problem der Todesstrafe, wissenschaftich zu lösen versucht* [1848] that for the state the scaffold was no less than a sacrificial altar).

One of the primary goals of the penal reform promised by Prussia's Friedrich Wilhelm IV (Zhukovskii's confidant and admirer) was the achievement of a compromise between these views. The final draft of the new Prussian Criminal Code (1847) mandated that executions were no longer to be held in the open. Instead, they would take place "in an enclosed space invisible to the public." Executions were to be announced by the ringing of a bell, "while in the meantime clergy shall address the people gathered round the execution place." Parents were to be encouraged "to gather their families around them in this hour for religious and moral contemplation."[16]

Preparation of the new criminal code was interrupted by the March 1848 violent public disturbances in Berlin. The question of capital punishment now appeared to be within the competence of the liberal Frankfurt Parliament, which was preparing the constitution for a united Germany. Here the abolitionists had an overwhelming majority, and the death penalty was abolished on December 27, 1848. By the spring of the following year, capital punishment had been outlawed in almost all the states of Germany, including the Grand Duchy of Baden, to which Zhukovskii had fled with his family from revolutionary Frankfurt. King Friedrich, of course, did not agree with the abolition of such an important "symbol of the state's determination to restore the social and political order."[17] By 1850 the Revolution had collapsed, and the death penalty was reinstated by virtually every German state.

Such are the ideological, judicial, and political contexts of Zhukovskii's article. The "semi-pietistic" draft version of the Prussian Criminal Code proposed by the king and rejected by the revolutionary parliament almost certainly served as a background for Zhukovskii. His article is a kind of a free translation from German into Russian. However, the differences between his interpretation and the original are extremely significant.

The opposition between visible and invisible is central to Zhukovskii's article (as well as to his later works in general): the "spectacle for the eyes" is counterpoised against the "spectacle for the soul," the visible (public) execution against the invisible presence of execution, and "material eyes" against "eyes of the imagination," as Zhukovskii puts it. He believes everyone possesses this kind of inner vision. It is significant the article was composed by a blind man (Zhukovskii lost his sight in early 1850). It is also essential to note that, for Zhukovskii, the article deals not with the best way to punish (a set of recommendations), but with the right way to perceive capital punishment, previously darkened by the false and ugly ceremonies of public executions. He hoped to see executions not as disgusting and bloody spectacles, but magically beautiful acts. To paraphrase Robert L. Jackson, Zhukovskii's article deals with "mystical vision" rather than the "ethics of vision" ("the moral-psychological experience of looking at violence"[18]) inherent in Dostoevsky, Turgenev, or Tolstoy.[19] It is impossible to understand the article by viewing it as a mere project, a proposal, and not as a "picture for the inner vision."[20]

We may easily divide the article into two parts. In the first part, Zhukovskii depicts the terrors and the corrupting effects of public executions. In the second he outlines the ideal (invisible) execution, providing a great moral and religious lesson for the public. Although the structure of the article appears perfectly logical, a close reading reveals striking contradictions and gaps.

In its first part, Zhukovskii depicts in minute detail the terrors of the gibbet, the guillotine, and quartering. Yet, in his actual proposal, he is silent regarding the means of the *invisible* execution. Will they hang the offenders or break them on the wheel, behead them or crush them to death, burn them alive or shoot them? He describes in detail the rite of the holy execution—the spectacle for man's soul—but gives no hint as to technicalities. The scaffold remains hidden from his readers. And there is no executioner.[21] Zhukovskii says nothing about a priest, as if the religious rites were carried out by themselves. There is not a single word about the country in which the execution is to take place. He says nothing about authorities, judges, or a military convoy: the offender, Zhukovskii writes, leaves the solitude of his prison for the solitude of the coffin, accompanied by sublime singing. Who is singing? It is not specified.

In his article Zhukovskii describes the overarching processes and actions rather than their "physical" sources. The real "plot" of the article is not a logical sequence of arguments or proposals, but rather an exposition of the inner development of the author's emotions inexorably approaching the final revelation of the execution. (It is not surprising that the article, as Zhukovskii stated himself in a letter to his sister, "was written by itself").[22] The theme of the agonizingly beautiful transition from life to death, from our wicked world to the bosom of merciful God, is central to this strange narrative. It is the very spectacle of transition that should compel people to recognize their solidarity with the offender in the eyes of the Lord. This is not a "utilitarian" project: it is a poetic vision. None of Zhukovskii's critics believed that the glorification of a scaffold could belong to a poet. Nevertheless, this project was deeply rooted in the poetical consciousness of its author.

Retribution is the central theme in Zhukovskii's poetry. Execution in his works is inevitable, terrible, but blessed, for its source is Almighty God, who punishes criminals according to their crimes. In his so called "terrible ballads," which gave him a reputation as a bard of ghosts and devils, Zhukovskii presents a catalog of execution methods: burning, drowning, consumption by mice, and abduction by Satan. It is noteworthy that Zhukovskii often depicts the execution of a sinner as secret, invisible.

The depiction of the inner world of the sinner occupies a central place in Zhukovskii's ballads. The sinner experiences unbearable remorse. He feels that he will be inevitably punished. Terror pursues him day and night in the form of ghosts or corpses. A terrible arm rises from the abyss to seize him. The furious, sullen, and dreadful Devil appears before him in all his might. The psychological sufferings of the sinner at the moment of his punishment are the culmination and denouement of Zhukovskii's ballads. The site of execution is a central point in Zhukovskii's balladic world.

In Zhukovskii's 1850 article, in accordance with his ballad aesthetics, the author likens capital punishment to "a ghost haunting a criminal" (971). Fear of retribution controls the villains. Zhukovskii focuses on the offender's remorse, but fear is not the prevailing emotion in his vision of capital punishment. The emotional atmosphere of the article is moving and ceremonial, with this sentiment making the article particularly unbearable to its critics. The theme of retribution slowly morphs into another theme that is also essential to Zhukovskii's ballads: redemption. How can the sinner's soul be saved? In his search for a convincing solution Zhukovskii considered various means of salvation—prayer (insufficient), saintly intercession (only occasionally helpful), and, finally, miracle—the most effective method. It is important to note that Zhukovskii depicts the redemption of the sinner as a mysterious and invisible process. The mystical conflict between soul and body is resolved when the sinner's soul escapes its material prison and passes into God's hands. Execution signifies redemption, the only possible way for the sinner to be saved. For him it is grace and hope, and it should be welcomed.

Zhukovskii's article of 1850 is a vision of a sinner's death. The place of execution is no less than a sacrificial altar, an inner sanctum resolving the passions of one's soul. Zhukovskii projects the contemporary problem of capital punishment onto the Christological plane, encompassing the ideas of torments, sacrifice, redemption, and resurrection. This is the spiritual context in which the image of the scaffold appears and then disappears.

The scaffold is among the most favorite images of Western pre-Romantic and Romantic culture: in painting (A. Wiertz) and music (H. Berlioz's *Symphonie Phantastique*), in the Gothic novel (M. Lewis) and the "medieval" literary ballad (R. Southey, W. Scott), in tragedy (J.-W. Goethe) and the "frenetic" novel (V. Hugo, J. Janine, E. Sue). The site of the scaffold represents a zone of "public saturnalia, when nothing remains to prohibit or to punish,"[23] a symbolic representation of social disease and man's lower passions, an aesthetically attractive locus of evil. In Foucault's words, the Western "gallows-literature" "from the *Castle of Otranto* to Baudelaire" manifested "a whole aesthetic rewriting of crime."[24]

In Zhukovskii's works, the image of the scaffold went through a long development. In his first free interpretation of Bürger's "Lenore" in 1808 (the Ur-text of Russian Romanticism), Zhukovskii demonstratively omitted the famous scene of a scaffold surrounded by demonic creatures *(das Gesindel)*. Instead, he depicted a crowd of flying specters howling above the body of the violated Liudmila: "Your hour has come. The end is nigh."[25] In 1831, Zhukovskii retranslated "Lenore." His second interpretation was much closer to the original. This time he left the scaffold in its place. Instead of Bürger's skeletons and devils, Zhukovskii depicted a mysterious swarm of ethereal creatures singing at the ballad's end: "Go to the grave, your corpse. God have mercy on your soul."[26] The spiritual nature of those creatures was not specified. Finally, in a short article, "Two Scenes from *Faust*" (1848) he gives a bizarre commentary on the famous episode concluding the first part of the tragedy *("Nacht, offenes Feld")*.[27] Faust and Mephisto rush on black horses across an open plain at night. Faust sees a scaffold—the very platform where his Margaret will be executed the next day. Witches and skeletons flit about, apparently engaged in some unholy rite. "Who are they?" Faust asks Mephisto. "A company of witches [*Eine Hexenzunft*]," the latter replies. "Onward! Onward! [*Vorbei! Vorbei!*]"[28]

Zhukovskii's article is directed against depictions of the scene by the German Romantic illustrators (F.-A.-M. Roetsch and P. von Kornelius), featuring devils and skeletons around a scaffold. The Russian poet insists that there are no witches here; holy angels are preparing a bed for Margaret. This is a holy place, and this symbolic vision means that she will be redeemed.[29]

The vision of the scaffold, borrowed from German eighteenth-century poetry and directly associated with *Faust* as an Ur-text, slowly developed in Zhukovskii's consciousness as a kind of "spiritual photography." Zhukovskii insisted upon the sacred status of the scaffold *in spite* of the powerful European Romantic tradition, that is, his background. In his later works, Zhukovskii deliberately rejects the portrayal of infernal orgies near a scaffold so popular in the French "frenetic" school.[30] For him, these bloody rites represent the absolute fall of contemporary literature, the triumph of materialism, an aesthetic inferno.[31] This aesthetic credo determines his invectives against the "disgusting scenes of corruption and bestiality in a numberless crowd of people who have gathered to feast their eyes with a spectacle of convulsions of the hanged" (971). Characteristically, he refers to a London execution in his article; England was popularly perceived at the time as a "classical country of capital punishment" (A. F. Kistiakovskii) and modern abolitionism. In other words, Zhukovskii's article is a polemical response to the Western aesthetic and social practice of visualizing capital punishment.[32] It is no surprise that he pairs the opposition "infernal-holy" ("material-spiritual") with "Western-Russian."

Indeed, the idea of symbolic purification of the site of a scaffold reflects both Zhukovskii's aesthetic convictions and his historic and patriotic reminiscences. The scaffold is one of the central symbols of the French Revolution. "Public excesses around the guillotine" (972) is a traditional motif in the portrayal of revolutionary events. In Russian Romantic historiosophy, the site of Louis XVI's execution represented the Alpha and Omega of the bloody historical epoch. Alexander I staged a triumphal military and religious spectacle in France on March 29, 1814 (Easter Sunday on the Russian Orthodox calendar). Eighty thousand allied troops and the French National Guard lined up around a special altar erected on the Place de la Concorde at the site of Louis XVI's execution. Alexander knelt at the altar, praying with his people, according to Orthodox ritual. "It was as if they purified the bloodied place of the innocent royal victim." As early as 1814 Zhukovskii praised this event in his poem "To the Emperor Alexander," where he "dramatized the spectacle of purification and forgiveness for the Russian public."[33] One may say that Zhukovskii saw the purification of the scaffold as an act of "Russian exorcism" directed against both the demons of the godless and bloody revolution and the dangerous literary tradition it begot. This is the impetus for his "master idea" of the providential mission of Holy Rus' and Holy Russian Poetry, whose calling it is to expel evil and return the sacred *(sviatoe)* to contemporary (Western) civilization.

The article on capital punishment is the culmination of the scaffold's unusual journey through Zhukovskii's work. The scaffold has left the material world and become a mystical incorporation of earthly and divine power, sin and redemption, contemporary ideological conflicts and Russia's spiritual mission; and it is visible only with the inner eye of the imagination. The "image of execution" evokes the idea of Golgotha and the Crucifixion. Zhukovskii refers to the execution as a sacrament. In fact, his project is a virtual projection of the holy liturgy onto social practice. Thus, "the Assembly of the faithful" is equivalent to the singing procession approaching the place of execution. The "Tsar's Gates," concealed during the moment of the sacrament, become the hidden site of execution. The redemptive cup passed to the criminal transfigures the whole scene, imagined by the audience as a kind of collective virtual Eucharist. Finally, the cross over the prison transforms the prison itself into God's church.

"And what a spectacle!!" the poet exclaims at the end of the article. "No eyes can see what the imagination can show one's soul at this moment. And when the singing suddenly stops—what then will this moved imagination see?" (972–73). Apparently the "vision" that is opened wide before the public is no less than a collective vision of Divine Glory, the Revelation, so central to Zhukovskii in the late 1840s.

The last period of Zhukovskii's life coincides with stormy historical events in Western Europe—hunger, rebellions, revolutions, and massacres. The idea of the restoration of order (political, moral, aesthetic, natural) is central to his letters and literary work from 1848 into the 1850s. His final works deal with such illustrative themes as the Egyptian plagues and destruction of Jerusalem, the slaughter of the suitors in the *Odyssey*[34] and the Apocalypse. Unlike his ballads, where the villains are punished individually, in his later works we find an entire collection of mass executions. From Zhukovskii's letters, poems and diary, we can easily reconstruct a gigantic apocalyptic picture: modern history becomes the final battle between the forces of good and evil. Political history and poetry express this crucial mystical conflict in equal measure. The rhetoric of Zhukovskii's later works reminds us of the apocalyptic poems and articles of the Napoleonic era, as if he had returned in his last years to the terrors and aspirations of his poetical youth. The comparison of two satanic uprisings—the French Revolution of 1789 and the German Revolution of 1848—occupies a central place in his works of the period. Only Holy Russia, its Emperor, and Providence can save the world from the Devil's hands.

Zhukovskii expressed his most radical eschatological views in his political letters to his former student, the Grand Duke Alexander Nikolaevich.[35] Here he gives free play to his mystical imagination. The awful claw of Satan hangs over Europe. The revolution is an infernal, stinking abyss. The "hydra of communism" is "a demonic effigy made by lawyers, Jews, and ambitious professors."[36] Zhukovskii interprets every political event as a mystical sign. The people must be awakened and struck by the extraordinary example of holiness. Zhukovskii argued that Russia should liberate Jerusalem from the Turks by the power of its moral beauty (not its army). The Russian tsar should summon his Christian colleagues to organize a holy host to liberate Jerusalem from the pagans, reviving Alexander I's Holy Alliance.

It is noteworthy that Zhukovskii describes his Jerusalem project in the same letter in which he discusses capital punishment.[37] In the context of his general apocalyptic project (an Alliance of Kings), the proposal to reform capital punishment attains a peculiar, symbolic meaning. Zhukovskii argues that in the modern age forces of good and evil collide at the scaffold. Public executions are dreadful events, profaning the holy ritual and leading to satanic corruption. But this corruption is visible, for more difficult to fight is evil hidden in the philanthropic guise of abolitionism, since the abolitionists are striving to eliminate the very symbol of the Last Judgment: the holy scaffold. For Zhukovskii, a true Christian must see and reveal Satan's tricks. "The only salvation is to purify [the] atmosphere."[38]

Zhukovskii's capital punishment article is a poetic endeavor to exorcize the Western demons of revolution and liberalism (to "purify [the] atmosphere") and to pull aside the veil of mystery, showing people what they need to see on the eve of the final denouement: the approaching execution. As mentioned, Zhukovskii was highly praised by his adherents as a Christian poet who said at the end of his life: "Poesy is God in the holy dreams of Earth." His critics argued that his unusual capital punishment project discredited his famous motto. But the critics misunderstood Zhukovskii's maxim. It is much more than a traditional Romantic apotheosis of poetry as divine revelation, since, in Zhukovskii's vision, these poetic dreams of Earth were the dreams of death brought on by a holy, beautiful, and final execution.

Notes

1. V. A. Zhukovskii, *Sochineniia v stikhah i proze*, ed. P. A. Efremov (St. Petersburg: Glazunov, 1901), 963. All the subsequent references to this edition are given in the text. The italics are mine.

2. The polemics started during Zhukovskii's lifetime. See *Utkinskii sbornik. Pis'ma V. A. Zhukovskogo, M. A. Moier i E. A. Protasovoi*, ed. A. E. Gruzinskii (Moscow, 1904), 85–87; N. P. Koliupanov, *Biografiia A. I. Kosheleva*, vols. 1–2 (Moscow: O. F. Koshelevoi, 1889–92), 2:211. The first printed responses appeared after the publication of the article in 1857 and belong to I. S. Aksakov and N. G. Chernyshevskii.

3. L. N. Tolstoy, *Polnoe sobranie sochinenii* (Moscow: Khudozhestvennaia literatura, 1957), 28:358.

4. See Zinaida Hippius, "Khristianin i kazn'," *Rech'* 54 (23 February 1909).

5. Brian Boyd, *Vladimir Nabokov, The Russian Years* (Princeton, N.J.: Princeton University Press, 1990), 34–36.

6. On the Russian history of public executions in seventeenth- and eighteenth-century Russia see, especially: Evgenii Anisimov, *Dyba i knut. Politicheskii sysk i russkoe obshchestvo v XVIII veke* (Moscow: Novoe literaturnoe obozrenie, 1999), 523–87; Evgenii Anisimov, "Narod u eshafota," *Zvezda* 11 (1998): 129–42.

7. The suspension of capital punishment in Russia was often interpreted in the late eighteenth and the first half of the nineteenth century as a triumph of Russian humanity over Western moral degradation (see, for example, Denis Fonvizin's letters from France). On Russian writers' views concerning capital punishment, see I. Malinovskii, *Russkie pisateli-khudozhniki o smertnoi kazni* (Tomsk, 1910).

8. On the history of the crime and punishment of the Mannings, see *The Progress of Crime, or The Authentic Memoirs of Maria Manning, by Robert Huish Esq.* (London, 1849). On the cultural consequences of the execution, see: Albert Borowitz, *The Bermondsdey Horror: The Murder That Shocked Victorian England* (London: Robson Books, Ltd, 1988); David D. Cooper, *The Lesson of the Scaffold: The Public Execution Controversy in Victorian England* (Athens: Ohio University Press, 1974), 11–12.

9. *The Letters of Charles Dickens*, ed. G. Storey and K. J. Fielding (Oxford: Clarendon Press, 1981), 5:644–45.

10. Ibid., 5:652–53.

11. M. Vaiskopf, *Siuzhet Gogolia: morfologiia, ideologiia, kontekst* (Moscow: TOO "Radiks," 1993), 465.

12. See the description of the ceremony of Petrashevskii's "mock execution" in I. Volgin, "Propavshii zagovor. Dostoevsky i politicheskii protsess 1849 goda. Konets pervoi knigi . . . ," *Oktiabr'* 5 (1998): 95–135.

13. See Michel Foucault, *Discipline and Punish. The Birth of the Prison*, trans. A. Sheridan (New York: Vintage Books, 1995). For a discussion of Nicholas I's project of execution in the light of Foucault, see Jeremy Tambling, *Dickens, Violence and the Modern State: Dreams of the Scaffold* (London: Macmillan Press, 1995), 132.

14. Foucault, *Discipline and Punish*, 46.

15. On a pietist vision of capital punishment, see James J. Megivern, *The Death Penalty: An Historical and Theological Survey* (New York: Paulist Press, 1977), 213; and, especially, Richard J. Evans, *Rituals and Retribution: Capital Punishment in Germany 1600–1987* (Oxford: Oxford University Press, 1996), 85–86.

16. Evans, *Ritual and Retribution*, 263–65.

17. Ibid., 265.

18. Robert Louis Jackson, *Dialogues with Dostoevsky: The Overwhelming Questions* (Stanford, Calif.: Stanford University Press, 1993), 4.

19. Characteristically, Zhukovskii drew the information about the London execution from the newspapers, rather than from the actual experience of looking at the scaffold. We have no evidence whether he had ever attended public executions in Germany.

20. This makes Zhukovskii's vision radically different from Prince Myshkin's famous project, the painting of the last moment of a condemned man.

21. This is what most distinguishes his idea from the mystical conception of another defender of capital punishment, the Sardinian count Joseph de Maistre: a terrible executioner is a central figure ("honor and bond") of his Manichean world.

22. *Utkinskii sbornik*, 85.

23. Foucault, *Discipline and Punish*, 60.

24. Ibid. 68.

25. V. A. Zhukovskii, *Stikhotvoreniia,* Biblioteka poeta, Bol'shaia seriia (Leningrad: Sovetskii pisatel', 1956), 286.

26. Ibid, 440. See Gerhardt Dietrich, "Faust und die Folgen: V. A. Zhukovskijs Aufsatz 'Zwei Szenen aus *Faust,*'" in *Mnemozina: Studia Literaria Russica in Honorem Vsevolod Setchkarev,* ed. Joachim T. Baer and Norman W. Ingham (Munich: Wilhelm Fink Verlag, 1974), 130–52.

27. V. A. Zhukovskii, *Estetika i kritika* (Moscow: Iskusstvo, 1985), 355.

28. Johann-Wolfgang Goethe, *Sämmtliche Werke,* vol. 7/1 (Frankfurt am Main: Deutscher Klassiker Verlag, 1994), 191.

29. V. A. Zhukovskii, *Estetika i kritika,* 355.

30. See: V. V. Vinogradov, *Evoliutsiia russkogo naturalizma. Gogol i Dostoevsky* (Leningrad: Academia, 1929), 168–69.

31. Zhukovskii even criticizes Michelangelo's *Last Judgment* for "the disgusting scenes with criminals and devils [that] corrupt the sublime meaning of the subject." See V. A. Zhukovskii, *Sochineniia v stikhakh i proze* (St. Petersburg: Glazunov, 1901), 941. Symptomatically, he refers here to the most authoritative portrayal of an execution in Western culture.

32. A. I. Koshelev, who visited Zhukovskii in 1850 in Frankfurt, noted that Zhukovskii's attitude toward capital punishment was closely linked with his total negation of Eugene Sue "i drugikh kommunisticheskikh romanistov," as well as "vsekh romanov, gde vystavliaetsia khudaia storona" (Koliupanov, *Biografiia A. I. Kosheleva,* 2:211).

33. Richard S. Wortman, *Scenarios of Power* (Princeton, N.J.: Princeton University Press, 1995), 1:226.

34. See Ilya Vinitsky, "'Theodyssey' by Vassilii Zhukovskii: The Homeric Epic and the Revolution of 1848," abstract, *AATSEEL 2001* (New Orleans, 2001), 146–47.

35. *Russkii arkhiv 1885,* no. 1–2, 252, 258, 339.

36. This is a polemic paraphrase of Marx's "spirit of communism." On a political subtext of a "ghost theme" in Zhukovskii's works of the 1840s, see I. Iu. Vinitsky, *Nechto o privideniiakh* (Moscow: MKL, 1998), 64–68.

37. *Russkii arkhiv 1885,* 337–40.

38. Ibid., 339.

The Wounded Young Heart

Dostoevsky's Netochka Nezvanova *as Bildungsroman*

ELENA KRASNOSTCHEKOVA

Netochka Nezvanova (1849) stands out within the evolution of Dostoevsky's early work, following *Poor Folk* (1846) and *A Weak Heart* and *White Nights* (both 1848). In Dostoevsky's other works, events are concentrated within a short span of time, a feature that has been characterized as "more characteristic of a drama or a novella than the traditional forms of the novel," whereas the almost ten-year span of *Netochka Nezvanova* suggests "something different, reminiscent of the structure of the bildungsroman from the end of the eighteenth century."[1] In the bildungsroman, an individual's maturation is revealed gradually, from one period of life to the next. In the best novels of the genre this process is, by its very nature, multifaceted, and when violence is involved it further complicates the picture.[2] In the context of this discussion I take violence to mean "any denigration of a person, everything that leads to the degradation, either physically or mentally, of an individual's potentiality, [and] that interferes with him attaining the full extent of his personal development."[3] Within the context of the bildungsroman, violence may cause a character's development to be either stunted or accelerated—for him to grow up too soon—but it may also be a catalyst to resistance. This is the case, I will argue, with *Netochka Nezvanova.*

Analyzing the aesthetic meaning of the bildungsroman, Mikhail Bakhtin sees "the image of the person who is becoming" as its defining characteristic: "Here, the dynamic unity of the hero's image is in opposition to statistical unity. The hero himself and his character become the variable in the construction of the novel. The hero's changes take on the significance of a plot, in relation to which the novel's entire plot is fundamentally rethought and restructured. Time is internalized within the person, incorporated into his very image, fundamentally altering all the events of his life and fate."[4] Bakhtin characterizes the "biographical" and "autobiographical" types of bildungsroman, noting that in such works "development occurs in biographical time; it undergoes unrepeatable, individual stages. . . . Here, development is the result of cumulative changing life conditions, events, activity, and work. An individual's destiny is created, and he himself and his characters along with it. The development of his life, his fate, merges with the development of the individual himself. Fielding's *Tom Jones* and Dickens's *David Copperfield* are examples of this."[5] The work of Dickens, so beloved by Dostoevsky,[6] certainly corresponds more to his writing than that of Fielding; but what is notable is that the names of the central characters are included in the titles, insofar as this genre is by its very nature monocentric. *Netochka Nezvanova* is the only one of Dostoevsky's works that employs a name as its title. The author's attention is specifically focused on the heroine and the development of her personality as it progresses through deeply "unrepeatable individual stages," as the "totality of changing life conditions" becomes the most important factor of her education in the harsh school of life. Nonetheless, the title is typical for Dostoevsky insofar as it metaphorically expresses the core idea of the work. The very sound of the heroine's name, Netochka Nezvanova (with its double "ne," a negation), suggests the idea of the world's violent rejection of this being, a rejection that defines the most difficult formative (and, under normal conditions, joyous) period of her life. "Nezvanova" means "nameless,"[7] but may also suggest "nezvanyi," "uninvited," in a metaphorical sense, unloved.

The first version of the novel that was published in a journal bore the subtitle "One Woman's Story," linking it to popular contemporary works about strong women from the lower classes of society who overcome a multitude of obstacles on the path to self-determination.[8] However, it was just this connection that inspired the negative reactions to the novel, as the subtitle led readers to expect a confession exploring the romantic and professional upheavals of a mature woman. Instead, one such critic found merely "excessive monological digressions, tedious moralizing, [and] monotonous, tiresome analyses of personal feelings."[9] Another decried the lack of structural elements and action, so that "the work's balance is clearly violated by excessive detail concerning the heroine's childhood."[10] When Dostoevsky published his two-volume *Works* in 1860, he made fundamental changes in the novel. He included the three existing parts of the novel, abridging and editing them in light of his decision not to complete the composition.[11] Although the author now chose to eliminate the titles of the three sections (formerly "Childhood," "A New Life," and "The Mystery"), three stages of life (childhood, adolescence, and youth) are still reflected in the final version, which spans almost ten years of the narrator's life. These alterations of the journal publication and the author's decision not to continue with the additional two parts that were originally planned resulted in what may be seen a change in the work's genre. The text acquired the more distinct form of a bildungsroman, something that helps put the criticisms of the early version into better context. Weakening of the plot is characteristic of such a work, as is the analysis of the feelings of a maturing person presented within a chronological framework, and the inclusion of a great deal of moralizing and didacticism (an inheritance from the Age of Enlightenment).

As is usual for a bildungsroman, *Netochka Nezvanova* begins with a tale of childhood (as noted, the first part was originally entitled "Childhood"), but its departures from this tradition are also immediately apparent. First of all, the starting point for the heroine's recollections seems strange. It is only at the age of nine years that the girl "comes to" and sees the pitiful attic room where her family lives in horrifying poverty and discord. This abnormally long "sleep"—which saves her from reality—increases the horror of her awakening and the acuity of her perception of the world around her: "But from the time I became aware of myself, I developed at a surprising rate, and many emotions that were by no means childlike were for some reason terribly accessible to me."[12] The adult Netochka acknowledges that her perception and experience of everyday life, imbued as it was with extreme misfortune, "cast a strange, dark shadow over the entire time I lived with my parents—over my whole life in fact" (28). Indeed, extreme need and deprivation threaten to stunt or suppress the heroine's personality, making her a victim of violence, which, according to our definition leads to "the degradation, either physically or mentally, of an individual's potentiality" and "interferes with him attaining the full extent of his personal development." It is no coincidence that Dal"s definition of violence is equated with the word "need": "need—poverty, extreme; lack of the most basic life needs; hunger, cold; bondage; a difficult, bitter life."[13] In a world where existence itself is synonymous with doing violence to someone, there is no chance for normal familial relationships—yet it is these that are at the center of the bildungsroman. In this "accidental family," so typical of Dostoevsky, the mother and stepfather—the primary figures in the child's life—are overwhelmed by misfortune and need, and torture each other. An atmosphere of desperation and anger, verging on physical abuse, reigns in the household. The situation is beyond the comprehension of the innocent Netochka, who is more afraid of her mother than of "any fear." The unfortunate woman buries her love for her daughter beneath her severity and exactitude, and they only alienate each other.

Netochka's first experience of parental affection is paternal. It is this that made her stepfather Efimov, a naturally gifted musician who wasted his talent in aimless pursuits, the most influential person in her life: "He was the strangest, most extraordinary man I have ever known . . . His influence on the earliest impressions of my childhood was far too powerful—so powerful in fact that these impressions have affected my entire life" (1). The crux of Netochka's childhood story is the dramatic destruction of this fantastic love for her father, which is almost romantic in nature. Efimov's drinking forces Netochka to deceive her mother by conspiring to steal her hard-earned money. When Netochka realizes what is going on, the result is intolerable suffering: "I was so appalled by what had happened that I could not look at father and for the first time did not go near him all evening . . . I was tormented by morbid dreams" (47–48). Efimov's outrageous behavior leads to a tragic denouement. Netochka's heart is crushed when, after Efimov convinces her to steal a large sum, he promises her a treat as a bribe. He has clearly not understood the depth of her love. He treats her like a three-year-old while he himself behaves like a cruel child. Netochka recalls: "I was suddenly heart-stricken. I felt that he was merciless, that he did not love me, because he could not see how much I loved him and thought I was willing to do what he asked of me only for the sake of presents. At that moment I, a child, understood him through and through, and I felt that this realization had wounded me forever, that I could no longer love him, that my papa was lost to me" (60).

If the concept of "violence" may be applied to human degradation, to damaging a person's physical and emotional potentiality, then

Netochka's situation is the result of such a level of violence that it does not simply wound her heart, but almost destroys it: "In my entire life, I had never spent more agonizing hours; they will remain in my memory forever. What I lived through during that time! There are moments in one's life in which one consciously experiences far more than in whole years . . . Was it really possible that he could not understand how difficult it is to deceive an impressionable nature, one who at an early age had felt deeply and comprehended a great deal of good and evil? Yet I realized that it was obviously his desperation that had made him decide again to lead me into sin, thus sacrificing my poor defenseless childhood and once more throwing into confusion an unstable conscience" (62).

Netochka's chaotic emotions concerning her father almost overshadow her mother's unexpected death, which occurs during one of her parents' quarrels. She is not immediately able to follow her long-time dream of leaving home with her father and starting another, wonderful life—a dream that had been opposed by her mother. She is almost paralyzed in the presence of her mother's dead body: "I quickly knelt down and folded my hands in prayer, but I was so overcome with horror and despair that I fell to the floor and lay there for several minutes as if dead. I tried to concentrate all my thoughts and feelings in prayer, but was overcome by fear. I got up, exhausted by my anguish. I no longer wanted to go with him. I was afraid of him now; I wanted to remain where I was." Finally, turning to her mother, "I frantically flung myself on her and embraced her lifeless body" (72). There is in this embrace an intuitive acknowledgement that they were both deceived, and when father and daughter do in fact finally flee, Efimov treacherously abandons the girl right on the street.

The next stage in Netochka Nezvanova's fate unfolds with another awakening, this time from a fainting spell. The original title of this part, "A New Life," in the logic of the bildungsroman corresponds to "Adolescence." Netochka's fading childhood memories have left a poignant impression, "a feeling of melancholy, as yet unclear to me, that was constantly growing in my heart. Fear and confusion overwhelmed me" (77). The girl wanders alone through the house of the kind Prince who has taken her in, dreaming of meeting, befriending, and forming a relationship with someone her own age. As Bakhtin says of Dostoevsky's heroes from "accidental families," "they are deprived of the real interaction within which their lives and relations would have developed. This interaction is thus transformed from a necessary part of life to a postulate, becoming the utopian goal of their endeavors."[14] In the "new life," two adolescents appear alongside Netochka, permitting her character to emerge more fully for the reader, whose perception is no longer limited to the heroine's self-descriptions. One, the boy Laria or Laren'ka (from the journal version only), is almost Netochka's double. Like her, he is a defenseless victim and orphan. "This was a boy of about eleven, pale, quite thin, with reddish hair, who crouched and shook all over."[15] The favorite child in a poor official's family, following his parents' death he ends up in the home of Fedor Feropontovich, his "benefactor" who is actually an oppressor. Almost every evening this man "would start to rail against his entire household because of the inexplicable indifference of people and society towards his domestic and civil virtues, and every evening he would turn his house into a small hell." When Laria makes an awkward joke, Fedor Feropontovich, "glaring and stomping, described all the vileness of his behavior to him, saying that he was insensitive, that he was a tyrant, that he was depriving his children of their bread; that he, and no one else, had driven his careless parents to their grave, suggesting to Laria that he was obstinate and unruly, and thoroughly intimidated and exhausted Laria, who was left with the conviction that he was an insensitive and ungrateful boy." "I'm an unlucky boy," the orphan sighs; "everyone becomes angry at him and abuses him." Laria/Laren'ka's state mirrors and helps explicate Netochka's own feelings. She notes, "I understood how deeply wounded the heart of this child was, who was mature beyond his years, but abnormally mature, mature emotionally, in his heart, at the same time that his mind was clouded by dreams and fantasies, and some sort of fatalism burdened his poor head."[16] This is characteristic of the "young person with a wounded heart" who is the hero of Dostoevsky's bildungsroman. The child grows up burdened by circumstances, fraught with the tyranny of the powerful, who elicit constant fear. The heart matures beyond its years, while the mind is delayed in its development, clouded by fantasies of salvation, and the will suppressed by hopelessness.

Netochka's brief encounter with the poor Laria/Laren'ka, who is even more unfortunate than she herself, further deepens her depression. In contrast, Netochka's experience of meeting little Princess Katia at first suggests the appearance of an angel: "my weakened nerves began to ache with a sweet ecstasy"; "this was love, true love, with its tears and joys, passionate love" (91–92). The novel's first critic noted: "children who have grown up in adverse circumstances are exceptionally prone to such premature, eccentric passions."[17] Katia's charm affects Netochka so strongly because here was a person of her own age, yet completely "different." This difference is mainly in Katia's lack of inhibition, her mischievousness and willfulness, her ease in social situations and complete absence of timidity. She has a "straightforward, naively frank nature, a true and noble grace" (95–96) derived from confidence in herself, from the realization that she is surrounded by love, and from complete indifference to anyone's opinion. Netochka remarks that "Hers was a fine, good little heart . . . which always led her to find the right path simply by instinct" (106), which is confirmed in the dramatic subplot of the development of their friendship.

"Though the results of all she [Katia] undertook were beautiful and true, they were obtained at the cost of continual deviations and errors"—these words are the key to the princess' contradictory behavior (108). Scorn and attraction: the first overcomes the second, as Katia, so used to command, turns her scorn for Netochka into a wicked game—torturing "the lost lamb." Netochka suffers immeasurably: "This new loneliness became almost as painful to me as my former solitude; again I grew pensive and melancholy, and somber thoughts preyed on my mind" (96). The despotic scorn of the adored Katia creates precisely such a crisis, as from the depths of depression "a sense of righteous indignation rose up in my wounded heart" (113). The crisis is overcome in part by Netochka's sacrifice, but primarily thanks to the Prince's influence. He addresses the governess, who has unjustly punished the unhappy girl: "How have you been treating this poor child? This is barbarous, absolutely barbarous—it's savagery! A weak, sick child, a dreamy, easily frightened little girl with such an active imagination,—and to put her in a dark room and leave her there all night! Don't you know what her life has been like? . . . This is barbarous, it's inhuman, I tell you, madam! How can one administer such a punishment? Who devised it—who could possibly have devised such a punishment?" (122).

The third and final part of *Netochka Nezvanova,* entitled "The Mystery," could have been called "Youth." The "mystery" itself, however, is the "wounded heart" of Aleksandra Mikhailovna, the Prince's daughter from his first marriage, although it could also refer to the miraculous awakening of Netochka's character. At first Netochka again seems traumatized and alienated: "I entered another family, another house with new people, and once more I was uprooted from all that had grown dear to me and to which I felt I belonged. I arrived completely exhausted and racked by heartfelt anguish" (135). But for the first time she finds tranquility, of which her traumatized organism is so in need, and spends "more than eight years" in peace and quiet. The girl from an "accidental family" has finally achieved the "utopian goal of her efforts"—a true, loving relationship. Aleksandra Mikhailovna becomes deeply attached to the girl: "She was mother, sister, friend, everything in the world to me, and took the most devoted care of me in my youth" (137).

In the bildungsroman, there is usually a wise mentor who instructs the young hero, like Mentor himself in Fénélon's *Adventures of Telemachus* (1699), a work that many take as the first example of the genre. Aleksandra Mikhailovna, Netochka's new teacher, "maintained that it was useless to stuff my head full of dry facts, and that our success would depend entirely on my instinctive understanding and her skill in stimulating my desire to learn—and she was right, as was proved by her success" (144). This recalls the system described in Jean-Jacques Rousseau's "pedagogical novel," *Emile, or Education* (1762). For the humble Netochka, the absence of coercion was of paramount importance: "In the first place, the usual pupil-teacher relation did not exist. We worked together like two friends from the very start, and sometimes, though I was unaware of the ruse, it was made to appear that I was teaching Aleksandra Mikhailovna. In fact, arguments often sprang up between us, and I became quite vehement trying to prove my point, yet all the while she was imperceptibly leading me onto the right path" (144). A melancholy beauty, Aleksandra Mikhailovna knew from her own experience how silent suffering from an undeserved slight can wound one's heart. The time had arrived for Netochka to acknowledge her emotional experience and to evaluate it, and to refuse the role of patient victim. This goal is attained through dialogue with her teacher: "everything which formerly had surged up in me with abnormal and precocious violence, everything which had so lacerated my young heart that it was embittered by all the unjust cruelty and cried out against the pain without knowing its source—all this was little by little being smoothed out and brought into harmony" (145).

Reading is another source of Netochka's "lessons in living." The world of books had first been revealed to her while she was still living in the attic. That helped her to endure, since she had "lost all judgment, all sense of the present, of reality." "Books were the happiest period of my life"—such was the bitter experience of her childhood. At thirteen years of age, they served a different purpose. Not knowing how to deal with new subconscious desires, a longing for movement, intolerable anguish—all signs of physical maturation—she searched in books for "the correct path." The road or path is a primary motif in the bildungsroman, as is that of the threshold from which the path begins. In evaluating her reading, Netochka employs these metaphors: "It was as though fate had brought me to the threshold of the new life to which I had been impelled and had dreamed of day and night, and before setting me on the new path had led me to the summit to show me the future in a magic panorama, a dazzling perspective. . . . Almost every page I read was in some way familiar to me . . . it was as if I had some foreknowledge of it, as if something prophetic had been brewing in my soul, fortifying my hopes" (150–51).

Netochka's inevitable coming of age crisis occurs at age sixteen, when living in books is no longer sufficient: "suddenly an inexplicable apathy came over me; I was afflicted with an unbearable, depressing lethargy which I myself could not understand. All my fantasies and enthusiasms subsided, my daydreaming suddenly waned from lack of vitality" (158). She accidentally discovers a farewell letter to Aleksandra Mikhailovna from her admirer, and this jolts Netochka out of the world of books into reality: "From that moment my life was shattered" (161). At first glance, her reaction seems exaggerated, but it adheres to the emotional logic of the "wounded heart." The letter reveals the true reason for the beautiful woman's moral slavery. Petr Aleksandrovich has maintained his despotic power over his wife's shattered heart because of his position as "savior" and her sense of sin and shame. His wife had accepted him as her "benefactor," but the cost was great. Netochka is caught up in her mentor's drama—"the mystery was now linked to my whole existence." The girl who had been for so many years an aloof observer now becomes an active participant, and—by virtue of the ensuing circumstances—Aleksandra Mikhailovna's defender from her husband's hypocritical ridicule. This incident elicits an abrupt change in her character. Her peaceful youth ends, and restless young womanhood approaches: "What I was going through at that time was comparable to the experience of a man who, as he leaves forever the home where he has led a calm, untroubled life, sets out on a long journey to an unknown region, and before departing looks about him for the last time, mentally saying farewell to his past, sick at heart and full of misgivings about the unknown, perhaps harsh and hostile, future that awaits him" (167–68).

The images of the abandoned home and the unseen path foretell the bildungsroman's finale. In the last pages Netochka is a resolute young woman, bravely challenging the husband of her unhappy friend. Pale, with trembling lips that have turned blue with rage, Petr Aleksandrovich confronts Netochka: "'Enough!' he said in a voice weak with emotion. 'I suppose you don't want me to use force, so give me the letter of your own accord.' Only then did I stop to think, and I was outraged, filled with shame and indignation at the idea of brute force. . . . 'You are behaving contemptibly, dishonorably. You forget yourself! . . . Let me pass!' He again advanced toward me, but looking into my eyes saw such determination that he hesitated" (186–87).

Netochka, using the strongest and most precise words she can think of, accuses Petr Aleksandrovich of playing a cruel game with a poor woman's heart: "This is brutal—it's shameless, vile . . . it's beneath contempt" (190–91). A miracle of liberation has occurred; the "scab" of denigration, which had covered her vivid personality during the years of deprivation, falls away. The "wounded heart" that had not healed not only did not deprive Netochka of her force of will, but exactly the opposite: the experience of suffering strengthened her opposition to evil. The suffering of her early years did not drive Netochka to "dullness" or antisocial behavior, as some critics claimed, and did not stifle her self-respect.[18]

This upbeat ending links Dostoevsky's book to the classic Enlightenment bildungsroman, which stresses more the achievements of intellect and emotional development than losses in the "school of life." The open ending of *Netochka Nezvanova* is also characteristic of the bildungsroman. The final scene is very short. After reciting her accusatory monologue, Netochka runs into her room: "I was stopped at the door by Ovrov, who had been assisting Petr Aleksandrovich with his business affairs." The young man wants to speak with Netochka about something. "Tomorrow, then" (201). If the monologue had marked the end of the novel about childhood-adolescence-youth, then the meeting with Ovrov is a portent of "tomorrow"—young adulthood.

Netochka Nezvanova has always been regarded by Dostoevsky scholars as being of only marginal interest, mostly because of its alleged inconclusiveness. However, it is my opinion that the specific framework of the bildungsroman offers a more satisfactory and "conclusive" interpretation. It is known that Tolstoy, while planning *Childhood, Boyhood, Youth,* the first part of which appeared three years after *Netochka Nezvanova,* had originally thought to encompass "The Four Stages of Growth." He ended up completing only three parts, those during which Nikolen'ka grew up—that is, until the point when this "young person" became simply a "person."[19] Despite the fact that work on *Netochka Nezvanova* was forcibly interrupted by its author's arrest in 1849, the novel *Netochka Nezvanova* may be considered to be complete in its revised version of 1860. In keeping with the tradition of the bildungsroman, this version of Dostoevsky's novel, like Tolstoy's trilogy, ends on the brink of adult life.

TRANSLATED BY LISA TAYLOR

Notes

1. *Istoriia russkogo romana,* ed. A. S. Bushmin et al. (Moscow: Akademiia nauk SSSR, 1962), 1:422.
2. For further discussion of this topic, see my book *Ivan Aleksandrovich Goncharov: Mir tvorchestva* (St. Petersburg: Pushkinskii fond, 1997), 49–57.
3. A. A. Guseinov, "Nenasilie i perspektivy obshchestva," in *Etika nenasiliia: Materialy mezhdunarodnoi konferentsii* (Moscow: n.p., 1991), 15.
4. Mikhail Mikhailovich Bakhtin, *Estetika slovesnogo tvorchestva* (Moscow: Iskusstvo, 1979), 200.
5. Ibid., 202.
6. See, for example, N. M. Lary, *Dostoevsky and Dickens* (London: Routledge and Kegan Paul, 1973), 43–46.
7. Charles Passage, *Character Names in Dostoevsky's Fiction* (Ann Arbor, Mich.: Ardis, 1982), 29.
8. While George Sand's influence is evident in the conception of *Netochka Nezvanova,* there is a more specific source, *Mathilde, the Memoirs of a Young Woman* (1841) by Eugène Sue, which Dostoevsky had thought of translating in 1844.
9. Fedor Mikhailovich Dostoevskii, *Polnoe sobranie sochinenii v 30-i tomakh* (Leningrad: Nauka, 1972–90), 2:52.
10. Ibid.
11. For the history of this work see ibid., 2:494–98.
12. Fedor Dostoevsky, *Netochka Nezvanova,* trans. Ann Dunnigan (Englewood Cliffs, N.J.: Prentice-Hall, 1970), 28. Further references to this edition will be given in the text of the article.
13. V. I. Dal', *Tolkovyi slovar' zhivogo velikorusskogo iazyka* (St. Petersburg: n.p., n.d.), 2:559.
14. Bakhtin, *Estetika slovesnogo tvorchestva,* 187.
15. Dostoevsky, *Polnoe sobranie sochinenii,* 2:440.
16. Ibid., 2:444, 445, 441, 445.
17. Ibid., 2:52.
18. This was the opinion of N. A. Dobroliubov; see *Sobranie sochinenii v deviati tomakh* (Moscow: Khudozhestvennaia literatura, 1963), 7:242. For an opposing view at the time see O. F. Miller, who considered that Dobroliubov's classification of Netochka with the "oppressed people" (e.g., Nelli from *The Insulted and the Injured*) was one-sided, since they "had not allowed all within

them that was human to be suppressed." O. F. Miller, *Publichnye lektsii* (St. Petersburg: Tipografiia M. I. Popova, 1878), 214.

19. Dostoevsky's accurate psychological description of the complexity of Netochka's development and his insight into the youthful heart are fully worthy of comparison with those of Tolstoy.

Violence and the Word

Dostoevsky

HARRIET MURAV

The violence in Dostoevsky's text is sudden, sparse, and powerful. When Raskolnikov hits the old pawnbroker on the head with the dull side of his ax, her blood spills out "as if from an overturned glass."[1] Petr Verkhovenskii's battle with Kirillov is uncannily shocking: the otherwise impassive Petr Verkhovenskii himself "shudders" as he enters the room in which his victim, Kirillov, stands dead quiet and corpse-like, ready to turn against him. In *A Writer's Diary,* contemplating the real-life crime committed by the actress Anastasiia Kairova, who assaulted her lover's wife with a razor blade, Dostoevsky asks what if Kairova had not stopped her attack, but had instead "not only finished killing Velikanova, but began cursing the corpse, cut off the head, the nose, the lips?" (23:10). Ivan Karamazov's descriptions of the abuse suffered by children are among the most difficult passages to read in Dostoevsky's entire corpus.

In all these examples Dostoevsky uses language to represent acts of violence. My focus, however, is not on violence as a theme or object of description, but on violence as an effect of language. The boundary between the two is not always stable, as I will later show. Dostoevsky represents language itself as a weapon. The recipient of a message may experience the message as if it were an act of physical violence, and the emotions and sensations the message provokes may include, for example, pain, humiliation, and fear. These messages have a relation to the philosopher J. L. Austin's performatives and to what the U.S. Supreme Court has defined as "hate speech" but they are not identical to either. In *How to Do Things with Words* Austin describes a set of "performative" statements that constitute the "doing of an action," as for example, in the naming of a ship, the placing of a bet, or the completion of the marriage ceremony.[2] Austin distinguishes performatives from statements that do not do anything, but only describe, and may be true or false. The deliberate use of language to inflict violence may certainly be thought of as the "doing of an action" but not in the same immediate and automatic sense as Austin's category of performatives. Performatives rest on a set of conventions, and their binding force flows from those conditions already agreed upon, and in certain cases, from a specific configuration of language, authority and power. There are circumstances under which, as Austin puts it, "things go wrong" and the performative does not produce the usual result. For example, when a person who names a ship *Mr. Stalin* is actually not entitled to perform the ceremony, the ship in question remains unnamed. Austin excludes from consideration statements made in a literary context, that is, language that is spoken by an actor on a stage or introduced in a poem, labeling these as performatives that are "hollow or void." But it is precisely these kinds of statements that we must consider in order to examine the problem of language as a form of violence in Dostoevsky's text, namely, language that while embedded in a certain set of literary conventions, for example, an author quoting the thoughts or utterances of a fictitious character, nonetheless *does* something not only to the other fictitious characters represented in the text, but to the readers of the text as well.

The best way to introduce the specific dimension of the problem brought forward by Dostoevsky is with the central event of his early years in St. Petersburg. This is a case of a performative issued by the right person in the right circumstances that while made hollow and void, nonetheless inflicted violence upon those who were its object.

In December 1849 Dostoevsky and other members of the political circle he was associated with were subject to a mock execution. The prisoners were lined up, the death sentence was read to them, the first three were tied to stakes, their heads covered, and the order was given to shoot. At the last minute the order was rescinded. In contrast to other mock punishments, in which prisoners were informed in advance that their death sentence would not be carried out, in this instance Tsar Nicholas I stage-managed the charade to maximum effect. He had ordered the reprieve in advance of the morning of execution but chose to keep the new sentence a secret. Dostoevsky, who was in the second group of prisoners, was certain that he had only minutes to live.[3] The death sentence was made void, transformed into something more resembling a performative that is uttered by an actor on the stage, but it inflicted injury nevertheless. At least one of Dostoevsky's fellow-prisoners lost his reason as a result of his experience that morning on the Semenovskii square.

In *The Idiot* (1868) Prince Myshkin focuses on the death sentence itself as the source of great pain for the condemned prisoner. There is "no greater torment of earth" than "the sentence which you surely will not escape" (6:20). A soldier who is brought in front of a cannon and shot at will still hope, "but read this same soldier a sentence which is certain and he will go out of his mind or begin to cry" (6:21). In what is in all likelihood an autobiographical reference, Dostoevsky has Prince Myshkin recall a conversation he had with a condemned man who reported that he carefully apportioned the amount of time he had remaining, reserving two minutes to think about himself, but in those minutes the terrible certainty that his life would end paradoxically engendered in him the desire that it end more quickly. The death sentence produces the desire for death, deforming the natural wish to live.

It is striking that Prince Myshkin refers to the death sentence as a particular form of speech, characterizing it as verbal abuse, "invective" *(rugatel'stvo)*. It is a specific use of language that produces the effect of violence on its object. In this case, however, the effect of violence does not come from the words alone, but from the power of the state to carry out the sentence on the bodies of the prisoners. As the legal scholar Robert Cover writes: "Legal interpretation takes place in a field of pain and death."[4] Actors in a theater performing a scene of execution presumably do not suffer the ill effects endured by Dostoevsky and his fellow prisoners, but part of the harm they suffered was a direct result of their transformation into actors performing the spectacle of their own execution. The gap between the tsar's power to change the meaning of his own words and the words of his officials and the prisoners' lack of power to effect the words and their meaning is part of the prisoners' suffering. It is as if the tsar does not recognize that he belongs to a community of speakers, but imagines himself as the single godlike speaker. The demonstration of the tsar's power not only shows his power over life and death, but his power over words. We can take this example of state-authorized violence and the use of language as an instrument of this violence as a limit case.

There are other instances in Dostoevsky's texts in which language and power work together to create an effect of violence on the recipient of the message. An episode takes place in *The Insulted and the Injured* (1861) written shortly after Dostoevsky's return to Russia after his Siberian exile. In this tale of multiple love triangles and contested property the first-person narrator Ivan Petrovich is in love with Natasha Ikhmenev, who loves Alyosha, the son of the villainous Prince Valkovskii. Valkovskii, scheming both against his own son and Natasha, plans to have his son marry someone else and then declare the couple mentally incompetent. The prince uses the narrator as his intermediary, inviting him to a restaurant. Their conversation is, at first glance, far removed from the conditions I described above with regard to capital punishment. But as we will see, power and the force of law enter this speech situation as well. The purpose of the dinner is for the prince to reassert his power, stemming from his legal rights as a father, his wealth, and his superior social status. As Ivan Petrovich readily admits, "I was in his power" (3:355). Prince Valkovskii, as I will show, uses language to augment his power, transforming the genre of confession into an assault on his listener. Austin excludes literary representations of speech acts from consideration, but what Dostoevsky shows in this episode is how the violence of language is in part the destruction of conventions governing the use of language in specific speech situations. The making hollow of a performative, in this case, the performative genre of confession, is itself an act of violence wrought in and by language.

In order to get a sense of the brilliance of Dostoevsky's representation of what may be called the inverted confession, it is helpful to rehearse Foucault's well-known analysis of the power-knowledge relation within which traditional confession finds itself:

> The confession is a ritual of discourse in which the speaking subject is also the subject of the statement; it is also a ritual that unfolds within a power relationship, for one does not confess without the presence (or virtual presence) of a partner who is not simply the interlocutor but the authority who requires the confession, prescribes and appreciates it, and intervenes in order to judge, punish, forgive, console, and reconcile; a ritual in which the truth is corroborated by the obstacles and resistances it has had to surmount in order to be formulated; and finally, a ritual in which the expression alone, independently of its external consequences, produces intrinsic modifications in the person who articulates it:

it exonerates, redeems, and purifies him; it unburdens him of his wrongs, liberates him, and promises him salvation.[5]

However, in literary confessions such as Rousseau's, as Paul de Man famously argues, the confessee may not desire absolution, but exposure, because exposure is pleasurable. When Rousseau confesses that he planted the theft of the ribbon on the servant Marion, according to de Man, his object was "neither the ribbon nor Marion, but the public scene of exposure which he actually gets . . . the more there is to expose, the more there is to be ashamed of; the more resistance to exposure, the more satisfying the scene."[6] In Rousseau's case, the possibility of a shift in the flow of power normally found in confession, a realignment of the relation between the confessee and the confessor (here understood as the reader) depends on his capacity to extract pleasure from the exposure of his own guilt.

The scene in *The Insulted and the Injured* turns the problem in another direction. Not only does the confessee use his confession for pleasure, he turns his own pleasure into an attack on his confessor. Dostoevsky was, of course, familiar with Rousseau's text. Like Rousseau, Dostoevsky's villain, Prince Valkovskii claims that he is no worse than other human beings, but only more "open" (3:362). The prince recounts, for example, how he beat one of his servants to death because he wanted the man's wife for himself; he describes his love affair with a woman who could "give the Marquis de Sade lessons in debauchery;" he makes a declaration of his own freedom from any moral obligation whatsoever; finally, he provides a metaphor for the strategy behind his own discourse. Prince Valkovskii tells the story of a Parisian "madman" who used to expose himself on the street, opening his coat to reveal his naked body to anyone who happened by. The prince's interlocutor, Ivan Petrovich, interprets the metaphor by concluding at the end of their conversation that the prince "truly resembled the madman in the raincoat" (3: 368). The prince's stories and revelations are comparable to the act of indecent exposure. The act of indecent exposure contains a passive and an active element: the passive pleasure of receiving the gaze of the spectator(s), and the active element of the attack on the passerby, akin to what the prince describes as the sudden removal of the mask of decency. The confession of his worst acts is not an admission of guilt or a plea for forgiveness but a new instance of an assault on another.

Ivan Petrovich describes his sense of injury: "You were not only not worried that you could compromise yourself before me with your revelations but were not even ashamed. . . . You did not consider me a person" (3:368). The prince fails to recognize the boundaries that at least in a liberal version of civil society normally separate one person from another. The prince's words are an attack on his interlocutor's status as a bounded, separate individual. The verbal intimacy that Prince Valkovskii forces on Ivan Petrovich is paradoxically invasive, as if the prince had not "exposed" himself to Ivan Petrovich, but instead forced Ivan Petrovich to expose himself to him. Prince Valkovskii's verbal behavior in this instance resembles Tsar Nicholas's: the prince, like the tsar, abrogates to himself the position of sovereign speaker whose power over speech seeks to eliminate others from the community of speakers. In both cases, the message makes the recipient passive and invisible.

In Ivan Karamazov's "Rebellion," in contrast, the violence of language spills over the boundaries separating the speaker from the listener, contaminating both. Furthermore, the distinction between the use of language to represent violence and the use of language to inflict violence is similarly unstable. Ivan has been "collecting" cases of child abuse from the newspapers, including the story of the Swiss boy Richard, who grew up neglected and starved, committed murder, and while on death row became a Christian; the Kroneberg case, in which a jury acquitted a father who whipped his daughter for up to fifteen minutes at a time; and the case of a five-year-old girl locked in the outhouse by her parents and forced to eat her own excrement. These instances serve a specific function in Ivan's philosophical dilemma about the possibility of human redemption, but my focus here is how they function as speech acts in relation to Ivan's listener, Alyosha: "'Am I tormenting you, Alyoshka, you don't seem to be yourself. I'll stop, if you want.' 'It's nothing, I want to be tormented too,' Alyosha muttered" (14:221).

Ivan's words cause a physical change in Alyosha, evident to Ivan, who remarks, "you don't seem to be yourself." Alyosha is in an analogous position with regard to Ivan's discourse as the children are with regard to their abusers. He is the passive and seemingly innocent recipient of Ivan's verbal violence, just as the children are the passive and, according to Ivan, innocent recipients of their adult abusers' physical violence. The analogy can be continued. Alyosha stands in the position of the reader of Dostoevsky's text.

The only difference between Alyosha and the children is the element of desire: Alyosha "wants" to be tormented. This tiny difference increases in importance as Ivan goes on to describe an episode involving a serf owner who had a little boy torn apart by his dogs, because the child accidentally injured one of them. In a manner similar to the early modern procedure of ordeal by torture, Ivan uses this episode to "test" or "try" Alyosha. Alyosha agrees that the serf owner should be shot. No longer in the position of a passive and innocent victim of violence ("I want to be tormented too"), Alyosha moves to the position of the active perpetrator of violence: "'Shoot him!' Alyosha said quietly" (14:221). The representation of violence produces the effect of violence both by causing pain and causing the desire for pain, but also by causing the desire to inflict violence on someone else. The shift in Alyosha from the passive to the active role may be compared to a similar shift that I discussed earlier with regard to Prince Valkovskii of *The Insulted and the Injured,* in whose verbal behavior elements of passivity and activity combine together in such a way as to intensify his pleasure. In so far as Alyosha pronounces a death sentence on the serf owner, and thus assumes a sovereign power over another, he may also be compared to Tsar Nicholas I.

The question may also be raised more generally about the complicity of the reader in relation to the violence Ivan describes. Dostoevsky blurs the boundaries between those who perpetrate violent acts, those who describe the acts in verbal statements, and those who receive the statements. The violence of language undermines the familiar and easy distinctions between the innocent and the guilty, and readers of Dostoevsky may find themselves struggling with an uncomfortable feeling of complicity, no matter how remote, in the acts that Ivan describes. Reading Ivan Karamazov's "Rebellion" may serve as a test or trial for the reader without a clear-cut outcome.

Austin stipulates a set of conditions limiting the efficacy of performatives, including the reservation that the right person has to utter the right words. In the example I cited earlier, only the person entitled to name a ship can complete the speech act of naming it efficaciously. Dostoevsky raises questions about who is speaking/acting and undermines our ability to delimit the speaking subject. Speech that constitutes the doing of an action is Austin's definition of a speech act, but in Dostoevsky, as we have seen in the case of Prince Valkovskii, speaking may be a form of doing that is at the same time a form of being acted upon, and in the case of Alyosha, being acted upon by speech may become a form of acting by speaking ("Shoot him").

Judith Butler's *Excitable Speech* provocatively responds to the question of the relation of speech to action by arguing that speech ought not to be reduced to conduct.[7] Her argument rejects the model of unitary sovereign subject wholly responsible for his or her speech. In contrast, according to Butler, speakers cannot be held fully responsible for their speech because, as David Campbell puts it, the "ambiguity and indeterminacy of language which means all speech is to some extent out of control."[8] Dostoevsky, like Butler, ultimately rejects the model of the sovereign subject, but for different reasons, which stem from his exploration of a religious and mystical model of the interconnectedness of human action. The clearest exposition of this rather confusing idea comes from the notorious chapter "At Tikhon's" in *The Devils*, although Zosima briefly mentions it in *The Brothers Karamazov*, when he says that each one is responsible all for all. Tikhon agrees to forgive Stavrogin only if Stavrogin will forgive him. Denying that such an agreement is merely a "monkish formula," as Stavrogin disparagingly describes it, Tikhon says that there is no such thing as "unitary sin," suggesting a critique of the model of the single, sovereign actor, and pointing toward an idea of the hidden linkages among human acts. In contrast to the violence of Prince Valkovskii and Ivan's speech acts, the potential for violence in Stavrogin's confession is mitigated by Tikhon's extraordinary capacity to respond to it with love. In Dostoevsky's text, as I have tried to show, the performatives "I confess," "I accuse you," and "I sentence you" may link speakers and their interlocutors together in a chain in which everyone is implicated in violence. "I forgive" breaks the chain of violence, reforging it as a chain of co-responsibility. The efficacy of the language of forgiveness in Dostoevsky remains, however, unpredictable and indeterminate, unlike the unidirectional power of divine revelation in Zhukovskii's poetry (see Ilya Vinitsky's essay in this volume, "The Invisible Scaffold").

Notes

1. F. M. Dostoevsky, *Polnoe sobranie sochinenii v tridtsati tomakh*, 30 vols. (Leningrad: Nauka, 1972–90), 6:63. Henceforward all references to be given parenthetically in the body of the text by volume and page number. Unless otherwise noted, all translations are my own.

2. J. L. Austin, *How to Do Things with Words*, 2nd ed. (Cambridge, Mass.: Harvard University Press, 1975), 7.

3. For a summary of various accounts of these moments, including Dostoevsky's remarks in a letter to his brother, see A. F. Budanova and G. M. Fridlender, eds., *Letopis' zhizni i tvorchestva F. M. Dostoevskogo 1821–1881*, 3 vols. (St. Petersburg: Akademicheskii proekt, 1994), 1:175.

4. Robert Cover, "Violence and the Word," *Yale Law Journal* 95 (1986): 1601–29.

5. Michel Foucault, *The History of Sexuality*, vol. 1, trans. Robert Hurley (New York: Random House, 1980), 61–62.

6. Paul de Man cited by Peter Brooks, *Troubling Confessions: Speaking Guilt in Law and Literature* (Chicago: University of Chicago Press, 2000), 20. Brooks provides a searing critique of the legal use of confession based on, among other arguments, the literary representation of the instability of confession.

7. Judith Butler, *Excitable Speech: A Politics of the Performative* (New York: Routledge, 1997).

8. David Campbell, "Performing Politics and the Limits of Language," *Theory and Event* 2 (1998):1. Available at http://muse.jhu.edu/journals/theory_and_event/v002/2.1r_campbell.html.

Nihilists and Terrorists

DANIEL BROWER

At the news of the first assassination attempt on Alexander II in 1879, Vera Zasulich reportedly "fell into a deep depression." One of her companions attributed her despondency to a notion that her attack on General Trepov the previous year had opened the way to political terror.[1] Her dismay did not reflect on her own deed, which she never regretted. Her scruples were programmatic, not moral; social revolution, not terror, was her chosen means of struggle. Still, her very personal reaction suggests how problematic terror appeared to Russian radicals. This ambiguity points to the major issue I address in this essay: How did the taking of human life in the name of revolution become imbedded in the radical movement by the late 1870s, at a time when bitter debates occasioned by fundamental disagreement on doctrinal and ideological principles left terrorism's role unresolved? I will argue that assassination became a preferred mode of action among some radicals because of historically specific conditions and social-cultural influences peculiar to Russia of the 1860s and 1870s. In my reading, the nihilists were the forerunners to terrorists; in a figurative sense, Ivan Turgenev's fictional Bazarov was blood relation to Alexander's eventual assassins of the "Land and Freedom" movement. The factors that I highlight bear a strong resemblance to those uncovered in studies of other terrorist movements in later years.[2] Russia can claim pride of place as the first in a long line of countries where terror became a recognized, and feared, expression of political opposition.

The sources for my analysis draw upon my own earlier work on the emergence of a radical subculture in the 1860s, the literature on the radical movement of the 1860s and 1870s, and the abundant memoir literature that the survivors of the late 1870s terrorist movement left of their words and deeds. There are problems with each. Almost all the secondary literature on Russian radicalism of that era is so sympathetic to the goals of the militants and so hostile to the tsarist regime of the time that it does not treat the issue of terrorism separately from propaganda and agitation. It is useful for factual background only. Philip Pomper's work on Nechaev is the exception, for he constructs a behavioral model (stressing psychological factors) for this destructively inclined rebel. My own research on the social and cultural roots of radicalism has no direct bearing on the turn to violence; my use of its findings here is in this sense an effort to infer connections where none are explicit.[3] The authors of the memoir literature, heavily focused on the years just prior to Alexander II's assassination in 1881, sought to preserve the aura of moral virtue that they had at the time accorded the terrorists by honoring the dead and sanctifying the cause that the authors themselves believed in. These records remain nonetheless a gold mine of information on the mentality of the radicals. Their vocabulary of sanctification offers insight into the individual motives and group behavioral patterns by which assassination became a tolerable, even worthy act of warrior-heroes. A noble cause justified ugly deeds.

That the nihilist was a new social as well as an ideological phenomenon was obvious to friends and foes alike in the mid-century. Colorful language proclaimed the onslaught of a cohort of iconoclasts. This was the gist of Dimitrii Pisarev's famous 1861 article, in which he issued his famous challenge to accepted truths in the form of an "ultimatum of our camp: what can be smashed should be; what stands up under the blows is acceptable; what flies into a thousand pieces is trash."[4] Pisarev's reference to "our camp" was for the time a flight of fantasy, but one that lent itself to warlike posturing. Even the question of how to identify the "new people" who manned the barricades was a matter of some discussion. Nikolai Chernyshevskii proposed a social portrait of the radical in his novel *What's to Be Done*, subtitled *Tales of the New People*. The stereotypical *nigilist* and *nigilistka* flaunted their personal resolve by adhering to a dress code that defied propriety. It was apparent to everyone that their distinctive appearance expressed their refusal to abide by social custom. Chernyshevskii's novel taught its readers, as one student reading group concluded a decade later, that (in the words of a police spy in their midst) "one must renounce traditions" to be able to "help the people."[5] This was a fairly colorless rendering of Pisarev's dramatic proclamation of defiance, but a reliable indicator that radical ideals had become rooted in ethical behavior.

Pisarev's appeal to "our camp" conjured up the image of a mythical bastion defended by "us" for battle against "them." The emergence of bonds of solidarity uniting Russia's young rebels proceeded with remarkable speed. These derived from shared convictions, the disowning of the institutional and moral authority of family, class (estate), and state, and the creation of communal institutions and practices useful for both survival and the recruitment of new members. By the mid-1860s the nihilists were far more often comrades in the manner of Chernyshevskii's Vera Pavlovna and her male companions than solitary heroes in the style of the author's Rakhmetov. Adoption of the new markers of comradeship, in dress, behavior, and vocabulary, assured those abandoning the comforts and protection offered by society of a new place of shelter and support. The groups of learning and mutual support, baptized "circles" [*kruzhki*], proved a phenomenally successful focal point for gathering disaffected students and emancipated women, and very soon for political agitation.

On a higher level of organization, the shared living arrangements of the communes offered the greatest security and the strongest ties of solidarity. Sergei Sinegub's personal exploit of saving in 1871 the oppressed sixteen-year-old daughter of a parish priest through a fictitious marriage made for celebratory storytelling. The success of the operation was a measure of the solidarity of the radical community, whose members' social conscience was usually (but not always) the assurance of selfless concern for their comrades' well-being. Sinegub's undertaking emerged out of his participation in the Chaikovskii circle, which took over the planning of the young woman's escape from paternal tyranny. Her flight had an assured destination thanks to the existence of women's communes, one of which became her new home in St. Petersburg.[6] The radical community had become a world apart.

The image of the rebel had by then been reinvented several times. The most threatening personification was that of the terrorist. It is surprising how quickly the urge to take blood manifested itself in radical literature, and how soon afterwards words led to deeds. Pride of place for first promoting terror probably belongs to Peter Zaichnevskii's 1863 pamphlet, *Young Russia,* which anticipated "rivers of blood" in a struggle in which "he who is not with us is against us; he who is against us is our enemy, and enemies must be destroyed by any means."[7] The words were melodramatic, but his readiness to consider the lives of "enemies," however identified, as forfeit proved a portent of the future. Melodrama became reality in 1864 in the conspiratorial organization that Nikolai Ishutin baptized "Hell," whose members talked of plotting the death of the tsar and eliminating unworthy members from their midst. Karakozov's attempt on Alexander II two years later, in 1866, was the only sequel to the talk of regicide, and over a decade passed before the cause was taken up seriously again. Yet in those few years a mode of terrorist discourse and practice had taken shape. The radical community had given birth to a new breed of rebels. They shared with the larger subculture the bonds of solidarity that protected and nurtured their activity. Their distinctiveness lay in their readiness to turn selflessness into a form of martyrdom, sacrificing if necessary their own lives to achieve the destruction of their enemies.

Shortly afterward, the image of the terrorist assumed a grotesque reality in the person of Sergei Nechaev. Philip Pomper has explored in detail Nechaev's writings and deeds, suggesting a psychopathological explanation for his extremism. Nechaev's actions and proclamations gave a particularly sinister character to the terrorist's profile. The radical terrorists of the late 1870s laid no claim to his heritage. Yet in two respects he deserves to be placed in their midst. In the "Catechism of a Revolutionary," he portrayed, more forcefully than any writer then or later, the "doomed revolutionary . . . ready to perish himself to destroy with his own hands everything that hinders [the success of the revolution]."[8] Self-sacrifice achieved an ugly apotheosis in his wild imagination. Secondly, by organizing and carrying out in 1869 the assassination of a comrade, accused of being a police spy in his revolutionary organization, People's Revenge (Narodnaia Rasprava), he made tangible the potential for violence that lay hidden within the radical movement. His actions demonstrated how the moral precept "the end justifies the means," could become the sanction for assassination. It reemerged a decade later at the core of the radical movement.

Just how an individual could act out this bloody scenario, in the name of utopian beliefs, was a preoccupation for the novelist Fyodor Dostoevsky. He used his novel *The Devils* (*Besy,* 1872), partly inspired by Nechaev's murder of a student comrade, to present a simplistic portrait of a terrorist in the person of Peter Verkhovenskii. Polemically the

Enemies Face to Face: *Interrogation of a Revolutionary,* 1904 by V. Makovskii.

novel was successful, but it presented a superficial psychological profile of a nihilist drawn to violent deeds. Earlier, though, he had looked far more deeply into the personality of a prototerrorist. In the person of Raskolnikov, the central character of *Crime and Punishment* (1866), he suggested that a complex interplay of personal needs and convictions lay behind a murder justified by ideological principle. Before the death of the moneylender and her sister, Raskolnikov's thoughts are of "exceptional men" whose great gifts make them "lords of the future" fit to "march over corpses or wade through blood." But after the murder, his tone changes dramatically. He admits that his claim to moral superiority, a common note among the radicals, is self-delusion, for he recognizes that he acted from a compelling desire to prove to himself that he indeed belonged among this elite. He could achieve that end, he confesses to Sonia, only by "transgressing." "To dare [*osmelit'sia*]" to murder was his personal act of initiation, an action to prove his liberation from the existing moral code by ridding the world of a creature he judged to be morally debased.[9] The novelist terminates Raskolnikov's foray into daring deeds with his confession; for others not prone to religious qualms, the need to act in so decisive a manner could be repeated many times over.

Though Dostoevsky's aim was to pinpoint the fatal flaw in Raskolnikov's character, his analysis offers a valuable clue to the link between nihilists and terrorists. The radicals' claim to a rightful place in the world apart from, and superior to, the despicable, brutal tsarist regime depended not only upon acts of renunciation, but also upon meaningful deeds that attested to their rejection of that regime. Ishutin and Nechaev, each in his own way, had made known their conviction that those deeds should include political assassination. It was for them the ultimate act of defiance, and thus of revolutionary legitimation. Intellectually and morally it remained a bitterly contested option. Nonetheless, by the end of the 1870s it had acquired its own mystique within radical circles.

The failure of the populists' propaganda campaign among the peasant population set the stage in the late 1870s for the turn to violence. The massive arrests and the trials that followed were both a crushing blow to the radical movement and a public demonstration of the repressive powers of the state. So it appeared to the radicals, whose vocabulary of combat became more militant than ever before. So too did their deeds. Vera Zasulich's shooting in January 1878 of General Trepov was only one among several modes of attack on the regime. Radicals had already begun to prepare for battle by arming themselves with daggers and revolvers. Once visions of armed uprising had dissipated, these weapons served as the means of eliminating spies planted by the secret police among the radicals. It was enough that suspicion fall upon an individual to bring retribution. In one of the first known incidents, Lev Deich and a comrade hunted down a presumed police spy in Odessa, knifed him, poured acid on his face to prevent identification, and left a note proclaiming "Such is the fate of any spy."[10]

And for the first time, the use of firearms became an accepted means to resist arrest. The first shoot-out between radicals and police occurred in early 1878 in a violent confrontation in Odessa. The resistance was unsuccessful, and as a result two of the armed rebels were sentenced to death by hanging. Shifting the target to high police officials came very quickly. In retaliation for the hanging of the Odessa radicals, in mid-1878 Sergei Kravchinskii stabbed to death the head of the secret police, N. V. Mezentsev. The title of his pamphlet, written immediately after the assassination, was eloquent justification: *A Death for a Death.* Lev Tikhomirov, at the time one of the key activists in the Death or Freedom group in St. Petersburg (later a renegade and tsarist publicist), concluded after his renunciation of radicalism that these acts appeared to his comrades "the sole means to begin the revolution, to prove to themselves that it really is beginning and not just empty phrases."[11] The humiliation inflicted upon the radicals by mass arrests and the despair at the collapse of the "to the people movement" had combined to sanction revenge by terror. Retribution had become a revolutionary deed; the compelling urge to take action recalled Raskolnikov's decision "to dare."

The memory that these militant radicals left behind among the survivors was of "champions [*bogatyri*] of our time, ready for death at any moment." The words are those of V. Debogorii-Mokrievich, whose lukewarm sympathy for terrorism was overwhelmed by his admiration for the "daring" of the armed comrades in the Kiev radical circles. The calls that he heard "to terrorize the government" led to the assassination in Kiev of the assistant state procurator that fall. Debogorii-Mokrievich was quite unconvinced by the "deductive logic" used by his comrades, who explained the turn to "political action"—that is, terror—as a strategically necessary move away from the unwelcoming peasantry to confront the repressive state. Instead, he saw in it the product of "passion and circumstances," the latter principally the arrests and trials of the populists, the former generated by anger at the apparent impunity with which the authorities could imprison and punish their comrades.[12]

Their proclaimed justification was "vengeance." Not the principled "*rasprava*" by which Nechaev had baptized his group, for that term had a general sense of legitimate violence. The term used by the terrorists of the late 1870s was that for blood feuds, "*mest'*," an act of reprisal. Zasulich's shots at General Trepov earned her among Moscow radicals the accolade of "political avenger," who acted to fight "this terrible system of lies and repression."[13] So it was for Kravchinskii, and as well for Deich. Kravchinskii claimed that his assassination of Mezentsev was an "exceptional episode," since "we will never go beyond the limits of self-defense. Murder is a horrible thing!"[14] These moral qualms quickly dissipated.

For the terrorist process had a dynamic of its own that permitted only surrender or further violence. The police were determined to eliminate the radical opposition and had no qualms about infiltrating the movement. In 1878 some of the leaders of Land and Liberty were swept up by police arrests as a result of information that their comrades believed came from one of these traitors. Alexander Mikhailov immediately ordered what he termed "the elimination" of the spy and "vengeance" on the chief of the secret police. The assassins placed on the agent's body a note stating that "this spy is punished by the orders of the central executive revolutionary committee."[15] The act of revenge acquired an aura of institutional authority; the fact that no such executive committee existed mattered little. Toward the end of the year, Kravchinskii carried the argument one step further in proclaiming, in the first issue of the underground bulletin of Land and Liberty, that the terrorists were the "defensive force" whose mission was "to defend the comrades from the traitorous blows of the enemy."[16] The avengers had placed themselves on the front lines of a war without mercy. Moral qualms had no place there.

As the conflict grew in intensity, so too did the vocabulary that ennobled political violence. The image of secular martyr informed the idealized self-portrait of the assassins. The voluntary acceptance of one's own death represented in its terrible way the ultimate proof of selflessness and of absolute dedication to the cause. Its associations with Christian hagiography did not trouble Kravchinskii. Writing a decade later for a Western audience, he claimed that "the terrorist" was "beautiful, terrifying, inexpressibly alluring, since he unites in himself the highest type of human grandeur: the martyr, and the hero." This martyrdom did not resemble the Christian model, in Kravchinskii's opinion, for here was "a warrior with only one aim: to destroy the hated despotism and to give his homeland political freedom."[17]

A second distinction, one that the author did not mention, was that terrorists treated the death of their victims and unfortunate bystanders as a necessary consequence of their battle with tsardom, a means justified by their noble (utopian) goal. Lev Tikhomirov recalled that adoption of this moral precept had aroused among radicals a passionate debate in the 1870s, and most (including himself) resolved it by concluding that their ideals constituted the "greatest good." Terror's brutal methods paled to insignificance by comparison.[18] They lived by an absolutist ethical code whose hold on them as individuals and on the group as a whole made their own deaths a tolerable event, and the destruction of "the enemy" an unquestioned necessity. Leo Tolstoy was amazed at their disregard for human bloodshed. Writing about them later in his novel *Resurrection,* he claimed to find within their circle an "exalted opinion" of their deeds that sustained their conviction that

A Nihilist "Circle": *The Evening Party*, 1875 by V. Makovskii.

"their cruel acts were not only not bad [*durnymi*], but rather were valorous exploits."[19] The solidarity created by the nihilists had generated extraordinary, terrible deeds.

The terrorists had come to constitute a warrior band by 1879. The depredations on their ranks by tsarist arrests were not serious enough to weaken the movement, since new recruits arrived continuously to volunteer for battle. Their social profile still resembled the archetypical nihilist—young, studying or at the very least studious, from a family of noble or urban estate, and persuaded that the most heroic task, indeed the only viable life, was service in the revolutionary cause. But the dress code had changed, at least for the men. No longer the scruffy nihilists, or the populists in village garb, the terrorists adopted in public, as Sergei Aptekman recalled, the guise of "the 'gentleman,' very correctly dressed. And in his belt is a dagger, and in his pocket a revolver."[20] Probably Aptekman had most closely in mind Sergei Kravchinskii and Alexander Mikhailov, both of whom were "barin" by birth and "barin" by choice of appropriate disguise. As well, for terrorists to walk about in the likeness of gentlemen may well have been an act of provocative defiance, gratifying to their self-image as destroyers of the old order.

That year, 1879, marked the emergence of terrorism as the principal tool of the revolutionaries. After bitter debate, Land and Liberty militants gave their backing to Sergei Solov'ev's attempt early that year to assassinate the tsar. Their decision set the stage for the formation of People's Will, solely dedicated to regicide. Defenders of terrorism spoke out on the pages of the Land and Liberty bulletin, arguing that "we have accepted the challenge, we do not fear the struggle and in the end will destroy the government, no matter how many on our side are lost."[21] Historical heroes buttressed their cause. Not Karakozov, who was outside the nihilist-terrorist filiation and too close to the euphoric times when Alexander II was the "tsar-emancipator," but those glorious semimythical figures from the West, Charlotte Corday of French Revolution notoriety, and the legendary Swiss Wilhelm Tell.

There really was little doubt among the radicals that terrorism had become the *mot d'ordre* of their movement. The 1879 Lipetsk meeting of St. Petersburg radicals (preceding the Voronezh gathering of militants from across the country) was a moment of consecration of the terrorist as crusader/warrior. Alexander Morozov spelled out the targets for assassination, whom he described as "our enemies, all those who aid the government and are against us." And Alexander Mikhailov, by common agreement the most "rigorous" among the backers of terror, read out the condemnation of the tsar in a setting that resembled a miniature show trial. After praising Alexander II's emancipation of the serfs and judicial reforms, then detailing the repression of the radicals of recent years, he concluded with the rhetorical query: "For the sake of these two good deeds at the beginning of his reign, should we forgive him for all the evil that he has done and will do?"[22] His audience sat as jury and executioners. Their unanimous "No" was a declaration of war.

They had created out of the amorphous ideas and practices of the nihilists a world of absolute good and evil, had selected from the radical image of the selfless idealist those ingredients suitable to the role of the warrior-crusader, and had refashioned the spirit of martyrdom to be the mark of the Russian terrorist. Alexander II's death in 1881 ought to have been their moment of triumph. From our post-Soviet perspective, it appears a step toward the defeat of the admirable ideals by which they justified their deeds. The halo of martyr has passed to their victim. The interior setting of the magnificently restored Church of Christ in the Blood, centered on a baldachin built over the exact cobblestones where the tsar was assassinated, commemorates the tsar's martyrdom.

Notes

1. Olga Liubatovich, "Dalekoe i nedavnee," in *Five Sisters: Women against the Tsar*, ed. and trans. Barbara Engel and Clifford Rosenthal (New York: Schocken, 1975), 163.

2. An interesting effort at dissecting the commonalities of terrorist movements is J. M. Post et al., "The Radical Group in Context," *Studies in Conflict and Terrorism* 25 (March–April 2002): 70–82.

3. Philip Pomper, *Sergei Nechaev* (New Brunswick, N.J.: Rutgers University Press, 1979); the paragon of apologists is David Footman, *Red Prelude: A Life of A. I. Zhelyabov*, 2nd ed. (London: Barrie and Rockliff, 1968); my own work is *Training the Nihilists: Education and Radicalism in Tsarist Russia* (Ithaca, N.Y.: Cornell University Press, 1975).

4. D. Pisarev, *Izbrannye sochineniia* (Moscow: Khudozhestvennaia literatura, 1934), 1:66.

5. Quoted in B. Itenberg, *Dvizhenie revoliutsionnogo narodnichestva* (Moscow: Nauka, 1965), 68.

6. The subsequent renown of this affair among sympathizers in and beyond Russia is apparent in the detailed account of their adventure given in Jaakoff Prelooker, *Heroes and Heroines of Russia: Builders of a New Commonwealth* (London: Simpkin, Marshall, Hamilton, Kent, 1908), 51–77.

7. B. Koz'min, ed., *Istoriko-revoliutsionnaia khrestomatiia* (Moscow: Novaia Moskva, 1923), 1:59.

8. Quoted in Pomper, *Sergei Nechaev*, 91.

9. Fedor Dostoevskii, *Prestuplenie i nakazanie* (Moscow: Nauka, 1970), 202–3 (pt. 3, ch. 5), 323–24 (pt. 5, ch. 4).

10. V. Debogorii-Mokrievich, *Ot buntarstva k terrorizmu* (Moscow: Molodaia gvardiia, 1930), 1:316. The story of Land and Liberty's choice of terrorism is Deborah Hardy, *Land and Freedom: The Origins of Russian Terrorism, 1876–1879* (New York: Greenwood, 1987), esp. ch. 6 ("The Mystique of Terrorism").

11. Lev Tikhomirov, *Nachalo i konets* (Moscow, 1890), 91.

12. Debogorii-Mokrievich, *Ot buntarstva*, 373–78.

13. V. Anzimirov, *"Kramol'niki": khronika radikal'nykh kruzhkov 70kh gg.* (Moscow: I. D. Sytin, 1907), 10.

14. Cited in Osip Aptekman, *Obshchestvo Zemlia i volia semidesiatykh gg.: po lichnym vospominaniiam* (Petrograd: Kolos, 1924), 329.

15. Quoted in Mikhail Popov, *Zapiski zemlevol'tsa* (Moscow: Vsesoiuznoe obshchestvo Politkatorzhan i ssyl'no-poselentsev, 1933), 140.

16. *Zemlia i volia* 1 (25 October 1878), quoted in Aptekman, *Obshchestvo*, 329.

17. Sergei Stepniak (Kravchinskii), *Podpol'naia Rossiia* (London: Fonda russkoi vol'noi pressy, 1893), 23–25; Barbara Engel makes a persuasive argument that the women terrorists measured up to the ascetic standards of martyrdom better than the men (*Mothers and Daughters: Women of the Intelligentsia in Nineteenth-Century Russia* [New York: Cambridge University Press, 1983], ch. 9 ["Morality Becomes Absolutism"]).

18. Tikhomirov, *Nachalo*, 94.

19. L. Tolstoy, *Voskresenie* (Leningrad: Khudozhestvennaia literatura, 1980), 403 (pt.3, ch.5).

20. Aptekman, *Obshchestvo*, 333.

21. *Zemlia i volia* 2 (April 1879), quoted in Aptekman, *Obshchestvo*, 357.

22. Alexander Morozov, "Sobytie v kruzhke Zemlia i volia," *Povesti moei zhizni* (Moscow: Akademmia nauk, 1947), 2:512, 517.

Violence and the Legacy of "Bakuninism" in the Russian Revolution

J. FRANK GOODWIN

Among the many legendary revolutionists of nineteenth-century Russia, none became more closely associated with the idea of violent rebellion than the "apostle of universal destruction," Mikhail Bakunin (1814–76). By means of militant rhetoric and inexhaustible agitation for the complete demolition of the large European states, Bakunin represented the most outstanding spokesman for a massive, merciless uprising of the Russian peasantry against the autocracy. Notwithstanding their enormous respect for his revolutionary pathos, the pioneers of Russian Marxism also identified Bakunin with retrogressive political tendencies of "adventurism" and "anarchism," which they had to oppose and resist for many years in order to win support for the concept of a proletarian revolution. The eventual birth of the Russian Social-Democratic Labor Party and the growth of an organized proletariat, conscious of its socialist aims and willing to take advantage of legal means of struggle, gave encouragement to those who placed no faith in the ultimate success of anarchic revolts, terrorism, or other primitive forms of revolutionary activity traditionally linked to Bakunin. By 1905, however, as the legacy of Bakunin's radical thought found new adherents among anarchists, some Russian Marxists warned against a revival of its appeal. When the Bolshevik wing of the party took advantage of mass discontent to seize power in 1917, critics accused it of "Bakuninism," which remained a common metaphor for the violent impulse within the Revolution.

The notion of "Bakuninism" in the Russian revolutionary movement arose during the final years of the International Working Men's Association (1864–76), whose general council, led by Marx and Engels, called upon the working class to fight for political power and to reject Bakunin's anarchist appeal for the destruction of all political power. Their most detailed critique of Bakuninism appeared in the 1873 pamphlet *The Alliance of Socialist Democracy and the International Working Men's Association*, which exposed several of the most violent aims of Bakuninism as spelled out in Bakunin's own pamphlets: to eradicate completely all vestiges of the existing order so that "not a stone shall remain standing," as Bakunin wrote; to instigate "popular anarchy," already "prepared over a long time in the instinctive consciousness" of the masses; and to unleash "evil passions," which "must from the very first day destroy, radically and totally, the state and all the state's institutions." Describing Bakunin's Alliance as a backward tendency in which "the economic and political struggle of the workers for their emancipation is replaced by universal pan-destructive acts of heroes of the underworld," in other words, by a plan "to let loose the street hooligans," the authors also attempted to demonstrate that the anarchist principles of Bakunin provided the formula for the violent crimes of his agent in Russia, Sergei Nechaev, including the murder of a political associate. They called attention to Bakunin's appeal for traditional Russian "brigandage" *(razboi)* in two proclamations, *Several Words to Our Young Brothers in Russia* and *Posing the Revolutionary Question*, which glorified the bloody popular uprisings led by the Cossack brigand Stenka Razin during the seventeenth century and called for a ruthless popular rebellion in the same spirit. They also noted the direct appeal for "systematic assassination" in the proclamations *Beginnings of Revolution* and *Catechism of a Revolutionist*, both of which they attributed to Bakunin.[1] In another work, Engels held Bakuninism responsible for the failure of uprisings in Spain in 1873. By their refusal to participate in political activities when possible and by their tendency to "drift into sporadic, desultory and senseless uprisings," Engels insisted, the Bakuninists merely caused a "senseless fragmentation of revolutionary resources," which allowed the state to crush the movement. "In short," he wrote, the Bakuninists demonstrated "how a revolution should *not* be made."[2]

Despite the efforts of Marx and Engels to disassociate Bakuninism from the program of the International Working Men's Association and to warn against its dangers, in Russia a certain revival of Bakunin's ideas occurred during the second half of the 1870s, when a new program of "buntarstvo," or agitation for spontaneous uprisings, made its appearance in the movement. According to one leading representative, V. K. Debogorii-Mokrievich, the "southern rebels" *(iuzhnye buntari)* not only accepted the need "to go to the people and organize revolts," as dictated in Bakunin's influential work of 1873, *Statism and Anarchy,* but also believed that the only path to a socialist order in Russia would be "revolutionary and bloody," by way of a spontaneous uprising of the masses.[3] Another leading "southern rebel," L. G. Deich, confirmed that the main inspiration for their program and tactics came from Bakunin, whose views many were prepared to adopt uncritically, even his notion of "the brigand as a people's protestant."[4] While the doctrine of "buntarstvo" began to decline soon after Bakunin's death in 1876, a Bakuninist spirit and belief in the necessity of violent action against the autocracy persisted within Russian populism throughout the next decade.[5]

The founders of Marxism came to recognize Bakunin's legacy as one of the chief obstacles facing the future proletarian movement. Looking back at the 1870s and early 1880s, G. V. Plekhanov and V. I. Zasulich informed the Socialist International some years later that they had reached the correct understanding of scientific socialism only after a difficult fight with Bakuninism and its false belief in backwardness as the key to progress in Russia.[6] The need to combat Bakuninism in Russia and anarchism in Europe led to two important works by Plekhanov on the question of violence during the 1890s, particularly the violent "propaganda by the deed" practiced by the French anarchists. In "Anarchism and Socialism" (1894) Plekhanov characterized the anarchists' use of terrorism and opposition to political struggle as "complete Bakuninism" *(usovershenstvovannyi bakunizm),* thanks to which, "in the name of revolution," Plekhanov emphasized, the anarchists merely "serve the cause of reaction."[7] In "Strength and Violence", Plekhanov ridiculed the anarchists' faith in the tactics of violent acts and uprisings as the only truly "revolutionary" form of action. Its complete failure to advance the cause of revolution demonstrated the inferiority of violence to the strength derived from the willingness to take advantage of legal means when available.[8]

Although Marxist ideas had begun to take root toward the end of the nineteenth century, increasing social unrest in Russia soon favored a resurgence of Bakunin's legacy as well. Ignited by the state's massacre of demonstrators on Bloody Sunday (January 9, 1905), when one Social-Democratic observer perceived the "monstrous dark force of spontaneity" at work, revolts erupted throughout 1905 among the urban proletariat, the rural peasantry, and the military,[9] while radicals of various affiliations contributed to an escalation of terrorism.[10] Bakuninist convictions found clear expression within the emerging anarchist movement, which desired the complete destruction of the autocratic order.[11] The violent, maximalist dimension of Bakunin's thought seems to have appealed strongly to many Russian anarchists, for his familiar pronouncement, "the urge to destroy is also a creative urge," appeared in the flyers of several groups, including the "Anti-Authoritarians," the "International" group of Anarcho-Communists in Riga, the "Commune" group of Anarcho-Communists in Georgia, and groups in Belostok, Kiev, and Odessa.[12] While the anarchists remained divided on the question of revolutionary tactics, one of the broad divisions of anarchists, the Anarcho-Communists, perceived in Bakunin's motto mainly the idea of destruction, which motivated their aspiration to eradicate the state and their indiscriminate means of fulfilling it. Thus a southern Russian group of Anarcho-Communists with the Bakuninist name "Rebel" *(Buntar')* called upon Russian workers and peasants to "fight for the destruction of Capital and the State by means of fire and sword!" and to "remember the testament of the great Bakunin and the first Russian anarchists, brought up on the ideas of the left wing of the International."[13]

Recalling the historic conflicts with Bakunin within the International Working Men's Association, Plekhanov and others continued to denounce the tactics of anarchism and disassociate it from Marxism. On the eve of 1905 Plekhanov renewed his offensive against the anarchists in a new edition of "Anarchism and Socialism," in which he called the anarchists the "most irreconcilable enemies" of the Social-Democrats and warned the latter to avoid any collaboration with them in the workers' movement.[14] As another party veteran suggested a few years later, the Anarcho-Communists' inclination toward terrorism tended to blur the distinction between the politically conscious anarchist and the common "bandit" or "hooligan." The "theoretical foundations" of Russian anarchism, he observed, lay in traditional "Bakuninism," which demonstrated "the same praise of the 'lumpenproletariat,' the same preaching of immediate social revolution, the same attitude toward the political struggle, toward parliamentarianism, democracy, etc."[15] Regardless of traditional opposition to Bakuninist tactics, however, the violent circumstances of 1905 encouraged militancy among all revolutionary parties, including the Social-Democrats. In principle, the Russian Marxists were not opposed to revolutionary violence. Insofar as the immediate goal of the working class, as Marx and Engels had spelled it out in the *Communist Manifesto*, was to conquer political power through "the forcible overthrow of the bourgeoisie,"[16] the means chosen for that end, as Plekhanov emphasized in "Strength and Violence," should be those that best guarantee a successful revolution.[17] In the history of the socialist movement, the seizure of power by the Paris Communards of 1871 had illustrated the necessity of armed struggle in an attempt to vanquish a bourgeois state. Marx had defended their actions passionately and without criticism, save for the Communards' "conscientious scruples" and their failure to start a civil war.[18] When, in the immediate wake of Bloody Sunday in St. Petersburg, anticipation of armed uprisings by the Russian proletariat raised the likelihood of violent confrontations with the state, the leaders of both Social-Democratic factions readily began to consider the technical details for an insurrection. The need for party agitators in Russia to defend themselves and their fellow demonstrators against attacks by hostile forces like the Black Hundreds led to the formation, training, and arming of militia units within the local party committees.[19]

Once the revolutionary situation of 1905 passed and opportunities for legal reform arose, the use of militant tactics again became an issue of concern within the Social-Democratic Party. While the creation of the first Duma in October of 1905, together with the bloody suppression of the Moscow workers' revolt in December, convinced some of the need to abandon illegal forms of struggle, Lenin refused to disavow the need for violence in the war with the autocracy. His willingness to sanction it became evident after a series of armed "expropriations" in the Caucasus carried out by agents of his underground Bolshevik center, which utilized the proceeds of bank robberies to finance Bolshevik operations, including the purchase of weapons abroad. Presided over by a majority of Mensheviks who generally wished to unify the party and advance the revolutionary cause by legal means, the Unity Congress of Social-Democrats in April 1906 formally condemned expropriations of private funds for their demoralizing effect on the revolutionary movement and resolved "to fight against the actions of individuals or groups of individuals who seek to seize money under the name or slogan of the Social-Democratic Party," a decision that Lenin ignored.[20] A few months after the Unity Congress, Lenin defended the tactics of guerrilla warfare and its funding through expropriations. To those fellow Social-Democrats who would accuse the Bolsheviks of "demoralizing methods," "anarchism," "terrorism," and the like, Lenin wrote that guerrilla warfare was an inevitable form of struggle during a period of civil war between the state and the masses, one that would not succeed in disorganizing the proletariat so long as it did not serve as the "chief" or "exclusive" tactic, in other words, the tactic of "vagabond elements, the lumpenproletariat and anarchist groups."[21] Meanwhile, opposition to terrorism and to illegal methods increased further and led to an even stricter prohibition against expropriations at the Party's London Congress of 1907.[22]

The horrific bloodshed of World War I exacerbated differences among Marxists in Russia on the eve of 1917. The mass slaughters of the war, which caused over three million Russian deaths and over seven million additional casualties[23]—incomparably higher than the casualties of revolutionary violence throughout the previous five decades—further radicalized the position of Lenin and his supporters with respect to the majority of Social-Democrats. Whereas most Mensheviks supported policies of national defense and reform, a small but determined group of Bolsheviks called for a transformation of imperialist war into civil war.[24] The real extent of their division appeared with the return of Lenin to Petrograd (formerly St. Petersburg) in April of 1917 and the public declaration of his theses "On the Tasks of the Proletariat in the Revolution." Lenin's call for the rejection of the Provisional Government, an immediate end to the war, and other radical changes[25] shocked fellow socialists and brought on new charges of political heresy. Through his apparent disregard for Russia's insufficient development and his appeal to elemental social forces, Lenin convinced many opponents that he had effectively jettisoned Marxism and embraced Bakuninism. Describing the reception of Lenin's "reckless anarcho-seditious system" at a unifying conference of Social-Democrats in April, the Menshevik N. N. Sukhanov recalled one party veteran's remark that Lenin wished to occupy "a European throne which has been vacant for thirty years—the throne of Bakunin!" Lenin's theses provoked a similar reaction from Petrograd Soviet member Iu. M. Steklov, another veteran Marxist, who found in them "only abstract constructions that prove that the Russian Revolution has passed [Lenin] by."[26] Having denounced Lenin's program of expropriations and isolated "explosions" *(vspyshkopuskatel'stvo)* as "Bolshevik Bakuninism" a decade earlier,[27] in the newspaper *Unity* Plekhanov once again declared that Lenin followed "the logic of anarchism," and that Lenin's desire for the overthrow of the Provisional Government amounted to *"an insane and extremely harmful attempt to sow anarchist turmoil on the Russian Earth"* (Plekhanov's italics). In his article "Marxism or Bakuninism?" he claimed, finally, that the issue facing Russia in 1917 was not "whether Bolshevism or Menshevism will prevail in Russia," but rather "which ideas will prevail in our socialist milieu, the ideas of Marx or the ideas of Bakunin."[28]

Despite the Bolshevik triumph in October under the banner of Marxism, the anarchy and ruthless violence of the ensuing Civil War merely reinforced the Bolshevik-Bakuninist analogy. In *State and Revolution,* composed on the eve of October, Lenin had clarified the distinction between Marxist and anarchist opposition in the state, insisting that Marx refused to remove "organized violence, *that is, the state*" (Lenin's italics) until all resistance to the "transitional" dictatorship was crushed.[29] Within months of taking power, moreover, the Bolsheviks showed ever diminishing tolerance for the elemental spontaneity that helped to drive events of the preceding year. Yet as the many early Soviet studies of his career suggest, Bakunin remained arguably the most vital of the Bolsheviks' pre-revolutionary forerunners. Valuable studies of Bakunin by Steklov, Gorev, M. N. Pokrovskii, and V. P. Polonskii, to name a few, all reflect the significance which Bakunin's legacy held for Communists throughout the first decade of their rule. The notion of "Bakuninism" in late imperial and early Soviet Russia continues to provide an important ideological context for the study of the October Revolution and its aftermath.

Notes

1. Karl Marx and Friedrich Engels, *Collected Works* (New York: International Publishers, 1988), 23:466, 470, 518, 520–21, 545, 555, 568–70, 706. The pamphlet is attributed to Marx and Engels, with the assistance of Lafargue. As defenders of Bakunin have repeatedly emphasized, the calls for assassinations and murders in the quoted proclamations likely belong to Nechaev rather than to Bakunin, whose authorship of "Beginnings of Revolution" and the so-called "Catechism of a Revolutionist" was only partial, at best. For a close and insightful

analysis of the proclamations cited by Marx and Engels in their pamphlet on Bakunin's Alliance, see the excellent study by Stephen Cochrane, *The Collaboration of Nechaev, Ogarev, and Bakunin in 1869: Nechaev's Early Years* (Giessen: W Schmitz Verlag, 1977).

2. Marx and Engels, *Collected Works*, 23:595, 597–98.

3. V. K. Debogorii-Mokrievich, *Ot buntarstva k terrorizmu. S predisloviem S. N. Valka*, book 1 (Moscow: Molodaia gvardiia, 1930), 164, 242–43.

4. Lev Deich, *Za polveka*, vol. 2: *Torzhestvo Bakunizma v Rossii* (Berlin: Izd-vo "Grani," 1923), 209, 211.

5. Franco Venturi, *Roots of Revolution: A History of the Populist and Socialist Movements in Nineteenth-Century Russia* (New York: Grosset & Dunlap, 1960), 571–72.

6. Neil Harding, ed., *Marxism in Russia: Key Documents 1879–1906*, trans. Richard Taylor (Cambridge: Cambridge University Press, 1983), 93–94; Samuel H. Baron, *Plekhanov: The Father of Russian Marxism* (Stanford, Calif.: Stanford University Press, 1963), 114–15.

7. G. V. Plekhanov, "Anarkhizm i sotsializm," in G. V. Plekhanov, *Sochineniia*, ed. D. B. Riazanov (Moscow: Gosizdat, 1923), 4:236, 237, 239, 242, 243.

8. G. V. Plekhanov, "Sila i nasilie," in G. V. Plekhanov, *Sochineniia*, 4:250, 253, 256.

9. J. L. H. Keep, *The Rise of Social Democracy in Russia* (Oxford: Clarendon, 1963), 158.

10. For a close examination of terrorism in Russia during this period, see Anna Geifman, *Thou Shalt Kill: Revolutionary Terrorism in Russia, 1894–1917* (Princeton, N.J.: Princeton University Press, 1993).

11. Paul Avrich, *The Russian Anarchists* (Princeton, N.J.: Princeton University Press, 1967), 69.

12. V. V. Kriven'kii, ed., *Anarkhisty. Dokumenty i materialy, 1883–1935*, 2 vols. (Moscow: ROSSPEN, 1998), 1:104, 106, 119, 132, 166.

13. Kriven'kii, ed., *Anarkhisty*, 1:69–70; Avrich, *The Russian Anarchists*, 44, 48, 85–86.

14. G. V. Plekhanov, "Mezhdunarodnoe tovarishchestvo rabochikh," in G. V. Plekhanov, *Sochineniia*, 2nd ed., ed. D. B. Riazanov (Moscow: Gosizdat, 1928), 16:191–92.

15. B. I. Gorev, "Apoliticheskie i antiparlamentskie gruppy (Anarkhisty, maksimalisty, makhaevtsy)," in *Obshchestvennoe dvizhenie v Rossii v nachale XX-go veka*, vol. 3, book 5, ed. L. Martov, P. Maslov, and A. Petrosov (St. Petersburg: Tipografiia tovarishchestva Obshchestvennaia pol'za, 1914), 491, 498.

16. For comparative translations of this passage in the *Manifesto*, see Hal Draper, *The Adventures of the Communist Manifesto* (Berkeley, Calif.: Center for Socialist History, 1994), 132–33, 233.

17. Plekhanov, "Sila i nasilie," 256.

18. Marx and Engels, *Collected Works* (Moscow: Progress Publishers, 1989), 44:132.

19. Keep, *The Rise of Social Democracy*, 173, 187–88.

20. B. I. Nikolaevskii, "K istorii 'bol'shevistskogo tsentra,'" in *B. I. Nikolaevskii. Tainye stranitsy istorii*, ed. Iu. G. Fel'shtinskii (Moscow: Izdatel'stvo gumanitarnoi literatury, 1995), 26–27.

21. V. I. Lenin, "Guerrilla Warfare," in V. I. Lenin, *Collected Works* (Moscow: Foreign Languages Publishing House, 1962), 11:216, 219–20.

22. B. D. Wolfe, *Three Who Made a Revolution: A Biographical History* (New York: Dell, 1964), 378–79, 393–95; Robert Williams, *The Other Bolsheviks: Lenin and His Critics, 1904–1914* (Bloomington: Indiana University Press, 1986), 106, 112–16, 154.

23. A. I. Stepanov, "Obshchie demograficheskie poteri naseleniia Rossii v period pervoi mirovoi voiny," in *Pervaia mirovaia voina. Prolog XX veka*, ed. V. L. Mal'kov (Moscow: Nauka, 1998), 480.

24. E. H. Carr, *The Bolshevik Revolution, 1917–1923* (New York: Macmillan, 1950), 1:66–67.

25. V. I. Lenin, "O zadachakh proletariata v revoliutsii," in V. I. Lenin, *Polnoe sobranie sochinenii*, 55 vols. (Moscow: Politicheskaia literatura, 1962), 33:113–18.

26. N. N. Sukhanov, *Zapiski o revoliutsii*, 3 vols. (Moscow: Politizdat, 1991), 2: 16, 21.

27. Nikolaevskii, "K istorii bol'shevistskogo tsentra," 51–52.

28. G. V. Plekhanov, "God na rodine," in *Polnoe sobranie statei i rechei, 1917–1918*, 2 vols. (Paris: J. Povolozky, 1921), 1:28, 111.

29. V. I. Lenin, *Selected Works in Three Volumes* (Moscow: Progress Publishers, 1977), 2:281.

On Blood, Scandal, Renunciation, and Russian History

Il'ia Repin's Ivan the Terrible and His Son Ivan

KEVIN M. F. PLATT

On January 13, 1913, a young man named Abram Balashev, armed with a dagger and unhinged by psychosis, committed a scandalous act of violence that set the Russian public reeling. Balashev plunged his dagger not into a person, but rather into a painting—I. E. Repin's famous 1885 historical canvas *Ivan the Terrible and His Son Ivan, 16 November 1581.* Interestingly, the subject matter of this painting was itself violence—its place in Russian history and its consequences. Balashev's attack was only an extreme example of a general pattern of "violent" reactions that this work elicited from the time of its first showing. In the following essay, I will investigate this intriguing concatenation of historical bloodshed, Repin's artistic meditation on that violence, and a series of violent responses to that meditation. My analysis evokes a recurrent motif of Russian history and culture: the ironic resurgence of violence despite all efforts to transcend it, and the peculiar intersection of aesthetic violence and political violence in the Russian experience.

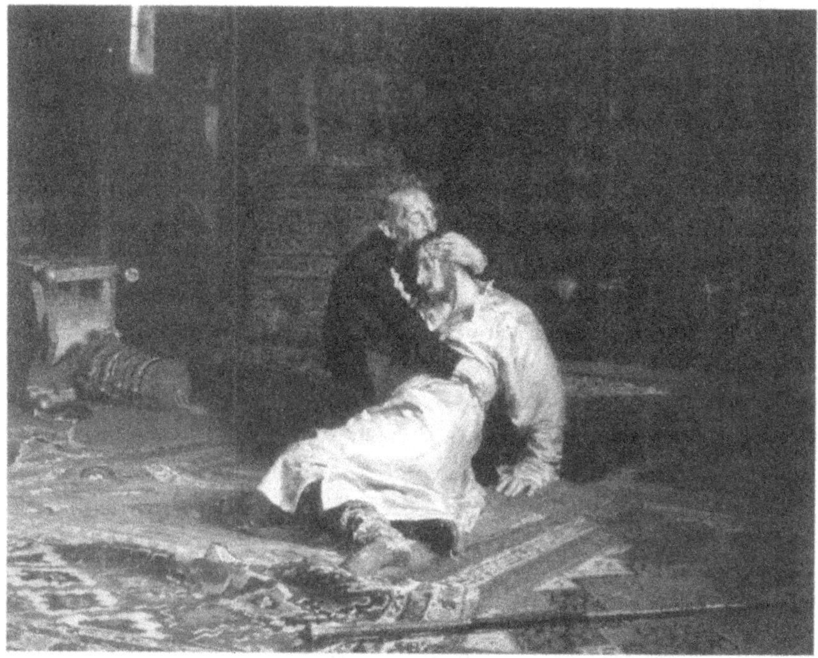

Ivan the Terrible and His Son Ivan, 16 November 1581, 1885, by I. E. Repin. State Tretyakov Gallery, Moscow.

At the time of its first exhibition Repin's bloody depiction of the Russian past evoked heated critical controversy and public scandal. The subject of Repin's work is Ivan the Terrible's apparently unintentional killing of his son and heir in a fit of rage with a blow of his staff. The episode is historically significant in that this act determined that Ivan's successor as tsar would be the "feeble-minded" Fedor, who died without producing an heir, thus dooming Muscovite Russia to the decades-long crisis of succession known as the Time of Troubles. When Repin's painting was first exhibited in the Itinerant exhibition of 1885, its gory representation of royal bloodshed shocked elite Russian society. A leitmotif of the response to the painting was the assertion that, above and beyond the "obscenity" of the subject matter, it simply depicted far too much blood—the Imperial Academy of Arts in fact invited a professor of anatomy to deliver a lecture in which he claimed the actual impossibility that so much blood could result from such a wound.[1] Defenders of the painting such as the influential critic V. V. Stasov and the liberal-leaning publisher A. S. Suvorin ridiculed such "anatomical" critiques of the painting and argued that its subject was in fact the tsar's repentance and self-castigation following his act of passionate violence—a morally edifying theme that was intensified by its dramatic depiction.[2] The painting so outraged the Director General of the Most Holy Synod Konstantin Pobedonostsev that he used his influence over Tsar Alexander III to bring about a prohibition on public display of the work.[3] However, in subsequent decades the public furor surrounding the painting died down, giving way to a celebration of Repin as a Russian artistic genius and of the painting in question as one of his finest masterpieces.

Nevertheless, it was undoubtedly the same element of graphic violence in this disturbing work that had offended the Russian public in 1885 that provoked the madman's assault on the canvas in 1913. According to newspaper accounts, Balashev, the son of an icon-painter and an Old Believer, in the weeks before the attack had visited the Tret'iakov Gallery a number of times and obsessively contemplated Repin's work and one other less explicit representation of a violent episode from the Russian past.[4] Finally, he drew his weapon and threw himself at the painting, crying out, "Blood! Why the blood? Down with blood!"[5] Balashev's attack on the painting elicited a torrent of editorial outrage at the act and sympathy to Repin. I. S. Ostroukhov, director of the Tret'iakov Gallery, retired in disgrace, to be replaced by the young I. E. Grabar'. Experts in art preservation and restoration from the State Hermitage Museum in St. Petersburg were brought in to repair the damage to the fabric of the canvas, and Repin came to Moscow from his retreat in Kuokalla, Finland, in order to restore the painting itself.

Yet Balashev's attack was not the only act of violence perpetrated on Repin's painting in early 1913. Three days later the young artist, poet and critic Maksimilian Voloshin published a short essay entitled "On the Significance of the Catastrophe that Befell Repin's Painting."[6] The essay argued that the madman's attack had been instigated by the painting itself, and that its gory representation of violence had shocked and tormented viewers for two decades before finally pushing the poor Balashev over the edge. A month later Voloshin elaborated on his argument in a public lecture and debate at the Moscow Polytechnic Museum, sponsored by members of a futurist artistic group called Jack of Diamonds. Among the other participants in the debate that followed was the futurist artist David Burliuk, and among the members of the audience in the packed auditorium was none other than Repin himself, who was then visiting Moscow in order to repair his work. Like the original essay, Voloshin's lecture was an act of avant-garde provocation or *epatage* calculated to offend the bourgeois sensibilities of the public.

Repeating his argument that Repin's work was an irresponsible application of the techniques of illusionistic naturalism in order to evoke the viewer's horror, Voloshin argued that "in the figure of Balashev we are dealing not with a criminal, but with a victim of Repin's painting," and that "the evil brought about by Repin's painting in the course of thirty years has been great indeed." The critic concluded that *Ivan the Terrible and His Son Ivan* was a dangerous work of art that caters to the mass taste for sensationalism and cheap thrills, and that it "has no place in the National Gallery, which forms the artistic tastes of the young. Its real place is in some grand European Panopticon like the Musée Grévin [a famous wax museum in Paris]. There it would be a magnificent example of its genre. There, it would deceive no one, for everyone who goes to such a place knows what he is after. But since this is impossible, the curators of the Tret'iakov Gallery must certainly, at the very least, place this painting in a separate room marked with the sign 'entrance for adults only.'"[7] Following Voloshin's outrageous lecture, Repin himself ascended to the podium and offered a rather disjointed but clearly enraged response. Other participants in the debate, apparently as shocked as everyone else, offered their own awkward comments. Wild clapping, booing, and foot-stamping punctuated the entire evening.

Voloshin's lecture and the public discussion that followed it rivaled Balashev's attack in the frenzy of outraged responses they provoked. Many compared Voloshin's intentionally "appalling" words to Balashev's dagger as analogous acts of criminal aggression, as did Repin himself in his own response to Voloshin following the lecture. According to Voloshin, Repin dismissed the critic's major arguments as "rubbish" and "tendentiousness," steadily losing self-control as he worked himself up to an accusatory conclusion: "And now they are saying that the painting should be sold abroad. They will never commit such an absurdity. Some Russians want to finish what Balashev started . . . Balashev is a fool . . . a fool like that is easy to pay off."[8] As Voloshin pointed out in his published version of his lecture, Repin's denigrating comments suggested that Balashev's act followed from modernist rhetoric that denied the art and culture of the past.[9] Critical voices in the press agreed, pronouncing Voloshin's lecture a simple continuation of Balashev's violence. Some who equated the madman and the critic saw more hopeful implications. A letter from sixteen prominent members of the Union of Russian Artists to Repin announced that "two events of no real significance—the act of a lunatic and the tactless pronouncements of a few individuals—gave rise to an occurrence of huge public import and lucid spiritual beauty," in that the resultant outpouring of public support and recognition of Repin expressed "the blood ties linking the artist and the nation."[10]

These hyperbolic attacks and counterattacks, exchanged by the painting's critics (or assassins?) and its champions, are founded on a rather paradoxical divergence of opinions concerning the ultimate source of the violence that marked the episode. On one hand, Voloshin links Balashev's assault to the aesthetic violence of the painting itself: Balashev "did to the painting precisely what the painting has done to the souls of visitors of the Tret'iakov Gallery for thirty years."[11] On the other hand, Repin and his supporters identify Balashev's assault on the painting with the attacks of Voloshin and "unbridled" avant-garde artists in general, ready to destroy the masterpieces and values of past generations. One newspaper response to the affair explicitly invoked the scandalous formula of the best known futurist manifesto by way of explanation of Voloshin's behavior: "A slap in the face of public taste! The Burliuks announce, shamelessly: 'The past is too small for us. The Academy and Pushkin are incomprehensible hieroglyphs. And therefore, throw overboard from the steamship of modernity Pushkin, Dostoevsky, Tolstoy, and so on and so forth.'"[12] So how are we to sort out this bout of finger-pointing and blame? That is, what in fact is the source of the violence of 1913, and how are we to interpret it?

The answers to these questions may be found in a closer consideration of the painting itself, of the historical events that it depicts, and of other events to which it arguably refers. For these violent reactions to the painting as an aesthetic object were preceded by and predicated on the actual bloodshed of Russia's past and present. Repin's associate Ivan Kramskoi reported that one of the first viewers of *Ivan the Terrible and His Son Ivan* cried out in outrage "It's regicide, after all!"[13] In fact, the painting does not depict an act of regicide (although Repin had considered calling it "Filicide" [*Synoubiistvo*], and then abandoned this title, likely considering it to be too sensational), yet the remark reveals what many viewers had in mind upon seeing the canvas. Any mention of regicide in 1885 could not but recall the assassination of Alexander II four years earlier on March 1, 1881. The full title of the work, *Ivan the*

Terrible and His Son Ivan, 16 November 1581, goes to awkward lengths to include a date exactly three centuries prior to the regicide of 1881, and suggests that Repin had precisely this connection in mind himself. At the time of Balashev's attack, Repin explicitly recalled that he had begun the canvas as a reaction in part to the assassination and to the public execution of the conspirators, at which he was himself present.[14] The work was thus calculated to draw an allegorical tie between royal bloodshed in Russia's past and present, and to suggest that the violence of the present is a legacy of the violence of the past.

However, the precise meaning of this allegorical connection is somewhat difficult to unravel, for it involves a strange reversal, or mirror-imaging: how can the murder of the tsarevitch at the hands of his father be comparable to the murder of the tsar at the hands of his subjects? It would seem that Repin's painting was intended as an interpretation of the assassination of Alexander II: by holding up this strangely distorting allegorical lens to the events of the present, Repin was asserting that the true culprits of the murder of the tsar were not criminals or revolutionaries, but rather the rulers of Russia themselves, for whom violence and repression were almost a genetic inheritance. This is to say, the bombs that exploded on March 1, 1881, were elicited by the brutality and cruelty of the state and were a logical (if perhaps not just) response to state violence. Furthermore, the painting's focus on the transcendent moment of repentance following the tsar's brutal outburst instructs contemporaries in the proper response to political violence. Whereas Alexander III inaugurated an era of reaction and political repression in response to the murder of the tsar, Repin's painting suggests that the current tsar, and perhaps all Russians, like Ivan the Terrible, must accept responsibility for the blood of confrontation, repent of their sins, and enter into a new era of peace. In this, *Ivan the Terrible and His Son Ivan* may be seen as a pictorial equivalent to the famous appeals of L. N. Tolstoy and V. S. Solov'ev to Alexander III in the immediate aftermath of the tsar's father's assassination, urging that repentance and forgiveness were the proper response of the throne to revolutionary violence, and not harsh measures and executions.[15]

Voloshin's critique aptly captures a peculiar dimension of Repin's painting: its paradoxical inclination to use violence to overcome violence. This is to say, while the painting was intended as a call to overcome violence, its lesson is inculcated by means of violent shock tactic. The bloody scene of the tsarevitch's gushing blood and the tsar's frenzy of anguished remorse, which reportedly caused some viewers to faint, hits viewers at a visceral level in order to force them to confront the bloodshed of their own epoch in a new way. The moral lesson of the painting—concerning the need to transcend violence and confrontation—arguably also demonstrates that great moments of repentance and growth may be reached precisely by means of great acts of brutality. Of course, Repin's violence is brutality of an aesthetic sort, but it is brutality nonetheless. Ironically, the history of the work's reception also seems to illustrate that impassioned condemnations of violence are capable of evoking physically violent reactions. As Voloshin points out, Balashev's attack, accompanied by his shriek ("Down with blood!") is entirely analogous to the main expressive significance of the painting: each rejects violence with an act of violence.[16] In this, both follow the pattern of the acts of political violence on which these aesthetic gestures (if one may call Balashev's attack an aesthetic response) were based: the terrorist bomb that killed Alexander II and the horrific murder of the tsarevitch. Voloshin quite aptly points out that all of these events (if we have correctly interpreted Repin's conception) were moments that should make possible a transcendence of historical violence. Instead, however, they seem to have the paradoxical result of perpetuating it.

Yet we cannot be too quick to side with Voloshin against Repin, for the paradoxical interpretational space around this painting may be exited through a number of different fissures. Repin and his supporters were of course absolutely right in pointing out that Balashev's attack and Voloshin's scandalous lecture were in many ways analogous acts of aggression. Of course, Balashev was not "paid off" by the avant-garde, and one suspects that his attack had more to do with the apocalyptic anarchical tendencies and hatred of imperial authority characteristic of Russia's religious dissenters, among whom the belief that Russia's rulers were allied with the Antichrist circulated well into the twentieth century.[17] Yet Voloshin's critique of the painting in the name of a condemnation of Repin's aesthetic violence toward his audience is entirely analogous to Balashev's attack on the painting in the name of a condemnation of the violence of Russian history. And in general, other representatives of the avant-garde themselves recognized that Balashev's attack on the painting was a splendid metaphor for their own iconoclastic rejection of past aesthetic and political life: while critics of Voloshin had invoked one futurist manifesto in their accusations of complicity between the madman in the gallery and the artistic madness of modernism, soon enough another avant-garde manifesto proudly claimed Balashev as an iconoclastic kindred spirit.[18]

So both sides of the debate occupy quite defensible positions. What neither seems to recognize, however, is that the interpretational space of the painting places all of them together in a common position. Voloshin, for all of his incisive critique of Repin's sensationalistic work, failed to acknowledge that his own lecture undertook "shock therapy" on its audience and engaged in cruelty toward the listener (that is, toward Repin) that was completely comparable to the cruelty and violence which Voloshin saw in Repin's canvas. Repin, for his part, failed to recognize how much Voloshin was his cultural heir. At the time of the first exhibition of *Ivan the Terrible and His Son Ivan,* Repin and his Itinerant colleagues constituted the avant-garde of the Russian art world, and his intentional provocation of his original audience was analogous to Voloshin's *epatage.* It serves a similar purpose—to call for a reevaluation of the Russian past, a transcendence of history and the violence inherent in it. In fact, all of the figures involved in this interpretational history of Repin's painting share an ironically violent rejection of violence—Repin, the early critics who accused him of showing too much blood, Balashev, Voloshin, and Repin's later defenders. One of these last, in fact, ended his commentary on Voloshin's lecture with the ominous words: "A congress of Governors will shortly take place in Petersburg to consider the matter of the battle with people of a certain sort. All power to the administration. One can only look ahead with hope to a time when there will no longer be elements in Russian society capable of insulting Repin. And that time is near."[19]

Backing away from this particular episode, let us consider what it can tell us about violence in Russian culture in general. The fundamental pattern we have observed is the attempt to overcome the violence and bloodshed of history by means of its forceful, even brutal, rejection. Perhaps needless to say, this stance toward the past was characteristic not only of avant-garde aesthetics from the end of the nineteenth century through the first decades of the twentieth, but even more so of political revolutionary activity in Russia during this same period. It was this shared taste for gestures of radical, even bloody renunciation of the past that underwrote the shaky relationship of artistic and political revolutionaries—of V. V. Maiakovskii and the Bolsheviks, for instance. The insight that eluded the majority of political and cultural revolutionaries alike (or at least eluded them until it was too late) was that the application of violence in order to fight violence ironically turns those who would banish bloodshed into people little different from those they seek to overthrow. Repin rejects Ivan's violence, but with such violence that Repin becomes conflated with the bloodshed he rejects, becoming a target for Balashev's and Voloshin's violent attacks, which repeat this same irony. The Bolsheviks reject the violence of the Imperial Russian state, yet they do so with such murderous zeal and fanaticism that they ultimately create a system of political repression that far outdoes anything the most reactionary tsar could have imagined. Here, then, is the ironic tendency of violence, even violence in the name of peace, always to give birth to more violence—an irony that, while it may appear banal to us at the start of the twenty-first century, certainly runs deep in the soil of both Russian cultural life and Russian history.

Finally, we should note the peculiarly close intertwining of cultural and political life in this episode—a feature especially characteristic of the modernist epoch in Russia. Consider a brief recap of the story I have outlined above: first, we have Repin's allegorical commentary on contemporary politics in the form of a historical painting, which calls for national reconciliation following the bloody violence of the assassination of Alexander II. The painting evokes a scandalized response from the state and the public so extreme that it culminates in a physical attack on the painting. But then, the scandalous secondary response to this episode in cultural life is itself so extreme that it ends in celebration of the "blood ties linking the artist and the nation," on the one hand, and calls to crush those "elements in Russian society capable of insulting Repin" on the other. There is a fascinating mirroring effect in this story, where an artistic response to political life is echoed by a political response to artistic life—a conflation of the murder of people with the murder of paintings, of real blood and horror with aesthetic violence and criticism. This imbrication of art and politics reveals, first of all, the hypertrophied role of cultural life in late-nineteenth- and early twentieth-century Russia as a forum for political and social expression, which may be traced to the structure of the intelligentsia, the history of censorship, and other factors. Yet also, and perhaps more importantly, the high drama of the Repin affair reveals the modernist conviction, shared by artists and revolutionaries alike, that the revolutionary rebuilding of the world was a task that must be viewed both in aesthetic and in political terms—that the task of the ages was not only a political transfer of power, but also an artistic recreation of human life.[20] Of course, the circularity of the relationship between art and politics we have observed in the Repin affair may be seen on a larger scale in history of early-twentieth-century Russia in general, which began with such hopes for an artistic transformation of politics, and by the thirties arrived at a violent and bloody politically engineered transformation of cultural life. The irony is perhaps best captured in the poet Osip Mandel'shtam's famous comment: "Only in our country is poetry truly respected—they even kill people for it."

Notes

1. The lecture was by Prof. Anatolii Landtsert. I have not been able to obtain the original publication of the lecture: A. Landtsert, "Po povodu kartiny Repina 'Ioann Groznyi i ego syn Ivan 16 noiabria 1581 g.'," *Vestnik iziashchnykh iskusstv* 3:2 (1885): 192–98; excerpts from the lecture are reprinted in M. Voloshin, *O Repine* (Moscow: Ole-Lukoie, 1913), 59–64.

2. Neznakomets (A. S. Suvorin), "Kartina Repina," *Novoe vremia* 3218 (12 February 1885): 1 (Suvorin was the publisher of *Novoe vremia*); V. V. Stasov, "Po povodu lektsii professora Landtserta o kartine Repina," *Novosti* 126 (9 May 1885), reprinted in V. V. Stasov, *Sobranie sochinenii*, 4 vols. (St. Petersburg: Tipografiia M. M. Stasiulevicha [vol. 4: Energiia], 1894–1906), 2:857–59.

3. See K. P. Pobedonostsev, letter of 15 February 1885 to Aleksandr III in *Tainyi pravitel' Rossii: K. P. Pobedonostsev i ego korrespondenty; pis'ma i zapiski, 1886–1895; stat'i, ocherki, vospominaniia*, ed. T. F. Prokopov (Moscow: Russkaia kniga, 2001), 176–77; I. E. Grabar', *Repin* (Moscow: Zhurnal'no-gazetnoe ob"edinenie, 1933), 155.

4. This was V. Surikov's *Boyarynia Morozova* (1887). See "Izurodovannaia kartina Repina" (unsigned article), *Russkie vedomosti* 14 (17 January 1913): 4; "V Tret'iakovskoi galeree" (unsigned article), *Russkie vedomosti* 15 (18 January 1913): 4; "Kartina Repina" (unsigned article), *Russkie vedomosti* 16 (19 January 1913): 3; "V Moskve" (unsigned note), *Pravitel'stvennyi vestnik* 14 (17 January 1913): 2.

5. "Izurodovannaia kartina Repina."

6. The essay is reprinted in Voloshin, *O Repine*, 5–10.

7. Voloshin, *O Repine*, 31–32, 33.

8. Ibid., 40.

9. For another indication that Repin expressed such a theory publicly, see "V Tret'iakovskoi galeree."

10. Cited in S. Iablonskii, "Pokushenie na 'Ioanna Groznogo,'" in *Novoe o Repine: Stat'i i pis'ma khudozhnika, vospominaniia uchenikov i druzei, publikatsii* (Leningrad: Khudozhnik, 1969), 334.

11. Voloshin, *O Repine*, 10.

12. *Moskovskii listok*, cited in Voloshin, *O Repine*, 53. The manifesto in question is, of course, "A Slap in the Face of Public Taste." See Anna Lawton, ed., *Russian Futurism through Its Manifestoes, 1912–1928*, trans. Anna Lawton and Herbert Eagle (Ithaca, N.Y.: Cornell University Press, 1998), 51–52.

13. Grabar', *Repin*, 155.

14. "Beseda s Repinym," *Russkoe slovo*, 17 January 1913; see also: Grabar', *Repin*, 151.

15. In a public lecture delivered on March 28, 1881, which was something of a scandal in its own right, Solov'ev pronounced that the proper response to the assassination was to pardon the assassins in the spirit of Christian forgiveness. Otherwise, the new emperor would "embark on a bloody cycle" and the Christian, Russian people would turn away from him. Tolstoy made much the same point in a letter addressed to the emperor at about the same time. See: V. I Fatiushchenko and N. I. Tsimbaev, "Vladimir Solov'ev—kritik i publitsist," introductory essay in V. S. Solov'ev, *Literaturnaia kritika* (Moscow: Sovremennik, 1990), 12; L. N. Tolstoy, letter to Aleksandr III (draft), in his *Sobranie sochinenii v dvadtsati dvukh tomakh*, 22 vols. (Moscow: Khudozhestvennaia literatura, 1978–85), 18:879–87. The final draft of the letter is not extant.

16. Voloshin, *O Repine*, 10.

17. In this connection, recall that the other focus of Balashev's obsessive gaze in the Tret'iakov Gallery, Surikov's *Boyarynia Morozova*, is a representation of the state persecution of Old Believers. The attack on Ivan, whose name has often been linked to arbitrary violence and demonic forces, might therefore be a rejection of "unholy" state violence. However, it should also be noted that Ivan was not generally a target of vilification by Old Believers—why should he be, given that his reign ended nearly a century before the schism? On twentieth-century views of contemporary leaders as "antichrists," see M. M. Beliakova and T. V. Chertoritskaia, "Krug chteniia staroobriadtsa-spasovtsa pervoi poloviny XX v., ili tri biblioteki Dorofeia Utkina," in *Traditsionnaia dukhovnaia i material'naia kul'tura russkikh staroobriadcheskikh poselenii v stranakh Evrony, Azii i Ameriki*, ed. N. N. Pokrovskii and R. Morris (Novosibirsk: Nauka, 1992), 306–12. For more discussion of Old Believer views of Ivan, see my "Antichrist Enthroned: Demonic Visions of Russian Rulers," in *Russian Literature and its Demons*, ed. Pamela Davidson (Oxford: Berghahn Books, 2000), 87–124.

18. See the manifesto "The Trumpet of the Martians," in Lawton, *Russian Futurism*, 103–5.

19. N. V. Glob in *Golos Moskvy*, cited in Voloshin, *O Repine*, 55.

20. The *locus classicus* for discussion of the relationships between art and politics during the Modernist epoch in Russia is Boris Groys, *The Total Art of Stalinism: Avant-Garde, Aesthetic Dictatorship, and Beyond*, trans. Charles Rougle (Princeton, N.J.: Princeton University Press, 1992).

Alimentary Violence

Eating as a Trope in Russian Literature

RONALD D. LEBLANC

SONIA: Isn't nature incredible?

BORIS: To me nature is, you know, I don't know, spiders and bugs and . . . and big fish eating little fish and . . . and plants eating, uh, plants . . . and animals eating, uh . . . it's like an enormous restaurant, that's the way I see it.

Woody Allen, *Love and Death*

Everything in a human being is an animal epos.

Vasilii Rozanov, "Balet ruk"

Modern Russian literature, considered in gastronomical terms, is perhaps best known for the memorable scenes of eating and feasting depicted in the works of a long line of Russian writers who excelled at celebrating enjoyment of the culinary pleasures of the table on the pages of their prose fiction. Readers are not likely to soon forget the descriptions of the tasty foods prepared by Pul'kheriia Ivanovna in Gogol's *Old-World Landowners* (1835), the fragrant pies enjoyed in childhood by the eponymous hero in Goncharov's *Oblomov* (1859), the elegant dinner served to Konstantin Levin and Stiva Oblonskii at the restaurant of the Hotel Angliia in Tolstoy's *Anna Karenina* (1879), or the fond reminiscences of their favorite dishes evoked by the salivating government officials in Chekhov's story "The Sirens" (1887).[1] But food and eating in Russian literature have been portrayed in decidedly less benign ways as well: not as a source of epicurean pleasure, but instead as an illustration of violence, aggression, and destruction. This is especially true in the case of those writers who tend to use the language and imagery of eating mainly as a metaphor for other human appetites, such as sexual desire. As Ronald Tobin has argued, in literature our physical appetite for food, as well as for sex, can be made to abide not by the semiotic code of pleasure *(goûter)*, but rather by the code of power *(manger)*. Fictional characters, as eaters as well as lovers, can be shown not so much to "taste" the objects of their desire as to "devour" them.[2]

In Russian literature, eating as a trope for physical and emotional violence is perhaps most closely identified with the works of Fyodor Dostoevsky, many of whose fictional characters are notorious for the bestially cruel and willfully violent behavior they are capable of manifesting. As concerns their libidinal appetites, these Dostoevskian characters are voluptuaries who seem impelled mainly by "carnivorism" *(plotoiadnost')*, a word that in Russian can denote both sensuality and rapaciousness. Literally the word suggests a craving to taste and devour "flesh" *(plot')*; thus it captures nicely the dual aspect of carnality as both a sexual and an alimentary concept in Dostoevsky's fictional works. Indeed, the Russian novelist's penchant for depicting human brutality was characterized by one of his contemporaries precisely in terms of animal predation: that is, of wolves devouring sheep. In a famous essay where he attacks Dostoevsky's allegedly "cruel" talent, the populist critic Nikolai Mikhailovskii acknowledges the author's keen insight into human psychology, noting that "no one in Russian literature has analyzed the sensations of a wolf devouring a sheep with such thoroughness, such depth, one might say with such love, as Dostoevsky." This Russian writer's artistic specialty, Mikhailovskii notes, is his uncanny ability to dig "into the very heart of the wolf's soul, seeking there subtle, complex things—not the simple satisfaction of appetite, but precisely the sensuality of spite and cruelty." Indeed, Dostoevsky's works, he asserts, provide readers with "a complete nursery of wolves of different breeds."[3] Early in the twentieth century, Maxim Gorky would likewise assail this so-called Karamazovism, going so far as to assert that Dostoevsky was a cruel, sadistic, and misanthropic writer, an evil genius who portrayed man as a "wild and evil animal," not in order to refute this primordial human bestiality, but to justify it.[4] Robert Louis Jackson, who challenges Ivan Turgenev's charge that Dostoevsky was his country's Marquis de Sade, characterizes the motivation behind the Russian novelist's keen interest in human bestiality much more fairly and accurately when he writes that "Dostoevsky finds in the human propensity for violence and cruelty only a partial truth—a truth that is counteracted by fundamental moral and spiritual strivings of man."[5]

Although we live in a world where a term like "sexual predator" now seems quite natural (indeed, hardly metaphorical at all), the widespread use of animal metaphors to describe cruel, violent, and rapacious human behavior began in earnest only with the appearance of Darwin's writings in the second half of the nineteenth century. Prior to this time, such metaphors were largely restricted to works of Gothic fiction. Many intellectuals in Russia took serious issue with what they saw as the pernicious social implications of Darwin's evolutionary theory. They were particularly upset when such notions as the "struggle for existence" and the "survival of the fittest" were transferred from the realm of the animal or vegetable kingdom and applied to human society. The drive to obtain food that Darwin posited as underlying the struggle for existence among animals in the natural world seemed to them a not entirely appropriate analogue for human behavior within a civilized society.[6] Moreover, such a soulless, materialistic European ideology severely tarnished the self-image of a collectivist and spiritual Russia. As Daniel Todes has observed, the Russians' sense of communitarianism, their cooperative social ethos, and their vision of a cohesive society emblematized by the traditional peasant commune *(mir)* were seriously threatened by Darwin's Malthusianism, which in their eyes exalted individual conflict, competition, and disharmony at the expense of cooperation, brotherhood, and mutual aid.[7] Nevertheless, in post-emancipation Russia, where the reception of Darwin's theories during the 1860s and 1870s coincided with the onset of wide-scale capitalist development and western-style economic modernization, discussion of the famous scientist's biocentric ideas (especially his notion of the "struggle for existence") led to a marked increase in the use of predatory animal imagery by writers seeking to describe the new forms of socio-economic exploitation that were making their appearance in Russian society. In addition to Dostoevsky, several other contemporary writers—such as Aleksei Pisemskii (*The Predators*, 1873) and Aleksandr Ostrovskii (*Wolves and Sheep*, 1875)—regularly invoked the imagery of predatory beasts swallowing their prey as a way to depict not only the socio-economic exploitation by new capitalist entrepreneurs of impoverished gentry and liberated serfs alike, but also the sexual exploitation of women by men.[8] If post-emancipation Russia was seen by many to be a world where man was a wolf to man *(homo homini lupus est)*, man was especially a wolf to woman, upon whom he seemed to feed for purposes of his own sexual gratification and sense of psychological domination.

In Dostoevsky's case, bestial images of human behavior begin to make their appearance in his writings immediately following the author's return from Siberian exile, where his intimate contact with hardened criminals and ruthless murderers seems to have had a profound effect upon his view of human nature. Indeed, Dostoevsky's fictionalized account of his penal servitude is the first of his writings that contains in considerable quantity the kind of language and imagery that emphasizes how people can derive a cruel and sadistic pleasure from satisfying their base animalistic desires. In *Notes from the House of the Dead* (1862), we read about how some of the prisoners possess "bestial inclinations," a "bestial insensitivity," and a "bestial character." We also read about how a man in prison can grow morally depraved, lose his basic humanity, and "turn into a beast."[9] The narrator speaks, for example, about the monstrous Gazin, who, when drunk, would reveal "all the bestiality of his nature," a man who would slowly and voluptuously slit the throats of young children solely for the pleasure, deriving great enjoyment from the terror and anguish felt by his wretched little victims (56). The prisoner Korenev, meanwhile, is characterized as a totally "wild beast" whose spiritual torpor is so great that there is nothing left inside him except "a fierce thirst for bodily pleasure, sensuality, and carnal satisfaction" (66). No doubt the most loathsome and disgusting example of moral degradation in a human being, however, is provided by Aristov, an inveterate sensualist who has become addicted to the coarsest, vilest pleasures. Dostoevsky, appropriately enough, describes this convict's spiritual degradation and moral corruption in predominantly anatomical and animalistic terms: "Aristov was simply a lump of flesh, with teeth and a stomach, and with an insatiable thirst for the grossest and most bestial physical pleasures, for the satisfaction of the least and most capricious of which he was capable of the most cold-blooded violence, murder, or, in short, anything at all, provided he could hide his traces. I am not exaggerating anything; I knew Aristov well. He was an example of the lengths to which the purely physical side of a man could go, unrestrained by any internal standard or discipline. . . . He was a monster, a moral Quasimodo" (90). Inside the stockade at the Omsk prison, Dostoevsky thus came to meet a large number of cruel and violent murderers—the real-life prototypes for Gazin, Korenev, Aristov and the other fictionalized inmates he later portrayed in *Notes from the House of the Dead.* Their lack of remorse over committing even the most atrocious crimes certainly did much to shape the author's view of egoistic human desire in the modern secular world as being rapacious and bestial in nature.

The worst excesses of cruelty and brutality that Dostoevsky witnessed at the Omsk prison were not exhibited solely—or even primarily—by his fellow convicts, however. Even more "bestial" than the behavior of these fearless and determined convicted murderers, some of whom had killed simply for pleasure, was the perverse tyranny displayed by the camp "executioners," such as Lt. Zherebiatnikov, whose pleasure in administering floggings and birch-rod beatings to the prisoners amounted to a sick passion. This mean-spirited lieutenant, the narrator tells us (with a revealing metaphor), was something of a "refined connoisseur" when it came to matters of inflicting corporal punishment. "He loved, passionately loved, the art of the executioner, loved it purely as an art," the narrator writes. "He relished it highly and, like some jaded patrician of Imperial Rome, sated with pleasures, invented various refinements and unnatural variations in order to provide some small stimulus and pleasurable titillation for his soul, lapped in its layers of fat" (226). Indeed, the narrator openly compares the cruel feeling of pleasure enjoyed by Siberian executioners such as Lt. Zherebiatnikov to the perversities of the Marquis de Sade and Madame de Brinvilliers, speculating that there must have been "something in those sensations, at once sweet and painful, that made these gentlemen's hearts swoon with pleasure" (236). In his attempt to explain the perverse psychology of these bestial sadists, the narrator directly links their intoxicating will-to-power with the behavior of wild animals: "There are people who, like tigers, thirst for blood. Any man who has once tasted this dominion, this unlimited power, over the body, blood, and spirit of a human creature like himself . . . this boundless opportunity to humiliate with the deepest degradation another being made in the image of god, becomes despite himself the servant instead of the master of his own sensations. Tyranny is a habit; it has the capacity to develop and it does develop, in the end, into a disease. I maintain that the best of men may become coarsened and degraded, by force of habit, to the level of a beast. Blood and power are intoxicants; callousness and perversity develop and grow; the greatest perversions become acceptable and finally sweet to the mind and heart" (236–37). As we clearly see, Dostoevsky's narrator is here describing the psychology (or, more accurately, psychopathology)—rather than the sociology—of this bestial lust for power that intoxicates certain human beings. But Dostoevsky seems to have had the socioeconomic environment of modern capitalism specifically in mind when he writes that "the executioner's nature is found in embryo in almost every contemporary man. But the feral characteristics do not develop equally in all men" (238).

In his major novels about life in post-emancipation Russia that were to follow *Notes from the House of the Dead* during the 1860s and 1870s, Dostoevsky reveals quite graphically the extent to which human nature was being perverted by the new secular ethos of dog-eat-dog capitalism that was rapidly replacing the traditional Christian ethos of compassion, brotherly love, and self-sacrifice. In gastronomical terms, Dostoevsky's post-Siberian fiction shows us how commensalism (the fraternal sharing of bread) has now given way to carnivorism (the rapacious devouring of flesh) and how the pyramidal "food chain" from zoology has permeated an increasingly secularized Russian society and left its indelible mark on the national psyche.[10] In this regard, Dostoevsky's use of masticatory imagery anticipates in many ways the gastropoetics of Joris-Karl Huysmans, in whose works eating is made to serve as "an outlet for cruel, sadistic impulses whose expression reduces a human being to a primitive and savage level."[11] In Dostoevsky's novels, we watch, accordingly, as the rich proceed to devour the poor, the strong to devour the weak, and the proud to devour the meek. People with strong, rapacious natures are repeatedly likened to such predatory creatures from the animal kingdom as hawks, kites, hyenas, tigers, tarantulas, spiders, and reptiles. In his notebooks for *A Raw Youth,* which Jacques Catteau has characterized as a "novel of the predator," Dostoevsky frequently refers to the "predatory" *(khishchnyi)* type of personality.[12] This zoological view of human interaction is clearly evident when Ivan Karamazov comments rather cynically in regard to the deadly oedipal competition being waged between his father and his elder brother Dmitrii in *The Brothers Karamazov:* "Let one reptile devour the other."[13] Indeed, Ivan's intimation here about primal man's essentially cannibalistic nature, much like Raskolnikov's frightful dream about people eating each other in the epilogue to *Crime and Punishment* (1866), reminds us how readers of Dostoevsky's fiction are repeatedly provided glimpses of the gloomy apocalyptic future that awaits mankind, a dark and somber period of the Antichrist characterized by widespread anthropophagy, if human beings persist in abiding by the laws of Darwin rather than following the teachings of Christ.[14]

In many cases, psychological exploitation or socioeconomic parasitism merges with gender domination in Dostoevsky's fiction; thus we encounter numerous instances where rich and powerful males take advantage of poor, meek, defenseless females. Indeed, Dostoevsky's Gothic fictional world, as contemporary feminist critics point out, is filled with men—such as Prince Valkovskii, Svidrigailov, Stavrogin, Fyodor Karamazov—who ruthlessly exploit the privileges granted them by their gender and/or their socioeconomic class by committing acts of sexual violence against women.[15] As one might well expect, Dostoevsky likewise expresses the dynamics of this sexual domination, violence, and brutality through the language of eating: he repeatedly invokes certain masticatory terms—such as "to swallow" *(proglotit')*, "to eat up" *(s"est')*, and "to devour" *(zhrat')*—that reinforce the ethos of alimentary violence that reigns among the moral nihilists who populate his fictional world. Dostoevsky himself firmly believed that in a godless secular world—an atheistic world that believes in Darwin and science rather than in Christ and religion—there can be neither love nor compassion. "There is only egoism," he writes, "that is, the struggle for existence."[16] In his writings, therefore, this highly Christian writer used predatory animal imagery and cannibalistic tropes as a way to characterize, with marked disapproval, the mercenary relations that had developed between human beings in this new "dog-eat-dog" world of capitalism, commerce, and consumption.[17]

By the 1890s and 1900s, Darwinism had begun to give way to—or, more accurately, merge with—Nietzscheanism as the ideology of metaphysical and moral nihilism that seemed best to capture the spirit of emergent capitalism and the values of the nascent bourgeoisie in Russia. What was perceived to be Nietzsche's joyful, Dionysian affirmation of the dark and cruel psychic urges in human nature led many Russian critics and readers at the time to identify this new amoral philosophy closely with Dostoevsky's "cruel talent" and especially with the sadistic hedonism of his rebellious heroes, who were seen to have liberated themselves from the slave morality of the weak and mediocre herd surrounding them.[18] Svidrigailov, Stavrogin, and other "master" personality types from Dostoevsky's novels were now perceived as Russian incarnations of the fierce and fearless "blond beast of prey" *(blonde Bestie)* of vulgar Nietzscheanism who, in liberating his primal instincts, abandons himself to cruel and violent pleasures. The critic Nikolai Grot, for example, considered Nietzsche a social Darwinist who views people as "beasts whose only purpose in life is the struggle for existence, power, and strength," while Mikhailovskii asserted that "those gloomy depths of cruelty, limitless love of power and malice, into which Dostoevsky loved to look" had become the basis for Nietzsche's ideas.[19] In largely distorted form, some of Nietzsche's central notions—in particular, his belief, espoused in such works as *The Genealogy of Morals* (1887) and *The Anti-Christ* (1895), that the legacy of Christian culture has been the unfortunate reduction of the strong, aggressive, and daring beast of prey within human beings to a tame, domesticated, civilized animal—were now voiced by a number of fictional characters in Russian literary works that either popularized or, as was more often the case, vulgarized the German philosopher's beliefs. Matvei Prispelov, the central character in Petr Boborykin's *The Cruel Ones* (1901), for example, is a self-proclaimed Nietzschean who, in imitation of Dostoevsky's amoral "superman," seeks to assert his dominance over others through sexually aggressive behavior.[20] Brutish sexual aggression of a predatory nature likewise characterizes the behavior of the strong, rapacious male figures one finds in such popular and sensational boulevard novels as Mikhail Artsybashev's *Sanin* (1907), Evdokiia Nagrodskaia's *The Wrath of Dionysus* (1910), and Anastasiia Verbitskaia's *Keys of Happiness* (1912), where the search for pleasure and the quest for self-determination seem to be accompanied by the exercise of a Nietzschean will to power.[21] In fin-de-siècle Russia, where, it was feared, an ethos of self-love and a cult of the individual personality were now replacing the traditional Russian moral values of self-abnegation, Christian compassion, and civic duty, rapacious behavior of this sort almost invariably characterized the search for sexual liberation and personal self-discovery.

The Communist takeover in 1917 may well have ushered in a vastly different moral climate for early-twentieth-century Russia, especially concerning the issue of sexual relations, but tropes of alimentary violence and images of sexual predation continued, nonetheless, to make their appearance in works of Soviet fiction. Bolshevik commentators during the immediate post-revolutionary period, much as Mikhailovskii, Gorky, and other radical democrats had done before them, assailed the cynical evaluation of human beings as blood-thirsty and power-hungry beasts of prey, an ontological view that was considered to be the direct legacy of "bourgeois" writers and thinkers such as Dostoevsky,

Darwin, and Nietzsche. Nonetheless, this ethos of human carnivorism was revived during the 1920s and 1930s, when "eating" others continued to serve as a way of expressing metaphorically the inherently competitive and conflictual nature of social life in the modern world. The trope of alimentary violence is encountered very frequently, for instance, in the prose works of Boris Pil'niak, since it appealed so strongly to this writer's abiding interest in the biological and instinctual nature of human beings, particularly their deep-seated primitive, elemental urges, which he believed had been unleashed by the forces of revolution and civil war in early Soviet Russia. Irina Ordynina, a vocal adherent of the Darwinist notion of the survival of the fittest in Pil'niak's *Naked Year* (1922), champions the idea that might makes right: that only those people whose muscles are strong, whose will is resilient, whose mind is free, and whose beauty is godlike will succeed in vanquishing life during these primitive and troubled "Varangian" times. "I wish to drain the entire cup that freedom and intellect and instinct have given me," Irina proclaims. "Instinct, too, for are not these present days, after all, a battle of instinct?!"[22] Indeed, words such as "rape," "beast," and "instinct" become recurring verbal refrains in Pil'niak's novel, especially during the violent and disturbing scene of primitive brutality at the Mars loop station. In *Machines and Wolves* (1925) as well, Pil'niak captures vividly the rapacious inclinations of human beings during this chaotic time in Revolutionary Russia, when the collapse of stable governance and the disappearance of humane values implicitly encouraged people to treat each other like beasts: for men to become lupine *(liudi ovolchilis')*, to become like a wolf to other men *(volkom stal liudiam)*.[23]

Like the primitivist Pil'niak, a number of independent-minded writers—including Isaac Babel' and Andrei Platonov—portrayed the unleashing of violent animal instincts within human beings that accompanied the Revolution and Civil War in Russia. Most writers in the early Soviet period, however, seem to have preferred to employ beast metaphors and tropes of alimentary violence along the lines of social class rather than individual personalities, depicting the conflict between the Old World and the New World—in Marxist terms, the class warfare between the proletariat and the bourgeoisie—in terms of animal predation.[24] Thus, Ivan Babichev, in Iurii Olesha's *Envy* (1927), who seeks to preserve all the old world emotions commonly associated with the bourgeois age in the "battle of the epochs" he claims to be waging against his brother Andrei, imputes to the members of the new order a bestial appetite for power, violence, and destruction. "They're devouring us like food," he complains at one point to Kavalerov, "they're drawing the nineteenth century into themselves like a boa constrictor draws in a rabbit. . . . They chew and digest. What's of use—they imbibe, what's injurious—they throw away. . . . Our feelings they throw away, our technology—imbibe."[25] In Alexander Afinogenov's early Socialist Realist play about academic politics, *Fear* (1931), meanwhile, each side in the conflict accuses the other of acting in a predatory manner. Professor Borodin, a widely respected scholar of human behavior from the bourgeois era, claims that the new administrative leadership at the sociology institute where he works (made up mainly of proletarian cadres) has created a widespread atmosphere of terror and fear among the faculty and staff, who are constantly afraid of being accused of committing an ideological error and thus deviating from the party line. "The rabbit who has seen a boa constrictor is unable to move from the spot," writes Professor Borodin about the average member of the institute. "His muscles petrify. He waits submissively, until the rings of the boa constrictor squeeze him and crush him." "All of us are rabbits," he sadly concludes. His working-class colleague, Klara, however, claims that all they have done is refuse to live in fear of, or be frightened by, bourgeois specialists. "Fear has lived on earth for many hundreds and thousands of years," she explains. "Ever since the earth has known a world of slavery and oppression, fear has existed as a mighty weapon for the suppression of man by man. To frighten, to paralyze the will, to break the opposition of those who are oppressed, to transform people into obedient rabbits—that is what the boa constrictors of all times and all peoples have striven for. To frighten!"[26] Fazil' Iskander's satire of Soviet life during the Brezhnev era, *Rabbits and Boa Constrictors* (1982), attests to the fact that terror and fear did not disappear in later twentieth-century Russia with the liquidation of the proletariat's class enemies.[27]

Although beast metaphors and tropes of alimentary violence occasionally make their appearance in Soviet literature written during the Stalinist and post-Stalinist years, especially in beast allegories such as Iskander's and in the literature of exposure written by some of the more ecologically minded writers (such as Valentin Rasputin and Chingiz Aitmatov), the dominance of the Socialist Realist aesthetic tended to make the artistic depiction of beastly cruelty, conflict, and struggle obsolete. After all, if Soviet literature's task under Socialist Realism was to portray exclusively the positive aspects of socialist society in its imminent development, then images of violence and aggression would seem to be categorically out of place in a writer's depiction of contemporary social life. The advent of glasnost and perestroika during the Gorbachev years and the subsequent collapse of communist rule in 1991, however, witnessed not only the emergence of pornography, lurid pulp fiction, and the "dark literature" of morbidity *(chernukha)*, but also the return of tropes of alimentary violence. The purported romanticization of violence that many critics observe in post-Soviet Russian literature, film, and culture has, in fact, been attributed by some directly to the legacy of the "cruel talent" of the recently rediscovered Dostoevsky.[28] Despite the Supreme Soviet's April 1991 resolution calling for urgent measures to curb the propagation of pornography and dismantle the new "cult of violence and cruelty" in Russia, images of violence (especially sexual violence against women) greatly proliferated not only in post-Soviet film and fiction, but in daily life as well.[29] Contemporary Russia has become, according to Viktor Erofeev, "a paradise for sadists." "I do not know of another country," he explains, "where women would be so strongly aroused by the prospect of rape and where men would so naively confuse the sexual act with fighting."[30] As Igor' Kon puts it, "the beast has broken loose" in post-Communist Russia, where the end of censorship and the advent of a market economy have led to sex becoming grotesquely deromanticized, commercialized, and commodified. We can only hope that Kon, who continues to insist that "Russia is not a zoo," ultimately proves correct in his optimistic assertion that "the beast is not as terrible as it is made out to be."[31]

One postmodern writer whose work exemplifies the Dostoevskian brand of human bestiality that has reemerged in the New Russia is Viktor Pelevin. In his novel *The Life of Insects* (1994), which one scholar has interpreted as a polemic with such works as Karel and Josef Čapek's play *From the Life of Insects* (1921) and Franz Kafka's "Metamorphosis" (1916),[32] characters seem to morph back and forth between human and various insect forms, taking the shape of mosquitoes, flies, dung beetles, flying ants, moths, hemp bugs, cockroaches, and so forth. One of the more prominent predatory characters in the novel is an American entrepreneur, Sam Sucker, a human mosquito who is visiting the Crimea in hopes of setting up a joint business venture with a pair of Russian investors. All three of these venture capitalists, of course, are really doing nothing other than "sucking" Russian blood. "We suck everybody's blood," one of them openly acknowledges. Another central character, the female ant Marina, marries an army major in hopes of attaining a comfortable, middle-class existence for herself. But during the intermission of Glinka's opera, *A Life for the Tsar* (performed in its insect version, of course), her husband trips on the stairway, strikes the back of his head against one of the steps, and dies without regaining consciousness. Some of his fellow officers proceed to gnaw off and devour parts of his torso with their mandibles, saving a few of the choicest portions for his pregnant widow, who is soon driven by poverty, hunger, and dire need to cannibalize not only her dead husband's body parts, but also some of her own unhatched eggs. "Life is a struggle," she later instructs her surviving daughter Natasha, "and the strongest win." The earlier, nineteenth-century Darwinian notion that "man is a wolf to his fellow man" *(chelovek cheloveku—volk)* is thus transformed in Pelevin's late-twentieth-century novel into the insect idiom: "the ant is a beetle, cricket, and dragonfly to his fellow ant" *(muravei murav'iu—zhuk, sverchok i strekoza)*.[33] "Pelevin's evocation of a Russia confronted by the first pangs of capitalism," one scholar correctly observes, "seems to recall—and perhaps not accidentally—Dostoevsky's polemics with the popular Darwinist ideas of society as composed of predators and prey that accompanied Russia's initiation into capitalism during the 1860s and 1870s." Eating and drinking, this scholar notes, "emerges as the ultimate act of predatory power" in Pelevin's insect novel about post-Communist Russia, which portrays a grotesque world where "one's relationship to the Other is predicated entirely on the act of eating or devouring."[34]

Let me conclude this brief survey of bestial imagery and tropes of alimentary violence in post-Dostoevskian Russian literature with the reminder that comparing human beings to rapacious beasts of prey who seek to swallow up and devour weaker creatures is patently unfair to the animals so figurated. After all, predatory creatures such as wolves, lions, and boa constrictors are merely following their natural instincts of self-preservation and obeying the law of survival of the fittest as they seek to win the struggle for existence in the animal kingdom. "People talk sometimes of bestial cruelty, but that's a great injustice and insult to the beast; a beast can never be so cruel as a man, so artistically, so artfully cruel," Dostoevsky's Ivan Karamazov reminds us. "The tiger only tears and gnaws, that's all he can do. He would never think of nailing people by the ears, even if he were able to do it. These Turks took a pleasure in torturing children, too; cutting the unborn child from the mother's womb, and tossing babies up in the air and catching them on the points of their bayonets before their mother's eyes. Doing it before the mother's eyes was what gave zest to the amusement." The intoxication of cruelty that inflames the vile blood in some human beings, Dostoevsky would insist, is, in the final analysis, a pathologically human trait, not a natural animal one. Ivan Karamazov is perhaps not telling us anything radically new when he asserts that "in every man a beast lies hidden," but he significantly adds that it is "the beast of rage, the beast of lustful heat at the screams of the tortured victim, the beast of lawlessness let off the chain."[35] This inner beast, Dostoevsky is telling us, is the cruel, sadistic, "artistic" face of the dangerously sensual and instinctual creature that only human animals are capable of becoming.

Notes

1. "Chekhov, Gogol, Bunin, Shchedrin, and countless memoirists have devoted no small number of pages to descriptions of oblivious gorging, a process that literally becomes orgiastic, virtually a sexual activity," writes Tatyana Tolstaia. "Russian literature's reserve in regard to eroticism and carnal love is compensated for many times over by the lengthy unbridled epic poems devoted to the joys of the stomach." See "The Age of Innocence," *New York Review of Books* 40:17 (October 21, 1993): 24.

2. In his study of Molière's *L'Ecole des femmes* (1662), Ronald W. Tobin interprets the central romantic plot in this French play as a semiotic collision between the code of power, communicated by the verb *manger* ("to devour"), and the code of pleasure, with its concomitant notion of *goûter* ("to taste"). Whereas the carnivoristic and predatory Arnolphe seeks to "devour" Agnes, hoping to dominate and control her as soon as she becomes his wife, Horace wishes instead to enjoy a "taste" of Agnes's sexuality and tender affection as a love partner. See Tobin, "Les mets et les mots: Gastronomie et sémiotique dans *L'Ecole des femmes*," *Sémiotique* 51 (1984): 133–45.

3. N. K. Mikhailovsky, *Dostoevsky: A Cruel Talent*, trans. Spencer Cadmus (Ann Arbor, Mich.: Ardis, 1978), 12. Mikhailovskii maintains that during Dostoevsky's early career the writer's talents were devoted mainly to studying the psychology of the sheep being devoured by the wolf, while in his later career Dostoevsky turned his attention almost exclusively to the psychology of the wolf devouring the sheep. Erich Fromm later incorporates Dostoevsky's dichotomy between human predators and their prey in his psychological study *The Heart of Man: Its Genius for Good and Evil* (New York: Harper & Row, 1964); see esp. ch. 1, "Man—Wolf or Sheep?" 17–23.

4. Maksim Gor'kii, "O 'Karamazovshchine,'" *Russkoe slovo* 219 (September 22, 1913), and "Eshche o 'Karamazovshchine,'" *Russkoe slovo* 248 (October 27, 1913). Both of these essays are reprinted in Maksim Gor'kii, *O literature* (Moscow: Khudozhestvennaia literatura, 1961), 66–69, 70–75.

5. "Dostoevsky and the Marquis de Sade: The Final Encounter," in R. L. Jackson, *Dialogues with Dostoevsky: The Overwhelming Questions* (Stanford, Calif.: Stanford University Press, 1993), 145. See also F. Kaufman, "Dostojevskij

a Markyz de Sade," *Filosoficky časopis* 3 (Prague, 1968): 384–89; and Sergei Kuznetsov, "Fedor Dostoevskii i markiz de Sad: sviazi i pereklichki," in *Dostoevskii v kontse XX veka*, ed. Karen Stepanian (Moscow: Klassika Plius, 1996), 557–74. As I have tried to show elsewhere, the larger and more important truth for the purportedly sadistic Dostoevsky is that human predatoriness and carnivorism, both of which are disturbing manifestations of a godless egoism, must be transcended by returning to Christ and his law of active, self-sacrificing love. See my essay "An Appetite for Power: Predators, Carnivores, and Cannibals in Dostoevsky's Fiction," in *Food in Russian History and Culture*, ed. Musya Glants and Joyce Toomre (Bloomington: Indiana University Press, 1997), 124–45.

6. For studies of the reception of Darwin (and Darwinism) in nineteenth-century Russia, see Alexander Vucinich, *Darwin in Russian Thought* (Berkeley: University of California Press, 1968); Daniel Todes, *Darwin without Malthus: The Struggle for Existence in Russian Evolutionary Thought* (Oxford: Oxford University Press, 1989); James Allen Baker, "The Russian Populists' Response to Darwin," *Slavic Review* 22:3 (1963): 456–68; and "Russian Opposition to Darwinism in the Nineteenth Century," *Isis* 65:229 (1974): 487–505; and George L. Kline, "Darwinism and the Russian Orthodox Church," in *Continuity and Change in Russian and Soviet Thought*, ed. Ernest J. Simmons (Cambridge, Mass.: Harvard University Press, 1955), 307–28.

7. Todes, *Darwin without Malthus*, 29. As Peter K. Christoff points out, one of the leading Slavophiles maintained that "the best way to constrain man's animal, jungle proclivities was to raise him in a commune." See *K. S. Aksakov: A Study in Ideas*, vol. 3 of Christoff's monumental study, *An Introduction to Nineteenth-Century Russian Slavophilism* (Princeton, N.J.: Princeton University Press, 1982), 368. The peasant commune, according to another Slavophile, "does not comprehend the personal freedom of man alone, which for it is a *wolf's* freedom, not human freedom." See A. Gilferding, *Sobranie sochinenii* (St. Petersburg, 1868), 2: 478. Gilferding, in Christoff's words, "saw in the Russian communal principle salvation from jungle-like individualism and social Darwinism" (368n).

8. For a brief discussion of these novels, see LeBlanc, "An Appetite for Power," 128–29. "The wolves devour the sheep," observes the landowner Lyniaev in Ostrovskii's play when describing the society around him, "and the sheep peacefully let themselves be devoured." See *Volki i ovtsy* in Aleksandr Ostrovskii, *Sobranie sochinenii* (Moscow: Khudozhestvennaia literatura, 1960), 7:121–223.

9. Fyodor Dostoevsky, *Memoirs from the House of the Dead*, trans. Jessie Coulson (Oxford: Oxford University Press, 1983), 14, 18, 293. All further references to this work (whose title we will render as *Notes* rather than *Memoirs*) will appear parenthetically in the text. For a study of animal imagery and "bestiality" in Dostoevsky's works, see V. P. Vladimirtsev, "Poeticheskii bestiarii Dostoevskogo," in *Dostoevskii i mirovaia kul'tura*, Al'manakh no. 12 (Moscow: Klassika plius, 1999), 120–34.

10. For a discussion of this shift from commensalism to carnivorism, see Ronald D. LeBlanc, "Food, Orality, and Nostalgia for Childhood: Gastronomic Slavophilism in Mid-Nineteenth-Century Russian Fiction," *The Russian Review* 58 (1999): 244–67.

11. Edward Rossmann, "The Conflict over Food in the Works of J.-K. Huysmans," *Nineteenth-Century French Studies* 2:1–2 (1973–74): 61. "Eating here is an act of neurotic frenzy," Rossmann explains, "rather than the normal pursuit of pleasure."

12. Fyodor Dostoevsky, *The Notebooks for "A Raw Youth,"* ed. Edward Wasiolek, trans. Victor Terras (Chicago: University of Chicago Press, 1969), 21–28. Jacques Catteau discusses *A Raw Youth* as "the novel of the predator" in *Dostoevsky and the Process of Literary Creation*, trans. Audrey Littlewood (Cambridge: Cambridge University Press, 1989), 265–68.

13. Fyodor Dostoevsky, *The Brothers Karamazov*, trans. Constance Garnett, revised by Ralph E. Matlaw (New York: W. W. Norton & Company, 1976), 170.

14. For a fuller treatment of the theme of cannibalism in Dostoevsky's fiction, see LeBlanc, "An Appetite for Power," 131–40.

15. See, for example, Nina Pelikan Straus, *Dostoevsky and the Woman Question: Rereadings at the End of the Century* (New York: St. Martin's Press, 1994).

16. "Notebook for *Diary of a Writer*, 1875–76," in Dostoevsky, *Polnoe sobranie sochinenii* (Leningrad: Nauka, 1982), 24:164. For discussions of Dostoevsky's reaction to Darwin and Darwinism, see G. M. Fridlender, *Realizm Dostoevskogo* (Moscow-Leningrad: Nauka, 1964), 157–63; B. E. Lewis, "Darwin and Dostoevsky," *Melbourne Slavonic Studies* 11 (1976): 23–32; and Dmitrii Shlapentokh, "Dostoevsky, Darwinism and Fedorovism," *Rusistika* 2 (1990): 3–9.

17. Dostoevsky himself was not especially fond of Darwin's teachings. Like his fellow "native soil enthusiasts," the *pochvenniki* Nikolai Strakhov, Apollon Grigor'ev, and Nikolai Danilevskii, Dostoevsky fervently championed the so-called Russian idea, believing that the tendency in the West to seek scientific and materialistic solutions to fundamental problems of human life posed a grave threat to the moral and spiritual values that traditionally had nurtured the Russian soul. In his *Diary of a Writer*, Dostoevsky on a number of occasions refers quite openly to Darwinism, the "struggle for existence," and the instinct for self-preservation in a highly negative way, as ideas that were implicitly alien (and even antithetical) to basic Russian and Christian sensibilities. In some of his letters, meanwhile, Dostoevsky repeatedly links the Darwinian notion of the "struggle for existence" with the socialists' misguided belief that the socio-economic "environment" is to blame for human vices and that a revamping of the political system in Russia—by "turning stones into bread"—would rectify their country's most pressing social problems. "Today's *socialism* in Europe, and with us too," he writes to Vasilii Alekseev on June 7, 1876, "eliminates Christ everywhere and worries first of all about *bread*, calls on science, and asserts that the single reason for all human problems is *poverty*, the struggle for existence, and 'people prey to the environment.'" Unlike the current theories of Darwin, Dostoevsky adds, Christ's message insists that "in addition to the animal world there is a spiritual world in man as well." In a letter to Pavel Polotskii, written just three days later, in which he discusses Pisareva's recent suicide, Dostoevsky complains that young people in Russia today are being assured that there is no spiritual life and no generosity, that "there is only the struggle for existence." If you tell a person "that there is no generosity, but that there is the elemental struggle for existence (egoism)," Dostoevsky explains, you effectively deprive

that person of both personality and freedom. See Fyodor Dostoevsky, *Complete Letters*, ed. and trans. David A. Lowe (Ann Arbor, Mich.: Ardis, 1991), 4:285–87.

18. For examinations of Nietzsche's reception and influence in late-nineteenth-century Russia, see Edith W. Clowes, *The Revolution of Moral Consciousness: Nietzsche in Russian Literature, 1890–1914* (DeKalb: Northern Illinois University Press, 1988); and Ann Marie Lane, "Nietzsche Comes to Russia: Popularization and Protest in the 1890s," in *Nietzsche in Russia*, ed. Bernice Glatzer Rosenthal (Princeton, N.J.: Princeton University Press, 1986), 51–68.

19. N. Ia. Grot, "Nravstvennye idealy nashego vremeni: Fridrikh Nitsshe i Lev Tolstoi," *Voprosy filosofii i psikhologii* 16 (January 1893), 129–54; and Nikolai K. Mikhailovskii, *Literaturnye vospominaniia i sovremennaia smuta* (St. Petersburg, 1900), 2:434.

20. Petr D. Boborykin, "Zhestokie," *Russkaia mysl'* (1901).

21. Edith Clowes examines Nietzschean elements in Mikhail Artsybashev's *Sanin* (as well as in Leonid Andreev's "The Story of Sergei Petrovich," 1900) in her essay "Literary Reception as Vulgarization: Nietzsche's Idea of the Superman in Neo-Realist Fiction," in *Nietzsche in Russia*, 315–29.

22. Boris Pil'niak, *Golyi god* (Chicago: Russian Language Specialties, 1966), 142, 143–44.

23. Boris Pil'niak, *Mashiny i volki* (Munich: Wilhelm Fink, 1971), 34, 138.

24. In their illuminating study of the language, motifs, and symbols of revolutionary Russia, Orlando Figes and Boris Kolonitskii show how images of the class enemy during this period were often zoological (especially predatory) in nature. The widely distributed pamphlet *Spiders and Flies* (1917), for instance, portrayed the privileged classes as "spiders" who were sucking the blood of the working class (the "flies"). See *Interpreting the Russian Revolution: The Language and Symbols of 1917* (New Haven, Conn.: Yale University Press, 1999), esp. ch. 6, "Images of the Enemy," 153–86. A. M. Selishchev notes that images of predatory beasts (especially the "hydra" of counterrevolution) likewise appeared at this time in the speeches of revolutionary activists. See *Iazyk revoliutsionnoi epokhi: Iz nabliudenii nad russkim iazykom poslednikh let (1917–1921)* (Moscow: Rabotnik prosveshcheniia, 1928; rpt. Letchworth, Hertfordshire, England: Prideaux Press, 1971), 133–34.

25. Iurii Olesha, *Envy*, trans. T. S. Berczynski (Ann Arbor, Mich.: Ardis, 1975), 87. Ivan feels the same way about human progeny. "You don't have to love one another. There's no need to be united," he preaches to a pair of newlyweds at their wedding banquet. "Bridegroom, forsake the bride! What sort of fruit will your love bring you? You'll bring your own enemy into the world. He'll devour you" (68).

26. Alexander Afinogenov, *Fear*, trans. Charles Malamuth, in *Six Soviet Plays*, ed. Eugene Lyons (Boston: Houghton Mifflin, 1934), 451–52. At play's end, Professor Borodin finally sees the error of his ways and vows to make amends by radically changing his social and ideological consciousness. "I will tell the whole world how I protected the rabbits and how the rabbits proved to be boa constrictors" (468).

27. Fazil' Iskander, *Rabbits and Boa Constrictors*, trans. Ronald E. Peterson (Ann Arbor, Mich.: Ardis, 1989). Irina Ratushinskaia, meanwhile, provides a

parodic deconstruction of this paradigmatic Soviet predator in her short story "On the Meaning of Life," where the main character is a vegetarian boa constrictor whose "all-consuming" (*vsepogloshchaiushchaia*) passion is to watch rabbits, not to eat them. See Irina Ratushinskaia, *A Tale of Three Heads*, trans. Diane Nemec-Ignashev (Tenafly, N.J.: Hermitage, 1986), 12–19. I am extremely grateful to Professor Gitta Hammarberg of Macalester College for drawing my attention to this delightful little tale.

28. See, for example, Jane T. Coslow, Stephanie Sandler, and Judith Vowles, introduction to *Sexuality and the Body in Russian Literature*, ed. Costlow, Sandler, and Vowles (Stanford, Calif.: Stanford University Press, 1993), 30. "Dostoevsky foreshadowed much of the dark literature *(chernukha)* in recent Soviet writing," they write, "and his novels explored the psychological complexities of sexual desire and sexual dread a generation before the advent of Freudian psychoanalysis."

29. See, for example, Tat'iana Zabelina, "Sexual Violence towards Women," in *Gender, Generation and Identity in Contemporary Russia*, ed. Hilary Pilkington (London: Routledge, 1996), 169–86.

30. Viktor Erofeev, "Markiz de Sad, sadizm i XX vek," in Erofeev, *V labirinte prokliatykh voprosov* (Moscow: Soiuz fotokhudozhnikov Rossii, 1996), 280.

31. Igor' S. Kon, *The Sexual Revolution in Russia: From the Age of the Czars to Today*, trans. James Riordan (New York: The Free Press, 1995). See ch. 7, "The Beast Has Broken Loose," 107–25.

32. Alexander Genis, "Borders and Metamorphoses: Viktor Pelevin in the Context of Post-Soviet Literature," in *Twentieth-Century Russian Literature: Selected Papers from the Fifth World Congress of Central and East European Studies*, ed. Karen L. Ryan and Barry P. Scherr (New York: St. Martin's Press, 2000), 301–3.

33. Victor Pelevin, *The Life of Insects*, trans. Andrew Bromfield (New York: Penguin, 1999), 14, 159, 71.

34. Keith Livers, "Bugs in the Body Politic: The Search for Self in Viktor Pelevin's *The Life of Insects*," *Slavic and East European Journal* 46:1 (2002): 4, 5.

35. Dostoevsky, *The Brothers Karamazov*, 219, 222.

Russian-Jewish Writers Face Pogroms, 1881–1917

BRIAN HOROWITZ

Violence against Jews in Russia from 1871 to the end of tsarism in 1917, so-called pogroms, brought death to many Jews, wounded and maimed others, and caused millions of rubles in property damage.[1] In nearly all cases the responsible parties were never punished for their crimes. In the few instances where perpetrators of pogroms were brought to justice, Jewish defenders were also arrested and in some cases convicted.[2] In addition to Jewish losses, pogroms damaged Russia's international prestige. After the pogroms of 1881–82, and again after the Kishinev pogrom in 1903, there were demonstrations in London and New York against the Russian government's inhumanity. Increased state oppression against Jews after 1882 made it increasingly difficult for the tsarist government to get foreign loans. Jews themselves, faced with danger to their lives and property, confronted existential questions: What was the future for Jews in Russia? Should they stay or emigrate? Was there any hope for improvement? Would the Russian government ever defend them, or was it itself complicit in these crimes? Debates over these issues inevitably found their way into creative literature by Jews.

Jewish culture in nineteenth-century tsarist Russia was trilingual, with Yiddish and Hebrew texts intended exclusively for Jewish readers, while writings in Russian were accessible to everyone, Jews and non-Jews alike.[3] Russian-Jewish literature developed out of political needs, as a voice for expressing what the Jewish community wanted from the government. There was, at least until the second quarter of the twentieth century, a genre known as Russian-Jewish fiction. Stories, poetry, feuilletons—observations on the political or social scenes—were published in so-called Russian-Jewish journals. The first of many appeared in 1860, in the context of liberalization and expansion of the public sphere. These journals inspired hopes of equality and integration and presented an alternative way of life from religious orthodoxy. Jews were encouraged to seek secular education, learn Russian, and integrate in the surrounding community.

In 1881, following the assassination of Alexander II, pogroms broke out. For nearly two years, these pogroms swept the Russian Southwest, even reaching Warsaw. In response the government did not blame the pogromists, but the victims, the Jews themselves. The reason for the pogroms, the government argued, was Jewish exploitation of the peasantry. In order to protect the peasants, Jews must be kept out of the countryside. The government of Alexander III published a decree of new and particularly strict restrictions regarding where Jews could live and what professions they could hold. These decrees, known as the May Laws, were meant to be temporary, but they lasted until the fall of tsarism.

The new situation following the pogroms of 1881–82 created a crisis for Jewish authors in the Russian language. A virulent anti-Semitic discourse became firmly entrenched in leading Russian newspapers, especially *Novoe vremia*, which served as a mouthpiece for the government's attitudes. For many Jews, the pogroms represented an unmitigated tragedy because their hopes had been shown up as delusion. Having put their faith in integration and progress, they now had to find an alternative. Not wanting to return to religious piety, acculturated Jews often had little interest in or knowledge of Hebrew and Yiddish.

With regard to formal literary issues, Jewish authors writing about Jews in tsarist Russia retained a preference for realism, for the most part rejecting decadence, symbolism or bold experimentation with form. Because writers wanted to emphasize political value, they were loath to create texts that were complicated formally. Thus, these writers tended to identify with Russians who were politically left-wing and involved in the political struggle against tsarism.[4]

The pogroms demanded a response. Literature played a large role in acting as a forum for formulating that response. It is not surprising, then, that Russian-Jewish literature contains contradictory qualities, such as appeals to Jewish nationalism, discrete calls for revolution, expression of homage for the Russian people, and patriotic exhortations about Russia.[5] Treatment of the pogrom theme in Russian language Jewish literature inevitably serves as a gauge of the attitudes of Jewish writers toward Russia, the Russian government, the press, and the Russian people.

One of the first treatments of a pogrom appears in the story "Early Grave (From a Sketchbook)" ("Ranniaia mogila [iz zapisnoi knizhki]"), which was printed in *Voskhod* in December 1881.[6] Focusing on the emotions incited by violence, the author Simeon Frug describes how a young Jewish girl, a medical student in St. Petersburg, is raped and her father murdered during a pogrom. Depicting the pogrom with a naturalistic paintbrush, Frug uses broken syntax and a lexicon associated with confusion, violence, and pain. The conversation we hear is between the father and his daughter, Sonia:

> Scream, howl, roar . . . A moan hangs in the air . . . The despairing cries of women and children, furious screams of drunken bandits in a frenzy . . . The crash of furniture breaking, ring of windows shattering. . . ."Break it! . . . Hit . . ." "Help! . . ." "Run away? . . . Where to hide? . . . They are already here! . . . They are breaking into my room . . ." "Sonia! Sonechka! . . . Where are you? Come here. . . . Hide! . . . My God, where are you? . . ." But it was in vain. A large blond guy fell on him. "Kike! . . . Hey, come here, here! . . ." The old man fell. A knot of grey hair fell from the hand of the man. Screams, a snap, a crash was heard from the street . . ."Sonia, Sonia! . . ." wheezed the old man, beaten and covered with blood, and trying to move through the crowd which was becoming more and more insane. But there something flashed in the darkness and got hidden behind the doors of the barn . . ."Sonia! . . . My God! Let me through! . . ." But a peasant, disgusting, wild from drink and carousing, entirely in dirty rags threw himself after him . . . An animal-like, despairing scream rang out from the barn . . . The struggle lasted ten minutes . . . [. . .] Suddenly the doors to the barn opened and a girl ran out, entirely full of dirt, bloodied in a shirt that was ripped apart . . . She ran to the gates of the house and tripped and fell on something warm, barely moving in a smoking, red puddle . . .[7]

The warm object is of course the girl's father.

Although the bulk of the story captures the actual events in medias res, Frug does not refrain from offering a coherent message. At the story's end he explains that Sonia had to suspend indefinitely her dream of becoming a doctor. Sonia's dream of leaping from the Pale of Settlement to St. Petersburg reflects the idealism of the Haskalah ideology that Jews can be both patriotic and productive. The dashed hopes end that dream. Frug, however, does not give a hint of what Jews should substitute for their mistaken optimism.

For Frug assimilation was not an alternative. In a story from 1886 Frug drew a portrait of Rebecca Abramovna, a young woman who rejoiced in the fact that she did not "look like a Jew."[8] Befriending two Russians, a colonel's widow and a district police chief, she took pride in their acceptance of her and her ostensible superiority over other Jews. At the end Rebecca Abramovna is raped during a pogrom. According to Frug, she was the victim of an illusion, the idea that one can overcome one's Jewish identity. Frug opens his story with the words "Rebecca weeps," which he repeats throughout. Showing the falsity of imagining one can become something other than what one is, Frug concludes that all Jews share a single fate.

> Weep, Rebecca Abramovna, give your sadness free rein. But do not forget this: the heart of the matter does not lie exclusively in the fact that previously you laughed, as your dear mother thinks. Those who never even thought of "laughing" are weeping together with you. Gershon the melamed did not laugh sitting all day bent over his book. The tailor Jankel and the carpenter Motka from whose hands their needle and axe were ripped and who have run away to starve were not laughing either. They too are weeping! At least that is how we suppose things are. But there is a large difference between your pain and theirs. Both Gershon the melamed and Jankel the tailor never forget even for a second that, whether or not they look like a Jew, they are exactly those lucky ones, the souls of those who a thousand years before appearing in a body wandered in the Arabian sands, at the foot of Sinai, and each of them immediately understood at the first blow why they were struck, even if neither the colonel's widow, Khireeva, or the guard Ogloblia were aware of their existence, and consequently there was no one who would protect them . . . But you . . .
>
> Weep, Rebecca Abramovna, weep![9]

Frug was associated with the populist movement in Russia and was called the "Jewish Nadson"; Nadson was a poet famous for his melodramatic and world-weary thematics. A repentant populist, Frug withdrew his pity from the Russian peasant to the sad figure of the impoverished Jew. An early nationalist, he nevertheless could not find a positive mission for Jewish national identity. Everywhere he saw despair, pain, and tragedy, and he made these themes the central focus of his fiction. Although he began his life as an advocate of integration, the pogroms of 1881–82 transformed him. A supporter of Zionism, he never fully identified with the goal of a political state for the Jews, obviously preferring the tragic but emotionally rich fate of a Jew in Russia to a future dream on distant shores. Frug was not alone among Russian Jews in perceiving the pogroms as the central experience of his life. Others, including the journalist and writer Lev Levanda and the lawyer Mark Varshavskii, deeply lamented the failure of assimilation, carrying this disappointment around as a badge of Russian betrayal.[10]

In the next decade attitudes toward pogroms changed. Time to reflect about the causes of the violence and to contemplate solutions had an influence on fictional accounts. In his novel *The Migrants of Mezhepol'* (*Konets vykhodtsev,* 1896), Sergei Iaroshevskii offered a sociological portrait of attitudes among Russians and Jews.[11] Setting his story in a small city in Belarus, Mezhepol', and an area on its outskirts, Parogi, during the 1880s, Iaroshevskii treats a slice of life under the anti-Jewish May Laws.[12] According to the decree, Parogi is no longer part of the city, but belongs to the countryside, and, therefore, Jews are prohibited from living there. This law threatens to displace half of the Jewish population. Joseph Mezhepol'skii, a Jewish intellectual, has petitioned the authorities in St. Petersburg on behalf of the Jews. It turns out that the petition has no chance of success unless it contains the original decree of Jewish habitation, which is located in the personal archive of a certain Beliaev, a conservative landowner known for his anti-Jewish views. Frida, Joseph Mezhepol'skii's younger sister, has also returned to Mezhepol'. She is the object of love of the narrator, a Jewish doctor, who has devoted his life to social activism. Beliaev becomes interested in her too.

As the situation for Parogi's Jews becomes more and more desperate, violence breaks out when a Jewish storekeeper, who has lost his mind, returns to his former store, which he had been forced to sell for a fraction of its value. The new owners give him a beating, and one blow to his head kills him. The murder sets off a larger pogrom, which inflames much of the city. At exactly this time Frida realizes that she loves Beliaev, and Beliaev, who unexpectedly repudiates anti-Semitism, asks for her hand in marriage. Beliaev provides Joseph with the document necessary to save the Jews. Although everything seems to have worked out perfectly, Iaroshevskii ends the novel tragically. A local anti-Semite, Skal'kov, challenges Joseph to a duel and kills him, and Frida dies in a huge fire that devours the synagogue.

Iaroshevskii draws clear lines between good and evil for a purpose. He places blame on the government for enacting the new laws that force the Jews into such inhuman situations. He also indicts Russian merchants who exploit the misfortune of the Jews to acquire property and carry out pogroms. To these malicious figures he juxtaposes such kind characters as Beliaev, Beliaev's sister (who becomes Joseph's fiancé), Joseph, Frida, and the doctor. Love relations between Jews and Russians underscore a potential solution to anti-Semitism and Jewish nationalism. One also notices a subtext of the Esther story from the Bible, since Beliaev helps the Jews because of his love for the beautiful Frida. Nevertheless, Iaroshevskii does not allow the private happiness of a few to overcome the majority's power of hate. The duel and pogrom nullify everything. Instead of marriages we have funerals, instead of Parogi's Jews being rescued, they will be evicted.

Iaroshevskii can only treat issues negatively. Just as he emphasizes the impossibility of integration, he also mocks the striving for national exclusivity. The doctor confesses: "You see before you a fiery nationalist . . . I cannot explain to you how it happened. They say that narrow nationalism is a sign of regression. I admit this and feel it. My nationalism is just as vulgar and egotistical as those others who promulgate it. But it is a sweet poison and why shouldn't we, castoffs of humanity, not drink it to the full?"[13] Instead of nationalism uplifting the Jew, according to Iaroshevskii, it morally and intellectually lowers him. The highest level is cosmopolitanism and integration, but that is not offered as a potential solution.

Iaroshevskii's pessimism can be understood in terms of the generation from which he emerged. The two decades after the pogroms of 1881–82 were bitter times for intellectuals like Iaroshevskii, who neither wanted to sacrifice their old ideals of integration nor accept Jewish nationalism or political radicalism.[14] He was hostile to Zionism and was convinced that Western-style emancipation of the Jews of Russia was entirely possible. Because his views clashed with his environment, he disappeared from the literary scene many years before his physical death in 1907 (he published his last novel in *Voskhod* in 1899).

David Aizman, a politically left-wing writer, penned a series of stories dealing with pogroms from the viewpoint of Jews who had left Russia.[15] Instead of rejoicing in their escape from danger and chance to form new lives in Western Europe, the characters face a dilemma. Imbued with love for Russia, they cannot be happy outside her borders. Therefore, they suffer. In his story "Abroad" ("Na chuzhbine," 1901), Aizman eschews entirely the naturalist approach of Frug and the sociological scope of Iaroshevskii, focusing on the psychology of two Russian Jews, a married couple, who grapple with the question of whether Russia can be a real homeland for Jews. Setting his story in provincial

France, the location where the two live comfortably after having fled Russia, Aizman uses his characters to investigate the Russian-Jewish dilemma. A Jewish doctor, Joseph, and his wife, Sarah, argue about returning to Russia. Although Sarah had been nearly raped during a pogrom, she still wants to return home so that the family can be of service to Ukrainian peasants during an epidemic supposedly taking place in southern Russia. Joseph, the narrator of the story, shares none of her populist idealism. Instead he defends emigration. "'Return!' But what will meet us there! Have you forgotten? Now just recall a bit. Recall only this, what will happen to your son? What will become of him there? Here he will study wherever he wants, whatever he wants, his talents will be properly developed, without any obstacles, and perhaps he can become a famous person. What do I know. He's a very talented boy . . . And if he won't be famous, then he'll simply be a free citizen of a free country . . . But there, where will you teach him? Where will you find a place for Jacob Joselevich Izraelson? There you'll have to make him a money lender, make him work in the wheat business!"[16]

Despite such cogent reasoning about restricted opportunities for Jews in the 1890s, in the end Sarah wins, and the family returns to Russia. Even though she admits that the Ukrainians make pogroms, she exonerates them, saying that "they don't understand what they are doing." Even if the government is guilty, she and Joseph do not have the right to leave Russia for the sake of their own happiness. Although Joseph has better arguments, the decision to return demonstrates that idealism can be more powerful than reason. It also refutes the argument that Jews are unpatriotic. Against all self-interest and wisdom, Joseph and Sarah go to help the peasants, although this decision brings danger to themselves and their son.[17]

Aizman's stories allude indirectly to the condition of Jews in Russia after 1905, when they were accused of disloyalty. Even important "liberal" intellectuals, such as Andrei Bely and Konstantin Chukovskii felt threatened by the "onslaught" of Jews. In his article of 1908, "Jewish and Russian Literature," Chukovskii argued that Jews have no right to interfere in the creation of a national culture.[18] Aizman devoted his literary talent to emphasize the patriotism of Russia's Jews, their attachment to the natives and the Russian land. Therefore, unable to have security in Russia, they were also uncomfortable abroad. Their education and values, nourished on the soil of Russian populism, made them feel responsible for Russia's future. At the same time they could not expect full acceptance. Aizman's Jews are unable to rest easily with whatever decision they make.

This idea fits well with Aizman's left-leaning political views, which place the blame for anti-Jewish violence at the door of the government. Aizman was a contributor to the left-wing journal *Russkoe bogatstvo* and Maxim Gorky's journal, *Znanie*. Aizman believed the government was capable of stopping the pogroms if it wanted to do so and he equally chided the Russian people who at best were indifferent and at worse took pleasure in pogroms. In the story "Flow of Blood" ("Krovavyi razliv"), Aizman depicted Russians who descended to a subhuman moral level. While Aizman describes some Russians who are friendly with Jews, significantly he does not produce any Russian person who is deeply distraught by the pogroms.

The multifaceted depiction of pogroms by Jewish authors writing in Russian between 1881 and 1914 shows that Jewish authors felt the need to deal with contemporary events that affected Jews. At the same time, these stories reveal the attachment of Jewish writers to the political tradition of Russian literature. Because of government censorship that repressed free expression in politics, *belles lettres* became a place for the discussion of important social questions rather than a medium for purely formal experimentation.

As the small sample of stories here shows, Jews themselves were confused by the violence; they posed questions rather than answered them. They were confused because the pogroms called into question all their previous ideals and hopes. Jewish writers in Russia tended to seek integration, looking to Western Europe as a model that could work for Russia too. Rachel Khin described this attitude in her characterization of the hero of "Dreamer" ("Mechtatel'"), a story published in 1896. An educated Jew forced to leave his home of more than twenty years during the huge eviction of Jews from Moscow in 1891 writes, "Our common friends consider me a Jewish fanatic. This is a mistake. I consider Jews unconscious fighters for the freedom of the spirit, and perhaps no one as ardently as I yearns for that day when the word 'Jew' will disappear. This will occur when each person will say to the other, 'My brother, pray however your soul desires.' On that blessed day tortured Agaspherus will lay down his heavy staff."[19]

Khin means that Agaspherus, the wandering Jew, would be able to stop running and find love and acceptance among non-Jews. On that day, the word *Jew* would have no negative connotations and would be equal or the same as Russian. It is not a coincidence that Khin depicts a man whose entire self-identification is linked to Russia, since Russian-Jewish authors fully identified the fate of the Jews with the fate of Russia. Considering the Jew as a sign representing progress and liberalism, these authors portrayed pogroms as attacks on progress itself. In his powerful editorials written in response to the pogrom violence of 1881–82, Lev Levanda juxtaposed pogroms with everything that was good, decent, honest, and legitimate in Russia. Levanda, among others, also raised the question whether Jews could consider themselves real members of the Russian state—whether the patch of land where they were born was their homeland or whether they really were foreigners, as anti-Semites claimed. In one of his hard-hitting and despairing editorials written during the period of violence, Levanda chastised the Jews themselves. Juxtaposing the desire for abstract justice and the very real beating that was occurring, Levanda defended emigration and self-defense. He writes: "In my view this sheepish passivity makes the affair more complicated because when the fist, coarse physical strength is in high regard, passive thought, love of peace and a petition for legality, law and justice are pointless and hilarious in the highest degree. Therefore if Jews don't want to be beaten by the first son of a bitch who meets them, the more secure means is to not let it happen, and they have enough strength not to let it happen if they would only have more confidence in themselves. *Aid-toi; et Dieu t'aidera.*"[20]

The pogroms eventually would lead many to the same conclusion. If Jews wanted to have security they needed their own self-defense units. If they wanted schooling, they would have to create their own schools. If they wanted peace, they would have to find their own land, create their own state, and form their own government. Pogroms inevitably had the powerful effect of pushing Jews into the nationalist camp. But even as nationalists, their literary creations fell into the realist category. By and large, Jewish nationalism reflected conservative attitudes.[21]

What one can say about pogroms is that the Jewish nationalism it spawned slowed down the absorption of Jews into Russian literature but did not stop the process. Within a generation following Aizman, the most important Jewish writers in Russian, Osip Mandel'shtam and Boris Pasternak, did not bring attention to their ethnicity, preferring to compete in Russian literature as equals with Russians.[22] Isaac Babel' certainly drew attention to his identity as a Jew, but he did not give it the same meaning as did earlier writers. He did not seek political redress for Jews. Babel''s retreat from Jewish politics shows that Jews in culture were no longer defined according to ethnic lines and that their Jewish identity was neutralized at least in comparison with the generation earlier. To have a Jewish background no longer implied identification with the Jewish group or its political agenda.

Pogroms did finally come to an end with the consolidation of Soviet power in the late 1920s, and with them this literary theme vanished from Soviet literature until its resurrection in the work of Vasilii Grossman, Anatolii Rybakov, and more recently in *Two Hundred Years Together* by Alexander Solzhenitsyn.[23] Despite the treatment of anti-Semitism in post-1960s Russian literature, one has not seen the rise of a distinctly separate literary grouping for Jews. Jewish and non-Jewish authors writing about Jewish themes belong to the mainstream. Whether or not new Russian-Jewish journals appearing in today's Russia and in Israel will constitute a separate subcategory of Russian literature is difficult to say. If it did, it would signify a regression back to the pre-Revolutionary period, when Jews were not accepted as full members of Russian literature, but it also perhaps signals ahead to a new multicultural Russia in which every ethnic group would be free to cultivate its own national culture within the framework of a reconfigured and democratic Russian Federation.

Notes

1. The casualties in the pogroms of 1881–82 were not huge by today's figures (forty dead), but the numbers grew in later violence. For example, "in the pogroms that broke out after 1905 almost three thousand individuals were killed. Damage from pogroms between 1903 and 1906 is "estimated to be 57.84 million rubles within the Pale and an additional 8.2 million outside it" (Shlomo Lambroza, "Jewish Responses to Pogroms in Late Imperial Russia," in *Living with Antisemitism: Modern Jewish Responses*, ed. J. Reinharz [Hanover, N.H.: Brandeis University Press, 1987], 253–74, quotation from 268-69). For a good introduction to the scholarship, see John D. Klier and Shlomo Lambroza, eds., *Pogroms: Anti-Jewish Violence in Modern Russian History* (Cambridge: Cambridge University Press, 1992), 271.

2. Historians have widely debated who should take responsibility for the pogroms. Although at the time many believed the government had a hand in their preparation, scholarship over the last fifteen years or so has successfully repudiated this point of view. For a discussion of the literature, see Michael Aronson, *Troubled Waters: The Origins of the 1881 Anti-Jewish Pogroms in Russia* (Pittsburgh: University of Pittsburgh Press, 1990); Hans Rogger, "Government, Jews, Peasants and Land in Post-Emancipation Russia," *Cahiers du Monde Russe et Sovietique* 17:1, 2–3 (1976): 5–21, 171–211; Rogger, "The Jewish Policy of Late Tsarism: A Reappraisal," *Wiedner Library Bulletin* 25:1–2 (1971): 42–51;

John Klier, "The Russian Press and the Anti-Jewish Pogroms of 1881–82," *Canadian-American Slavic Studies* 17:1 (Spring 1983): 199–221; Shlomo Lambroza, "Plehve, Kishinev and the Jewish Question: A Reappraisal," *Nationalities Papers* 12:1 (1984): 117–27; Lambroza, "Jewish Responses to Pogroms in Late Imperial Russia," 253–74.

3. See Uzi Shavit and Ziva Shamir, eds., *In the Gates of Kishinev* (Tel Aviv: ha-Kibutz ha-meuhad, 1994) (in Hebrew and Yiddish). For more on the Jew in Russian literature see Brian Horowitz, "A Jewish Russifier in Despair: Lev Levanda's 'Polish Question,'" *Polin: A Journal Devoted to Polish-Jewish Relations* 17 (2004): 279–98; L. Katsis, *Osip Mandelshtam, Muscus Iudeistva* (Jerusalem: Gesharim, 2002); Alice Nakhimovsky, *Russian-Jewish Literature and Identity: Jabotinsky, Babel, Grossman, Galich, Roziner, Markish* (Baltimore, Md.: Johns Hopkins University Press, 1992); Gabriella Safran, *Rewriting the Jew: Assimilation Narratives in the Russian Empire* (Stanford, Calif.: Stanford University Press, 2000); and Maksim Shrayer, "Toward a Canon of Jewish-Russian Literature," in *An Anthology of Jewish-Russian Literature*, 2 vols. (Armonk, N.Y.: M. E. Sharpe, 2007), xxiii–xv.

4. Interestingly, Jewish philosophers and critics such as Akim Volynskii (Flekser), Lev Shestov, and Mikhail Gershenson affiliated themselves with the artistic avant-garde.

5. Among the works on Russian-Jewish literature, see Gabriella Safran, *Rewriting the Jew: Assimilation Narratives in the Russian Empire* (Stanford, Calif.: Stanford University Press, 2000).

6. S. Frug, "Ranniaia mogila (iz zapisnoi knizhki)," *Voskhod* 12 (written in June) (1881): 79–82.

7. Ibid., 81–82.

8. "Sluchainyi fel'etonist," "Itogi," *Nedel'naia khronika Voskhoda* (1886): 43, 44, 46; republished in S. G. Frug, *Iudeiskaia smokovnitsa: Izbrannaia proza* (Jerusalem: Hebrew University, 1995) 127–45.

9. Frug, *Iudeiskaia smokovnitsa*, 134 (in Hebrew).

10. Yehuda Slutzsky, *The Russian-Jewish Press in the Nineteenth Century* (Jerusalem: Bialik Institute, 1970), 174.

11. S. Iaroshevskii, *Konets vykhodtsev* (St. Petersburg: Voskhod, 1896), 1, 2, 3, 4, 8, 9, 10 12. In the encyclopedia article in *Evreiskaia entsiklopedia* the author gives as the date for the novel 1891–92 and gives it a different title, *Vykhodtsy iz Mezhepolia*. See *Evreiskaia entsiklopediia*, 16 vols. (St. Petersburg: Brokgauz and Efron, 1907–13), 16:408.

12. Named after the decrees of 2 May 1882, these laws limited where Jews could live and what professions they could practice.

13. Iaroshevskii, *Konets vykhodtsev*, 29.

14. V. Lvov-Rogachevsky, *A History of Russian Jewish Literature*, ed. A. Levin (Ann Arbor, Mich.: Ardis, 1979), 121–22.

15. Among such stories are "Na chuzhbine," "Vragi," "Zemliaki," and "Krovavyi razliv."

16. D. Aizman, "Na chuzhbine," *Krovavyi razliv i drugie proizvedeniia*, 2 vols. (Moscow: Institut Russkogo Evreistva, 1991), 2:80.

17. One critic wrote about "Abroad," "I don't know a more penetrating and deeply felt depiction of irrational love for this land [Russia], this people who, it

would seem, have done everything to inspire hate" (M. Vainshtein, "Svidetel'stvo ochevidtsa," *Krovavyi razliv,* 245).

18. Chukovskii, "Evrei i russkaia literatura," *Rassvet* (1908): 9.

19. R. Khin, "Mechtatel'," in *Sbornik v pol'zu nachal'nykh evreiskikh shkol* (St. Petersburg, 1896), 243.

20. L. Levanda, "Mimokhodom (letuchie mysli nedoumevaiushchego)," *Ezhenedel'naia khronika Voskhoda,* 17, 23 April 1882, 464.

21. Hebrew and Yiddish writers grew closer to the Decadent and Symbolist movements, according to Hamutal Bar-Yosef, *Decadent Trends in Hebrew Literature: Bialik, Berdychevski, Brener* (Jerusalem: Bialik Institute, 1997), 13–21.

22. Pasternak apparently converted to Christianity. See C. Barnes, *Boris Pasternak: A Literary Biography,* 2 vols. (Cambridge: Cambridge University Press, 1989), 1:27–28.

23. V. Grossman, *Zhizn' i sud'ba* (Lusanne: L'Age de homme, 1960); A. Rybakov, *Deti Arbata* (Moscow: Sovetskii pisatel', 1988); A. Solzhenitsyn, *Dvesti let vmeste,* 2 vols.(Moscow: Russkii put', 2000–2002).

The Origins of Soviet State Terrorism, 1917–21

ANNA GEIFMAN

A cardinal feature of the newly established Soviet rule was its unremitting dependence on state-sponsored political violence—evident in the regime's very origins, as the first frantic weeks following the Bolshevik takeover in November 1917 escalated into sanguinary years of the Russian Civil War of 1918–21. Indeed, Lenin and his associates relied on and zealously defended a policy they called "Red Terror"—an instrument of repression by the revolutionary government—as a precondition for success in a seemingly visionary endeavor by a handful of political extremists to establish control over Russia's enormous territory and population. In the Bolshevik view, state "terror from above" was also an expedient tool in restructuring traditional society in accordance with the Marxist doctrine. This was allegedly not because of some intrinsic feature of Marx's creed, or a principle inherent in the very basis of Lenin's party. Rather, the Bolsheviks justified the necessity to rely on the Red Terror as a rejoinder to a wide range of anti-Soviet activity perpetrated by a myriad of their internal and foreign enemies, Russian reactionaries, foreign interventionists, and counterrevolutionaries of various leanings—all determined to destroy the communist regime. In the ensuing decades, scores of Soviet historians followed this required official interpretation, and many of their Western counterparts echoed with analogous conclusions. Yet, much in the conventional analysis of the Bolshevik Red Terror does not stand serious scrutiny.[1]

Even prior to the Bolshevik takeover, Lenin had declared on numerous occasions that his conspiratorial "Jacobin" party "never rejected terror on principle," nor could it do so.[2] In the era of the 1905–7 revolution the Bolsheviks did not shun from taking part in terrorist attacks and were frequently engaged in expropriations ("exes"), or politically motivated robberies of banks and other financial institutions for the sake of procuring funds for their faction.[3] Having taken over the Russian administration in November 1917, Lenin and Trotsky labeled opponents of violent methods "eunuchs and pharisees"[4] and proceeded to implement government-sponsored machinery of state terror—projecting the conspiratorial and criminal nature of the Bolshevik party onto their vision of the new dictatorial state. Its targets were to be exterminated not because they committed, or even might commit, crimes, but because the Bolsheviks envisaged Jacobin-like terror as an essential element of their blueprint for a new order. In their rhetoric, Lenin's followers presented the Jacobin Terror of 1793–94 as a model for their own Red Terror policy, and themselves as descendents of Robespierre and his fellow-extremists during the French Revolution. For their part, the Bolsheviks pursued "class-based" political violence, directed against any group of individuals designated as "class enemies" of the proletarian dictatorship. In one of the earliest references to their new course, on December 2 (15), 1917, Trotsky declared before a revolutionary gathering: "There is nothing immoral in the proletariat finishing off the dying class. This is its right. You are indignant . . . at the petty terror which we direct against our class opponents. But be put on notice that in one month at most this terror will assume more frightful forms, on the model of the great revolutionaries of France."[5]

Contrary to all subsequent claims about the use of violence in self-defense against counterrevolution, from the outset, the Bolsheviks thus set in motion the policy of state repression as an ideological weapon. The notorious Cheka (Extraordinary Commission for Combating Counterrevolution and Sabotage), which would become a primary instrument of the Red Terror, was formally, if secretly, established almost immediately after the Bolshevik takeover—on December 7 (20), 1917.[6] It came into existence months before any organized opposition to the Soviets had had a chance to form. By the first half of 1918, when the Cheka had already had its debut in terror, according to its deputy director, Ia. Kh. Peters, "counterrevolutionary organizations . . . as such were not observed."[7] Nevertheless, in early June 1918, the first Cheka head, "Iron Feliks" Dzerzhinskii announced that terror was "an absolute necessity," and that the repressive measures must go on in the name of the revolution, "even if its sword does by chance sometimes fall upon the heads of the innocent."[8]

Originally, the Bolsheviks had envisaged the Cheka as an investigative, rather than repressive agency; its primary function was to gather intelligence and prevent offenses against the state. Having no official judiciary powers, the Cheka was legally required to leave prosecution, indictment, and final sentencing of political offenders to the new Soviet courts, the so called revolutionary tribunals, introduced in late November 1917. It soon turned out, however, that the tribunals' tendency to linger on proprieties threatened the efficiency of Lenin's envisaged rule "unrestricted by any laws." As a solution, the Bolshevik leadership extended the Cheka's original mandate. Whereas the central Cheka offices in Petrograd and Moscow temporarily abstained from executing political undesirables, on February 23, 1918, Dzerzhinskii urged provincial and district Soviets to set up local Cheka bureaus, arrest counterrevolutionaries, and "execute them wherever apprehended." The authorities also announced publicly that enemies of the revolution would be "mercilessly liquidated on the spot." Accordingly, the Cheka's bureaus on the periphery began to resort routinely to summary judiciary procedures: unlimited by even the most cursory legal norms, they meted out arbitrary, often impetuous and unwarranted punishments, including death sentences. Significantly, much of the Cheka's efforts at the time centered around combating such economic crimes as "speculation," which "encompassed practically any independent commercial activity," and "sabotage," that is, refusal of technical experts and professionals to offer their services to the Bolshevik-controlled economy.[9]

The July 1918 massacre of the Russian imperial family—an event of supreme political and psychological significance—also took place six weeks before Red Terror was inaugurated as an official policy of the day. For decades to come, the Soviets relegated responsibility for the decision to murder the Romanov family in Ekaterinburg to local revolutionary activists. In fact, the secret order to execute former tsar Nicholas II, his wife Alexandra, their five children, three servants, and family doctor was issued in the Bolshevik headquarters in Moscow and carried out by a special Cheka squad.[10]

On August 30, 1918, the head of the Petrograd Cheka, Moisei Uritskii, was killed as a result of an assassination attempt; on the same day, Lenin was severely wounded in an unrelated terrorist episode. The Bolsheviks, however, perceived these attacks as part of a large-scale conspiracy—an assumption that elicited instantaneous and inundating fear. Overwhelmed by anxiety, Lenin's followers sought to mitigate their apprehension by unleashing a mass campaign of violence. The Red Terror did not begin but dramatically escalated at this time, encompassing retaliation, revenge, and infinite cruelty against real, alleged, and potential enemies.

The Bolsheviks now resorted to repressive measures much more openly than ever before. As an initial step, "512 hostages, most of them 'high notables' of the Tsarist regime, were shot in reprisal." Simultaneously, a "government decree declared that class enemies were to be sent to concentration camps and that members of counter-revolutionary organizations were to be executed."[11] Frightened people in power who sought to intimidate those under their control in order to reassure themselves of the legitimacy, strength, and longevity of their regime, the Bolsheviks then continually broadened the category of their class enemies: "Without mercy, without sparing, we will kill our enemies by the scores of hundreds, let them be thousands, let them drown themselves in their own blood. For the blood of Lenin and Uritskii . . . let there be floods of blood . . . more blood, as much as possible."[12]

The Bolshevik reprisals against other political parties had begun as early as November 1917 with the arrest of nonsocialist moderates, the Constitutional Democrats (Kadets). By late summer of 1918, Lenin's formula "those who are not with us are against us" already applied to the Bolsheviks' former comrades in the socialist camp, who were apprehended en masse and incarcerated. Of course they were not counterrevolutionaries, Lenin frankly admitted to Swiss socialist Fritz Platten, "but that's exactly why they are dangerous—just because they are honest revolutionists."[13] Before long, persecution extended from renowned figures of the socialist opposition to members of their families.[14]

By the fall and winter of 1918–19, Bolshevik terror achieved "a level of indiscriminate slaughter never before seen."[15] Arrests were now "based solely on social origin rather than a specific offense";[16] persecutions were aimed at virtually anyone representing the old regime's upper classes, the bourgeoisie, and the intelligentsia. Vicious atheistic campaigns against the Russian Orthodox Church and religion in general brought about unremitting violence against the clergy and the devout adherents of all persuasions.[17] Impelled by their perpetual dread of military conspiracies, the Bolsheviks made a special effort to locate and apprehend former imperial army officers, thousands of whom were executed without trial. Their family members found themselves in prisons and concentration camps, which initially came into being in Russia in 1918 and increased in number dramatically in 1919. Besides being used as cheap labor, these civilians served as hostages, or potential "execution material"; the Cheka firing squads shot them frequently as part of mass reprisals against opposition. Quickly, the practice of hostage-taking became routine, as the Cheka personnel arrested civilians randomly and executed them arbitrarily, typically in mass actions against the loosely defined category of "class enemies."[18]

Indeed, one did not need to be an officer, nobleman, or property owner to qualify as an enemy of the proletariat. Individuals from any social stratum whose viewpoints and activities were contrary to those of the Bolshevik party were likely targets of the Cheka. Faced with a wave of workers' strikes and peasant uprisings, the government directed its wrath even against the very groups whose alleged, if in fact very questionable, support had always served as the Bolsheviks' raison d'être and as an argument for their political legitimacy. In one of numerous cases, in December 1918, the central Cheka office in Moscow issued orders to its subordinates in the periphery "to stop terrorizing workers and peasants" and to end "terror against the peaceful population."[19] Relentless terror, however, continued to be the policy of the day, with the total number of its victims ranging between 50,000 in some estimates and 140,000 in others. Political violence "served the Bolsheviks . . . as a surrogate for the popular support which eluded them. The more their popularity eroded, the more they resorted to terror."[20]

Among perpetrators of state-sponsored terrorism, sincere idealists rationalized their behavior with an ideology-based determination to annihilate "class enemies." Along with the visionaries, however, there were bona fide representatives of the "seamy side" *(iznanka)* or the "lower depths" *(dno)* of the revolution, dominated, as it was by a new breed of extremists—"a blending of revolutionary and bandit."[21] A wide variety of hooligans, common criminals, and the riffraff of society joined the Bolshevik ranks and were now in the position to justify felonious acts with lofty slogans of freedom fighting. Soviet authorities were well aware that the very nature of Cheka activities attracted "corrupt and outright criminal elements," and Dzerzhinskii bluntly complained:

"only saints and scoundrels" offer their services to the Cheka, but "the saints are running away from me, and I am left with the scoundrels."[22]

It was especially difficult to differentiate between revolutionary and criminal practices in the periphery, where mass murder, robbery, blackmail, rape, beatings, torture, and startling sadism assumed astounding proportions—the "Red banditry," accompanied by incessant drinking and drug use by members of the Cheka and the tribunals.[23] Few regional or district Cheka officials were held accountable for their actions, and the only criteria for appointment to the revolutionary tribunals were undivided loyalty to the new regime and the ability to read and write. Consequently, 60 percent of the judges were individuals with incomplete secondary schooling; many used their positions "to pursue personal vendettas" and to extort bribes from families of the accused. A prominent Bolshevik, Mikhail Olminskii, protested in 1919: "what now goes on in the provinces is not Red Terror at all, but crime, from beginning to end."[24]

Strikingly, the behavior of numerous practitioners of terror was characterized by manifest psychiatric impediment, with psychological or mental derangement serving as a catalyst for violent, often sadistic behavior that in the prevailing circumstances of the day happened to take revolutionary form.[25] We may or may not opt to brand these radicals as psychopaths, but a contemporary reporter revealed that some individuals who took part in daily acts of violence became addicted to gore as if to narcotics; they "contracted the execution habit. . . . [They] volunteer for the service and cannot sleep unless they have shot someone dead."[26] Dzerzhinskii himself had reportedly been treated for a mental illness referred to as "circular psychosis,[27] and many of his chief lieutenants included drug addicts and unquestionable sadists.[28]

It was hardly a trivial matter for the Bolsheviks to find enough individuals willing to jail, guard, interrogate, torture, and execute. In fact, the Cheka's Deputy Director Peters conceded that he and his colleagues had trouble recruiting rank-and-file cadres because people were too "sentimental." The Bolsheviks solved this problem at least partly, however, by filling the Cheka staff vacancies with former employees of the tsarist secret police, the Okhrana. In addition, among the newly recruited Cheka officers, a disproportionate number were non-Russians, most commonly Armenians, Jews, and Latvians, many of whom had joined the struggle against Russian imperial authorities prior to 1917. Lenin seemed to favor these activists strongly, demonstrating ill-disguised bigotry in considering them to be "more brutal and less susceptible to bribery" than the "soft Russians."[29] Still more revealing was that among extremists promoting state-sponsored terror of the Bolsheviks, many had previously participated in terrorist ventures against the tsarist regime.

Lenin's regime was indeed founded on, and owed a great deal to, terrorist pathology. For many professional terrorists whose primary occupation before 1917 was bloodletting, the revolution presented an opportunity to return from their places of imprisonment or foreign exile and apply themselves once again to what they did best. Hence, after the Bolshevik takeover, they joined and often led the provincial and district sections of the Cheka, worked in the revolutionary tribunals, and after 1922, in the repressive organs of the GPU (Gosudarstvennoe politicheskoe upravlenie or State Political Administration).[30] Dzerzhinskii and his two Moscow Cheka associates, Martyn Latsis and Mikhail Kedrov, earlier in their political careers had been involved in extremist practices against the tsarist authorities and the bourgeoisie.[31] Likewise, in the periphery, especially in the Urals, where Bolshevik terrorist activities had been especially widespread after 1905, the Soviets were most successful in reassembling their old combat cadres, who after 1917 executed terror-related tasks of special importance.[32]

Significantly, former terrorists who volunteered as participants in the Red Terror came not exclusively from the Bolshevik ranks. The Left SRs, dissenters from the mainstream Socialist Revolutionary organization, played active roles in the Cheka during the period of their short-lived collaboration with the Bolsheviks prior to July 1918. Some maximalists, anarchists, and extremists of obscure ideological affiliation, as well as isolated Social Democrats, determined to preserve a united revolutionary front, also helped to build the Bolshevik-controlled machinery of repression—the would-be instrument of their own demise.[33]

During the Russian Civil War, the Bolsheviks were not, of course, the only political group responsible for raging violence, and the Red Terror may be compared with an array of atrocities perpetrated by the Whites. "The difference between the Reds' and the Whites' war on the internal front was perhaps that Lenin's government used terror as a method of social engineering." The Whites, although responsible for appalling acts of cruelty against the Bolsheviks, their sympathizers, and the population at large, "had never cherished a goal of recasting Russian society." Lenin's policy of repression thus fundamentally differed from all other sorts of "traditional" cruelty: it was ideology-based and theory-justified, applied not necessarily to real enemies, but to entire groups that the party in power considered to be ideologically impure or obstacles to the Bolshevik version of socialism.[34] Indeed, according to Left SR Isaac Steinberg, Commissar of Justice during the initial months of the Soviet rule, terror was an all-encompassing "system . . . a legalized plan of the regime for the purpose of mass intimidation, mass compulsion, mass extermination . . . The concept keeps on enlarging until . . . it comes to embrace the entire land, the entire population, and, in the end, all with the exception of the government and its collaborators."[35]

Whereas it is commonly assumed that fear became a dominant factor of Russian life only during Stalin's reign of terror, contemporaries remember otherwise: "the new regime mowed people right and left without discriminating much" between the guilty and the innocent, and already during the early months of the Soviet rule people lived in terror of random house searches, arrests, and imprisonment.[36] The apparent irrationality of repression was in fact part of Lenin's goal of creating the atmosphere of general intimidation—hence his belief that the Bolsheviks "must execute not only the guilty. Execution of the innocent will impress the masses even more." Yet, unlike Stalin in his day, Lenin's associates did not feel the need to embellish their actions or conceal the extent of their repressive policies. "We must," declared Grigorii Zinov'ev, "carry along with us 90 million out of the 100 million of Soviet Russia's inhabitants. As for the rest, we have nothing to say to them. They must be annihilated."[37]

The Red Terror did not end with the Bolshevik victory in the Civil War—as it might have had it been a reluctantly adopted weapon of self-defense and not a quintessential component of the Soviet regime. Although the Bolsheviks "did put an end to the indiscriminate massacres of 1918–19, they made certain to leave intact the laws and institutions which had made them possible." Indeed, already by 1920, "Soviet Russia had become a police state in the sense that the security police, virtually a state within the state, spread its tentacles to all Soviet institutions." In addition to a growing staff of investigators, interrogation officers, guards, and other prison personnel, the secret police relied on the Armies of the Internal Security of the Republic (Voiska Vnutrennei Okhrany Respubliki), which by the middle of 1920 consisted of nearly a quarter of a million men. Aside from its other duties, this internal army guarded concentration and forced labor camps, of which by the end of that year there were 84 with approximately fifty thousand prisoners. Only three years later, the number of camps increased to 315 with seventy thousand inmates. Thus, when "Stalin became undisputed master of Soviet Russia all the instruments which he required to resume the terror on an incomparably vaster scale lay at hand."[38]

Notes

This chapter first appeared in *Terror: From Tyrannicide to Terrorism in Europe, 1605–2005*, ed. Brett Bowden and Michael Davis (St. Lucia, Australia: University of Queensland Press, 2007).

1. To date, there is no comprehensive scholarly study of the Bolshevik Red Terror. The only book ever written specifically on the topic is an outdated and less-than-analytical treatise by Sergei Mel'gunov, *"Krasnyi terror" v Rossii, 1918–1923* (Berlin: Vataga, 1924). The most thorough shorter treatment of the subject may be found in Richard Pipes, *The Russian Revolution* (New York: Vintage Books, 1990). See also an important comparative study by Arno J. Mayer, *The Furies: Violence and Terror in the French and Russian Revolutions* (Princeton, N.J.: Princeton University Press, 2000).

2. V. I. Lenin, *Polnoe sobranie sochinenii* (Moscow: Izdatel'stvo politicheskoi literatury, 1959), 5:7.

3. See Anna Geifman, *Thou Shalt Kill: Revolutionary Terrorism in Russia, 1894–1917* (Princeton, N.J.: Princeton University Press, 1993), 90–96.

4. Walter Laqueur, *Terrorism* (Boston-Toronto: Little, Brown, 1977), 68. Cited in Pipes, *The Russian Revolution*, 791–92.

5. Cited in Pipes, *The Russian Revolution*, 805, 790.

6. On the general history of the Cheka see Leonard D. Gerson, *The Secret Police in Lenin's Russia* (Philadelphia: Temple University Press, 1976), 215; and George Leggett, *The Cheka: Lenin's Political Police* (Oxford: Clarendon Press, 1986).

7. Anna Geifman, "Cheka," in *The Modern Encyclopedia of Russian and Soviet History* (Gulf Breeze, Fla.: Academic International Press, 1978), 6:218.

8. Pipes, *The Russian Revolution*, 789–90.

9. Cited in ibid., 800–801, 804–5.

10. For a vivid description and exceptionally cogent analysis of the Romanov massacre see Pipes, *The Russian Revolution*, ch. 17.

11. Geifman, "Cheka," 218.

12. Cited in Pipes, *The Russian Revolution*, 820, 812.

13. Ibid., 792.

14. In one revealing case, in January 1920, the Cheka arrested the wife and three daughters of Victor Chernov, wanted as the underground leader of the outlawed Socialist Revolutionary party. His family spent weeks of semistarvation in an icy cell of the infamous Lubianka prison; the youngest girl was eleven years old (Olga Chernov-Andreyev, *Cold Spring in Russia* [Ann Arbor, Mich.: Ardis, 1978], 209–30).

15. Pipes, *The Russian Revolution*, 792.

16. Geifman, "Cheka," 219.

17. In recent years, historians in post-Communist Russia published important research on Bolshevik regional policies with regard to religion. See, for

example, M. G. Nechaev, *Krasnyi terror i tserkov' na Urale* (Perm': Izdatel'stvo Permskogo gosudarstvennogo pedagogicheskogo instituta, 1992).

18. See, for example, Mikhail Osorgin, *Vremena* (Ekaterinburg: Sredne-Ural'skoe knizhnoe izdatel'stvo, 1992), 577.

19. Vladimir Brovkin, *Behind the Front Lines of the Civil War* (Princeton, N.J.: Princeton University Press, 1994), 46.

20. Pipes, *The Russian Revolution*, 838, 792.

21. Referred to, for example, in A. Serebrennikov, ed., *Ubiistvo Stolypina: Svidetel'stva i dokumenty* (New York: Teleks, 1986), 319.

22. Cited in Geifman, "Cheka," 218.

23. See, for example, V. I. Shishkin, "Krasnyi banditizm v sovetskoi Sibiri," in *Sovetskaia istoriia: Problemy i uroki* (Novosibirsk: Nauka, 1992), 3–79.

24. Cited in Pipes, *The Russian Revolution*, 798–826.

25. Perhaps one of the most notorious representatives of this category was Bolshevik-terrorist Semen Ter-Petrosian, better known by his alias, Kamo. Dubbed by Maksim Gor'kii "an artist of the revolution," Kamo was a diagnosed psychopath. For discussion of his case see Geifman, *Thou Shalt Kill*, 167–68; I. Dubinskii-Mukhadze, *Kamo* (Moscow: Molodaia gvardiia, 1974), 5, 195–96; and Medvedeva-Ter-Petrosian, "Tovarishch Kamo," *Proletarskaia revoliutsiia* 8–9 (1931–32): 141–42.

26. Cited in Pipes, *The Russian Revolution*, 823.

27. G. A. Aleksinskii, "Vospominaniia," 15, in Boris I. Nicolaevsky Collection, Hoover Institution Archives, Stanford, California (cited hereafter as Nic.), 302–3.

28. Chernov-Andreyev, *Cold Spring in Russia*, 215. The inmates in the so called Extinction Boat (*Korabl' smerti*) prison of the Moscow Cheka found themselves in the hands of a former criminal turned hero of the Bolshevik terror, a raging "terror of the jail," nicknamed the "commissar of death" (Osorgin, *Vremena*, 575).

29. Pipes, *The Russian Revolution*, 802. Many former prisoners seem to remember their Latvian guards as particularly primitive and rough (see, for example, Osorgin, *Vremena*, 584).

30. See, for example, T. I. Vulikh, "Osnovnoe iadro kavkazskoi boevoi organizatsii," 7, in Nic. 207–11; S. M. Pozner, ed., *Boevaia gruppa pri TsK RSDRP (b) (1905–1907 g.g.) Stat'i i vospominaniia* (Moscow-Leningrad: Gos. Izdatel'stvo, 1927), 170n; Aleksandr Sokolov-Novoselov, *Vooruzhennoe podpol'e* (Ufa: Bashkirskoe knizhnoe izdatel'stvo, 1958), 39n; Kh. I. Muratov and A. G. Lipkina, *Timofei Stepanovich Krivov* (Ufa: Bashkirskoe knizhnoe izdatel'stvo, 1968), 111; *Soldaty leninskoi gvardii* (Gor'kii: Volgo-Viatskoe knizhnoe izdatel'stvo, 1974), 201; V. Iakubov, "Aleksandr Dmitrievich Kuznetsov," *Katorga i ssylka* 3:112 (1934): 134, 138; G. Shidlovskii, "O. G. Ellek (Pamiati starogo bol'shevika)," *Katorga i ssylka* 9:106 (1933): 143–44.

31. George Leggett, *The Cheka: Lenin's Political Police* (Oxford: Clarendon Press, 1986), 269.

32. T. S. Krivov, *V leninskom stroiu* (Cheboksary: Chuvashskoe knizhnoe izdatel'stvo, 1969), 110–12, 128; S. M. Pozner, "Rabota boevykh bol'shevistskikh organizatsii 1905–1907 gg.," *Proletarskaia revoliutsiia* 7 (1942): 85; Ivan Myzgin,

So vzvedennym kurkom (Moscow: Molodaia gvardiia, 1964), 21; G. Z. Ioffe, *Krakh Rossiiskoi monarkhicheskoi kontrrevoliutsii* (Moscow: Nauka, 1977), 150. A. Miasnikov (who, incidentally, had become mentally unbalanced while serving a term at hard labor for his combat activities in 1905–7) was a member of the Cheka in 1918, and in June of that year was personally responsible for the murder of Grand Duke Mikhail Aleksandrovich Romanov ("Kommentarii V. I. Nikolaevskogo k knige," in L. Shapiro, "The Communist Party of the Soviet Union" [1958 manuscript], 4, in Nic. 519–30B). Former Bolshevik combatant Konstantin Miachin (V. V. Iakovlev) escorted the family of Nicholas II from Tobol'sk to Ekaterinburg in 1918, where they were subsequently executed (Letter from B. I. Nicolaevsky to T. I. Vulikh dated 25 May 1956, in Nic. 207–16; Ioffe, *Krakh Rossiiskoi monarkhicheskoi kontrrevoliutsii*, 149–51). And Petr Ermakov, another terrorist active in 1905–7, was a member of a three-man firing squad that massacred the imperial family and their servants on 16 July 1918; in the spirit of a true revolutionary fanatic, he later boasted to have shot and killed empress Alexandra, the family doctor, and the cook using his own revolver (Nikolai Ross, ed., *Gibel' tsarskoi sem'i: Materialy sledstviia ob ubiistve tsarskoi sem'i [avgust 1918–fevral' 1920]* [Frankfurt: Posev, 1987], 586; Richard Haliburton, *Seven League Boots* [Indianapolis: Bobbs-Merrill, 1935], 120, 140).

33. For examples of former terrorists of various ideological trends using their past experience for the benefit of Soviet organs of repression, see William J. Fishman, *East End Jewish Radicals, 1875–1914* (London: Duckworth, 1975), 291; Henry J. Tobias, *The Jewish Bund in Russia from Its Origins to 1905* (Stanford, Calif.: Stanford University Press, 1972), 348; R. M. Aslamova-Gol'tsman, "Svetloi pamiati I. Ia. Bartkovskogo," *Katorga i ssylka* 48 (1928): 158–59; "Vospominaniia byvsh. okhrannika," *Bessarabskoe slovo* (1930), in Nic. 203–25; and P. P. Zavarzin, *Rabota tainoi politsii* (1924; rpt. Orange, Conn.: Antiquary, 1986), 157.

34. Brovkin, *Behind the Front Lines*, 408–9.

35. Cited in Pipes, *The Russian Revolution*, 793.

36. Osorgin, *Vremena*, 575, 578.

37. Cited in Pipes, *The Russian Revolution*, 822, 820.

38. Ibid., 829, 832, 836, 790.

The Problem of Revolutionary Violence in Isaac Babel''s Stories

VICTOR PEPPARD

Russian literature from the early 1920s about the Civil War in Russia is usually called "revolutionary romanticism," because it often portrays the Revolution as an elemental force, at once beautiful and terrible, that tosses the contesting forces and the civilian population around in a kind of whirlwind they have no control over.[1] This characterization cannot be accepted without qualification, however, since such depictions of the Revolution in the works of writers like Vsevolod Ivanov, Nikolai Nikitin, Boris Pil'niak, and others were likely to be found in stories that "ironized" the Revolution as much as they "romanticized" it. Furthermore, descriptions of the war, its combat and violence, far from being romantic could be exceptionally graphic and naturalistic. Stories about the Russian Civil War and Revolution often depict successive invasions of towns by Reds, Whites, and sometimes marauding bands, in which the different sides can scarcely be distinguished from each other, as they treat the local population with equal cruelty and violence. The ideological differences between Reds and Whites, so closely associated with this period in history, may figure hardly at all outside of various slogans and proclamations. Particularly in the Russian countryside, local people may be entirely clueless about the programs the combatants claim to represent.

Isaac Babel″s stories that he first wrote and published separately in the early twenties and then published as a cycle called *Red Cavalry (Konarmiia)* in 1926, together with several related stories published later, constitute an extremely provocative and problematic exposition of the question of violence committed in the name of the Revolution.[2] Of particular interest here are two interrelated questions: to what degree does Babel′ romanticize the Revolution, and does he ultimately justify its violence? Babel′ occupied an especially interesting vantage point from which to deal with this question as a so-called "fellow traveler," that is, a writer who was not a party member but who nevertheless sympathized with, or at least "went along with" its general revolutionary aims. In Babel″s case the term fellow traveler assumes a literal meaning in that he worked as a newspaper correspondent who traveled with the Red Cavalry on the Polish front.

Although Babel′ believed that "without elevated ideas and without philosophy there is no literature," far from containing open philosophical declarations, his stories usually set us the task of discovering what their philosophical significance might be.[3] As Andrei Siniavskii puts it, Babel′ "purposely disguised his thought, refused to impose it, or to present it circumstantially in grandiloquent and ostentatious declarations."[4] Even so, Babel′ challenges us to contemplate questions of value and encourages us to make judgments, however cagily and circumspectly he may operate. This is especially relevant, perhaps, in his depiction of the Revolution. Although Babel″s stories contain many of the elements typically found in the stories of the period, he creates a fictional world that is uniquely his own. Part of Babel″s genius was his great elusiveness: just when we think we have Babel′ pinned down on a particular question he is likely to slip out of our grasp and lead us suddenly on a chase in quite a different direction. Edward J. Brown has warned that we will be misreading Babel′ if we look in his stories "for open or hidden commentary on the Revolution . . . Babel″s irony reaches well beyond the immediate and the topical."[5] At the same time, however, Babel′ continually challenges us to make judgments. It is impossible to resist the attempt to try to define Babel″s conception of the Revolution, if only because Babel′ tempts us to do this so ubiquitously and so tantalizingly.

In his work as a newspaper correspondent on the Polish front Babel′ used the pseudonym Kiril Vasil′evich Liutov, and he also used the name Liutov for the narrator in his *Red Cavalry* stories. The name Liutov, from the Russian word for cruel, "liutyi," reflects the narrator′s desire to be tough, while his real nature is (usually) quite mild. Liutov is the main but far from the only perspective through which the central questions of violence and revolution are refracted, and he appears in a number of different guises. The story "Gedali" shows just how complex and subtle is Babel''s treatment of these questions. In conversing with the shopkeeper Gedali, Liutov plays a role that might be termed rabbi to the revolution. Gedali wants desperately to believe in the Revolution; and he wants to say "yes" to both the Revolution and the Sabbath. He thinks that "the Revolution is the good deed of good people" and that good people do not kill, therefore he cannot reconcile the fact that both sides kill and asks, "Who is going to tell Gedali where is the Revolution and where is the Counter-Revolution?" (30). He longs for a "sweet Revolution" and an International of "kind people" in which everyone will have first class rations. Liutov, who has earlier confirmed Gedali's idea that the Revolution cannot help shooting, answers that "they eat [the International] with gunpowder and season it with the best blood" (31). Thus we see in this story that Gedali, while romanticizing his delectable versions of the Revolution and the International, is troubled by the fact that both sides seem to behave alike. The Poles are "evil," but the revolutionaries also want to take away his beloved gramophone, and one of them even threatens to shoot Gedali when he resists giving it up. Here Liutov, whose sad reminiscences of childhood Sabbath eves draw him inexorably to the synagogue and the Jews of Zhitomir, and who is himself hungry—for some "Jewish short-cake, a Jewish glass of tea, and a little of that retired god in a glass of tea" (31)—adopts the guise of a wise rabbi, who helps the infinitely earnest and naïve Gedali, "the founder of an unrealizable International," to understand the inexorable hardness and cruelty of the Revolution.

The encounter between Liutov and Gedali encapsulates the archetypal situation depicted in the Russian Civil War stories mentioned above, in which Reds and Whites alternately take control of towns, each time displaying essentially the same harsh tactics, including shooting people and "appropriating" their property. In "Gedali" Babel' gives us two versions of "the story of the revolution." One is the romantic view in which there is plenty of killing, shooting, and looting, but all in a good cause that will allegedly result in a better life. The other is a more down-to-earth and sober version in which the combatants on both sides share many of the very same decidedly unromantic characteristics, including especially their brutal treatment of civilians. This then is one of Babel''s principal tactics, that is, to offer the reader two or more plausible "texts" within the framework of a single story and leave it to the reader to decide which of them might be the "genuine" one.

The next story in *Red Cavalry* after "Gedali," "My First Goose" ("Moi pervyi gus'"), provides a striking counterpoint to Liutov the wise counselor. He is shown here as a novice with the seemingly impossible task of ingratiating himself, a Jewish law student in spectacles, with a bunch of rough and ready Cossack soldiers he is billeted with. Acting out of a kind of mad inspiration, Liutov crushes the head of a goose under his boot and shoves around the elderly landlady in an attempt to impress the men. These acts, which are a profound betrayal of his own nature, have the desired effect, as the men invite him to eat soup and pork with them. Liutov then reads them an article from *Pravda* by Lenin, and finally sleeps in a hayloft, his legs entwined with theirs. Eliot Borenstein argues convincingly that Liutov's attempts to initiate himself into this soldierly society, which is both attractive and repellant to him, are ultimately frustrated in *Red Cavalry.*[6] Liutov underscores the gap between himself and the men when he writes that he sees the curve in Lenin's speech, whereas they see only its straight line. Nevertheless, Liutov clearly wants to be accepted into this fraternity of fighters for the Revolution, and Lenin's speech is both a symbol of this and a form of homage to the Revolution itself. Violence in "First Goose" is not directly related to the war, but is rather a rite of the passage Liutov is attempting to make. If his violent acts are in any sense mitigated, it is by the fact that he undertakes them as a kind of preemptive strike, since he has learned from the quartermaster that the Cossacks are fond of knifing people who wear glasses. As is almost always the case with Babel', a triumph contains within itself a loss, and we are told that in his sleep Liutov's "heart, crimson with the killing, creaked and leaked" (34).

It is apparent from a number of stories that Liutov has brought with him certain fundamental values that are tested to the limit in the conditions of civil war. First among these is a profound aversion to taking another person's life. The most graphic illustration of this occurs in "The Death of Dolgushov" ("Smert' Dolgushova"). Here, the dying Dolgushov, who is sitting with his guts spilled out before him, begs Liutov to put him out of his misery. The narrator, however, cannot bring himself to commit this act of violent compassion and rides away, leaving Dolgushov to his suffering. When the Cossack Afonka Bida, the first friend Liutov has made at the front, sees what Liutov has done, he is outraged and even threatens to shoot Liutov for his act of cowardice. The situation described in "Dolgushov" is made particularly poignant by the fact that the values Liutov has brought with him to the front—in this case his great reluctance to kill—have been stood on their head. In the context of war these values may be not only inapplicable, they may get their practitioner in trouble. Babel' is obviously fond of such contrapuntal motifs and themes. Whereas in "First Goose" the measure of the narrator's cowardice is his willingness to commit an act of violence, in "Dolgushov" his inability to commit violence when it would have been the right and merciful thing to do is proof of this cowardice.

The story "Squadron Commander Trunov" ("Eskadronnyi Trunov") contains one of the most complex and ambiguous treatments of the Civil War's violence in all of Babel''s work. The story begins and ends with the ceremonial burial of Trunov, who was killed earlier in the day. He is interred with all the honors befitting a "worldwide hero," including a full salute by a three-inch cannon; a speech by division commander Pugachov, in which he eulogizes other deceased members of the division as a "phalanx that was beating as the hammer of history on the anvil of future ages"; the playing of "The Internationale" by an orchestra; more shots; and a wreath of flowers (90). Liutov, who kisses the dead Trunov's forehead, is made to feel bad, because he had quarreled with him earlier that day. The argument had taken place after Trunov, wounded in the head and bleeding profusely, had executed two Polish prisoners and told Liutov to erase their names from the list of prisoners the latter is in charge of keeping. Liutov refuses to condone the killings, commenting, "Trotsky obviously doesn't write orders for you, Pavel" (94).

On the same morning that he killed the two prisoners Trunov insisted that the rules of war be followed when he prevented one of his men from making off with the clothing of an old man who had been bayoneted. In contrast, Trunov's final act is the epitome of bravery. He hands over command of the squadron, gives away his boots, and he and the man he has just reprimanded take on three American planes in a machine-gun battle that results in their deaths. At the end of the story Babel' refers to the ceremonial place in which Trunov is buried, as though to underline his genuine heroism in the cause of the Revolution. One might even say that this story embodies Babel''s most romantic treatment of the Revolution. With Babel', however, there is almost always a catch, which in this case is the fact that Trunov, for all of his manly courage, has committed the brutal, senseless murders of two men. Captured in their underwear, they were utterly defenseless and posed no threat to anyone. Babel''s description of the younger one is particularly interesting. The young man looks like "a German gymnast from a good circus with a white German chest and with sideburns" (93). Liutov also notices how the man turned toward him "two nipples . . . on a high chest and threw back his sweaty white hair" (94). The Red soldiers are particularly taken with the high quality underwear of this young man, whose nails are also well cared for. Without warning Trunov shoots the young man dead, shattering his skull and splattering his brains on Liutov. Babel″s description of this remarkable event is, as so often happens in his depiction of violent acts, devoid of any commentary or any emotion whatsoever, as though it took place in another place and time and had nothing to do with the narrator.[7] Liutov appears to remain calm and indifferent, but the reader may detect in his detailed, almost tender description of the young man both affinity and attraction. Understated homoeroticism, such as that found here, alternates with heterosexual eroticism in many of Babel″s stories.

Trunov's behavior here is extremely contradictory and disturbing. He is irritated that the prisoners don't immediately identify the officers among them, and suffering from his wound, he is in an agitated state and conscious of his imminent death. Yet, he has sufficient control of himself to write out a note in which he hands over command. His hostility toward the younger prisoner (who is a Pole and not a German) no doubt stems from class hatred for this handsome, well-cared-for gentleman. Ultimately, none of these considerations amount to a reasonable justification for his execution of the two men. We are left at the end of the story with a portrait of Trunov as both a genuine hero of the Revolution and a real brute, a man who is extremely scrupulous about certain rules of war and completely contemptuous of others. We receive no moralizing guidance, such as Tolstoy might have given, as Babel' leaves us to contemplate what these contradictions might mean.

The theme of making the Revolution appears in a number of different guises in Babel″s stories, as for example in one called "Berestechko." Here at a meeting of the townsfolk, who are tanners, Jews, and peasants, Division Commander Vinogradov tells them about the Second Congress of the Comintern in a rapturous voice. Liutov, meanwhile, was "wandering along the walls, where nymphs with their eyes cut out were dancing an ancient round dance" (71). Vinogradov continues to convince "the distracted petty bourgeoisie and the Jews who had been robbed" that "You are the power. Everything here is yours. There are no nobles. I'm starting the elections to the Revolutionary Committee . . ." (71). As Vinogradov carries on with his exhortation, Liutov finds and reads a letter written in French from 1820 by someone who is asking about Napoleon's death and announcing the birth of a child. It is hard not to conclude here that Liutov's wandering about the town suggests he is in search of something entirely different from the routine of war and revolution. What he longs for, judging by the things his attention fastens on, is the world of art and imagination, as reflected in the dancing nymphs, and indeed, life itself, as exemplified in the letter. The earnestness of Vinogradov in the face of his motley, indifferent audience can only make his strivings in the name of the Revolution seem fruitless, if not downright ludicrous.

As with his themes, Babel' plays variations on his character types, one of which is the true believer in the Revolution. Each of these expresses his fealty to the cause in different ways. Gedali is a romantic intellectual and scholar of the Talmud; Trunov is a man of action; and Vinogradov is a propagandist and organizer. "The Story of a Certain Horse" ("Istoriia odnoi loshadi") contains a similar character named Khlebnikov, whose idealistic beliefs in the aims of the Revolution cause him to resign from the Party when Division Commander Savitskii takes his horse away from him. In his resignation Khlebnikov writes that "the Communist Party was founded, I assume, for happiness and hard truth without limit, and it should also look after little people" (64). When Commander Savitskii rips up this statement, Khlebnikov appears to lose his mind, and eventually he is demobilized. Liutov is saddened by the loss of Khlebnikov, because "we were both moved by the same passions. We both looked on the world as on a meadow in May, as on a meadow where women and horses walked" (65). Liutov's evocation of a pure, lyrical romanticism here is another expression of what he longs for in the midst of the violence of war that surrounds him.

Liutov is acutely aware that he is unable to adapt his values and sensibilities to the exigencies of war, as we see in the story "After the Battle" ("Posle boia"). Here he has been ordered to send soldiers who are fleeing the scene of battle back into it. When one of them, Gulimov, tells him to go first and shoves the hilt of his sword into Liutov's chest, Liutov scratches him as hard as he can. This is only a prelude to another fight, as Liutov gets in an argument with the Cossack Akinfiev over the fact that he, Liutov, did not load his gun for battle. Liutov seems to get the better of the scrap as he knocks out one of his opponent's teeth, but at the end of the story he is still "begging fate for the simplest of abilities—the ability to kill a man" (124). In "After the Battle" it appears that whether Liutov follows orders and does the "right thing," as when he attempts to turn Gulimov back to the battle, or whether he goes against the code of battle and does the "wrong thing," as when he fails to load his gun, he will wind up in a life-threatening situation, usually a violent confrontation that he will have to claw his way out of. We may conclude therefore that in war there are various codes of conduct for different situations, but there is no larger scheme of justice in operation, only something more akin to the law of the jungle.

Keeping in mind Siniavskii's observation that Babel' does not force his ideas on us, I would like to return briefly to "The Death of Dolgushov," where he deals with questions about the value of life and death. In this story the character Grishchuk may be seen as the philosopher, as he keeps asking the question, "What do women work for?" He also asks, "What are courtings and weddings for, and why do godfathers play at weddings?" (44). Dolgushov first appears in the story when Grishchuk and Liutov see him dying, holding his innards in his hands. "'It's funny to me,' said Grishchuk sorrowfully and pointed at a man [Dolgushov] sitting by the road. 'It's funny to me what women work for'" (45). This glaring disjuncture between Grishchuk's repeating the words "its funny to me" *(smekha mne)* and his pointing to the fatally wounded Dolgushov is typical of Babel''s technique. I believe that the meaning of Grishchuk's observations is this: what is the point of women exerting themselves to go through the rituals of courtship and marriage when their men only wind up in a pool of blood and guts? Put another way, is not Babel' suggesting through the running commentary of his character Grishchuk on the horrific action around him that all of our human strivings are in vain, if we are likely to suffer a senseless and violent death despite them? As so often happens with Babel', he maneuvers by indirection but nevertheless forces us to confront an urgent question.

A number of Babel''s stories concern the innocent victims of the war's violence who are primarily women and Jews living in border towns such as Berestechko, Kozin, and Zhitomir. In the story "Berestechko" Babel' describes how some Cossacks execute an elderly Jew for espionage. As Richard Hallett observes, when Kudria slits the old man's throat, he does so "dispassionately," making sure not to spill blood on himself.[8] Although the old man in Berestechko struggles, the people who are objects of violence in Babel''s stories, such as the old landlady in "First Goose," usually remain passive. Her only reaction to the narrator's crude acts is to say that she wants to hang herself. Babel''s sketches of the plight of women in war, however brief they may be, contain an implicit but powerful indictment of the soldiers who abuse them. The story called "At Our Father Makhno's" ("U bat'ki nashego

Makhno"), from 1924, is about a woman named Rukhlia who has been gang-raped by six different men and on the next day has to suffer the taunts of a boy named Kikin, who participated in the rape by holding her head but refused his turn when he took offense at someone going before him. She does not respond but merely goes about her business, and as does the landlady of "First Goose," remains stoic in the face of the severest physical and psychological abuse. For the most part in *Red Cavalry* Babel' shows both the perpetrators and the victims of violence acting as virtual automatons, in this way underscoring the way in which it dehumanizes them.

The soldiers in Red Cavalry are typically indifferent to the plight of the local women and believe they have an absolute right to use them as they see fit, as happens in "A Hardworking Woman" ("Staratel'naia zhenshchina"), where three men arrange to pay Anelia two pounds of sugar for group sex. When she cannot finish with the third man, they blame her for being too greedy. (They had suggested she bring along a girlfriend, but she thought she could handle the job on her own.)

"The Biography of Pavlichenko, Matvei Rodionovich" ("Zhizneopisanie Pavlichenki, Matveia Rodionycha") stands out for its depiction of perhaps the most telling and far ranging critique Babel' makes of violence carried out (ostensibly) in the name of the Revolution. The violent culminating scene of this story is also one of the most powerful and provocative of the many in Babel''s works. Using the technique of skaz narration Babel' has Pavlichenko tell the story of how his landlord treated him during the years before the Revolution, how he held debts over him and (purportedly) took advantage of his wife. The climactic passages of the story describe how Pavlichenko, now a general in the Red Army, gets revenge on his former master. He has a letter from Lenin that reads, "In the name of the people and for the establishment of a brighter future, I command Pavlichenko, Matvei Rodionovich, to take various people's lives at his discretion." Pavlichenko then proceeds to kick his former master to death in front of the man's insane wife, who is holding a sword in her hand. Here is how Babel' describes this awful scene: "I stomped him for about an hour or more and during that time I got to know life to the fullest. With shooting, I'm gonna to tell ya, ya can only get rid of a person—shooting, that's a pardon for him and a cheap way out for yourself—with shooting ya don't get to his soul, where that soul is and how it shows itself. But me, sometimes I don't spare myself, and sometimes I'll stomp an enemy for an hour or more, as I want to get to know life, what this life of ours is all about . . ." (59).

Whereas some of Babel''s characters, such as Trunov and Kudria, kill without emotion, Pavlichenko, thirsting for revenge, does so with a sense of joy and duty, as he positively revels in pummeling his former master to death. It is telling that Pavlichenko rejects the more sudden methods of shooting or knifing in favor of trampling his enemy over an extended period of time. If a character like Grishchuk in "Dolgushov" appears to be a kind of stand-in philosopher for Babel' himself, then Pavlichenko appears in the role of a false philosopher. Not satisfied merely to carry out Lenin's orders, Pavlichenko has pretensions at attaining an understanding of life itself. Babel', of course, leaves it to the reader to conclude how profoundly perverted this philosophy is.

One can only wonder in retrospect how Babel' managed to have "Pavlichenko" published at all. Perhaps Babel' succeeded by using the ploy of putting the magic words "in the name of the people" and "for the establishment of a brighter future" in an order from Lenin. In any case, Babel' undermines the Revolution's own emblematic words by placing them in the mouth of a remorseless killer. (Pavlichenko's status as a Red general may also help to place him out of the censor's reach.) The story's last bizarre scene illustrates vividly and grotesquely what can happen when you place power over others' lives in the hands of a killer and thereby serves as a withering indictment of the mindless way in which the Revolution justified violence carried out it its name.[9]

Given that Babel''s mercurial prose is supremely resistant to finalizing interpretations, can we say nevertheless that Babel' ultimately justifies the violence of the Revolution? As we have seen here, Babel''s treatment of the Civil War is clearly romantic and heroic in places and decidedly ironic and skeptical in others; and in stories like "Trunov" these antinomies may alternate, coexist, or even compete with each other. I believe that this is the essence of Babel', that is, his ability to set out parallel philosophies, or possible philosophies for us to contemplate and/or debate. Even when we have decoded Babel''s philosophy in stories like "Dolgushov" and "Pavlichenko"—if indeed we have done that—we see that his real task is not to propose prescriptions about how better to conduct war and revolution, but rather to make us ponder such questions and other great questions of life anew.

Notes

1. I delivered a paper on this topic at the American Association for the Advancement of Slavic Studies National Convention, November 24, 2002. The

comments of Marcus Levitt were very helpful in focusing my ideas on the subject, but naturally I take responsibility for the way I have formulated them in this article.

2. Gregory Frieden, a major scholar of Babel', gives a fine overview of his life and works, including commentary on early reactions to his treatment of the Revolution in "Isaac Babel," in *European Writers: The Twentieth Century*, vol. 11, ed. George Stade (New York: Charles Scribners' Sons, 1990), 1885–1914. Charles Rougle illuminates the important themes of the art and the artist in Babel''s work in "Art and the Artist in Babel's 'Guy de Maupassant,'" *Russian Review* 48 (1989): 171–80. Alexander Zholkovsky's provocative and important investigation of Babel' includes "A Memo from the Underground (Babel and Dostoevsky)," *Elementa* 1 (1994): 305–20; and *Babel'* [in Russian] (Moscow: Carte Blanche, 1994), written together with M. B. Iampol'skii. This latter book is a wide-ranging treatment of Babel' that is particularly good on the many erotic and sexual aspects of his fiction.

3. Babel' said this in 1934 at the first Congress of the Soviet Writers' Union, and the quotation can be found in his *Sochineniia*, 2 vols., ed. A. N. Pirozhkova, (Moscow: Khudozhestvennaia literatura, 1990), 2:381. This and other translations from Babel' are my own. Subsequent quotations from Babel''s stories will be indicated by parenthetical references to page numbers from *Sochineniia* 2.

4. See Siniavskii's article "Isaac Babel" in *Major Soviet Writers: Essays in Criticism*, ed. Edward J. Brown (New York: Oxford University Press, 1971), 309.

5. See Brown's *Russian Literature since the Revolution* (New York: Macmillan Publishing, 1973), 177, where he also notes that each of Babel''s stories is based on a "grim incongruity."

6. See Borenstein's stimulating analysis of *Red Cavalry* in *Men without Women: Masculinity and Revolution in Russian Fiction, 1917–1929* (Durham, N.C.: Duke University Press, 2000), 73–124.

7. Gleb Struve was one of the first critics to note the detachment with which Babel' often describes violence in his *Russian Literature under Lenin and Stalin, 1917–1953* (Norman: University of Oklahoma Press, 1971), 71.

8. See Richard Hallett, *Isaac Babel* (New York: Frederick Ungar Publishing, 1973), 37.

9. I am grateful to Tatyana Novikov for her most perceptive comments about this story and the manner in which Pavlichenko carries out the killing.

State Violence in the Stalin Period

J. ARCH GETTY

Stalinism has become practically a synonym for state violence directed against the population. The massive scale and severity of this violence led many to put Stalinism into the same category with Nazi Germany: twentieth-century "totalitarian" states that recognized no limits to the use of harsh and sometimes arbitrary terror against their own people in order to retain power and accomplish their ideological goals. Linking the two regimes is controversial, but whatever one thinks of it, it is clear that Stalinism produced one of the greatest bloodbaths of an already bloody century.

Since the fall of the USSR and the opening of some of its secret archives, we have learned a great deal more about the nature of the regime and the violence it inflicted. Obviously, a complete new analysis of Stalinist violence is beyond our scope; here we seek to provide a rough overview of some of the interpretive views and new factual material on this grisly topic. Specifically, we shall confine ourselves to what we now know about the scope and scale of the main waves of terror and to current interpretations of Stalinist violence.

The numbers are staggering. Although we do not yet have precise figures, the best evidence tells us that from 1917 to Stalin's death, between nine and eleven million persons passed through the Gulag labor

Table 1. Political Arrests and Sentences by Soviet Security Police, 1921–1952

year	shot	to camps and prison	exiled	other sentences
1921	9,701	21,724	1,817	2,587
1922	1,962	2,656	166	1,219
1923	414	2,336	2,044	0
1924	2,550	4,151	5,724	0
1925	2,433	6,851	6,274	437
1926	990	7,547	8,571	696
1927	2,363	12,667	11,235	171
1928	869	16,211	15,640	1,037
1929	2,109	25,853	24,517	3,741
1930	20,201	114,443	58,816	14,609
1931	10,651	105,683	63,269	1,093
1932	2,728	73,946	36,017	29,228
1933	2,154	138,903	54,262	44,345
1934	2,056	59,451	5,994	11,498
1935	1,229	185,846	33,601	46,400
1936	1,118	219,418	23,719	30,415
1937	353,074	429,311	1,366	6,914
1938	328,618	205,509	16,842	3,289
1939	2,552	54,666	3,783	2,888
1940	1,649	65,727	2,142	2,288
1941	8,001	65,000	1,200	1,210
1942	23,278	88,809	7,070	5,249
1943	3,579	68,887	4,787	1,188
1944	3,029	70,610	649	821
1945	4,252	116,681	1,647	668
1946	2,896	117,943	1,498	957
1947	1,105	76,581	666	458
1948	0	72,552	419	298
1949	0	64,509	10,316	300
1950	475	54,466	5,225	475
1951	1,609	49,142	3,425	599
1952	1,612	25,824	773	591
Total	**799,257**	**2,623,903**	**413,474**	**215,669**

Source: State Archive of the Russian Federation, fond 9401, op. 1, delo 4157, ll. 201–3, 205.

camps. Already by 1934, half a million persons were in these camps, and at the time of Stalin's death in 1953 the number had grown to more than 1.7 million, with another 750,000 in less severe labor colonies. Although most inmates were in camp for nonpolitical criminal offenses and most were released after relatively short sentences, others were long-term inmates.

More than a million persons died in the camps during these years.[1] If we add to this the numbers of known executions, deaths of persons deported or forcibly "resettled," and probable deaths in prisons and in transit, we reach a rough total of at least 2.5 million deaths of persons while they were being held in detention during the Stalin period. In addition to these narrowly defined "custodial" deaths, one must add those who died from starvation (particularly in 1932–33 and 1946–47) and the "collateral" victims of wartime and postwar deportations. Although historians debate whether such additional deaths were intentional or ancillary results of regime policies and blunders, the most conservative estimates posit some six million deaths, intentional and indirect, directly attributable to Stalinist policies.

When we think of repression during the Stalin years, we usually think of those arrested for real or imagined political offenses ranging from real conspiracies and opposition to careless remarks critical of the regime. Although, as the table shows, large-scale repression was constant throughout the Stalin period, there were two great waves of political violence: the collectivization of agriculture (1930–33) and the Great Terror (1936–38). A later wave in 1945–46 was related to returning Soviets who had been German prisoners of war and who were temporarily held in camps for processing; most of these were freed in short order after investigation.[2] Both the collectivization and Great Terror periods saw mass arrests of people according to categories, rather than individual accusations, and both were of such a scale as to leave lasting marks in the psychological and social consciousness of Soviet citizens.

In a series of incremental steps that began in 1928, the Stalinist leadership sought to take control of agricultural production and marketing. Never comfortable with the private farming and free grain market the Bolsheviks had tolerated since 1921, Stalin by the end of the 1920s came to believe that peasants were deliberately withholding grain from the market in order to get higher prices from state purchasers, who bought grain for the army and for distribution in the cities. One-time "emergency" state seizures of grain from peasants in 1927 and 1928 at low fixed prices became more frequent. Moving next against "kulaks" (prosperous peasants whom the regime identified as ringleaders and troublemakers) in 1929 and 1930, the regime used increasing pressure and violence against those who resisted its confiscatory policies, culminating in Stalin's statement of November 1929 announcing the "liquidation of kulaks as a class." This was a signal for a general war of expropriation against kulaks, as well as other peasants who resisted or opposed the offensive and who, regardless of their property status, were classified as kulaks by the regime.

The campaign quickly took on a life of its own as local communist activists, eager to demonstrate their solidarity with Stalin's plans, encouraged the offensive with overly optimistic reports to Moscow. The Stalinist leaders accordingly raised targets, goals, and repression. Although it is not at all clear that Stalin had planned it from the beginning, by early 1930 the regime announced that the total collectivization of agriculture, the abolition of all private farming, was the new goal. Based on self-delusion, mendacity, or both, Stalin claimed that huge numbers of peasants were voluntarily joining the new collective farms.

With its expanding goals and changing targets, collectivization demonstrates a common feature of Stalinist repression: a wild, only loosely controlled campaign characterized by excess and improvisation more than tight control or planning. Local activists, taking their cues from Stalin, pushed the boundaries of the operation far beyond the original goals. Stalin, encouraged by their "achievements," pushed them even further in a kind of vicious circle of violence. For example, in the first days of 1930, Stalin's deputy Molotov announced that 60,000 kulaks were to be sent to camps and 150,000 kulak households (about 5 percent of all peasant households) were to be deported to far-off regions of the USSR and thus "dekulakized." In the event, by the end of 1931, 381,000 households had been dekulakized and exiled: an astounding two million persons violently uprooted, stripped of their property, and forcibly deported in boxcars; some 30,000 were executed in those two years alone.[3] The term "kulak" became a plastic, catch-all accusation that could be applied to anyone who opposed, or who might oppose, the regime. Eventually, as Stalin later told Winston Churchill, some ten million "kulaks" were expropriated and/or killed, imprisoned, exiled, or sent to labor camps.

The result of all this was disaster, and not only for those directly targeted by Stalinist plans. Local firebrands, stirred by the idea of "building socialism," attacked churches, village elders, and traditional peasant culture in general. Recent research shows that peasants resisted on a large scale, with pitched battles between peasants and regime forces and entire districts in revolt.[4] Peasants slaughtered their livestock and refused to sow crops in protest; the regime increased the pressure and refused to relent, going so far as to increase grain demands from the hungry peasants and to enact a law making it a capital offense to pilfer state property—even a single stalk of grain. The result was a catastrophic famine in 1932–33. We still do not have solid data on the numbers dying of starvation, but the best estimates are from two to four million. Peasants dropped dead in the streets. Children died in their mother's arms or beside the road. Stalin, through the Soviet press, denied to the country and the world that any famine existed.[5]

The other large-scale outburst of state violence was the Great Purges, or Great Terror, of 1936–38. As with collectivization, the opening of Soviet-era archives since 1990 has given us a fuller if not yet a complete picture of the violence.

From October 1936 to the end of 1938, the secret police (NKVD) arrested just over 1.5 million people.[6] We now know that the Great Terror of the 1930s actually consisted of several discrete but sometimes overlapping campaigns and operations. Until recently, the best-known of these was Stalin's purge of the party and state elite. Particularly in 1937 and 1938, military, economic, party, and state institutions were virtually decapitated. Prominent leaders in these fields were accused of being "enemies of the people," spies, and traitors and were arrested along with their subordinates in swift police sweeps. People were encouraged to denounce their chiefs and each other. The party leaderships of all the USSR's provinces and republics were destroyed, practically to the last person. Economic planning organizations were purged and re-purged: the leaders of the Commissariat of Heavy Industry, responsible for the country's rapid industrialization, were liquidated, and then their replacements were annihilated. A third wave purged the replacements of the replacements.[7]

On June 11, 1937, the world was shocked at the Soviet press announcement that eight of the most senior officers of the Red Army had been arrested and indicted for treason and espionage on behalf of the Germans and Japanese. In the ten days following, 980 senior commanders were arrested. Many were tortured and shot. In the months that followed, the Soviet military establishment was devastated by arrests and executions. In 1937, 7.7 percent of the officer corps were dismissed for political reasons and never reinstated; in 1938 another 3.7 percent were removed. The attrition rate was much greater at higher ranks, with senior officers falling in huge numbers. In 1937 and 1938, more than 34,000 military officers were discharged for political reasons, according to the latest estimates. Of these, 11,596 were reinstated by 1940, leaving the fates of more than 22,000 officers unknown; they simply disappeared.[8]

Although this purge of the USSR's elite is the best known aspect of the Great Purges, the wave of terror also hit ordinary people. From mid-1937 to mid-1938, the secret police carried out a mass terror, known as the "kulak operation," against ordinary peasants, common criminals, various marginal types (in the Soviet sense: priests, former members of other political parties, former tradesmen), and "socially dangerous elements": people who had committed no crime to that point but who might in the future. Based on a Stalin telegram complaining that disgruntled peasants and criminals "are the chief instigators of all sorts of crimes," this operation saw the arrest of just over 700,000 ordinary persons, about half of whom were summarily shot.[9] Additionally, a series of "national operations" targeted immigrants and Soviet citizens of German, Polish, Baltic, Korean, and other origins. In 1937 and 1938, 366,000 such persons were arrested, and the overwhelming majority of them were immediately executed.[10]

Of the 1.5 million secret police arrests in the 1936–38 Great Terror, 668,000 led to execution in 1937 and 1938. This two-year figure comprises 87 percent of all executions for the entire Stalin period (1929–53). Nearly all the rest of the 1.5 million people were sentenced to hard labor camps for terms up to twenty-five years. In all these cases, the victims were tried before summary special courts (often ad hoc troikas) in "expedited procedure," as the documents laconically attest, and quickly sentenced. Of the 1.5 million, only 13,000 were exonerated at trial.

The population of all labor camps, labor colonies, and prisons doubled during the Great Terror to 2,022,976 persons by the beginning of 1939. This means a total increase in prisoners in 1937–38 of 1,006,030.[11] Of course, aside from the 668,000 executions in the terror of 1937–38, many others died in the regime's custody in the late 1930s. If we add the figure we have for executions to the number of persons who died in Gulag camps, the few figures we have on mortality in prisons and labor colonies, and the number of peasants known to have died in exile, we reach a total figure of 1,473,424 immediate deaths during the two-year Great Terror.[12]

How do we explain such massive, repeated violence? One popular explanation centers on Stalin's personality. Through his political skill and cunning, Stalin emerged as the first among equals following Lenin's death and then as dictator. With total power concentrated in his hands, his troubled psychology—"sickly suspicion," as Khrushchev would call it—emerged. Insecure about his revolutionary credentials, his intellect, and the degree to which his comrades respected him, Stalin launched a paranoid terror to rid himself of those who knew too much about him, those who threatened or challenged his ego, those who were too independent to worship him.[13] Consistent with psychohistorical analysis of other historical figures, this explanation has become a powerful one.

Critics, however, wonder how well we can analyze the psychology of a person who left no diary and practically no personal letters or papers of any kind. Can we really know anything concrete about how he thought and felt? Other critics are prepared to grant a primary role in the terror to Stalin's personality, but note that this fails to explain how the eccentricities of one man could destroy millions of people. Even aside from sycophantic hero-worshippers, Stalin had plenty of help. Thousands of party members participated in the terror, and behind them millions to one degree or another accepted it. The social, mass dimension of the terror needs explanation beyond the psyche of one person.

One such social explanation sees Stalin in a particular social and historical context, reviving the argument that "great men" have a limited ability to make history and are rather products of their times. Here, the emphasis is on the complete breakdown of Russian society and economy resulting from World War I, the Russian Revolution, and the subsequent Civil War. This national collapse saw the destruction and discrediting of all kinds of authority in the wake of the fall of the tsar. It led to anarchy, chaos, unbelievably cruel violence, starvation, and the near-dismemberment of the country by foreign powers in 1918–21. With social collapse came a belief in violence as a valid means of social defense and a tool of politics. Thus, the cruelty and mass violence of Stalinism had strong and recent historical roots in popular belief and psychology. Stalin emerges as a kind of historical necessity, produced by violent times to use violence to pull the country together, to modernize it and to make it strong and able to resist dismemberment at the hands of its more prosperous neighbors.[14] Such a Stalin is presented to us without ideological or psychological characteristics, and even though he emerges here as a product of events more than maker of them, his purported accomplishments make him seem a bit too heroic, if not downright positive, to many critics.

Another influential set of explanations finds fatal ideological flaws in Bolshevism. Marxism and Marxism-Leninism laid claim to scientific infallibility. Their adherents believed that they had found The Truth about how societies work, about how they were evolving. This led them to conceive of their ideology, their movement, their party as infallible agents of history. Against this truth there could be no honest disagreement, no legitimate dissent or no loyal opposition. Anyone who stood in the way, or threatened to stand in the way, was an enemy to be destroyed without pity or remorse. Once a paranoid dictator seized control of such a fanatical movement of true believers, the logic of rooting out "enemies of the people" took hold on a broad scale and became a mass terror.[15]

This explanation also has its critics. Some historians wonder about the real power of ideology as an explanation. Bolsheviks tended to believe a variety of things, and even in its most monolithic periods, party members were rarely of one mind. Moreover, looking at the twists and turns of Bolshevik policy in the 1920s, 1930s, and 1940s on economic and social policy, it is not easy to find ideological consistency. Much more obvious is a kind of pragmatism in which the regime decides what it must do and then comes up with an ideological justification for it. For these critics, ideology is not the answer.

Another enduring explanation for terror, related to the ideological one, is the theory of totalitarianism. Here, the Stalinist system is one of a number of twentieth-century movements (the other notable one being Hitler's Nazi state) that sought to penetrate every aspect of life and society in order to mobilize a total society for some goal. No ties or social groupings outside the official ones are permitted; individuals are "atomized," and informal civil society is replaced by an all-encompassing official one. In order to maintain its momentum and justify its existence, the totalitarian state has to continually find, identify, and mobilize the persecution of enemies as a means of bonding society, purifying it, and drawing citizens into the prescribed monolithic pattern.[16]

The viability of a totalitarian movement would appear to depend on its ability to exert something like total control, and only with twentieth-century technologies of surveillance and control is it possible to make and control an entire society. Yet many students of both Nazi Germany and Stalinist Russia have noted the survival and thriving of very non-totalitarian elements within both systems. Bureaucratic infighting and factionalism, disobedience in the regimes' own chains of command, poor communications, and popular resistance all speak against total control. Further, the regimes' strong tendency to zig and zag, change their minds and policies, and in general to contradict themselves in a mass of improvisations also do not appear to support the view of a monolithic or even a new type of regime.[17]

A recent variant on the long-lived totalitarian theory uses tools from literary and philosophical analysis, finding the answer in "modernity."

With roots in the Enlightenment belief in the use of science and reason to perfect society and humanity, modernity as a mode of thinking and governing is used to explain a number of trends in twentieth-century politics. The new desire of states to measure their populations, spy on them, mobilize them rationally, and even purify them are aspects of modernity's drive toward perfection. Terror is seen as ideological, with modern states cultivating society as if it were a garden, pulling out "evil" weeds and nurturing "good" ones in order to build the perfect society.[18]

Such theories see modernity as a uniquely modern phenomenon, but critics have wondered about its novelty in history. The Domesday Book counted and ordered people and resources more than a thousand years ago. The ancient Assyrians and Byzantines were masters at pulling out evil weeds, moving and transplanting whole populations in a not irrational manner. The Spanish Inquisition also sought to perfect society, and it is arguable whether its goal of a uniform godly heaven on earth differs qualitatively from Nazi or Stalinist or Enlightenment goals of perfection. And, after all, Herodotus and Machiavelli used gardening metaphors to instruct their princely auditors to prune and weed in order to hold on to power. In other words, critics of the modernity explanation wonder if all these actions do not fall under traditional rubrics of statecraft. If all that separates modernity from such apparent antecedents is the modern technology of increased efficiency, then twentieth-century "modernity" becomes a matter of technological, quantitative degree rather than a qualitative innovation.

Another recent trend in understanding Stalinist violence (which, like those above, is not without its critics) is less interested in finding theoretical explanations and seeks a more empirical, typological, and contingent approach. According to this view, there were many forms of Stalinist violence; there was no single type and thus no single theory able to explain it.[19]

Sometimes Stalinist violence was straightforward and traditional, inflicted on those who opposed the current policies of the regime. Collectivization was a clear example of such suppressive, hegemonic violence. The regime decided on a drastic, revolutionary change in agriculture. Peasants resisted. The regime crushed them with massive and cruel violence. Mass violence was also used on occasion to punish entire ethnicities, as the Stalinist deportations of Chechens, Crimean Tatars, and others indicate.

Other times, state violence could be retaliatory. When in 1926 a Soviet diplomat was assassinated in Warsaw, Stalin and the Politburo decided to execute several dozen "anti-Soviet" people who had long been held in Soviet prisons and thus could have had no contact with the assassination. In their twisted counsels, the Stalinists decided that world imperialism had struck a blow against the socialist state by instigating the Poles to kill the Soviet diplomat. But the unfortunates dragged out of Soviet prisons and shot were not Polish. They were Russian anti-Bolsheviks and were executed as hostages to strike a blow of revenge against their fellow imperialists abroad. Precisely the same thing happened in 1934, when Stalinist intimate Sergei Kirov was assassinated. At first believing that the killing was another nefarious imperialist plot of foreign origin, the Bolsheviks executed several dozen long-term anti-Bolshevik prisoners already in Soviet jails. To the Stalinists, all prisoners were potential hostages against the unceasing evil plots of foreign capitalists, and their retaliation recalled the violence inflicted against innocent groups during the Russian Civil War.

Another kind of Stalinist violence was heuristic or demonstrative and is best seen in the various public trials of the Stalin period. We now know conclusively that Stalin personally selected victims, edited testimony, and determined sentences in advance. Heuristic violence involved contrived penal spectacles that, like medieval morality plays, presented good and evil for public (peasant) consumption. When, in the three famous Moscow show trials of the 1930s, former heroes of the Revolution stood in the dock and beat their breasts and confessed to astonishing crimes of treason and espionage, they were providing negative examples of the danger of oppositional opinions, consorting with foreigners, and conspiracy in general.

Demonstrative violence, also best conveyed in show trials, was a similar tool of administration. In 1937, for example, Stalin faced a problem with falling livestock production. He decided that the main problem was the carelessness of local agricultural and veterinary officials. Accordingly, he sent telegrams to several provinces ordering party officials to stage local show trials of randomly selected livestock officials, who were to be charged with sabotage and punished "with the application of the death penalty." Staging a grisly and lethal event, *pour encourager les autres,* was thus a means of stimulating administration and obedience.

It perhaps goes without saying that in both heuristic and demonstrative show trials, the guilt or innocence of the accused was entirely beside the point. In 1948 prominent Soviet Jews belonging to the Jewish Anti-Fascist Committee were tried and executed for espionage connections to the United States and Israel. It made no difference that the committee had been officially sponsored by the Soviet government just a few years before. It made no difference that the charges were so ludicrous that the handpicked judge found it necessary to report back to the Politburo that it was impossible to convict the accused. He was told that he was missing the point: the Politburo had already decided the lessons and conclusion of the trial and he should go back and convict and sentence as ordered.

On other occasions, Stalinist violence was preemptive and prophylactic. The massacre of the Soviet elite that formed part of the Great Purges seems to have been of this type. Stalin decided that significant numbers of his own subordinates and colleagues were potentially unreliable in the event of a coming war. In order to prevent future plots or fifth columns against his leadership, he decided to destroy the possibly unreliable. In his latter-day memoirs, dictated decades after Stalin's death, the dictator's unrepentant right-hand man Viacheslav Molotov admitted that most of the administrators and leaders killed in the 1930s had probably not done anything wrong. The problem was what they might do (or not do) in the future. "We were obligated in 1937 [to ensure] that in time of war there would be no fifth column. Really, among Bolsheviks there were and are those who are good and faithful when everything is good, when the country and the party are not in danger. But if anything happens, they shiver and desert . . . and the main thing is that in the decisive moment there was no relying on them. . . . If we did not take stern measures, the devil knows how these troubles would have ended up. . . . And we did not trust; that's the thing. . . . Of course, demands came from Stalin, of course things went too far, but I think that everything was permitted thanks to one thing: only to hold on to power!"[20]

Similar prophylactic violence was also applied in the form of the deportation and exile of large groups. In 1939 when the Soviets entered Poland, and in 1940 when they entered the Baltic states, large segments of the "bourgeois" (and thus potentially anti-Soviet) population were rounded up and deported to the Soviet interior.

Looking at the various impulses behind these various types of Stalinist violence, one notes two things. First, all of these modes of Stalinist violence have long unfortunate pedigrees in history. From the dawn of time, authoritarian regimes have butchered opponents and potential opponents, staged heuristic political spectacles, executed hostages, and uprooted suspect populations as matters of brutal statecraft. In this sense, Stalinist state violence seems rather traditional, primordial, and primitive if not atavistic. Second, regardless of the verbiage of its propaganda, within the leadership there was no attempt to justify violence by reference to theory, total control, scientific infallibility, purification, weeding or perfecting society, or even ideology. Stalinist leaders did exchange purportedly theoretical essays and "theses" on various arcane points of Marxist theory. But when it came to economic administration, social policy, and certainly to violence, the talk was hardheaded and practical, and ideology was not their guide. They were attacking opponents, shooting hostages, staging educational executions, and preempting treason. As Molotov noted so succinctly, it was all about one thing, "only to hold on to power."

It may seem strange at first glance that as late as 1937, when the Stalinist group had crushed any internal political challengers, when it had destroyed capitalism and the social groups connected with it, when it should have felt supremely confident, it would at that moment worry about holding on to power. Most of our theories of terror assume that the regime was confidently in control of the country.[21] But if we think about the kind of dictatorship that began forming even in Lenin's time and reached its apogee under Stalin, we can see that confidence and control were more the exception than the rule.

This was a regime that from its early days banned other political parties, newspapers, and the expression of any dissent in society and even inside its own party. It punished incautious speech, including the telling of political jokes or recitation of rhymes and singing of songs. It relied on a network of tens of thousands of informers to tell it what the people were thinking. It imprisoned or killed huge numbers of people who *might* become a threat. It was obsessed with conspiracy and secrecy and was chronically frightened of spies, foreigners, and even of its own population. We now know how in the 1930s political and social relations, the malfunctioning of government, and the activities of officials increasingly came to be understood as "omnipresent conspiracies" and subversion by dark forces.[22] Politburo members carried pistols in their overcoats as they went around on their daily business. These are not measures taken by a secure and self-assured regime and reflect an abiding fear and insecurity about its own position.

Reading various party texts in the 1930s, including the minutes of Central Committee meetings, Politburo memoranda, and official correspondence produces the impression of an abiding anxiety about the position of the regime. Its leaders felt themselves constantly on the defensive. Recalling in the 1930s their formative experiences in the Civil War, they always thought they were figuratively surrounded, constantly at war with powerful and conniving opponents. It is perhaps not without interest that twenty years after the event, they reflexively fell back on Civil War metaphors, branding all categories of enemies as "white guards," and thought in terms of taking hostages and shooting.

Fear is not a new aspect of Stalinist studies. We have long known that the population was afraid of the party, the party was afraid of the Central Committee, the Central Committee was afraid of the Politburo, and the Politburo was afraid of Stalin. However, fear also ran in the opposite direction: the party feared society, the Central Committee feared the party, Stalin feared his lieutenants, and so forth. The regime *as a whole* was chronically anxious about a multitude of political and social threats, and like those who suffer from chronic anxiety, seems to have been unable to evaluate them rationally, to distinguish between greater and lesser dangers, or to respond to them in balanced ways. As their anxiety grew in the 1930s, so did their exaggeration of dangers and their inability to sort out the minor from the major threats. The Great Terror was not only a matter of Stalin's decision. Within the elite as a whole there was a generalized consensus on the need for it. They disagreed about who the main targets should be, but their various anxieties and insecurities led them to agree that threats were real and could only be fended off with force.[23]

Increasingly frustrated with this situation and unable to manage their environment, they responded with the political equivalent of a psychotic break. Like the maniacally depressed person who has lost control of his environment—as he defines it—and climbs a tower with a rifle, or a postal employee who enters his workplace with a machine gun, they began shooting wildly. Strong and confident governments, with efficient and loyal bureaucracies and sure of the support of most of the population, do not need to resort to terror to accomplish their policies or to stay in power.

None of this is to say that theirs was a weak regime. The Bolsheviks were able to inflict violence of an unimaginable scale to secure their ends and, after all, they succeeded in collectivizing agriculture, frustrating anti-state conspiracies, and staying in power. The point is, however, that they could think of no way of governing without resorting to massive force. They lacked the tools, the information, and the popular support that other regimes took for granted, and they knew it. We are used to imagining and theorizing the Stalinists as larger-than-life monsters, confidently pulling the levers of a well-oiled totalitarian machine in order to implement their ideological plans. But they were also nervous little monsters, hysterically reacting to real threats caused by their disastrous policies or to imagined conspiracies by dark and sinister forces.

Notes

1. J. Arch Getty et al., "Victims of the Soviet Penal System in the Pre-War Years: A First Approach on the Basis of Archival Evidence," *American Historical Review* 98:4 (1993): 1017–49.

2. Although a minority of scholars continues to defend much higher numbers, the figures in the table, with only small variations, reflect a clear consensus among historians working in Soviet-era archives. Researchers in the Memorial Society in Moscow with unparalleled access to secret police archives have presented nearly identical numbers: A. I. Kokurin and N. V. Petrov, eds., *Gulag (Glavnoe Upravlenie Lagerei), 1917–1960* (Moscow: Izd. "Materik," 2000). For close analysis of these grim statistics, see the work of S. G. Wheatcroft, "The Scale and Nature of Stalinist Repression and Its Demographic Significance: On Comments by Keep and Conquest," *Europe-Asia Studies* 52:6 (2000): 1143–59, and "The Scale and Nature of German and Soviet Repression and Mass Killings," *Europe-Asia Studies* 48:8 (1996): 1319–53; M. Ellman, "Soviet Repression Statistics: Some Comments," *Europe-Asia Studies* 54:7 (2002): 1151–72; and Getty et al., "Victims."

3. On collectivization in general, see R. W. Davies, *The Socialist Offensive: The Collectivization of Soviet Agriculture, 1929–1930* (London: Harvard University Press, 1980); Sheila Fitzpatrick, *Stalin's Peasants: Resistance and Survival in the Russian Village after Collectivization* (New York: Oxford University Press, 1994); Lynne Viola, *Peasant Rebels under Stalin: Collectivization and the Culture of Peasant Resistance* (New York: Oxford University Press, 1996).

4. Viola, *Peasant Rebels.*

5. There is a lively debate among historians about the nature of the famine. Some argue that Stalin deliberately created the famine to destroy the Ukrainian peasantry. See Robert Conquest, *The Harvest of Sorrow: Soviet Collectivization and the Terror-Famine* (New York: Oxford University Press, 1986). Others have argued that although Stalinist policies played a key role in it, the famine was unintentional. See Mark Tauger, "The 1932 Harvest and the Famine of 1933," *Slavic Review* 50:1 (Spring 1991): 70–89.

6. In addition to the 1.5 million secret police arrests, another 1.5 million persons were prosecuted for various nonpolitical infractions, especially crimes against public order and property. It should be noted, however, that in a state where the government prescribes the social order and owns virtually all the property, the difference between political and nonpolitical crimes is hard to judge. There seems to be considerable overlap in the sources between these two groups, and analysis suggests a total of approximately 2.5 million arrests of all kinds in 1936–38. See Getty et al., "Victims."

7. The standard account of the purge of the Soviet elite is Robert Conquest, *The Great Terror: A Reassessment* (London: Oxford University Press, 1990).

8. See Roger Reese, "The Red Army and the Great Purges," in *Stalinist Terror: New Perspectives*, ed. J. Arch Getty and Roberta Thompson Manning (Cambridge and New York: Cambridge University Press, 1993), 198–214.

9. J. A. Getty, "'Excesses Are Not Permitted': Mass Terror and Stalinist Governance in the Late 1930s," *Russian Review* 61:1 (2002): 113–38.

10. Terry Martin, "The Origins of Soviet Ethnic Cleansing," *Journal of Modern History* 70:4 (1998): 813–61.

11. During the Cold War and before the opening of Soviet-era archives in the 1990s, estimates of the numbers of purge victims were often dramatically higher, with some experts positing up to seven million arrests and ten to fifteen million camp deaths in these two years, and a camp population of 9.5 million by 1939. See Chris Ward, *Stalin's Russia*, 2nd ed. (London: Edward Arnold, 1999), 135–36.

12. Getty et al., "Victims."

13. See Robert C. Tucker, *Stalin as Revolutionary* (New York: Norton, 1973).

14. See Theodore Von Laue, "Stalin among the Moral and Political Imperatives, or How to Judge Stalin," *Soviet Union* 8:1 (1981); and Theodore Von Laue, "Stalin in Focus," *Slavic Review* 42:3 (Fall 1983): 373–89.

15. The classic ideological explanation is Aleksandr Solzhenitsyn, *The Gulag Archipelago 1918–1956*, 3 vols. (London: Harper and Row, 1973–78).

16. See Hannah Arendt, *The Origins of Totalitarianism*, new ed. (New York: Harcourt Brace Jovanovich, 1973); and Z. Brzezinski, *Ideology and Power in Soviet Politics* (New York: Praeger, 1962).

17. For an example of such "revisionist" treatments, see Gábor Tamás Rittersporn, *Stalinist Simplifications and Soviet Complications: Social Tensions and Political Conflicts in the USSR, 1933–1953* (New York: Harwood, 1991). See also Sheila Fitzpatrick, "New Perspectives on Stalinism," *Russian Review* 45 (1986): 357–73.

18. David L Hoffman, *Stalinist Values: The Cultural Norms of Soviet Modernity, 1917–1941* (Ithaca, N.Y.: Cornell University Press, 2003); Peter Holquist, "'Conduct Merciless Mass Terror': Decossackization on the Don, 1919," *Cahiers du Monde Russe* 38:1–2 (1997): 127–62; Amir Weiner, *Making Sense of War: The Second World War and the Fate of the Bolshevik Revolution* (Princeton, N.J.: Princeton University Press, 2001).

19. The following discussion is based on J. Arch Getty and Oleg V. Naumov, *The Road to Terror: Stalin and the Self-Destruction of the Bolsheviks, 1932–1939* (New Haven, Conn.: Yale University Press, 1999).

20. V. M. Molotov and F. I. Chuev, *Sto sorok besed s Molotovym: Iz dnevnika F. Chueva* (Moscow: Terra, 1991), 390, 401, 13–14.

21. Z. Brzezinski, *The Permanent Purge* (Cambridge: Cambridge University Press, 1956).

22. See Gábor T. Rittersporn, "The Omnipresent Conspiracy: On Soviet Imagery of Politics and Social Relations in the 1930s," in *Stalinist Terror: New Perspectives* (Armonk, N.Y.: M. E. Sharpe, 1992), 99–115.

23. Getty and Naumov, *Road to Terror.*

The Struggle against Treason

Stalin's Great Terror in the Mirror of Ivan the Terrible's Oprichnina

MAUREEN PERRIE

The years 1936–38 witnessed one of the most infamous episodes of state-sponsored violence in human history. The "Great Terror" (sometimes known as the "Great Purges," or as the Ezhovshchina, after N. I. Ezhov, the head of the Soviet secret police) involved not only the public show trials of many former leaders of the Communist Party, but also the mass arrests and executions of ordinary Soviet citizens. Reports of the arrests and trials in the contemporary Soviet press depicted a network of wreckers and saboteurs whose activities had been detected as a result of the vigilance of the security services. No one today accepts this picture of a dastardly conspiracy. It is surprising, however, that historians have paid so little attention to the ways in which the official presentation of the events of 1936–38 found its reflection in depictions of other times and places. Films, novels, and plays on contemporary topics promoted the themes of sabotage, espionage, and treason.[1] But in the late 1930s and 1940s the relevance of these themes went much further, pervading, for example, the writing of much popular (and even academic) history, and the creation of artistic works on historical subjects. The present article will analyze one example of this process, the representation of an earlier period of state violence: the reign of terror conducted by the sixteenth-century Russian tsar Ivan IV ("the Terrible").

Let us start by reminding ourselves of the way in which political developments in the 1930s were officially presented to the Soviet public. A convenient example of this is the notorious *Short Course* history of the Bolshevik Party, first published in 1938, at the height of the terror. According to this work, the murder of S. M. Kirov, the Leningrad Party boss, in December 1934, was carried out by a group of counterrevolutionaries who were funded by foreign capitalist states. The trial of L. B. Kamenev, G. E. Zinov'ev, and others in August 1936 brought the leaders of this conspiracy to justice. The trials of 1937 revealed further ramifications of the plot. A joint band of party oppositionists ("Trotskyites and Bukharinites") had conspired against the Soviet state from its foundation, at the behest of the espionage services of foreign states. The "annihilation" of this "gang of spies, wreckers and traitors to the country," in accordance with the sentence of the court, had met with the approval of the Soviet people.[2]

Of course, there was widespread skepticism among the Soviet public about this official story.[3] Many disbelieved in the real existence of the ruinous network of foreign agents, and their doubts provided cause for concern both to the security organs and to the propaganda agencies.

Because of the state monopoly of the press and the media in Stalin's Russia, such dissident opinions could not be publicly and explicitly voiced. One way in which dissent could be expressed, however, was in "Aesopian" language—the allegorical use of subversive parallels.[4] Such methods had been employed before 1917 in order to evade the tsarist censorship, and they were soon adopted in similar circumstances in the Soviet period. The authorities, of course, were ever-vigilant in their search for "subtexts" and "allusions" in historical and literary works; and they often overreacted by banning "innocent" works whose dissident content lay in the eyes of the censors rather than in the intentions of the authors. *On the Rack*, Aleksei Tolstoi's play about Peter the Great, was suspected by some at its preview in 1929 of being an allegorical critique of the human costs of the First Five-Year Plan, and Mikhail Bulgakov's plays about Molière and Pushkin were suppressed in 1936 because their depiction of famous writers' troubled relationships with rulers who sought to control them provided an uncomfortably close analogy to the contemporary Soviet situation.[5]

Not only was there considerable skepticism in the late 1930s about the official version of the Ezhovshchina, but various alternative explanations were put forward. One of these came from Nikolai Bukharin, the prominent leader of the "Right" opposition. In his last letter, "To a Future Generation of Party Leaders," written shortly before he was arrested, subjected to a show trial and executed, Bukharin argued that the secret police had spun out of control. "I feel my helplessness," he wrote, "before a hellish machine, which, *probably by the use of medieval methods,* has acquired gigantic power, fabricates organized slander, acts boldly and confidently." "At present," Bukharin continued, "most of the so-called organs of the NKVD are a degenerate organization of bureaucrats, . . . who . . . cater to *Stalin's morbid suspiciousness* . . . in a scramble for rank and fame, concocting their slimy cases. . . . Any member of the Central Committee, any member of the Party can be rubbed out, turned into a traitor, terrorist, diversionist, spy, by these 'wonder-working organs.'"[6]

When he referred to Stalin's "medieval methods," Bukharin was probably thinking of the extraction of confessions by the use of torture: at his trial he stated that "the confession of the accused is a medieval principle of jurisprudence."[7] Some later historians have developed this idea and compared the Stalinist show trials with witch-hunts and the persecution of heretics in early modern Europe.[8] For those contemporaries who shared Bukharin's opinion of the terror as the work of a morbidly suspicious tyrant, other historical parallels were not hard to find. According to Isaac Deutscher, even in the early 1930s oppositionists had referred to Stalin as "the Genghiz Khan of the Politbureau, the Asiatic, the new Ivan the Terrible."[9] In this context, it would not be surprising if Soviet historians thought very carefully before writing about Tsar Ivan, lest they be suspected of providing an Aesopian critique of Stalin and his campaign against "spies, wreckers and traitors."

The grounds for such an analogy were strong. In 1565 Ivan IV divided Russia into two sections, the *oprichnina,* which was to be the tsar's own domain, and the *zemshchina,* which was at least nominally governed by his aristocratic counselors, the boyars. Ivan recruited his personal bodyguard, the *oprichniki,* who came to perform the functions of a security-police force. The *oprichniki* were given free rein to eradicate treason in the territory of both the *oprichnina* and the *zemshchina.* The term "*oprichnina*" came to be used to designate not only the tsar's domain, but also the reign of terror that ensued, and which lasted for seven years, until Ivan abolished the division of his realm in 1572. The worst atrocity in this period was Ivan's punitive raid on Novgorod in 1570, when he massacred the city's population on suspicion of their treasonous links with Poland-Lithuania. This was followed by mass public executions in Moscow of other alleged traitors, who were accused of abuses of power and of contacts with the Crimean Tatars and the Turks, as well as with Russia's western enemies in the Livonian War.

Of course, Ivan's "Great Terror" should not be seen as an exact counterpart to Stalin's. The sixteenth-century context was very different from that of the twentieth century. Ivan's *oprichniki* raped, looted and murdered with relative impunity, but there was no equivalent of Stalin's vast network of labor camps in which so many Soviet citizens died of cold and hunger. Unlike Ivan, Stalin did not stage public executions in order to intimidate the population (although the show trials performed a comparable function). But there were, undoubtedly, a number of similarities between the two regimes. Both rulers used torture as a means of obtaining confessions, and these confessions were often the only form of evidence against the accused. Perhaps the closest parallel between the two periods can be found in the atmosphere of fear and suspicion created by allegations of treason, and by the official encouragement of denunciations of traitors.

Historians still debate whether there really was any conspiracy against Ivan the Terrible.[10] In the pre-revolutionary period, Russian scholars provided a wide range of interpretations of the *oprichnina*. Few, however, accepted that Ivan faced a real danger. Some thought that the accusation of treason was a cynical pretext on the tsar's part for launching a campaign to weaken the old aristocracy and hence strengthen the centralized power of the monarchy. Others believed that Ivan was clinically mad, suffering from paranoid suspicion of his closest associates, and that the *oprichnina* episode (like similar behavior on Ivan's part in subsequent years) was a senseless and motiveless blood-letting. Depictions of the tsar as a crazed tyrant tended to predominate in nineteenth-century artistic representations of his reign, some of which were designed as Aesopian critiques of contemporary autocrats such as Nicholas I.[11] Such negative images of Ivan were deeply rooted in the historical imagination of the pre-revolutionary Russian intelligentsia, and they were to persist well into the Soviet period. When Stalin's critics compared him with Ivan the Terrible, they implied that both rulers had invented the alleged plots in order to rid themselves of their opponents.

In the 1920s the dominant trend in Soviet historiography was the "school" of the Marxist historian M. N. Pokrovskii (1868–1932). In the mid-1930s, however, Pokrovskii was criticized for the damaging effect that his "abstract sociological schemes" had had on the teaching of history. At a time when Russian history was increasingly being harnessed to the cause of Soviet patriotism, Pokrovskii was considered to have provided too negative a depiction of the tsarist past. Following the campaign against Pokrovskii, state-building tsars such as Peter the Great were rehabilitated as "progressive for their time," new textbooks were commissioned that would familiarize school pupils with dates and facts, and popular artistic works were expected to draw instructive patriotic parallels between historical events and the contemporary situation. In the late 1930s, when Germany and Poland were regarded as the main potential enemies of the Soviet Union, Alexander Nevskii's defeat of the Teutonic Knights in 1242, and Minin and Pozharskii's liberation of Moscow from the Poles in 1612, were celebrated in literature and on the cinema screen.[12]

Ivan the Terrible was not such an obvious candidate for rehabilitation in the mid-1930s, but the commissioning of new textbooks meant that his image could not be ignored. By 1937 it would clearly have been problematic to depict him as a paranoid tyrant obsessed with the eradication of nonexistent plots. We find instead that Ivan's terror is depicted in a manner consistent with the official presentation of the events of 1936–38—the necessary eradication of despicable spies and traitors implicated in complex webs of conspiracy with foreign enemies of the state. The textbooks all asserted or implied that the tsar's campaign against treason was well founded. A. V. Shestakov's *Short History* for primary schools, published in 1937, stated that, "After the first defeats in the [Livonian] war, Ivan discovered that he was being betrayed by the big boyar landowners. These traitors entered the service of the Poles and Lithuanians."[13] The textbooks for secondary schools and higher education, which appeared in 1940 and 1939 respectively, were rather more nuanced, but the message was basically the same. The secondary-school textbook described the defection of Prince Andrei Kurbskii and other prominent figures to Lithuania and presented the *oprichnina* as Ivan's legitimate response to their "treason." S. V. Bakhrushin, in his chapter on Ivan in the university textbook, argued that the tsar's undoubted cruelty was "provoked by the stubborn resistance of the big feudal lords to his endeavors, and by direct betrayals on their part."[14]

Before 1940 there is no evidence of specific directives "from above" concerning the rehabilitation of Ivan the Terrible. In the late 1930s the generally positive assessment of the tsar as a "progressive" state-builder was, of course, in line with the anti-Pokrovskii campaign and with the adoption of a more patriotic approach to pre-revolutionary Russian history. But the prevalent theme that Ivan was not pathologically suspicious, and that his campaign against treason was justified by the existence of plots and conspiracies against him, seems to have been improvised "from below" by individual historians.

Direct intervention by the authorities in the depiction of Ivan the Terrible dates from the end of 1940, when a play about the tsar was commissioned from Aleksei Tolstoi, and a film from Sergei Eisenstein. These commissions followed the issuing of instructions from the Central Committee "on the restoration of the true historical image of Ivan IV in Russian history."[15] From around 1941 we have intriguing anecdotal evidence of Stalin's own view that Tsar Ivan had been "insufficiently terrible": he had repented of his cruelty and had not persecuted the boyars decisively enough.[16] The message clearly was that Stalin did not intend to make the same mistake. Tolstoi and Eisenstein, however, were to face great difficulties in their attempts to depict the tsar on stage and screen.[17]

The first version of the script of Tolstoi's play "Ivan the Terrible" was heavily criticized in the weekly arts paper *Literatura i iskusstvo* (Literature and Art) in May 1942, apparently on Stalin's personal instructions, for failing to "rehabilitate" the tsar sufficiently. The author revised the play, turning it into a two-part work that illustrated Ivan's harshness towards traitors more graphically than the original script had done. This time the text met with Stalin's approval; and although the first production of the first part, "The Eagle and His Mate," in October 1944, was condemned for its melodramatic devices, the play subsequently won a Stalin Prize and became a standard part of the repertoire of the late-Stalinist theatre.

In the case of Eisenstein's film, by contrast, an initial success story subsequently turned sour. Stalin personally approved the screenplay, and *Part One*, released in 1945, won a Stalin Prize. *Part Two*, however—which dealt with the period of the *oprichnina*—provoked Stalin's displeasure. A Central Committee resolution of September 4, 1946, criticized the film for depicting the *oprichniki* as "a gang of degenerates on the lines of the American Ku-Klux-Klan" and for presenting Tsar Ivan as "weak in character and lacking in willpower, something on the lines of Hamlet." The film was not shown publicly until after Stalin's death. The official criticisms of *Ivan the Terrible: Part Two* were probably not the only reason for the ban: many have seen it as an Aesopian attack on Stalin and his terror; and its highly artificial, visually dense style defied the aesthetic norms of Soviet "socialist realism."[18]

Since Stalin himself apparently regarded the historical Ivan as "insufficiently terrible," it was somewhat inconsistent of him to criticize Tolstoi and Eisenstein for depicting the tsar as weak and indecisive. In fact it seems that Stalin wanted to see Ivan portrayed in the theatre and cinema as an analogue of his own self-image as a heroic and farsighted ruler. The tsar's "repressions" had to be presented as essential to the interests of the state. In a conversation with Eisenstein and others in 1947, Stalin told the director that Ivan's executions could be depicted on screen: "Ivan the Terrible was very cruel. You can show that he was cruel, but you must show why it was necessary to be cruel."[19] An implicit justification of the violence of the purges is very obvious here.

By a curious irony, the most successful Stalin-era account of Ivan's reign (in terms of the degree of official approval that it received) was a revised version of a work that had first been published in 1922 by R. Iu. Vipper, a "bourgeois" historian who subsequently emigrated to Latvia. Vipper's unusually positive view of Ivan the Terrible had been criticized in the early Soviet period, when Pokrovskii's approach to history predominated, but it had become fashionable by the late 1930s. After the Soviet occupation of the Baltic states in 1940, Vipper returned to Moscow, and in 1942 he published a revised edition of his biography of Ivan. The most significant amendment in the new edition was the addition of a chapter entitled "The Struggle against Treason." In the discussion of the *oprichnina* in the first edition of his book, Vipper had referred to "real or imaginary traitors," leaving the question open as to whether the victims of the repressions were or were not guilty of the treason of which they were accused. In subsequent editions, however, Vipper provided a detailed justification of the most intensive period of terror, in 1568–72. He claimed that new sources which had become available since 1922 (the writings of the German *oprichniki* Albert Schlichting and Heinrich von Staden) conclusively demonstrated that Ivan faced real threats in 1567–71. The tsar had not been excessively suspicious—if anything, he was too trusting, and had underestimated the dangers posed by the reactionary opposition. Russian traitors were in league with the Poles, the Turks and the Tatars, so that the struggles against internal and external enemies were interrelated parts of a single crusade, and patriotism could be invoked as a justification and legitimation of both. This theme clearly had particular resonance during the war, and Vipper's book enjoyed great success: it was favorably reviewed; a third edition was published in 1944, and export-quality foreign translations, including an English version, followed.[20]

The textbook-writers of the late 1930s may simply have sought to avoid suspicion of subversive analogy when they insisted that Ivan had faced real conspiracies; by the 1940s, however, depictions of the *oprichnina* were expected to provide an allegorical legitimation of Stalin's Great Purges as a ruthless "struggle against treason." The fact that Stalin personally oversaw the creation of a "correct" historical image of Ivan the Terrible by Tolstoi and Eisenstein indicates that he was concerned to justify the "medieval" methods which he had used in the 1930s in order to maintain himself in power: to "show why it was necessary to be cruel."

Notes

1. See, for example, Peter Kenez, *Cinema and Soviet Society, 1917–1953* (Cambridge: Cambridge University Press, 1992), 164–65.
2. *History of the Communist Party of the Soviet Union (Bolsheviks): Short Course* (London: Cobbett Publishing Co., 1943), 298–301, 317–19.
3. See, for example, Sarah Davies, *Popular Opinion in Stalin's Russia: Terror, Propaganda and Dissent, 1934–1941* (Cambridge: Cambridge University Press, 1997), 113–23.
4. A classic study of this phenomenon is Lev Loseff, *On the Beneficence of Censorship: Aesopian Language in Modern Russian Literature* (Munich: Verlag Otto Sagner, 1984).
5. Maureen Perrie, *The Cult of Ivan the Terrible in Stalin's Russia* (Basingstoke: Palgrave, 2001), 51–53, 73–74.
6. Roy A. Medvedev, *Let History Judge: The Origins and Consequences of Stalinism* (London: Spokesman Books, 1976), 183. My emphases.
7. *Report of Court Proceedings in the Case of the Anti-Soviet "Bloc of Rights and Trotskyites"* (Moscow: People's Commissariat of Justice of the U.S.S.R., 1938), 778.
8. See, for example, Moshe Lewin, *The Making of the Soviet System: Essays in the Social History of Inter-War Russia* (London: Methuen, 1985), 309–10.
9. Isaac Deutscher, *Stalin: A Political Biography*, rev. ed. (Harmondsworth: Penguin Books, 1990), 349. For other similar comparisons, see Perrie, *Cult of Ivan the Terrible*, 78, 84.
10. For historiography to 1934, see Perrie, *Cult of Ivan the Terrible*, 5–21. A new assessment of the reign can be found in Andrei Pavlov and Maureen Perrie, *Ivan the Terrible*, Longman "Profiles in Power" (Harlow: Pearson Education, 2003).
11. On this point, see also Kevin Platt's article in this volume, "On Blood, Scandal, Renunciation, and Russian History."
12. On these developments, see Perrie, *Cult of Ivan the Terrible*, 25–69; and David Brandenberger, *National Bolshevism. Stalinist Mass Culture and the Formation of Modern National Identity, 1931–1956* (Cambridge, Mass.: Harvard University Press, 2002), 27–112.

13. *Kratkii kurs istorii SSSR. Uchebnik dlia 3-go i 4-go klassov*, ed. A. V. Shestakov (Moscow: Gosudarstvennoe uchebno-pedagogicheskoe izdatel'stvo, 1937), 40.

14. *Istoriia SSSR. Uchebnik dlia VIII klassa srednei shkoly*, ed. A. M. Pankratova (Moscow: Gosudarstvennoe uchebno-pedagogicheskoe izdatel'stvo Narkomprosa RSFSR, 1940), 134–35; *Istoriia SSSR*, vol. 1. *S drevneishikh vremen do kontsa XVIII v.*, ed. V. I. Lebedev, B. D. Grekov, S. V. Bakhrushin (Moscow: Gosudarstvennoe sotsial'no-ekonomicheskoe izdatel'stvo, 1939), 390.

15. Perrie, *Cult of Ivan the Terrible*, 85–86.

16. Ibid., 86–87.

17. Ibid., chapters 6 and 7.

18. On the stylistic features of the film see Joan Neuberger, *Ivan the Terrible*, KINOfiles Film Companion 9 (London: I. B. Tauris, 2003), especially 96–124.

19. G. Mar'iamov, *Kremlevskii tsenzor: Stalin smotrit kino* (Moscow: Kinotsentr, 1992), 85.

20. R. Iu. Vipper, *Ivan Groznyi* (Moscow: Del'fin, 1922; 2nd ed., Tashkent: Gosudarstvennoe izdatel'stvo UzSSR, 1942; 3rd ed., Moscow and Leningrad: Izdatel'stvo AN SSSR, 1944); published in English as R. Wipper, *Ivan Grozny* (Moscow: Foreign Languages Publishing House, 1947).

A Substitute for Writing

Representation of Violence in Incidents *by Daniil Kharms*

MARK LIPOVETSKY

Daniil Kharms (a pen-name of Daniil Ivanovich Iuvachev, 1905–42), one of the most brilliant and enigmatic representatives of absurdist literature, is equally important for the history of the Russian avant-garde and even postmodernism. The group OBERIU (Ob"edinenie real'nogo iskusstva, The Union of Real Art), organized by Kharms and his friends, was probably the last page of the avant-garde as a visible part of Soviet culture, and one of the first experiments in underground culture, which, despite constant political pressure, survived into the 1980s. The majority of Kharms's works of the 1920s and 1930s were not published during his lifetime—only his works for children appeared publicly—and, moreover, he did not intend them to be published. Kharms clearly realized the incompatibility of his artistic experiments with mainstream Soviet culture, and he lived in extreme poverty on the periphery of the Leningrad literary scene; he was arrested several times and died in prison.[1] In the 1960s Kharms's absurdist works began to be published in Russia for the first time and were released in full over the next three decades.[2] By the 1990s Kharms had become one of the most highly revered classics of unofficial culture, having already influenced several generations of experimental writers, including those who shaped the course of Russian postmodernism, such as Venedikt Erofeev, Dmitrii Prigov, and Vladimir Sorokin.

Violence plays an incredibly significant part in Kharms's works. He frequently depicts acts of cruelty, fights, mutilations, murders, and so forth in great detail, equally funny and terrifying. This prominent element of Kharms's narratives has either been ignored or interpreted as the writer's indirect reaction to Stalinist terror. I would like to focus on the function of violence in one of Kharms's most famous and representative works, a collection of minimalist stories and plays entitled *Incidents*. Compiled by Kharms himself as a collection, *Incidents* comprises thirty numbered texts, written between 1933 and 1939 (but placed in nonchronological order), supplied with a table of contents and title page. I would like to explore the association between violence and Kharms's representation of writing. In modernist aesthetics the act of writing and literary creation arguably presents a manifestation of artistic freedom and power. The purpose of this essay is to show how in *Incidents* Kharms allegorically presents the very process of artistic creation, but replaces it with a series of absurdist signifiers, among which motifs of violence play the key role. Allegory, according to Walter Benjamin, "represents precisely the non-being of that which it represents,"[3] and Kharms focuses precisely on the problem of non-being and representation.

The majority of the "incidents" display extremely weakened referentiality—they do not happen in "real" time and space. Kharms does not even bother to create an illusion of "reality." Minimized individuation of the authorial voice (the majority of the texts are impersonal, even protocol-like in their narratives) equally rules out the possibility of interpreting the "incidents" as acts of self-expression. The "self" behind these texts appears as abstract as the time-space references: the *incidents* happen nowhere and "express" no one's inner world. In a way, Kharms's prose represents the first Russian example of what Roland Barthes later called "writing degree zero."[4] If "the world" and "the self" are excluded, then the incidents' main subject can only be language itself, or more precisely, writing in its pure, "zero degree" form, supposedly cleansed from the traces of history and subjectivity. The most illuminating evidence of this philosophy of writing may be found in the very first text, "Blue Notebook No. 10": "There was once a red-haired man who had no eyes and no ears. He also had no hair, so he was called red-haired only in a manner of speaking. He wasn't able to talk because he didn't have a mouth. He had no nose either. He didn't even have any arms or legs. He also didn't have a stomach, and he didn't have a back, and he didn't have a spine, and he also didn't have any insides. He didn't have anything. So it's hard to understand whom we're talking about. So we'd better not talk about him any more."[5]

This text not only sets the tone for the entire cycle, but also justifies the reader's perception of the cycle in its entirety as an allegory of writing. The single positive statement of the story, "There was once a red-haired man," is deconstructed to the degree that it offers a demonstrative rejection of the entire narrative: "So it's hard to understand who we're talking about. So we'd better not talk about him any more."[6] In terms of philosophical convention, this text clearly demonstrates how a narrative about something can transform it into nothingness. A red-haired man with no eyes, ears, hair, mouth, nose, hands and legs, spine, stomach and intestines, is, in fact, a defamiliarized description not only of each and every one of the characters in *Incidents*, whose individuality is exhausted by their nomination—first names and surnames—but also of any literary "object," which does not exist in reality, which is not tangible, yet is still a living entity. This literary object can be represented by a character but also by the author, appearing in a text as a summation of narrative figures and rhetorical devices. In short, literature emerges as an apotheosis of nonexistence, and writing itself appears to serve a solitary purpose—to expose the emptiness behind its own product, that is, to erase the subject of the representation and by this means to undermine its own ontology.

The similarity of this deconstruction to an act of violence sets the stage for the cycle as a whole. The programmatic meaning of "Incidents," the miniature following "Blue Notebook No. 10," is emphasized by the eponymy of its title with that of the entire collection. The title "Incidents" is usually interpreted as a metaphor for "the world of determinism," in which death appears as the sole logical product of life.[7] True, death, insanity, destruction appear in this miniature as the result of any action by a subject, however arbitrary: "Once Orlov ate too many ground peas and died. Krylov found out about it and died too. Spiridonov up and died all by himself. Spiridonov's wife fell off the cupboard and also died. . . . Mikhailov stopped combing his hair and caught a skin disease. Kruglov drew a picture of a lady with a whip in her hand and lost his mind. Perekhrestov was sent four hundred rubles by telegram and put on such airs that they fired him at his office." Death and degradation emerge here as the core of existence, the ultimate result of any life effort. Yet the reiteration of this "formula" in every sentence of the text only serves to emphasize the final statement:

"Good people, but they don't know how to take themselves in hand"[8] (literally: how to put themselves on firm footing). This statement belongs to the narrator, or better to say, a writer-character. The obvious tone of superiority toward the "good people" seems to demonstrate his immunity to the laws of destruction. Yet the only premise that could make him immune to this universal principle is his writing, which, supposedly, protects the subject from dangerous indeterminism, from the forces of chaos. Writing, according to this logic, provides a safe haven against "outsideness" (Bakhtin[9]), or a position that Kharms in his philosophical treatise "On Existence, Time, and Space" (1940) had defined as "something" *(nechto):* "neither time, nor space, an 'obstacle' that creates the Universe's existence,"—"a knot of the Universe."[10]

The same "triad" (life efforts resulting in destruction, and the outside position supposedly provided by writing) is reproduced in the ministory "Falling-Out Old Women." Old women are falling out of windows because they are "too curious"—that is, possessed by excessive vitality. Their curiosity, however, is invoked by an attraction to death.[11] Thus, again life activity gravitates to death and to death only, with serial repetitiveness. Although the narrator's voice, appearing in the final phrase only, demonstrates no less curiosity than that of the falling-out old ladies, it reflects the position of an outside observer who is not affected by the same force of gravity: "When the sixth old woman fell out of the window, I became fed up with watching them and went to the Maltsevskii Market, where they said a blind man had been presented with a knit scarf."[12] Again the "writer" is invincible to the destruction, protected by writing itself.

In "A Sonnet," Kharms simultaneously complicates and undermines the philosophical model represented in the two previous stories. Schematically, the structure of this text may be represented by two symmetrical triangles having one common side. The major "axis" connecting life efforts with death is transferred here into the "intellectual" dimension and is represented through the impossibility of the mind overcoming disorder (chaos). The latter crisis is comically represented by the incapability of the narrator, his neighbors, and a store cashier to detect "which came first, 7 or 8 . . ." By analogy to "Incidents" and "Falling-Out Old Women," the power of life/mind fails to prevent death/chaos, and is overcome by the latter. In this story, human consciousness is not only unable to restore the lost order, but it becomes a direct manifestation of entropy, losing its own identity as well. Characteristically, the narrator's "I" appears only in the first line of the text ("An amazing thing happened to me: I suddenly forgot which came first, 7 or 8"[13]), then it is dissolved within the "we" of the collective mind, equally unable to resolve this problem, and never reappears again. (The last line of the text reads: "Then we all went home.")

If the narrator's voice is not immune to the power of chaos, then what can confront it? Kharms suggests two seemingly incompatible answers to this question. One is located on the text's metalevel—this is the narrative's *formal order.* As A. Dobritsyn has demonstrated, "this tiny story contains 14 sentences—equal to the number of lines in a sonnet, wherein these sentences form two 'stanzas' and two 'tercets'; the thematic composition of 'A Sonnet' precisely corresponds to the classical model of a sonnet (thesis—its development—antithesis—synthesis). Besides, there are 14 words in the first sentence of the story, while the entire text counts 196 words, i.e., 14 squared." Hence "a text in which the characters suffer from difficulties in calculation . . . was obviously thoroughly calculated by the author."[14] This contradiction raises the reader who is able to detect it to the level of the "outside" author, who can overcome the world's disorder by the invisible, yet strict and beautiful order of writing.

On the other hand, within the narrative, Kharms suggests quite a different opposition to disorder: "We argued for a long time, but fortunately, a little boy fell off a park bench and broke both jaws. This distracted us from our argument. Then we all went home."[15] Paradoxically, these lines form the sonnet's synthesis; the formal order supports this "resolution" by the authority of the sonnet tradition! In the structure of the text, injury/violence ("broke both jaws") appears as a functional synonymy to the formal order, here in reference to the author's outsideness. Within the plot, injury/violence can produce the same effect that the formal order produces on the textual metalevel. In other words, a boy breaking both jaws can *substitute* for writing, or at least can lead to an effect analogous to that suggested by the grand literary tradition of a sonnet. However, if the order of writing implies the possibility to transcend chaos, the broken jaws negate it completely. These two mutually exclusive components shape the philosophical concept of "A Sonnet" and foreshadow the function of violence in other stories of the cycle.[16]

Violence, then, functions as a necessary component of any act of communication. A characteristic example: at the end of "The Story of the Fighting Men," Aleksei Alekseevich, after beating and disfiguring Andrei Karlovich, suddenly and in amazement notices that his "partner" has fled. Aleksei Alekseevich "looked around and, not seeing Andrei Karlovich, left to seek him."[17] If it had been just an ordinary fight, Aleksei Alekseevich would have been totally satisfied with his victory, but the fight appears here as a form of communication, and therefore, the disappearance of his "interlocutor" appears as the unnecessary interruption of a civil conversation. Significantly, Aleksei Alekseevich beats Andrei Karlovich with his prosthetic jaw, again associating violence and speech.

According to the logic of *Incidents*, not only does communication imply violence, but any violence is communicative. Violence offers Kharms's characters the most accessible form of transcendence, since in acts of violence Kharms's characters are *literally not themselves:* they expand their being toward the other, taking the notion of "getting in touch with your fellow man" to an extreme. Naturally, if the expansion of the "self" outside its limits into the territory of the "other" is consistent enough, it leads either to the ousting of the other or, more frequently, to his or her complete elimination. The equivalence between violence and communication excludes the necessity of a cause for the former. Sometimes Kharms depicts something that *triggers* violence, however, the majority of violent acts in the cycle have no motivation whatsoever. Violence in Kharms's stories typically exceeds its immediate motivation, usually leading to the death of one of the characters.

One may characterize the violence in *Incidents* in the following ways: It is always excessive and self-sufficient. It is ecstatic, and the ecstatic excitement caused by violence can be passed from one subject to another ("A Lynching," "Hunters," "The Beginning . . ."). Violence is practically universal as a "signifier"—Kharms's characters use it to express such things as irritation ("What They Sell . . ."), vitality ("The Beginning . . ."), and grief for dead friends ("Hunters"); it can satisfy wild passions ("A Lynching"); and resolve intellectual problems ("A Sonnet"). Violence is extremely diverse in its forms and means (a vast variety of beatings, dismemberments, psychological humiliations, and offensive gestures). For example:

The peasant Khariton stopped, picked up a stone, and threw it at Timofey. Timofey disappeared somewhere. "That is a clever one!" the herd of people shouted, and Zubov ran full speed and rammed his head into a wall. "Oh!" a woman with a swollen cheek shouted. But Komarov beat up the woman, and the woman ran howling through the doorway. Fetelushin walked past and laughed at them. Komarov walked up to him and said, "Hey you, greaseball," and hit Fetelushin in the stomach. Fetelushin leaned against the wall and started to hiccup. Romashkin spat from the top-story window, trying to hit Fetelushin. At that moment, not far from there a big-nosed woman was beating up her kid with a trough. A fattish young mother rubbed a pretty little girl's face against a brick-wall. . . . The peasant Khariton got drunk on denatured alcohol and stood in front of the women with unbuttoned trousers and said bad words.

Thus began a beautiful summer day. ("The Beginning of a Beautiful Summer Day [A Symphony]")[18]

All these features make violence in Kharms's presentation akin to art, which is also self sufficient and does not need an external reason for its existence. It is universal in its means and emotional triggers, and ecstatic as well. Ecstatic exaltation as specific to both art and violence is emphasized in the "anecdote" about Pushkin throwing stones: "Pushkin loved to throw rocks. As soon as he saw a rock, he would throw it. Sometimes he became so excited that he stood all red in the face, waving his arms, throwing rocks, simply something awful."[19]

Thus, violence appears in *Incidents* as an integral allegory of writing, since it functions as the most accessible (and almost flawless) form of communication, as well as a no less easily attained version of art.

One may isolate within the cycle such texts that directly deal with the theme of violence and, thus, provide insightful commentary to the specificity of violence as a form of transcendence akin to writing, or rather as a deconstruction of any transcendence. The "violent" texts of the cycle constitute several pairs: "A Meeting" is paralleled with "What They Sell in the Stores Nowadays"; and detailed descriptions of fighting link "The Story of the Fighting Men" with "Mashkin Killed Koshkin." Especially significant are the pairs "A Lynching" and "The Beginning of a Beautiful Summer Day (A Symphony)," as well as "Hunters" and "Pakin and Rakukin." The first pair is focused on the ecstasy of collective violence, while the second presents violence as an individualized and almost psychologically motivated act.

There are three "personages" in "A Lynching": Petrov, "on horseback," delivering a speech; a "man of medium height" who starts an argument with Petrov *(nachinaet raspriu)* because Petrov refuses to explain what he has written in his notebook; and the crowd, which initially "takes the side of the man of medium height" and then, when Petrov, "to save his life urges on the horse," "for the lack of another victim seizes the man of medium height and tears off his head." In this triad, one may detect a parody on dialectics: an exceptional Petrov (on horseback, with ambitious projects, and on top of this, writing something in his "little notebook" and, thus, supposedly immune to destruction) is opposed by the average "man of medium height." The crowd in this configuration operates as a "dialectical synthesis"—by supporting the "man of medium height," it eventually kills him. Yet, the main component of this "synthesis" is violence; it manifests the crowd's essential needs and motivations: "The crowd, having satisfied its passions, disperses." This is of course pseudo-dialectics, since violence is absolutely arbitrary as well. Everything is whimsical here, even Petrov's speech in which he informs the crowd that for some unknown reason "in place of the public park there is to be built an American-style skyscraper."[20] The violence alone is not accidental: it is driven by a clear *ritualistic* logic and exemplifies the *correct* response to Petrov's announcement. The creative impulse (modernist? utopian?—these overtones are detectable in Petrov's project) demands a ritualistic sacrifice for its realization. What we see in Kharms's story directly corresponds to the logic of sacrifice, as described by Rene Girard: the "man of medium height" acts as a "surrogate victim" of the leader (Petrov), and by this means fulfills the main function of ritualistic violence. Here "the function of sacrifice is to quell violence within the community and to prevent conflicts from erupting." Thus, the murder not only symbolically confirms the realization of Petrov's project, but also produces harmony within the community. As Girard points out: "This is the terrible paradox of men's desires. They can never agree on the preservation of their object, but they can always agree on its destruction. They are never in accord except at the expense of the victim."[21]

The ritualistic meaning of violence appears even more clearly in "The Beginning of a Beautiful Summer Day." Critics usually interpret the genre definition "A Symphony" and the text's finale ("Thus began a beautiful summer day," concluding a long list of various acts of violence) as an expression of Kharms's irony toward literary as well as ideological models of harmony in the life of "simple people." In my view, these interpretations are only partially valid. The joyful vitality of the acts of violence, plus the closed-up, circular structure of the narrative (a peasant Khariton appears at both the beginning and the end) indicate the ritualistic character of the collective and spontaneous activity depicted in the text. It is tempting to read this text through Bakhtin's theory of the carnival and to deduce the self-mutilation of the "people's collective body" as a condition of its resurrection for a new life cycle, in this case, "the beginning of a beautiful summer day." However, a more relevant approach may be found in the rituals of "potlatch" as described by Georges Bataille.[22] Much as in "potlatch" rituals, in Kharms's story the chain reaction of violent acts and gestures produces the effect of expenditure and excess that, in turn, serves as a guarantee for the "goodness" of the beautiful summer day. Sacrificial victimization provides a flourishing and vital force, as if charging life's engine with energy. Violence as a "potlatch" also generates social harmony, and through this again demonstrates its similarity to acts of creativity.[23]

"Hunters" and "Pakin and Rakukin" stress another aspect of violence that is no less important for the representation of writing: these texts are about the *power* of the author that erases the difference between writing and violence. The protagonist of "Hunters," Oknov,[24] appears when he mourns the deaths of his friends, but instead of translating his feelings into words (he "didn't want to talk to anybody"), he expresses his grief through violence toward Kozlov, who bothers him with his solace. In this skit, words and violence form tight, yet not very transparent relationships. For example, the first words that Oknov pronounces after three emphatic "no's," describe the act of violence that he had performed on Kozlov, as well as his "planning" for the next, no less violent, action: "It's not enough that I've just hit you on the back of your head with a stone, I'll also tear off your leg."[25] At the same time, the single authorial remark in this "play" is also about this act of violence: "*Oknov (tearing off Kozlov's leg):* I'm here, nearby." The absence of other remarks produces a strange effect: it seems that after this first act of violence Oknov becomes invisible to the other characters as well as to the reader. "Where is Oknov?" asks Kozlov, who has just been mutilated by him. "Looks like he tore off his leg!" exclaim Striuchkov and Motyl'kov, as if they can only see Kozlov. Oknov continues to voice violent sentiments and to commit unnamed horrible acts, but they are not specified, they are either beyond or before words.

One may suggest that the acts of violence make Oknov invisible because his presence in the text can be achieved through words only, and his violence places him *outside* of the realm of discourse and disables the speech of those in contact with him. Yet, Oknov has the final words—"God bless!" *(Gospodi blagoslovi!)*—over the body of a strangled Kozlov, and he pronounces them after the other characters have been subjugated to his will and have joined him in murdering Kozlov. It is possible to suggest that the power of Oknov over Kozlov (a victim) and over Striuchkov and Motyl'kov (accomplices to murder) is comparable with the author's power over the text and its readers. Violence momentarily transfers Oknov from a relatively "real" space-time continuum into a point of "something," located, as mentioned earlier, beyond the coordinates of time and space. Much like an author, he can control the words of the characters.[26] The transition of Striuchkov and Motyl'kov from supporting a victim into willing participation in the violent act of murdering him can also be compared with the author's power to dictate his or her will to all the figurants of the text, as well as to the reader. In this respect, violence appears as some kind of a transverbal language, or rather, a language of power that recalls Antonin Artaud's project for a "theatre of cruelty" operating by a supreme language of violent acts and thus making verbal expression superfluous.[27]

Violence as an allegory of the author's power is revisited in "Pakin and Rakukin," the last text of *Incidents*. Unlike the other "violent" stories, Pakin performs his act of violence and brings Rakukin to his death without laying a finger on him—only through verbal offences and commands. Rakukin's death, resulting from Pakin's verbal control, expresses itself in the victim's strange disfiguration: "Looking at Rakukin from Pakin's perspective, one could think that Rakukin was sitting with no head at all. Rakukin's Adam's apple was sticking out. Involuntarily, one could not help thinking of it as his nose."[28] The disappearance of Rakukin's head, the substitution of an Adam's apple with a nose—this is all reminiscent of the transformation of the "red-haired man" in "Blue Book No. 10." As a result of Pakin's verbal violence, in other words, of his power realized through words, Rakukin mutates into a purely literary character, which in turn leads to his death as a human being. This suggestion can be supported by the last paragraph of the text, where totally literary "characters" appear: Rakukin's soul and the Angel of Death, who "takes Rakukin's soul by the hand and leads him somewhere through houses and walls."[29] The Angel of Death echoes not only the "God bless!" pronounced by Oknov over the strangled Kozlov, but also words said by Rakukin throughout the text: "I believe, said Rakukin."[30]

These religious signals link the "authorial" power of Pakin over his victim with the power of the supreme "Author"—God—writing the destinies of humans. Violence assigns godlike power to the victimizer, because, according to Walter Benjamin, "mythical violence in its archetypal form is a mere manifestation of the gods. Not a means to their ends, scarcely a manifestation of their will, but first of all a manifestation of their existence."[31] Considering the traditional modernist mythology of the godlike power of the author—"a deity, named author" (Nabokov)—the suggestion of violence as the primary source of this power demonstrates the depth of Kharms's deconstruction of modernism.

Nevertheless, Kharms does share the modernist mythology of the godlike status of the author,[32] and he directly displays his power by depriving his own characters of individuality and psychology, transforming them into some kind of morbid clowns. As Robin Milner-Gulland writes, "In general terms, of course, Kharms belongs to the poetic works of modernism, as his 'collage' techniques, oddities and crudities of lexis, *sdvigi* (dislocations), sometimes fractured syntax, parodistic and bathetic effects and phonetic experimentation, often reaching 'transrational' word-invention, all bear ample witness."[33] Other researchers compare Kharms's works with those of Velemir Khlebnikov, French Surrealists, Kafka, Beckett, as well as Ionesco and Genette. Kharms's *Incidents* displays all the definitive features of the avant-garde in its mockery of traditions and cultural canons, experimentalism, and testing the limits of literature.

However, through the presentation of violence as a substitute for writing or authorship, Kharms arrives at the substitution of the God-creator, or in other words, creativity, with the Angel of Death, the direct representation of destruction and ultimate absence. Death in Kharms's *Incidents* appears as the ultimate signifier of the allegories of writing, among which violence plays the dominant role. It does not promise transcendence and it does not lead to the safe haven of "outsideness," or "something" *(nechto),* rather it manifests the complete and hopeless absence, disappearance and erasure of the subject and of meaning.

Thus, Kharms deconstructs the modernist avant-garde utopia of creativity and freedom, the idea of creating self-sufficient and individual models of the world, eternity, and history. His representation of violence as an allegory of writing presents a faultfinding analysis of modernist discourse *from within.* It is one of the most radical examples of modernist avant-garde self-critique, even to the point of self-destruction.

Notes

1. He was arrested at least twice, first in 1931, after which he was sent to the exile in Kursk, and in 1941—this arrest led to his horrible death in the prison psychiatric ward. Kharms's archive was saved from destruction by his close friend Iakov Druskin.

2. Jean-Philip Jaccard illuminatingly entitled his book on Kharms *Daniil Kharms and the End of the Russian Avant-Garde* (Bern: Peter Lang, 1991). In accord with this vision, Anthony Anemone isolates "three general stages" in Kharms's evolution: "[First], a revolutionary and nihilistic attack on the authority of bourgeois traditions in art and politics; second, in the exploration of what have come to be called post-modern problems of language and meaning; and, most importantly, an ethical critique of the Utopian project in modern Russian history and the role of avant-garde in preparing the way for the violence and immorality of Stalinism" ("The Anti-World of Daniil Kharms: On the Significance of the Absurd," in *Daniil Kharms and the Poetics of the Absurd: Essays and Materials*, ed. N. Cornwell [New York: St. Martin's Press, 1991], 88–89). The emphasis on the exploration of the problems of language and representation, as well as Kharms's "critique of the Utopian project," the approach to his absurdism as a philosophical dismantling of the most essential premises of literature and art, are characteristic for the recent works on Kharms, especially the monographs by Graham Roberts (*The Last Soviet Avant-Garde: OBERIU—Fact, Fiction, Metafiction* [Cambridge: Cambridge University Press, 1997]), Mikhail Iampolskii (*Bespamiatstvo kak istok [Chitaia Kharmsa]* [Moscow: Novoe literaturnoe obozrenie, 1998]), Aleksandr Kobrinskii (*Poetika "OBERIU" v kontekste russkogo literaturnogo avangarda* [Moscow: Izd-vo Moskovskogo kul'turologicheskogo lytsieia, 2000]), and D. Tokarev (*Kurs na khudshee—absurd kak kategoriia teksta u Daniila Kharmsa i Semiuelia Bekketa* [Moscow: Novoe literaturnoe obozrenie, 2002]). Roberts argues that "in his prose and drama, Kharms shows how language—at least certain language—can shape, even transform reality. In his fiction words are more powerful than things, yet words are never the same as things," which means that "language has a power to destroy as well as to create" (Roberts, *Last Soviet Avant-Garde*, 145, 144.) This perspective may help us understand the role of motifs of violence in Kharms's mature works.

3. Walter Benjamin, *The Origin of German Tragic Drama*, trans. John Osborne (London: Verso, 1990), 265.

4. "A style of absence which is almost an ideal absence of style; writing is then reduced to a sort of negative mood in which the social or mythical characters of a language are abolished in favor of a neutral and inert state of for; thus thought remains wholly responsible, without being overlaid by a secondary commitment to a History not its own. . . . If the writing is really neutral, and if language, instead of being a cumbersome and recalcitrant act, reaches the state of a pure equation, which is no more tangible than an algebra when it confronts the innermost part of man, then Literature is vanquished, the problematics of mankind is uncovered and presented without elaboration, the writer becomes irretrievably honest" (Roland Barthes, *Writing Zero Degree*, trans. Anette Lavers and Colin Smith [New York: Farrar, Straus and Giroux; Noonday Press, 1977], 77, 78).

5. George Gibian, ed. and trans., *The Man with the Black Coat: Russia's Literature of the Absurd: Selected Works by Daniil Kharms and Alexander Vvedensky* (Evanston, Ill.: Northwestern University Press, 1987), 57.

6. Robin Aizlewood argues that this strategy is characteristic for the cycle as a whole: "The divorce between signifier and signified is a recurrent theme in

Kharms where words can lose their accepted reference and turn into their opposite. . . . Thus fundamental categories such as life/death, waking/dreaming, and identity all become unsettled." (Robin Aizlewood, "Towards an Interpretation of Kharms's *Sluchai,*" in Cornwell, *Daniil Kharms,* 103–4).

7. See Jean-Phillippe Jaccard, *Daniil Kharms i konets russkogo avangarda,* trans. F. A. Petrovskaia (St. Petersburg: Akademicheskii proekt, 1995), 250.

8. Gibian, *The Man with the Black Coat,* 64.

9. About this category of Mikhail Bakhtin's philosophic aesthetics see Gary Saul Morson and Caryl Emerson, *Mikhail Bakhtin: Creation of a Prosaic* (Stanford, Calif.: Stanford University Press, 1990), 53–56; Michael Holquist, *Dialogism: Bakhtin and His World* (London: Routledge, 1990), 30–33.

10. Daniil Kharms, *Polnoe sobranie sochinenii,* ed. V. N. Sazhin (St. Petersburg: Akademicheskii proekt, 2001), 3:34.

11. See Iampolskii, *Bespamiatstvo kak istok,* 299–300.

12. Gibian, *The Man with the Black Coat,* 58.

13. Ibid. 60.

14. A. A. Dobritsyn, "'Sonet' v proze: *Sluchai* Kharmsa," *Philologica* 4 (1997): 163–64, available at http://rema.ru:8100/philologica/04rus/04rus_dobricyn.htm. Accessed 10 Aug. 2007.

15. Gibian, *The Man with the Black Coat,* 60.

16. Within the rest of the cycle, one may isolate the texts concentrated around different types of transcendence/transgression: *literature* ("Pushkin and Gogol," "Mathematician and Andrei Semenovich," "Four Illustrations of an Idea Shocking a Person Who Is Not Prepared for It," "Makarov and Peterson," "An Unsuccessful Show," "Tiuk!" "A Historical Episode," "Fedya Davidovich," and "Anecdotes about Pushkin's Life"); *a dream or trip outside of a usual habitat* ("An Optical Illusion," "Carpenter Kushakov," "A Trunk," "An Incident with Petrakov," "A Dream," "A Young Man Who Astonished a Watchman," "The Losses," and "Dream Teases Man"); and, finally, *violence* ("A Story of the Fighting Men," "A Lynching," "What They Sell in the Stores Nowadays," "Mashkin Killed Koshkin," "Hunters," "The Beginning of a Beautiful Summer Day [A Symphony]," and "Pakin and Rakukin"). The motif of violence/injury is present in all three groups of the *Incidents.* However, for obvious reasons, I will focus on the last group of stories.

17. Kharms, *Polnoe sobranie sochinenii,* 2:337.

18. Gibian, *The Man with the Black Coat,* 52.

19. Ibid., 71.

20. Ibid, 66.

21. Rene Girard, *Violence and the Sacred,* trans. Patrick Gregory (Baltimore, Md.: John Hopkins University Press, 1977), 14, 28.

22. "American tribes practice *potlatch* on the occasion of a person's change in a situation—initiations, marriages, funerals—and even in a more evolved form it can never be separated from a festival. . . . *potlatch* excludes all bargaining and, in general, it is constituted by a considerable gift of riches offered openly and with the goal of humiliating, defying, and *obligating* a rival. . . . But the gift is not the only form of *potlatch;* it is equally possible to defy rivals through the spectacular destruction of wealth. It is through the intermediary of this last

form that *potlatch* is reunited with religious sacrifice since what is destroyed is theoretically offered to the mythical ancestors of the donees. Relatively recently a Tlingit chief appeared before his rival to slash the throats of some of his own slaves. The destruction was repaid at a given date by the slaughter of a greater number of slaves. . . . It must be recognized, in fact, that wealth is multiplied in *potlatch* civilizations in a way that recalls the inflation of credit in banking civilizations; in other words, it would be impossible to realize at once all the wealth possessed by the total number of donors resulting from the obligations contracted by the total number of donees" (Georges Bataille, "The Notion of Expenditure," in *Postmodernism: Critical Concepts*, ed. Victor E. Taylor and Charles E. Winquist [London: Routledge, 1998], 1:6–7).

23. Bataille comments on art as one of the forms of *potlatch* in the modern world: "From the point of view of expenditure, artistic production must be divided into two main categories, the first constituted by architectural construction, music, and dance. This category is comprised of *real* expenditures. . . . In their major forms, literature and theater, which constitute the second category, provoke dread and horror through symbolic representations of tragic loss (degradation and death). . . . The term poetry is applied to the least degraded and least intellectualized forms of the expression of a state of loss [and] can be considered synonymous with expenditure; it in fact signifies, in the most precise way, creation by means of loss. Its meaning is therefore close to that of *sacrifice*. . . . The poet frequently can use words only to his own loss; he is often forced to choose between the destiny of a reprobate, who is as profoundly separated from society as rejects are from apparent life, and a renunciation whose price is a mediocre activity, subordinated to vulgar and superficial needs" (ibid., 4–5).

24. "Oknov" is a derivative from Russian "okno"—a window. This name contains a significant reference to Kharms's symbolism of a window as a sign of the transcendental world, referring both to light and writing (see Iampolskii, *Bespamiatstvo kak istok*, 42–73). In several texts, Kharms uses the monogram "window" composed of the letters of the name of his beloved Esther (a star); additionally, Oknov appeared in other Kharms texts as a figure of a visionary. See Il'ia Kukulin, "'Dvenadtsat' Bloka, zhertvennyi kozel i siuzhetoslozhenie u Daniila Kharmsa," *Novoe literaturnoe obozrenie* 16 (1995): 147–53.

25. Kharms, *Polnoe sobranie sochinenii*, 2:351.

26. The confrontation with Oknov causes some kind of verbal paralysis in Striuchkov: "*Striuchkov:* This is villainy! *Oknov:* Wha-at! *Striuchkov:* . . . -ainy . . . *Oknov:* Ho-o-o-w? *Striuchkov:* Nn . . nn . . nnn . . . nothing" (Kharms, *Polnoe sobranie sochinenii*, 2:351), as well as in Kozlov, who, after being mutilated by Oknov, responds to "Kozlov, where are you?" with inarticulate "Shasha . . . !" This "non-word" is interpreted by the initially compassionate Striuchkov and Motyl'kov as a "license to kill" Kozlov: "Look how things got with him! . . . Nothing to do now. Personally I think we should just strangle it" (ibid.).

27. Parallels between Kharms and Artaud are briefly addressed by Jaccard, *Daniil Kharms*, 205–6, 208.

28. Kharms, *Polnoe sobranie sochinenii*, 2:360.

29. Ibid., 361. In Kharms's text the soul (a feminine noun in Russian) is referred to as "him" rather than "her."

30. Ibid., 360.

31. Walter Benjamin, "Critique of Violence," in his *Reflections: Essays, Aphorisms, Autobiographical Writings,* trans. Edmund Jephcott (New York: Harcourt Brace Jovanovich, 1978), 294.

32. See, for example, his famous letter to Klavdiia Pugacheva of October 1933: "And yet I began to bring order into the world. And then Art appeared.... Now it is my duty to make a proper order. This goal enraptures me and I can think of nothing else. I try and say it, write it, draw it, dance it, build it. I am the world's creator and that is the most vital of my qualities. How can I not think of it incessantly? In everything I do, I am aware that I am the creator of the world" (Daniil Kharms, *O iavleniiakh i sushchestvovaniiakh* [St. Petersburg: Azbuka-Klassika, 2000], 235).

33. Robin Milner-Gulland, "Beyond the Turning Point: An Afterword," in Cornwell, *Daniil Kharms,* 244.

The Sadists' Club

Struggling with the Legacy of Stalinism in Vasilii Aksenov's The Burn

NINA EFIMOV

> Vasia had once asked me: "Mother, what's the fiercest of all animals?" Fool that I was! Why didn't I tell him the "fiercest was man—of all animals the one to beware of most."
>
> Evgeniia Ginzburg, *Journey into the Whirlwind*

In 1973 Alexander Solzhenitsyn, a former prisoner of the Stalinist labor camps, presented a systematic chronicle of KGB atrocities in his astonishing masterpiece *The Gulag Archipelago,* and in the summer of 1974 its English and French translations changed the world's view of the Communist regime. Although Solzhenitsyn's shocking estimate—sixty million victims of Communist terror—seemed to be overrated, current research indicates that this figure was low.[1]

Nonetheless in the last decade Stalin's approval rating in Russian public opinion poll has increased dramatically. A television poll on March 5, 2003—the fiftieth anniversary of Stalin's death—as well as several sociological surveys, showed that the majority of Russians approved of Stalin's role in Soviet history and regarded him as a "wise" leader who brought industrial strength to the Soviet Union and contributed to its development into a superpower. One may question the accuracy of such polls, but the rise of Stalin's popularity in post-Communist Russia is evident. The alarming question of why so many Russians are able to forget or ignore the scale of Stalin's crimes may be partially explained by the fact that most of his victims died in the camps, and that only 12 percent of the secret police's archives have been opened to the public; documents concerning such things as medical experiments on prisoners, the suppression of peasant unrest, and labor camp revolts are still classified. It seems as though the sudden collapse of the Soviet Union and the host of subsequent political and social changes in Russia have also served to obscure memory of the victims of "the Soviet experiment."

In the closed, undemocratic Soviet Union it was dissident writers who introduced the prison-camp theme into clandestine Russian literature. In Varlaam Shalamov's *Kolyma Stories* (1954–73) the horrors of everyday camp life are conveyed with narrative simplicity and a detached authorial voice. In *Faithful Ruslan* (1963–75) Georgii Vladimov describes the jailors' cruelty and the suppression of a prison revolt through the perception of a guard dog. Ius Aleshkovskii, in his novel *The Hand* (1980), creates a grotesque portrait of a KGB executioner confessing to his cruelties; himself a casualty of collectivization, he has used terror to take revenge on those who had victimized him.

KGB violence is also a major theme in the works of Vasilii Aksenov, whose biography was itself shaped by the Gulag. Born in Kazan' in 1932, in the pitiless year of collectivization, Aksenov shared the fate of other children of "enemies of the people." His mother, Evgeniia Ginzburg, a history professor at Kazan' University, was arrested in 1937 and charged with Trotskyism and participation in a terrorist counter-revolutionary organization. Her well-known memoir *Journey into the Whirlwind* (two volumes, 1967 and 1978) belongs to Russia's finest autobiographical literature. Aksenov's father, Pavel Aksenov, a leading member of the Tatar Province Party Committee, was also arrested in 1937. One night officers of the NKVD came after little Vasia and literally picked him up out of the cradle.[2] The writer remembers:

> The NKVD had taken me when I was four years old. . . . I was put with two other boys into a special compartment of a train going to the town of Kostroma. With me came a female security officer [*chekistka, baba*], who was in charge of us; and we were not allowed to leave the closed compartment. We were four-year-old child-prisoners.

I was in the children's home for about six months, until my relatives found me.

The NKVD gave no information of my whereabouts, but my uncle, my father's brother, came to Kazan': he was unemployed because as my father's brother he had lost his job at the university, and he spent his days simply waiting to be arrested. Since he had nothing to lose, he very bravely went there, pounded his fist on the door and shouted: "Give me the boy!" He then entered, boldly reclaimed me and took me to the home of my aunt (my father's sister) in Kazan', where I was brought up until I was sixteen—and at sixteen I went away to Mama in Magadan.[3]

After graduating from high school in Magadan, Aksenov returned to Kazan' where he was admitted to the medical school at Kazan' University, from which, soon after Stalin's death, he was expelled for not having disclosed in his application that he was the son of "enemies of the people." In fact, in 1953 the Kazan' KGB prepared documents for Aksenov's arrest, "simply because [his] 'coming of age' had drawn near,"[4] and had Stalin not died, he would have been sent to a labor camp. In 1956 Aksenov graduated from Leningrad University and began his medical career.

The appearance of his first novel, *Colleagues* (1960), in *Iunost'* (The Youth), the best literary journal for young Soviet readers, at the height of Khrushchev's Thaw, brought Aksenov fame and membership in the Union of Soviet Writers, and his next novel, *A Starry Ticket* (1961), made him one of the most popular writers. His works were translated into foreign languages, and a movie version of *Colleagues* was shown at a film festival in Argentina. Aksenov's early prose was remarkable for its absence of the kind of routine political conformity expected of all Soviet writers. His was labeled "youth prose"; young people—so ran the officious argument of the Thaw period—were impatient with Soviet state ideology, and their lukewarm ideological position could be tolerated. Political alignment was expected to come as Aksenov "matured," but at the time he was officially accepted as a "neo-romantic" Soviet writer.

In March 1963 at a meeting with young Soviet writers and artists, Khrushchev criticized the pro-Western orientation and lack of Communist ideals in "youth prose," and he singled out Aksenov as a bad example. Aksenov was forced to promise to change his ways. However, and surprisingly, neither his arrest in 1966 for demonstrating against the installation of Stalin's bust near the Lenin mausoleum; nor his public support for Solzhenitsyn's letter to the Fourth Congress of Soviet Writers, which contained criticism of the suppression of creativity in the Soviet Union; nor his public protest against the trial of the writers Iulii Daniel' and Andrei Siniavskii resulted in a ban on his works. Furthermore, as his prose evolved, Aksenov continued to refuse to allow the intrusion of Soviet discourse in his writing. His characters become more enigmatic and burdened with a personal mystery that they do not care to unravel, as in *Our Golden Hardware* (1966) or in *Surplussed Barrelware* (1968). They do communicate, but in ways that are beyond words, and their demeanor remains ostensibly non-Soviet and naively westernized.

The attempt by the Brezhnev establishment to cover up Stalin's atrocities and reintroduce him into Soviet culture was met by Aksenov with *The Steel Bird* (written in 1965, published in 1977), an allegory of life under Brezhnev and a warning about a return to Stalinism. The main protagonist, Popenkov or The Steel Bird, as he calls himself, is a hybrid man-bird-airplane and a symbol of Stalinism. Besides the assumed name, he has the psychological traits of a Soviet dictator, such as despotism, intolerance to freedom, and the desire to enslave and destroy the world. *The Steel Bird* revealed that the absence of Soviet realia in Aksenov's former works had been rooted in a conviction that the regime had no redeeming values.

In the 1970s, although Aksenov was allowed to accept invitations to lecture in the West, official publication of his new writings in the Soviet Union became problematic, and the writer himself was put under KGB surveillance. By 1978 the authorities prohibited the publication of works by and about Aksenov both on account of the interviews he had given in the West and for the unofficial publicity surrounding his unfinished novel *The Burn* (written 1969–75, published in 1980), his last novel before emigration. *The Burn* presents a world sharply split between the Soviet evil and the good that a few individuals spontaneously, sporadically, and ineffectively strive to accomplish. In 1978, in protest against the state monopoly on literary production, Aksenov edited *Metropol,* the first uncensored Soviet almanac intended as an alternative to samizdat—"self-published" underground works banned from publication by the regime. In January 1979 twelve copies of *Metropol* were completed and two were smuggled abroad to be published there, while the twenty-two *Metropol* contributors held an inauguration party with foreign reporters attending. The official reaction was merciless: Aksenov's books were removed from libraries, and in the summer of 1980 he was forced to leave the country, like many other writers of his generation. In January 1981 Aksenov learned from Soviet newspapers that the Supreme Soviet had deprived him of his Soviet citizenship.

He came to the United States, where he accepted a teaching position at George Mason University. The career of a writer in residence and professor of Russian literature suited him well. Aksenov's new novels confirmed his prestige both in Russia and in the West; they were studied in universities, discussed at Slavic studies conferences and in scholarly journals, and, most importantly, were also well received by readers. Aksenov's post-emigration writings before the collapse of the Soviet Union—*The Island of Crimea* (1981), *Paperscape* (1982), and *Say Cheese!* (1985)—all portray violence as the general background for his characters' development. At the same time, they make a clear distinction between good and evil, refusing to justify evil by recourse to some higher instance. *Say Cheese!*, an autobiographical novel evoking Aksenov's participation in *Metropol*, ends with the conversion of Brezhnev's Politburo to the side of good. In the novel's fictional world, there is no evil, and the Devil himself spontaneously mends his ways without punishment or purification.

After perestroika Aksenov frequently visited Russia, actively participating in its cultural and literary life. Although his Russian citizenship was reinstated, he preferred to remain in the United States, calling it his home country. Written alternatively in realistic and ironic styles, his later novels—*The Yolk* (1991), *The Moscow Saga* (1993–94), *The New Sweet Style* (1998), and *Caesarian Luminescence* (2001) are reflections on violence in the Soviet state and on recent developments in Russia.

Aksenov's view on Communist atrocities is far from simplistic. His villains, on the other hand, are completely black. Along with quintessential evil characters such as Taimyrskoe Rylo (Ugly Taimir Mug) in *Say Cheese!*, Smerdiashchaia Dama (Stinking Lady) in *Rendezvous* (1991), and Stepanida Vlasievna in *Our Golden Hardware* (1980), he creates a series of expressionistic images of KGB agents, party officials, and army officers who have no scrap of doubt in the rightness of mass executions. Their devotion to the Revolution and Communism has overturned the normal values of life, and they enthusiastically generate mountains of corpses. The most outrageous villains and perverts find the KGB the perfect place to unleash their sadistic instincts.

This is also true of *The Burn*, which, as the title suggests, deals with pain and suffering. Nauseating violence is at the core of the novel. *The Burn* has no plot; rather, it is a collage of self-contained, painful flashbacks of a young Soviet intellectual from childhood to his final status as Victim (*postradavshii*—"one who has suffered.") Set in the late sixties and early seventies, the novel is divided into three parts: "The Men's Club," "Five in Solitary," and "The Victim's Last Adventure." The first part describes the lives of five main protagonists—a scientist, a doctor, a sculptor, a writer, and a saxophone player—who share the same patronymic, Apollinarievich. The reader learns about their artistic and scientific work in Moscow from the Thaw through the late sixties, their lifestyles, drinking binges, women, and, most importantly, disillusionment with their talent and their subsequent professional decline.

Sometimes the five characters act simultaneously or talk and interact with each other, but most of the time the actions of one are continued by one of the others. They may be seen as "quintuplets"[5] or as a postmodern portrayal of a single individual with a split personality, seen from different angles.[6] In part 2 we realize that the five characters share the same past—all five grew out of one teenager, Tolia Steinbok, who had been reunited with his mother and his stepfather in Magadan in the late 1940s, after his mother's twelve-year stint in a labor camp was over. (The autobiographical subtext is clear.) Tolia's storyline is punctuated by episodes featuring the evil NKVD officer Cheptsov,[7] who had arrested Tolia's mother and had tortured Tolia's best friend, Sania Gurchenko, sadistically humiliating him. Memories of Cheptsov continue to haunt the five major characters in their adulthood as they recognize him in various guises—a cloakroom attendant, a literary censor, a major-general, an official, and so forth.

The third book is an alcoholic hallucination of the five protagonists who are now one and the same person—the Victim in search of salvation. Realistic historical episodes, such as the Soviet invasion of Czechoslovakia, alternate with fantastic fragments (for example, the story of a Soviet tank that gets lost on the way to Prague and travels through the West). In the end the Victim commits suicide and arrives in a surrealistic purgatory—the afterlife appears to be a pipe dream, a poster paradise with a pin-up God. The accumulation of violence and evil generates a spontaneous religion featuring an enigmatic and personal God who is himself more of a problem than a solution, a forsaken flower and the miasma of evil. This is an image of an all-forgiving, non-vengeful, but impotent God. The novel's ending—images flickering through the mind of the dying Victim—presents an inventory of methods of torture.

Violence, regular as clockwork, impels the characters, motivates them, and drives the plot while love, politics, and human interactions are associated with primal scenes of rape and sexual abuse. The protagonist, whose consciousness makes up the substance of the narrative, is prompted by recollections of Soviet evil—uncanny, demonic, destructive, suggesting horrors beyond what is recorded in the novel. The narrative also offers glimpses of the mindset of an abused child.

Aksenov's most brutal and predictably violent characters in *The Burn* are Stalinists—perverts and sadists. The female geometry teacher who harasses Tolia for hiding his "unhealthy origin" (i.e., that he is the child of an "enemy of the people") provides a good example. This grotesque episode transforms a sadist into a clown, one whose incoherent and incongruous speech results in a public orgasm. Its didactic climax is, in fact, a stream of consciousness, expressed in grammatically correct but illogical syntax, with a mixture of broken proverbs and Stalinist slogans justifying violence: "There is a pseudo-student here who is hiding his true face, who has fallen as an apple not far from the apple tree of his parentage in our Soviet cherry orchard, where the chips fly when we cut down such trees, and where the hammer is not answerable for what the saw does! With the cosine we are building gigantic hypotenuses, we are growing watermelons on compost in square greenhouses, under the guidance of our great leader we are changing the course of rivers by planting protective windbreaks of trees, but the snake-headed Hydra of the enemies of the people, stinking of putrefaction, slithers its way into our great friendly family of nations!"[8] In her political and sexual excitement, the teacher unconsciously employs images of objects and geometric figures with sharp edges, tools of torture, and verbs of stabbing and chopping, with suggest the violent nature of her desire.

Colonel Cheptsov, another Stalinist and supporter of large-scale violence, inflicts suffering on Sania Gurchenko and on his own stepdaughter Nina, whom he loves but nonetheless intends to denounce for her relationship with a dissident scientist. Cheptsov's unconditional belief in plots and conspiracies hatched by "enemies of the people" shapes his mentality as a serial killer: "'I'd squash them all and to hell with the regulations!' said Cheptsov, jumping on Sania's face. 'All their children, all their relations and friends! You know, I can't bear to look at all these bastards!'" (386). Cheptsov's appearance accentuates his naturally murderous personality: "imagine him undressed—huge, with resilient buttocks, a hairy protruding stomach, a heavy pendulous penis, like that of the dominant male of a heard of seals, a wrinkled old killer" (385). Cheptsov's sadism is aroused by Nina's betrayal of the Party (he catches her with anti-Soviet propaganda) and he rapes her. The equation of political and sexual violence is also realized through symbolic means. Cheptsov, half-naked and "in a green officer's shirt," whips Nina with a military belt and beats her with a buckle that has a red star on it. Keith Booker remarks that Cheptsov "functions more as a generalized embodiment of the ideology of Stalinism than as a realistic human figure."[9] Cheptsov's sadism and murderous desires are cultivated by his profession, suggesting that he personifies KGB brutality.

Cheptsov is addicted to "functional sadism"—getting satisfaction in torturing and humiliating helpless convicts. Having retired from duty, he satisfies his sadistic urges by stalking victims of Stalinism and reminding them of the past: "He would simply stand behind the backs of the giggling, wheezing, cackling old men and clasp his big, powerful hands in front of him. Inevitably his steady stare would make one of the domino players cringe, turn around, shiver with fear, and nudge his neighbors. They had recognized him! They knew! The older generation remembered that stare only too well and knew what it meant" (339).

In *The Burn* the author's response to Stalin's crimes may be observed in the scene of Cheptsov's possible salvation. After raping Nina and denouncing her to the KGB Cheptsov commits suicide and dies in the emergency room with Dr. Malkolmov on duty. Malkolmov recognizes him as his former torturer, but, guided by forgiveness, injects him with "Lymph D"—a magical elixir that gives life and moral knowledge. The elixir, however, is wasted because the life-giving injection cannot transform the genetically evil Cheptsov into a good person. It does bring him back to life, yet the resurrected Cheptsov is "not even a man at all" but "a philosophical construct." Nevertheless, forgiveness of the enemy is crucial in the Victim's psychological make-up and Aksenov's characters instinctively come to a realization that, while the evil must be stopped and revenge rejected, atrocities must be forgotten. This is further illustrated in the episode where the Victim makes a phantasmagoric escape to the countryside to meet his father, Apollinarii Bokov, an old Bolshevik. The Victim raises a white flag of capitulation next to his father's Red Banner: "Perhaps if we meekly accept those machine-gun ideas, we could stop any future bloodshed, shut off the artery?" (509). Like his non-punishing God, who is always love and who pities both Brezhnev and the Czechs, the Victim cannot prevent violence, and so Aksenov's novel offers no solutions.

In Aksenov's novel *The Moscow Saga* Lenin is reincarnated as a squirrel and a dog comes back as a boyar, suggesting that false, pseudoreligious justifications of violence are an inevitable part of human history. Whether moments like this are sarcastic comments on the cultural provincialism of Soviet life or ironic instantiations of postmodern kitsch, Aksenov's epiphanies are effective in preventing allegorical, historicist, or other "serious" readings that would explain his characters' victimization. Aksenov seems to suggest that violence is a fact of life and that there is nothing beyond that but unrewarded pain. Ordinary people can be weak and confused, and living in a totalitarian state entangles them in evil against their will. While the most efficient KGB agents might have been naturally vicious individuals who joined the organization for pleasure, ordinary people, left on their own, turn instinctively to the good. A grotesque reminder of Stalinism and crimes committed by Stalinists, Aksenov's writing is his legacy to a Russia in quest of a new post-Communist identity.

Notes

1. D. M. Thomas, *Alexander Solzhenitsyn* (New York: St. Martin Press, 1998), 443.

2. Throughout its existence, the name of the Soviet secret police changed as follows: Cheka, GPU, OGPU, NKVD, KGB.

3. Inger Lauridsen and Per Dalgard, "Interview with V. P. Aksenov," in *Vasily Pavlovich Aksenov: A Writer in Quest of Himself*, ed. Edward Mozejko (Columbus, Ohio: Slavica Publishers, 1986), 14.

4. Lauridsen and Dalgard, "Interview," 16.

5. Nina Efimov, *Intertekst v religioznykh i demonicheskikh motivakh V. P. Aksenova* (Moscow: Izdatel'stvo Moskovskogo universiteta, 1993), 105–14.

6. Per Dalgard, *The Function of the Grotesque in Vasilij Aksenov*, trans. Robert Porter (Arhus: Arkona, 1982), 95.

7. Cheptsov's prototype is a real NKVD officer, Chentsov, whom Evgeniia Ginzburg describes in her second volume, *Within the Whirlwind* (Milan: Arnoldo Mondadori, 1979), 164.

8. Vasilii Aksenov, *The Burn* (New York: Random House, 1984), 282. All further references to this novel are provided in the text.

9. M. Keith Booker and Dubravka Juraga, *Bakhtin, Stalin, and Modern Russian Fiction: Carnival, Dialogism, and History* (London: Greenwood Press, 1995), 35.

Circles of Hell, Circles of Life

Two Responses to Violence in Gulag Memoirs

NATASHA KOLCHEVSKA

The two subjects of this essay witnessed—and subsequently wrote about—one of contemporary history's most horrific occurrences: the incarceration of millions in the belt of forced labor camps as memorialized by Alexander Solzhenitsyn in *The Gulag Archipelago.*[1] The first of these, Evgeniia Ginzburg, penned a memoir, translated into English in two volumes, *Journey into the Whirlwind* and *Within the Whirlwind* (*Krutoi marshrut,* 1967, 1981), that was first published to much acclaim abroad, was translated into several languages, and has become a staple of courses and discourses on twentieth-century history and women's writing.[2] Like Ginzburg, after her release from the Gulag, Evfrosiniia Kersnovskaia began writing—and in her case also drawing—what would eventually grow to a dozen illustrated notebooks. Some seven hundred of her works were posthumously collected into "Cliff Drawings" *(Naskal'naia zhivopis')* a large-format book of images and text that was published in Russia in 1991. Kersnovskaia's unique work, with its visual documentation of suffering and degradation, its use of visual discourse alongside the more culturally regulated (in the Russian context) verbal narratives, and her adoption of a clearly "masculine" stance in her memoir set it apart from other Gulag writings by women.

The facts of the Gulag experience varied relatively little—inhumane conditions, cold, dirt, life-threatening disease and illness, hunger, crowding, and the full gamut of indignities, sadistic behaviors, and other forms of dehumanization committed both by camp officials and other prisoners, including criminals. As Leona Toker has recently enumerated, Gulag memoirs also share a distinctive set of topoi.[3] Nonetheless, the variations in the enormous number of narrative responses to those givens run the full range from self-serving cover-ups to meticulous exposés, from vast histories to personal stories. In more individualized tales, such as the two under scrutiny here, social background, ideology, temperament, and sexual identity—to name only a few—affect the survivor's ability or willingness to resist capitulation to the Gulag's inhumanity and then recapitulate their experience through narrative form. Of the survivors who wrote memoirs, most had little hope that their memoirs, typically written in journal form, would be published in their lifetimes. Those who chose that mode shared a common purpose: for them "writing was one of the ways to preserve self identity and integrity."[4] The implication for later generations is well summarized by Toker: "What most survivor accounts seek to make poignantly meaningful is not the death but the individual lives of the victims whose worth is denied by totalitarian regimes. History books or archival materials are of little help here—one needs more effective aids to imagination and thought. Quality writing about atrocities is ethically significant not only because it captures potentially reluctant audiences, but also because it stages and mediates a closer engagement with its material."[5] If we keep in mind a later statement by Toker, that "[a] famished *zek* [prisoner] finds it extremely hard to preserve the integrity of the moral self,"[6] implying that any writing that comes out of the Gulag does so in spite of serious damage to the body and mind, the fact that any of the writers were able to relay that experience to subsequent generations becomes all the more remarkable.

Those Gulag survivors whose narratives have proven to be the most enduring fused their ethical positions with a range of literary strategies and aesthetic devices. One common strategy used by memoirist-survivors of both the Gulag and the Holocaust has been the creative act of establishing a familial Other, a later witness who substitutes for the lack of actual surviving witnesses and serves as a prompt or precursor for their ultimately public testimony to the horrors and crimes they have witnessed. As was the case with Holocaust survivors, for those who went through the Gulag "the historical imperative to bear witness could not be met during its actual occurrence"[7] as the relentless struggle to survive overwhelmed any possibility of narrative re-enactment at the time. As Ginzburg writes in *Whirlwind:* "All those years I had no opportunity to write anything down, to prepare any preliminary sketches for a future book" (2:419). And in her preface, Kersnovskaia similarly observes that "my whole life during those years was a chain of nasty and ugly events that do not fit into the understanding of a normal person and cannot reach the feelings of someone who did not live through it."[8]

Reaching across the shattered bridge of the initial silence imposed by their expulsion from what they describe as Paradise (Ginzburg from a privileged, "socialist" lifestyle, Kersnovskaia from the pastoral idyll of her family's estate), each puts pen to paper first to restore the bond, textually if not experientially, between themselves and loved ones. The tradition, dating back to antiquity, of writing memoirs as family legacy, has gained particular poignancy in the twentieth century, as the family has become the first victim and last vestige of protection against war, exile, cultural displacement, and other violent ruptures. The first thing that Ginzburg does once her son Vasia (the future writer Vasilii Aksenov) has finally come to stay with her in Magadan in 1948, after a twelve-year separation, is to spend the night reading him a draft of what would eventually become *Whirlwind:* "he was my first listener," she confesses (2:268). In a similar gesture, Kersnovskaia attributes a dialogical intention for her drawings. Addressing her mother as "my first and last, sole and irreplaceable friend," she frames the journal as her response to her mother's request to write down the story of the seventeen years they were apart: "You would sometimes say—'a little piece from here, from there—I can't figure anything out. Write everything in order, and then maybe I'll understand everything that happened to you.'" Factually truthful or not, the authors in both cases would have us believe that the text we hold in our hands would not have come into being without that Other who could see things that they could not. While either author would have been horrified by the actual possibility of their mother or son literally "trading places" with them, the text, in a sense, allows them to do so. To paraphrase Michael Holquist, the excess of seeing experienced by survivors is defined by the lack of seeing by their loved ones, and vice versa,[9] and the text becomes the mediating structure through which they try to overcome this excess or lack, opening the floodgates to narrative memory.

The exploration and use of gender roles and their performance constitute another distinguishing strategy in these narratives. However, in this respect, Ginzburg and Kersnovskaia present very different subjectivities in their responses to what was a fact of life for millions of Soviet citizens. Both survivors were born in the first decade of the twentieth century (Ginzburg in 1904, Kersnovskaia three years later), both came from relatively privileged social backgrounds (Ginzburg's father was a Moscow pharmacist, Kersnovskaia's an Odessa lawyer and legislator) and were well educated. And both, as mentioned above, initially took up the pen to share their experiences with loved ones. Beyond these facts, the similarities diminish. For all of her exposure to the horrors of the Gulag and its henchmen (and a few henchwomen), Ginzburg, a member of the new Soviet "priviligentsia" of the 1920s and 1930s, remained until her death in 1975 a committed Leninist ideologically and a model of good breeding, compassion, and love throughout her eighteen years in the Gulag and exile. An air of personal generosity, moral uplift and optimism permeates her memoir. Married and a mother of two sons before her arrest, she remarries in the Gulag, adopts a daughter there and eventually receives permission for her one surviving son to come live with her. At the end of her memoir, she returns to Moscow, her birthplace. Motherhood and family ties—even if they have to be reinvented and reconstituted—and the concomitant attributes of femininity and culture play a defining role in her construction of herself as a subject. Whether she is resisting violence and suffering or falling in love in the Gulag, Ginzburg's responses rely on traditional Russian culture—high (poetry is her favored medium), middle (she is never far from home and coziness, no matter where she lands), and low (though not too low—folklore and ritual provide important subtexts throughout her tale, but she is duly horrified by the behavior and pastimes of the criminal prisoners).

Conversely, Kersnovskaia, born to a Russified Polish father and Greek mother in the Moldavian borderlands, never accepts the Soviet system, constructs herself as a "displaced" person wherever she goes, forms few lasting bonds during her years in the Gulag, and assumes a far more traditionally "masculine" stance when confronted by its savagery, which she describes in far more gruesome, graphic, and at times grotesque detail. While it is true that the mother/child matrix play a role in the genesis of her narrative, as they do for Ginzburg, that role is a more limited one: family and other relationships are constructed in "Cliff Drawings" as far more fleeting and fragmentary, and are destroyed more often than they are created. Where Ginzburg tends to find refuge in traditional gender, family, and cultural roles, Kersnovskaia's approach is that of a demythologizer, exposing the Gulag as a destroyer of these values.

A comparison of the two authors' attitudes toward the everyday experiences of violence and death in the camps will show the antipodal nature of these two approaches. As Alexander Zholkovsky perceptively argues, Ginzburg uses an incident of prisoner cannibalism, offset by the blossoming love affair between herself and Anton Walter, her future husband, "to reclaim the traditional values of love and culture, reintegrating them with Nature, Christianity and even official authority."[10] Here, the idyll of the author's life-affirming romance, complete with love poems à la Ovid in Latin and Russian, secret letters, books, and the exchange of lofty ideas, is juxtaposed to and, indeed, triumphs over, the ironically related tale of a prisoner who has cooked the flesh of a man he has murdered and whom she must muster all her nursing skills to save, so that he can be tried and executed. Ginzburg deftly combines high culture with folkloric rites of passage in this chapter to prepare her heroine for her second, more emotionally and ethically "genuine" marriage than her first, to a prominent Party functionary. Typical of Ginzburg's exceptional ability to endow actual experience with individual and archetypal resonance, "Paradise under the Microscope" (the title of the chapter) presents enough of a narrative trajectory for Zholkovsky to analyze it as a short story. With its extremes of the most debased human behavior (cannibalism), and its apogees (love and spirituality) acting as a foil to one another, it is paradigmatic of Ginzburg's repeated attempts at balance and integration as she struggles—within the text—to endow the depravity that confronts her everyday life with a larger meaning by bringing the forces of life and death into balance metaphorically, through literary cross-cutting and symbolism.

Kersnovskaia enters many of the same spaces inhabited by Ginzburg in the Gulag, including service as a surgical nurse in a camp hospital. She too expresses her indignation at the conditions she confronts in the course of her medical duties, but the content of her drawings (even more than the text) often draws for its "remembered" imagery on the dehumanized, the brutal, and the demythologized. Despite an abundance of cultural references through which she too, like Ginzburg, establishes her membership in the Russian intelligentsia, symbolism and metaphor are largely absent in Kersnovskaia's treatment of her nursing activities, which brutally portray the materiality of the body, especially in its dead state, as corpse, since she is soon reassigned from the operating theater to the hospital's morgue. In that liminal world, Kersnovskaia merges stereotypical gender roles, for she is not only a nurse, but also a keeper of the dead, one who shifts from the care and nurturing of the living (the gravely ill) to the dissection and disposal of corpses. In a chapter simply titled "Morgue," she combines some of her most graphic verbal and visual descriptions of death and morbidity with ironic, black humor. At one point, confronted with the task of burying two hundred corpses, she says half comically, half tragically, "I gutted you, I'll bury you." In an earlier carnivalesque scene, the horror of ancient taboos against corporeal desecration is mitigated by comic elements and laughter, as legal and medical personnel attending an autopsy to determine how a man was murdered begin "sneezing, crying, and covering their noses with handkerchiefs. I fell back on the stretcher as tears flowed from the formaldehyde and the laughter."

Kersnovskaia's acts of compassion are numerous, yet, in contrast to Ginzburg, she always positions herself as an outsider, often intervening physically to protect weaker prisoners. One of the key elements in Ginzburg's narrative is her sense of connection with the various communities of women she encounters during her eighteen years in the Gulag and exile, and her model for selfhood is "relational," rather than individuating, to borrow from the sociologist Nancy Chodorow's theory of gender differentiation.[11] She repeatedly reveals her vulnerability by expressing a range of human emotions—fear, bewilderment, as well as concern for her own survival and that of her fellow (female) prisoners. Emaciated after months of tree-felling and violently ill from acute diarrhea and fever before she is due to board a transit ship, Ginzburg conceals her condition not only because she knows that to be left behind as others board the ship that will take them to Magadan means a death sentence, but also because she did not want to be "parted from [her] friends" (1:353) Like her husband-to-be, she heals others and herself through empathy and participation in the common lot.

When Kersnovskaia is confronted by violent action, often as punishment for her brash attacks on guards and overseers, rather than proceeding from a position of lateral relationship she repeatedly casts herself in a heroic role, doing what those weaker or smaller cannot do in their own self-defense. Unlike Ginzburg's humanism and stoicism in the face of aggression, Kersnovskaia meets her violators with defiance, with physical, often violent action, and with an unwavering air of invulnerability. Moreover, in the verbal narrative and particularly in the

"I've gutted you, [now] I'll bury you. Forgive me my brothers. It's sheer happenstance that I haven't joined you," by Evfrosiniia Kersnovskaia. Reprinted by permission of the E. Kersnovskaia Foundation.

"Pavel Evdokimovich was sneezing, repeating, 'What a fool I am.' The prosecutor finally said, 'You're used to this but it's a bit hard for us.' And they all rushed to leave this 'hospitable institution,'" by Evfrosiniia Kersnovskaia. Reprinted by permission of the E. Kersnovskaia Foundation.

"They approach, crossing themselves, and bow to the ground . . ." by Evfrosinia Kersnovskaiia. Reprinted by permission of the E. Kersnovskaia Foundation.

"What do they mean, 'Wait for an easy death?' . . ." by Evfrosiniia Kersnovskaia. Reprinted by permission of the E. Kersnovskaia Foundation.

visual representation that is the distinctive feature of her memoir, she self-consciously counterpoises her physical presence (dominant in size and strength) to that of the women around her, who assume traditional passive feminine roles.[12] In one dramatic scene, in which the tree-felling has brought her, like Ginzburg, to "within a hair of death," she lies prostrate and is surrounded by devout women praying and keening for her. She, however, will have none of it, and their passivity only energizes her to action: "They walk up to me, make the sign of the cross, bow to the floor. I hear, 'You're dying, Frosia, you angelic soul. You stood up for the truth . . . Took pity on us and our children. Lord, be merciful to Thy servant, Evfrosiniia. Send her an easy death . . . Frosia, forgive us our sins . . . We won't forget to remember you in our prayers.' What do they mean, 'wait for an easy end'? To make that viper [the sadistic tree cutting foreman, Khokhrin] rejoice? What does he think, that I will obediently die? Or that, like Barzakh [a fellow inmate], I will kiss his feet?! No! And having mustered my strength I grabbed an axe and ran through the entire settlement to his office." Sorely tempted to attack the foreman ("killing such an evildoer would be a good thing," she speculates), nevertheless Kersnovskaia does not kill Khokhrin once she confronts him. As she enters, he sits with his back to the door, and "to strike someone from the back you need to be a killer." Knowing she is doomed, she runs off to a frozen lake, where she stares into a hole in the ice and contemplates suicide, yet manages—not for the first or last time—to attempt to escape.

Ginzburg's report of cannibalism is one of the more physically repugnant "events" of *Whirlwind:* in keeping with her focus on her heroine's "spiritual journey," and perhaps the squeamishness of her own consciousness, Ginzburg often excises the worst details of the Gulag's violation of the physical body. Kersnovskaia's memoir, on the other hand, is remarkable for its unflinching exposure of brutality and all of its intended and unintended consequences, and the drawings graphically expose the abuses caused by mixed-sex barracks with no provision for the most basic needs of hygiene or elimination; the degradation of repeated strip searches of women by male guards; the barbarity of a woman giving birth to a thirteenth child under camp conditions; waking up to the scurrying of rats on her back—to cite some of the most vivid incidents—as well as rape, infanticide, and various work-related fatalities. The wealth of accumulated human culture that plays a mediating role in Ginzburg's tale has little effect here, as Kersnovskaia is confronted (and we, through her) with the unadorned evidence of humanity's inhumanity.

In many western societies, women have traditionally played the role of cultural mediator, a role into which Ginzburg slips comfortably but that offers no shelter for Kersnovskaia. It is fair to assume that the motivations behind the memoirs of both authors were various and complex: cognitive, didactic, and ethical, as well as therapeutic. Yet, while Ginzburg's *Whirlwind* is restorative and reintegrative, for Kersnovskaia the wound never healed. We see this in the endpoints of the journeys traced in these two narratives, when both survivors have returned more or less to normalcy after their Gulag ordeals. *Whirlwind* begins and ends with two distinctive physical settings that lend the work its (outwardly) circular structure. In the opening pages, Ginzburg is awakened in her comfortable home by an early morning telephone call from party headquarters in Kazan', ordering her to appear by 6 a.m. This ominous call will launch the heroine/memoirist on her eighteen-year journey to the Gulag and beyond. At the end of that biographical and narrative journey, she returns to European Russia, to the familiar spaces and friends who, like her, had survived their journey into the archipelago. Although she returns to Moscow, Ginzburg underscores the circularity of her narrative—and her reintegration into normal life—through a "chance" encounter with some strangers, *provintsialy* ("country cousins") who ask her if she knows the way to Moscow's Kazan' station. She ends with a scene of profound *byt*—everyday life:

> Would you please tell us, young lady, how we get to the Kazan' station? This apparently trivial happening immediately put me in a good mood again. For one thing, they had called me "young lady," so even in my late fifties, I didn't look like an old woman . . . [and] I remembered that while I was rummaging in my handbag, looking for my mislaid [release] certificate, I had seen in the depths a square of chocolate. I ate it with relish and rose resolutely from the bench. I looked around me. The well nourished Moscow pigeons . . . were deep in conversation with one another. A little girl in a red dress was busily skipping. A constant stream of people was pouring into the subway. I was about to join them. I would merge with the general stream. Could I really do that? I was just like everyone else! (2:415)

Ginzburg thus completes her journey and returns to the everyday work of repair—of self and family, of reputation and profession. The end of her journey lies in her embrace of the ordinary.[13]

Kersnovskaia's book closes on a different note. Release from the camp comes in 1952, and she too, like Ginzburg, must wait several more years before she can return to European Russia. Her last chapter (*"Na vole"*—"Freedom") is filled with scenes of repose and reunion with her mother, who dies soon after Kersnovskaia's return. But unlike Ginzburg, reintegration is not possible for her. "The years passed," she writes. "Work was, without question interesting, but exhausting," since even as a free person, she works in the mines. "I decided to make use of my vacation time. I didn't try to go anywhere. Where [could I go]? Nowhere, and I have no one. The sanatoriums are not for me: I have been 'deprived of my rights' and I'm not even a union member. I spent my vacation wandering in the tundra" (359). Eventually she resettles in Mineral'nye vody, a resort in the south of Russia immortalized by the great Romantic poets Pushkin and Lermontov. "Cliff Drawings" ends on a note of loneliness, isolation—and adventure, as in her final drawings this self consciously "unfeminine" heroine chronicles her journeys through Russia's "wild south" and the Caucasus mountains, where she turns to nature and a monastic retreat for restoration (she visits the New Afon monastery in Abkhazia). The final drawings stand alone, uncaptioned, testimony perhaps, to their creator's search for a more direct expression of experience than language, deformed by totalitarian ideologies and practices, can provide. Among those ideologies we can include the prevalence of traditionally gendered roles in Russian and Soviet society. It is here that Kersnovskaia's bending of those roles to express, visually more than verbally, her own sexuality, that we can particularly situate the uniqueness of her Gulag memoir.

Notes

1. Figures in the large, and still growing, body of resources on the Gulag give estimates of between five and twenty million *zeks*, or prisoners, at any one time. Recent studies of the Gulag that have informed my thinking for this essay include those by Galina Mikhailovna Ivanova, *Labor Camp Socialism: The Gulag in the Soviet Totalitarian System*, trans. Carol Flath, ed. Donald J. Raleigh (Armonk, N.Y.: M. E. Sharpe, 2000); Robert W. Thurston, *Life and Terror in Stalin's Russia, 1934–1941* (New Haven, Conn.: Yale University Press, 1996); J. Arch Getty and Roberta T. Manning Getty, eds., *Stalinist Terror: New Perspectives* (Cambridge: Cambridge University Press, 1993); and Anne Applebaum, *Gulag: A History* (New York: Doubleday, 2003). Also see J. Arch Getty's chapter in this volume, "State Violence in the Stalin Period."

2. The first Russian editions of *Krutoi marshrut* were published outside the Soviet Union in Italy, Germany, and the United States. The two volumes in English were titled *Journey into the Whirlwind* (San Diego: Harcourt Brace Jovanovich, 1967) and *Within the Whirlwind* (San Diego: Harcourt Brace Jovanovich, 1981), respectively. Other tamizdat editions followed before the memoir was finally published in the Soviet Union, first in serialized form in 1989 in the Latvian

journal *Daugava,* and finally as a separate edition in 1990 (Moscow: Sovetskii pisatel', 1990). In the text, I refer to pages in *Whirlwind,* volumes 1 or 2.

3. See chapter 3 in Leona Toker, *Return from the Archipelago: Narratives of Gulag Survivors* (Bloomington: Indiana University Press, 2000).

4. Veronica Shapovalov, ed. and trans., *Remembering the Darkness: Women in Soviet Prisons* (Boulder, Colo.: Rowman and Littlefield, 2001), 2.

5. Toker, *Return from the Archipelago,* 3.

6. Ibid., 96.

7. Shoshana Felman and Dori Laub, *Testimony: Crises of Witnessing in Literature, Psychoanalysis, and History* (New York: Routledge, 1992), 84.

8. Evfrosiniia Kersnovskaia, *Naskal'naia zhivopis'* (Moscow, St. Petersburg: Kvadrat, 1991), 7. The translations from Kersnovskaia's memoir are mine throughout.

9. Michael Holquist in his introduction to M. Bakhtin, *Art and Answerability: Early Philosophical Essays,* trans. V. Liapunov, ed. M. Holquist (Austin: University of Texas Press, 1990), xxvi.

10. Alexander Zholkovsky, "Three on Courtship, Corpses, and Culture: Tolstoj, 'Posle bala'—Zoščenko, 'Dama s cvetami'—E. Ginzburg, 'Raj pod mikroskopom,'" *Wiener slavistischer Almanach* 22 (1988): 18. Reprinted in slightly different form as "Before and After 'After the Ball': Variations on the Theme of Courtship, Corpses, and Culture," in A. K. Zholkovsky, *Text Counter Text: Rereadings in Russian Literary History* (Stanford, Calif.: Stanford University Press, 1994).

11. I have found Susan S. Friedman's summary of Nancy Chodorow's feminist psychoanalytical theories to be very helpful in distinguishing between these two models of relationship formation. See her essay "Women's Autobiographical Selves: Theory and Practice," in *The Private Self: Theory and Practice of Women's Autobiographical Writings,* ed. Sheri Benstock (Chapel Hill: University of North Carolina Press, 1988), 34–62.

12. Indeed, one of the more interesting aspects of Kersnovskaia's narrative is that the visual text is more expressive than the verbal one, and that her drawings portray her sexual identity and issues of aggression, physical power, and raw emotions that her brief commentaries often leave out. For an illuminating recent discussion of Soviet attitudes toward female homosexuality, see Dan Healey, "Unruly Identities: Soviet Psychiatry Confronts the 'Female Homosexual' of the late 1920s," in *Gender in Russian History and Culture,* ed. Linda Edmonson (Basingstoke, U.K.: Palgrave, 2001), 116–38.

13. As Beth Holmgren has insightfully observed in the conclusion of her book *Women's Works in Stalin's Time: On Lidiia Chukovskaia and Nadezhda Mandelstam* (Bloomington: Indiana University Press, 1993), 171–79.

Violence in Viktor Astaf'ev's Fiction

JULIAN D. MOSS

One of Russia's best and most controversial novelists of the last fifty years, Viktor Astaf'ev was born on May 1, 1924, in the small Siberian village of Ovsianka, on the banks of the Yenisei River, around thirty miles from the city of Krasnoiarsk. His mother drowned in the Yenisei when he was seven years old, and after that he was brought up by his grandmother, and subsequently in a children's home. In 1942 he volunteered for the Red Army and fought to the end of the Second World War as a private. He was seriously wounded three times. After the war he settled in the Urals town of Chusovoi with his new wife, Maria Semenovna Koriakina-Astaf'eva, and took various manual jobs. Astaf'ev published his first story in 1951, and his writing career spanned half a century. In his later years Astaf'ev was as often feted as he was criticized, but he was always newsworthy and frequently pressed to comment on current affairs. In the last years of his life he was frequently called a living classic, and even the patriarch of Russian literature.[1] Ill health forced Astaf'ev to stop writing only in 2001, a few months before his death. He was, somewhat unfairly, seen as an anti-Semite and a chauvinist, but he was also a staunch defender of dissenters, including the Orthodox sect the Old Believers, toward whom he felt a great affinity. In his fiction Astaf'ev frequently returned to a few themes: war, ecology, Siberia, and village life, often with biting sarcasm directed against the Soviet system and the moral decline he perceived in Russian society. It is no surprise, given the inherent brutality of the Soviet state and the continued prevalence of violence in post-Soviet Russian society, that violence is another of the key features of Astaf'ev's prose. We will examine a number of examples of this, starting with a recent work set in 1942–43, continuing with a more abstract form of violence in a work of the 1970s and finishing with Astaf'ev's fictionalized social criticism of the 1980s.

Mainstream Soviet writing about the war, both fiction and nonfiction, tended to deal in positive depictions of resolute and heroic Soviet soldiers and officers and celebrations of the glorious sacrifices made by good Soviet soldiers, often in a triumphalist or bombastic tone, and with an emphasis on the leading role of the Communist Party and its members. Writers good and bad mined this seam extensively; indeed, World War II was "by far the most popular theme [in literature] throughout the 1960s and 1970s."[2] With time, growing numbers of works depicted less positive aspects of the war, and during the glasnost era more topics that had previously been taboo were explored: cowardice, the effects of the prewar purges of the officer class, the Nazi-Soviet pact, and the unpreparedness of the Soviet forces at the start of the war.[3] Debates raged around the "truth" of these varied depictions of the war.[4] Astaf'ev spoke often of the disdain in which he held much mainstream Soviet writing (fiction and nonfiction) about the war, criticizing it for its blandness, its heroic tone, its inaccuracy, its incompleteness;[5] at a conference in 1988 he said that he had been in a completely different war.[6]

In the 1990s Astaf'ev rejoined these debates by publishing two parts of an intended trilogy, *The Cursed and the Slain*.[7] This was a work Astaf'ev felt he had been preparing to write for many years.[8] In it he set out to tell what he saw as the whole truth about the war he had fought in; he depicts the war in unremittingly bleak tones. The work was criticized by many for its alleged lack of patriotism and lack of respect for the war dead. Recent estimates suggest that up to twenty-eight million Soviet citizens may have died during the conflict,[9] and their memory is still glorified in Russia, with the May 9 Victory Day holiday a major celebration every year with parades and concerts. One critic went so far as to describe Astaf'ev as a Satanic priest performing a black mass over the bodies of the dead.[10] But Astaf'ev was unrepentant and found a wide readership, not least amongst his fellow veterans. Many hundreds wrote to him to thank him for having the courage to tell the truth.

The first part of the trilogy, *Hell Hole,* short-listed for the Booker Russian Novel Prize in 1993, is set not at the Front, but at a training camp deep in Siberia in 1942, where newly conscripted youngsters are given minimal preparation for the battles ahead. The conditions are harsh and made worse for the new recruits by the violence inflicted on them by their officers. In the second part of the trilogy, *The Bridgehead,* set in 1943, the recruits are now battle-hardened soldiers. We follow them through a few days as they attempt to secure a bridgehead across the Volga as the German forces retreat. It is a bloody battle with many casualties.

Let us examine two strikingly violent episodes from *Hell Hole.* Arguably the most telling scene in the first section of *Hell Hole* is the death of a soldier, Poptsov, at the hands of the company commander, Pshennyi.

> Poptsov fell during the run. Yashkin turned back, lifted the whimpering goner up and dragged him through the gates onto the parade ground, into the ranks. Poptsov fell, curled up in the snow, folded his legs underneath himself, tried to thrust his hands into his sleeves and drag his neck into his collar.
>
> "Stand up, don't loiter!" bellowed the company commander, and from a running jump kicked the goner a couple of times, incensed; he couldn't stop or subdue his furious paroxysm. "Up! Up! Up!" With one swing he kicked the toe of his dully shining boot into the lad writhing on the snow, who at every blow tasted the saliva of his own sniveling. The company commander's face had turned puce, his eyes were full of frenzied malice, he could hardly breathe, his hatred had suffocated him and blinded his reason. . . .
>
> "You've got out of hand, you malingerers," he howled. "I'll show you! I'll show you! I'll . . ."
>
> Poptsov stopped bellowing, with childish defenselessness thinly cried out, "Ow!" and tried to straighten himself up strangely, toppling over onto his back. . . . With a martyr's relief Poptsov gave out a short breath, turned his head away from everyone and buried his nose in the sandy snow. (10:79–80)[11]

Poptsov is a weakling, ill-suited to the arduous life of the barracks, but he hardly deserves this. The attack can be considered nothing less than murder. The soldiers very nearly lynch Pshennyi in retaliation, an attack for which Zelentsov is court-martialed and sentenced to death. Pshennyi is not disciplined.

The second example is the exemplary shooting of the Snegirev brothers for desertion. The scene of their execution is long (it takes up some five pages, so is too long to quote at any length) and written as if in slow motion,[12] and it is harrowing in some of its detail.

Opposite the brothers, also on their knees, stood two soldiers holding at their elbows new carbines, with not removed but fixed bayonets. On the third cart came another three soldiers with carbines, the lieutenant sitting at the front, lightly and well dressed in quilted trousers and new grey felt boots; his pea-jacket was tightly belted; at his side, slightly tugging at his belt hung a holster from which the handle of a pistol worn by frequent use shone threateningly. . . . The battalion, it's true, paid no attention to the lieutenant; everyone from the completely frozen Petka Musikov to Battalion Commander Vnukov was staring at the condemned, ready at any moment to help them, to give them gloves, a hat, to light a cigarette, but nobody made, nobody could make, even the slightest movement toward them, and because of this it was hugely awkward and terrifying. Here they were, standing right alongside the doomed lads, our lads, Russian lads, brothers not only by class but also brothers in God's Testament—so why were they so unattainably distant, why was it impossible to help them? (10:200–205)

Astaf'ev again intends this as a condemnation of the officers responsible. The condemned brothers are portrayed as harmless teenagers who leave the training camp because they simply cannot cope—they are trying to return home to their mother. Of course, brutality towards army recruits continues to this day and readers saw in this work implied criticism of *dedovshchina* (bullying by older conscripts) and of the present-day officers who continue to let it happen.

Astaf'ev portrays the attack in *The Bridgehead,* the second volume of *The Cursed and the Slain,* as ultimately pointless; it is no more than a diversionary tactic. The main battles are taking place elsewhere, and establishing this bridgehead will have no effect on the course of the war. It is another example of the Soviet army's willingness to sacrifice the lives of its soldiers, this time on a grander scale than in *Hell Hole:* here only five hundred of the three thousand soldiers fighting across the river survive. This is one fictionalized example of what Astaf'ev sees as a common feature of Soviet commanders' behavior. Elsewhere in interviews and speeches he vigorously criticized other key decisions of the war: he believed Leningrad should have been surrendered to the Germans in 1941,[13] and that Zhukov should not have fought the Battle for Berlin in 1945;[14] in both cases Astaf'ev thought tens of thousands of Soviet lives had been needlessly sacrificed.

While another recent novel about the same war, Georgii Vladimov's *A General and His Army* (1994), has been described as having a general but almost no army, Astaf'ev's novel has an army but almost no generals.[15] The officers who are present are usually caricatured and condemned for their actions. What is more, for the first part of the trilogy Astaf'ev portrays the Red Army at war but without an enemy. There is only one German in *Hell Hole:* "It seemed, then, that through the blue-gray, greasy, ever greater, ever stronger suffocating fog he saw a German, a single one—the German was standing in the doorway of the *izba* and was talking about something with the owner, then he left and led out the orderlies Faya and Nelya. To be shot, presumably. But the girls returned with bundles, brought in some bread, salt, lard, a full bag of bandages, cotton wool, a flask of spirit and a bottle of iodine. This must have been a German from the ranks, from the trenches, who already knew suffering, pain, the soldier's lot. But he would later be numbered amongst the born villains, he would be mixed in and confused with fascist punishment squads, SS men, and various bone breakers in the rear, like our NKVD men, our SMERSH men, our tribunal men" (10:118–19).

Here the absence of violence is surprising: the only enemy soldier turns out to be a friend, a fellow human. We do find German soldiers in *The Bridgehead,* but again they are not the faceless, cruel enemy we might expect, but ordinary men. For Astaf'ev, the key divide is not between Soviets and Germans, but between officers and men. The German soldiers are presented sympathetically, as they too are just young men, fighting in a war they did not want for officers who do not care that they are dying. In this it might appear that Astaf'ev is, paradoxically, supporting the Marxist-Leninist critique of World War I, that imperialist wars are fought in the interests of the ruling cliques of the combatant nations and against the interests of workers in all countries. Astaf'ev, though, does not follow Lenin in promoting class war and revolution, but comes across as a pacifist.

What does Astaf'ev seek to show by these violent episodes? That the life of a raw recruit is worth nothing to the Soviet Army. That violence is commonplace. That the Soviet officer class is violently corrupt. We see that the Soviet system was more cruel to its own men than the Germans were to the Soviets, for we are shown violence inflicted, directly and indirectly, by Soviet officers on Soviet men, not by Soviets on Germans or vice versa.[16] By showing Soviet officers disposing of the lives of rank and file Red Army men, sometimes with a callous casualness, sometimes with a twisted and cruel inhumanity, Astaf'ev leaves the reader in no doubt about the moral equivalence of Nazism and Soviet Communism. In a 1997 interview Astaf'ev went further, asserting that in comparison with Russian despots the Nazis were merely children.[17] As one critic writes, "[t]he dark experience of the GULAG stands behind Astaf'ev's prose."[18]

It would be misleading to write any study of Astaf'ev's fiction without at least a brief consideration of rural life. Astaf'ev is often identified as a leading exponent of Village Prose [*derevenskaia proza*], a loose movement in Russian fiction of the 1960s and 1970s concerned with village life, ecological matters in the Russian countryside, and the protection of the natural environment, particularly that of Siberia. The story cycle *Queen Fish* (1972–75), one of Astaf'ev's best known works, is an archetypal Village Prose work and describes life by the Yenisei River. While there are concrete examples of physical violence committed by individuals, the overwhelming sense of the cycle is of a broader, more abstract, but no less devastating attack: Astaf'ev is decrying the rape of his native Siberia by the grasping urbanized Soviet state.

In the central story of the cycle, its "bright emotional centre,"[19] also called "Queen Fish," Man, specifically Soviet Man, represented by a poacher, Ignatych, does battle with Nature in the shape of a giant sturgeon. Ignatych snares the fish and at times appears to be winning in his struggle to reel her in. At other times the fish comes close to capsizing the fisherman's boat and drowning him. After several hours an exhausted stalemate is reached and they both escape with their lives. Ignatych takes the opportunity to reflect on his life and regret his violations, of a woman earlier in life, and of Nature, and he repents. Ignatych's violence here is unsuccessful because he has come up against a stronger adversary than a fellow human; it is also cathartic and rehabilitative. The lesson we should learn is that Nature, although powerful, is in grave danger because of Man's interference and violent disturbance of her natural equilibrium.

Village Prose was "the most aesthetically coherent and ideologically important body of published literature to appear in the Soviet Union between the death of Stalin and Gorbachev's ascendancy,"[20] and in creating a body of work that was not overly constrained by the demands of Socialist Realism it pushed back the boundaries of what was permissible in Soviet fiction.[21] The movement came to an end in 1970s and its exponents took their work and thought in different directions. Although some Village Prose writers moved toward extreme nationalism, chauvinism, xenophobia, and anti-Semitism (Astaf'ev made a small number of offensive pronouncements), many played prominent roles in the political debates of the 1980s and 1990s, exposing previously hidden social problems in the more open climate of the glasnost era. In common with some other Village Prose writers Astaf'ev moved away from the depiction of malign urban influences in a rural setting to an examination of urban life in provincial Russia and an increasingly despondent outlook in the face of the amorality and violence seemingly endemic to Russian society.

The publication of *A Sad Detective Story* catapulted Astaf'ev into the center of political and moral debate.[22] This was early in Mikhail Gorbachev's period as General Secretary of the Communist Party, when the concepts of glasnost and perestroika were still new. This novel, only Astaf'ev's second, tells the story of a forty-two-year-old man, Leonid Soshnin, who turns to writing after being invalided out of the police force of a fictional town in provincial Russia. He has seen much violence, and his recollections are the method Astaf'ev uses to regale the reader with almost endless stories of assault, rape, and murder, a depressing and uncompromising picture of contemporary Russian life. To give but three examples:[23]

1. A drunken young man climbs into a women's dormitory and is thrown out in disgrace. In revenge he decides to kill the first person he meets; it turns out to be a beautiful young pregnant woman. He beats her to death with a rock. His defense in court is that it was not his fault that the first person he came across was pregnant.

2. A couple, husband and wife, leave their baby at home while they go to the library for days. The baby dies of hunger and, in a particularly gruesome and naturalistic touch, Astaf'ev adds that the baby's corpse is infested with maggots.

3. A mother abandons her baby in an automatic luggage locker at the railway station, so that she does not have to feed him.

Some critics condemned Astaf'ev for describing such brutality in such a direct way, for failing to be optimistic or raise the spirits of his readers, or for failing to offer solutions to the problems he describes; others praised Astaf'ev for his courageous examination of serious issues facing contemporary society,[24] for his determination to tell "the truth, the whole truth" about social conditions, in order that solutions may be found by others.[25]

The novel is not without its artistic weaknesses. The characterization has been described as two-dimensional and unconvincing, and the fictionalization of Astaf'ev's criticisms is weak, leading one critic to describe the work as "a monologue with additional voices that constitute a sort of personification of the author's opinions, comments and tendencies,"[26] and another to write, "it is a crude vehicle for the direct expression of the author's own indignation as he parades and comments upon a succession of local drunks, pseudo-intellectuals, thieves, rapists, and cutthroats who are intended to represent the shortcomings of society at large. . . . Astaf'ev . . . was clearly willing to sacrifice aesthetic values in the effort to sermonize."[27] Despite these flaws the story remains powerful, and two things are particularly shocking: the matter-of-fact tone Astaf'ev employs to describe these horrendous crimes, and their mundanity—he is telling us that this is nothing out of the ordinary in Russia today.[28]

The themes explored in *A Sad Detective Story* are repeated in a long short story, "Liudochka," written in 1989.[29] While the story is often criticized on artistic grounds, "Liudochka," despite dealing with very similar subject matter, has been described as Astaf'ev's best work.[30] It is all the more impressive and disturbing for its close focus on one character, the young woman of the title, who comes to a provincial town from a depressed upbringing in a dying village, is raped by a gang of hoodlums, and subsequently commits suicide from shame. One of the story's strengths is that violence is not described in naturalistic detail; it is relatively restrained:

> Strekach grabbed her raincoat in his hand and crumpled it and Liudochka's dress, dragged the girl towards him, and tried to sit her on his knee. Liudochka pulled away from him more and more strongly, more and more urgently. . . . [He] threw [her] over the bench and then threw himself over too; snarling, he tried to catch her as she crawled away on all fours through the tall weeds. . . . Strekach caught Liudochka by her raincoat, dragged her toward him, and pushed her face into the ground. . . . With a crack he tugged open her dress. . . . Liudochka was still trying to cry out. From the suffocating darkness, from last year's tall weeds mixed with this year's, dirty wool fell into her gaping mouth, at least that's what it felt like, and overwhelmed her breathing, and the nausea that had been compressing her chest was suddenly released in a spasm. Her throat, seized by the spasm, jerked into life. . . . "The whore! . . . My jacket's covered in her vomit!" (9:403–5)

Again the violence is seen as normal, the police are shown to be helpless and uncaring. Perhaps most chilling is the story's conclusion:

> At the end of the quarter a small piece about the moral state of the town appeared on the fourth page of the local newspaper. They wrote that in the period in question there had been three murders, one hundred and five burglaries, and fifteen muggings aimed at taking the victim's clothing in the town, and an attempted robbery on the regional savings bank that had been prevented by the

vigilant forces of law and order. No major burglaries or crimes with particularly serious consequences had been recorded. There had been only eight rapes, thirty-two car thefts, and eleven robberies from dachas. . . . Compared with the same period in the previous year crime had fallen by 1.7 percent. Liudochka and Strekach [killed in revenge by Liudochka's step-father] were not included in the figures. The boss of the regional directorate of the Interior Ministry was only two years away from his pension and he didn't want to spoil the positive trend in the figures with doubtful cases. (9:428)

What conclusions can we draw about Astaf'ev's work? If in his stories of war Astaf'ev blames the Soviet system and its officer class for most of the violence he portrays, and in his works set in the 1960s and 1970s he castigates the Soviet state for its rape of Siberia, by the mid-1980s Astaf'ev had broadened his target to include most of Russian society. We should remember that Astaf'ev was not only the intolerant scold he might seem, and his writing can be lyrical and moving, as well as very funny. Nonetheless, much of Astaf'ev's fiction is written in a negative tone and shows his compatriots in a harsh light. The main role of violence in his work is to castigate some aspect of Russia: sometimes the Soviet system and its operatives, sometimes the state's destruction of Siberia, sometimes Russian Man's failure to live in harmony with Nature, sometimes contemporary Russia's sliding morals and casual violence.

Notes

1. V. P. Astaf'ev and Vladimir Karpov, "Doidem do propasti—vernemsia k zemle," *Literaturnaia gazeta* 3:5637 (January 22, 1997): 11.
2. David Gillespie, "Thaws, Freezes, and Wakes: Russian Literature, 1953–1991," in *Reference Guide to Russian Literature,* ed. Neil Cornwell and Nicole Christian (London: Fitzroy Dearborn, 1998), 61.
3. Rosalind Marsh, *History and Literature in Contemporary Russia* (Basingstoke: Macmillan and St. Anthony's College, Oxford, 1995), 99.
4. T. M. Vakhitova, "Narod na voine: Vzgliad V. Astaf'eva iz serediny 90-kh. Roman *Prokliaty i ubity,*" *Russkaia literatura* 3 (1995): 114–29.
5. V. P. Astaf'ev, "Polupravda nas izmuchila . . ." *Voprosy istorii* 6 (1998): 33–35.
6. Vakhitova, "Narod na voine," 117.
7. V. P. Astaf'ev, "Prokliaty i ubity (kniga pervaia: Chertovaia iama)," *Novyi mir* 10, 11, 12 (1992): 60–106 (10), 88–226 (11), 168–246 (12); V. P. Astaf'ev, "Prokliaty i ubity (kniga vtoraia: Platsdarm)," *Novyi mir* 10, 11, 12 (1994): 62–110 (10), 37–101 (11), 57–134 (12).
8. Astaf'ev and Karpov, "Doidem do propasti," 11.
9. Chris Ward, *Stalin's Russia* (London: Edward Arnold, 1993), 156.
10. Kseniia Mialo, "Mertvykh prokliat'ia," *Nash sovremennik* 6 (1995): 186–92.

11. V. P. Astaf'ev, *Sobranie sochinenii v piatnadtsati tomakh,* 15 vols. (Krasnoiarsk: Ofset, 1997–98). All translations are by the current author; reference is to volume and page of this fifteen-volume *Collected Works.*

12. Igor' Dedkov, "Ob"iavlenie viny i naznachenie kazni," *Druzhba narodov* 10 (1993): 185–202.

13. Vakhitova, "Narod na voine," 121.

14. V. P. Astaf'ev and Irina Rishina, "Razgovor na fone novoi knigi (iz dialoga Iriny Rishinoi i Viktora Astaf'eva)," in V. P. Astaf'ev, *Tak khochetsia zhit'* (Moscow: Knizhnaia palata, 1996), 9.

15. Lev Anninskii, "Za chto prokliaty?" *Literaturnaia gazeta* 9:5437 (March 3, 1993): 4; Igor' Zolotusskii "Ubity i voskresen'e: zametki o romane Viktora Astaf'eva *Prokliaty i ubity,*" *Literaturnaia gazeta* 12:5543 (March 22, 1995): 4.

16. Zolotusskii, "Ubity i voskresen'e," 4.

17. Astaf'ev and Karpov, "Doidem do propasti," 11.

18. Anninskii, "Za chto prokliaty?" 4.

19. T. M. Vakhitova, *Povestvovanie v rasskazakh V. Astaf'eva "Tsar'-ryba"* (Moscow: Vysshaia shkola, 1988), 40.

20. Kathleen F. Parthe, *Russian Village Prose: The Radiant Past* (Princeton, N.J.: Princeton University Press, 1992), ix–x.

21. Gillespie, "Thaws, Freezes, and Wakes," 60.

22. V. P. Astaf'ev, "Pechal'nyi detektiv: Roman," *Oktiabr'* 1 (1986): 8–74.

23. Igor' Zolotusskii, "Don Kikhot iz Veiska," *Novyi mir* 7 (1986): 248–55.

24. A. Kucherskii, E. Starikova, and V. Sokolov, "Viktor Astaf'ev's *A Sad Detective Story:* A Reader's Opinion and Two Critics' Replies," *Soviet Studies in Literature* 24:4 (1988): 4–43.

25. Ales' Adamovich, "Urok pravdy," *Literaturnaia gazeta* 12:5078 (March 19, 1986): 5.

26. Kucherskii in Kucherskii, Starikova, and Sokolov, "Viktor Astaf'ev's *A Sad Detective Story,*" 8.

27. Deming Brown, *The Last Years of Soviet Russian Literature: Prose Fiction 1975–1991* (Cambridge: Cambridge University Press, 1993), 88.

28. Starikova in Kucherskii, Starikova, and Sokolov, "Viktor Astaf'ev's *A Sad Detective Story,*" 14–17.

29. V. P. Astaf'ev, "Liudochka," *Novyi mir* 9 (1989): 3–27; in English as V. P. Astaf'ev, "Lyudochka," in *The Penguin Book of New Russian Writing,* ed. Victor Erofeyev and Andrew Reynolds (London: Penguin, 1995), 22–76. See also Nadya Peterson's discussion of this story in the next chapter.

30. Brown, *The Last Years,* 88.

Death and the Maiden

Erasures of the Feminine in Soviet Literature of the Fin-de-siècle

NADYA L. PETERSON

Representation of mortal closure as the central exegetic event of the narrative is a regular occurrence in the Russian literature of the later Soviet period. In a prescient vision of social upheavals to come Russian writers of the 1980s and 1990s link the deaths of their beloved characters to the imminent collapse of their society. In the literature of the perestroika period and after, death is everywhere—in the work of the writers of "alternative prose" (such as Anatolii Kim, Vladimir Makanin, and Liudmila Petrushevskaia), in "publicistic literature" (Chingiz Aitmatov and Iurii Bondarev), in "village prose" (Valentin Rasputin or Viktor Astaf'ev), as well as in the works of Russian postmodernists (such as Valeriia Narbikova or Victor Pelevin). A shared sense of disappearing moral shoring, of the futility of effort aimed at social change, of the end of a political era characterized by utopian dreams, as well as an anticipation of an apocalyptic catastrophe, pervade the writings of these authors.[1]

Manifestations of radical social collapse are portrayed metaphorically through the displays of the human body's impermanence in a multitude of death scenes. The link between the characters' demise and the cataclysmic events in their society remains constant if not always overt. Significantly, one can observe appreciable differences in the use of death as an exegetic device in the literature of this period, the differences stemming from the gender of the writers involved.

In this article I focus on the different strategies of representing mortal closure in the fictions of four Russian writers. These include Viktor Astaf'ev's story "Liudochka," Iurii Mamleev's "Tetrad' individualista" ("The Individualist's Notebook"),[2] Svetlana Vasil'eva's "Otets umer" ("The Father Is Dead"), and Elena Tarasova's "Ne pomniashchaia zla" ("She Who Does Not Remember Evil").[3] Each of the four sections of the article focuses on one work, and each investigates a particular function of the literary representation of death. All point to the different roles that women characters are made to assume in fin-de-siècle prose; all reveal a close connection between the stories of the women characters and the recent history of Russia.

Redemption through Sacrifice: Viktor Astaf'ev's "Liudochka"

Astaf'ev's story, written in 1988 at the height of perestroika, is a significant departure from the precepts of village prose, Astaf'ev's customary niche in literary histories. Astaf'ev, called by Thomas Venclova "the hater of the present," no longer exhibits in this work his former belief in the healing power of the traditional past of the Russian village. The first sentence of Astaf'ev's narrative indicates that the events of the horrific story that follows occur fifteen years earlier, in the relatively stable "period of stagnation." The violent resolution of the story, however, points to a different past—a primordial, pre-Christian, even pre-communal past where only the strongest survive.

The rupture with the ideals of village prose is made more pronounced by Astaf'ev's reliance on the familiar contours of the prodigal child story, a staple of literary accounts of life in the post-Stalin Soviet countryside. Liudochka, a displaced villager in a provincial town, a would-be hairdresser and bride, loses her virginity in a gang rape and her life in a suicide against the background of dying villages, morals, towns, and vegetation—amid the extinction of everything that formerly sustained Astaf'ev's ideal of possible goodness. Astaf'ev introduces two versions of the saintly mother of village prose into this story, and both are found wanting. Liudochka's adoptive mother in the provincial center takes advantage of the young girl's naiveté, using her as a servant and refusing to protect her from the town gang. Her own mother, reduced by Astaf'ev's characterization to a sole function of procreation (she is carrying a child by her ex-convict husband), is insensitive to Liudochka's anguish, even after she realizes that her daughter has been raped.

Astaf'ev grooms his young woman character for the sacrificial role from the very first. Liudochka is de-individualized, denied a connection with her kin: she is not even given a last name, and her full Christian name, Liudmila, is consistently used in its diminutive form. Astaf'ev's young woman is thus the epitome of a "pure maiden"—virtually anonymous, unspoiled, unsophisticated, and vulnerable. Astaf'ev emphasizes his protagonist's "artlessness"; she is a "simple soul," unable to adjust to the ways of the city. The writer contrasts Liudochka's natural astuteness in the village with her perilous ineptitude in town. It is in the corrupted environs of the town that Liudochka is invariably drawn to danger, moving increasingly closer to the final closure that will expiate the communal guilt.

Liudochka's journey toward sacrificial death begins when, in her teens, she comes down with pneumonia and is taken to a regional hospital. There she spends one night holding the hand of a dying youth who expects Liudochka to give up her life in the hope of mutual resurrection. He is, however, thwarted in his expectations:

> He hadn't been expecting from her a mere cold comfort, he'd been expecting a sacrifice from her, a willingness to be with him to the end, to the bitter end and perhaps even to die too. Then a miracle would have come to pass: the two of them together would have become stronger than death, they would have come back to life, and in this lad, already as good as dead, would have appeared a surge of such power that it would have swept away everything blocking the road to resurrection. But no one, not one single person on this earth had proved worthy of such an unprecedented act of bravery, such a desperate selfless, heroic sacrifice for his sake . . . for no, she was no Decembrist's wife, following an exiled loved one to the ends of the earth. And where are they anyway, today's Decembrists' wives? Standing in the queues for wine . . . [4]

A feeling of profound guilt before the young man for not sacrificing her life, for not being a "Decembrist's wife," never leaves Liudochka, until it is expiated by her terrible death. If the actual gang rape is concealed from the reader's view by an ellipsis, Liudochka's suicide is portrayed in painstaking detail. The omniscient narrator's description of Liudochka's last moments is focused on her erasure: "her heart soon got tired, it grew weak, started to contract, grow quiet, grow smaller, and when it had shrunk to the size of a walnut, it started to slow down,

down, and then disappeared without a sound and without a trace, borne away somewhere into the emptiness."[5]

The description of Liudochka's body after death is offered in the words of a gang member: "her whole body still trembling, swinging back and forth at the end of a rope, doing the twist in such a way that first her ass and then her front faced you, with a real whopper of a tongue sticking out, and something dripping from her naked legs." The grotesque aspect of the dead body, emphasized in the above description, and the verbal defilement of Liudochka's corpse, which accompanies it, serve several equally important purposes. The death scene offers the ultimate reduction of the female protagonist to an inanimate object of estranged contemplation. Furthermore, the ignoble death is a punishment for Liudochka's earlier inability to die in order to save the young man in the hospital. Finally, it is a sacrifice that unleashes the suppressed rage of the community, provides a motive for the violent murder of the rapist by Liudochka's ex-convict stepfather, and leads to a healing cleansing. Astaf'ev dwells on the animalistic nature of Liudochka's fierce avenger: "This was a two-legged creature formed by a merciless time, all stains had been removed from the bright whites of his eyes, and from their depths the sharpest crystals, his pupils, protruded. The sparks flashing from their facets were a metallic fire from the dark depths, wreathing not in consciousness, but beyond it, they came from that place in which a fury inherited from cavemen, a fury passed through the dark, thick woods to the ages, was bubbling away, an all-destroying, all conquering, merciless fury. A low, terrifying growl came from deep inside his belly, from under the swollen Neanderthal mounds of his forehead."[6]

The time has come when only an "all-conquering hero" from a primordial past can help save Astaf'ev's world. Significantly, both the rapist and, by extension, his society are denied a connection to the Christian God. Astaf'ev's hero rips a golden cross from the neck of the gang leader before he drowns Liudochka's rapist in a dirty ditch filled with boiling water. Contrary to the description of Liudochka's suicide and its aftermath, the gang leader's mangled body is spared the indignity of the readers' scrutiny. It is precisely the focus on the atrocity of the rape and suicide of an innocent girl that warrants for Astaf'ev the eradication of evil by means of violence.

If one presumes just for a second that Astaf'ev's position is ironic, if one fantasizes briefly about the author's desire to point to the artificiality of cultural constructs and to the incessant cultural recycling of clichés, then one can be justified in an attempt to label Astaf'ev an (unwitting?) postmodernist. This of course is not the case, and Astaf'ev would most likely be deeply offended by the inclusion of his work among the writings by cynical and playful intellectuals, some of them Jews. A profound reassessment of established ideologies that comes on the heels of the death of Communism links this "hater of the present" to the irreverent practitioners of postmodernism of the late Soviet period. Yet, in a radical opposition to the deliberately unfocused and emphatically antidogmatic stance of postmodernist writing, Astaf'ev's position is deeply moralistic and didactic.

Liudochka's propensity for finding herself in the wrong place at the wrong time is not motivated in the surface plot of Astaf'ev's story; it is, however, absolutely indispensable for the sacrificial role that Astaf'ev reserves for the feminine here. Astaf'ev's virgin is offered as a sacrifice necessary for the redemption of a society in the throes of dying.

Playing at Death: Iurii Mamleev's "An Individualist's Notebook"

In Mamleev's "An Individualist's Notebook" the narrator's wife, Zina, is shown to be a receptacle for his philosophical musings and a means of sexual release, in both instances providing a respite from the hero's obsession with dying. Zina's reduction to an object of sexual manipulation and of aesthetic contemplation is evident in the persistent use of the diminutive of her first name, Zinaida; in the atomization of this female protagonist (imagined as a set of body parts: cold beautiful feet, translucent skin, breasts); as well as in the experiments her narrator conducts on her, the experiments in which the near-death moment is arrested in a hypnotic trance: "Through the constant emphasis on the reality, and at the same time the horror, the absurdity of death, as the ultimate end of the 'I,' in tandem with the calculated arousal of unrestrained love for this doomed 'I' of mine—I brought her to a bizarre state of being, like that of a dream, in which someone is holding your hand, but you can't wake up, and never will wake up."[7]

The game with suspension on the edge of extinction occurring in someone else's body and as an image allows the narrator to dispel the reality of death for himself. For Mamleev's male hero, sex offers the optimal way of entering the hypnotic state that mocks death, enabling him to play at dying with another and returning to the living. The woman is the primary actor in this theater of death; she is the one who is able to provide a catharsis from the Individualist's fears of a personal dissolution. Yet she is not allowed to experience pleasure in the process. She has to accept unquestioningly the Individualist's control, as well as his vision of the cycle of death and rebirth inherent in a sexual congress—as the latter's sole purpose: "In the mounting squall of the sexual act I'd force [her] to see the entire life of man, fragile and doomed, like sperm itself, vile, decaying, in its rising, its clinging passionately to delicious pleasure, and its fall into nothingness. I made her imagine that the sweat of voluptuousness was the sweat of death, and that the exhausted end of the sexual act was also the symbolic end of our human life, a life just as ill-begotten and as doomed to speedy extinction, as an eruption of semen."[8]

Like a diligent student, Zina is made to internalize the lessons of her sadistic teacher, "getting into such a state that she would kiss the residual splashes of [his] sperm, tenderly, achingly, murmuring that they were the tears of a broken life."[9] Sex with Zina brings liberation from physicality and assuages the narrator's dread of mortality.

Similarly to Astaf'ev's youth who expects the virginal Liudochka to sacrifice herself in order to save him, Mamleev's hero wants his wife to offer herself as the final sacrifice to his continued existence. Yet in the end Zina is allowed to resist her husband's demands, and the marriage disintegrates. The narrator's needs for aesthetic enactment of the final closure, which would separate him from the dead, are fulfilled by the regular attendance of funeral services at a nearby cemetery.

Mamleev's libertarian pessimism, his interest in the shadowy margins and crevices of his characters' psychology, his intertextuality, and the obsession with the body are shared by many other writers of the late Soviet period. Like Aleksandr Ivanchenko, Petrushevskaia, and Valeriia Narbikova, Mamleev offers the reader a deliberately apolitical narrative, emphatically unanchored in the contemporary social debates about the future of the Soviet society. Yet the pointed focus on the absence of moral foundations and the primary emphasis of Mamleev's work on the issue of survival are indicative of a particular shared mood of a society on the brink of a drastic transformation. Both Mamleev and Astaf'ev, albeit in very different ways, reserve the role of a savior for a woman. Astaf'ev's story conceals the mythological dimension of a young woman's sacrificial death behind a customary format of a realistic village prose narrative. Mamleev strips his narrative of the familiar logic of a mimetic representation, offering instead a loosely plotted contemplation on the reality, and at the same time the horror, the absurdity of death, as the ultimate end of the "I," the reality and absurdity possible to diffuse, if only in a sexual trance, with a pliant, malleable, and expendable woman.

Resurrection: Svetlana Vasil'eva's "Father Is Dead"

In Vasil'eva's story the roles of the observer and the observed found in the fiction written by men and discussed above are reversed. If in Astaf'ev's and Mamleev's stories we find male protagonists fantasizing about or observing the death of a woman, here a woman narrator created by a woman author is shown to experience the death of her father. The portrayal of the death scene, and of the memories, dreams, and visions that come on the heels of the man's death, enable the narrator to "resurrect" her father, as well as to reconcile herself to the ubiquitous presence of death in life.

In contrast to Astaf'ev's and Mamleev's dying female protagonists, the narrator's father is individualized, given a full name and a distinctive personality. The various roles he played in his life—as a son, lover, husband, father, a juvenile delinquent, a war hero, a conscientious worker—are described in careful detail. If Astaf'ev deemphasizes the links of his virginal character to her kin in order to offer her as a sacrifice to the community, Vasil'eva accentuates the importance of the father's place within his kin and underscores his continuation in his children. Mamleev's narrator rehearses the death of a woman character to attain a distance from the reality of his own death. In Vasil'eva's story the purpose of the narration is to bring her father, now dead, closer to the narrator and to accept his physical end as a means to an eternal spiritual connection.

The ritualized process of taking leave of the dead delivers the narrator from her fear of dying. Vasil'eva's descriptions of the body at death are neutral and detached, yet pointing to the differences between the dead and the living. The narrator observes the ritualistic cleansing of the body of its corporeality and carnality in preparation for the next life where the spirit of the father can meet with his own ancestors. Remembrance of the dead father on the fortieth day leads to his appearance in the narrator's dream. The story concludes with an account of subsequent visits to the grave in which the living pay their respects to the dead.

Reverence for the dead is a theme found in many works of the fin-de-siècle Soviet literature, both in such nontraditional writings as Anatolii

Kim's, for example, and in the overtly realistic works of village prose. Vasil'eva's story, however, is one of the very few where a woman witnesses and records a death in a nonsacrificial gesture of reconciliation. Yet the site from which this woman narrator speaks is only superficially that of a woman; rather, in the face of death, she assumes an androgynous position. At one point the narrator identifies with a father-son relationship; and, in the discussion of death, her gender is mostly "unmarked."

In "Father Is Dead" the erasure of the feminine occurs as the result of an inclusiveness that allows for the presence of both masculine and feminine traits in a woman character confronted with mortal closure. The author points to a deeply felt spiritual connection of her narrator to the father who is viewed as a vital link between the generations of his kin. In Vasil'eva's vision it is the recognition of this connection that constitutes the essential means of dealing with the inevitability of a personal end and, by extension, with the end of her society.

Death as Punishment: Elena Tarasova's "She Who Does Not Remember Evil"

Tarasova's story is a tale of life as an enactment of death. A dynamic of reciprocity structures "She Who Does Not Remember Evil": that which wounds the body also wounds the soul. Like Astaf'ev's "Liudochka," this is a story of regression. But, if in Astaf'ev's story the narrator's community, through its avenger, regresses to the primeval past to rectify social injustices, here the regression is self-imposed, documented as physical, emotional, and spiritual disintegration, and is the result of the narrator's gender. An unnamed disease transforms this formerly beautiful and brilliant woman into a sexless creature whose longing for death is the only powerful desire of her life.

The disintegration of the narrator's body is shown to be accompanied by a descent into a spiritual void. The lack of spirituality in society *(bezdukhovnost')* was seen in the late Soviet period as a motive for "restructuring." In the public discourse of perestroika the blame for the spiritual void was placed on society and on the excesses of social engineering. In the works of Astaf'ev and Mamleev the solution to the problem of personal and social closure is predicated on casting a woman in a sacrificial role. Astaf'ev's sacrifice of a virgin, aimed at the salvation and renewal of a community, succeeds because it summons the arrival of the "all-conquering hero" who, together with Liudochka's pregnant mother, constitutes the primal family and represents the community to come. Mamleev's exploitation of his female character provides a relief from fears of personal extinction. In Tarasova's story, however, spirituality is intimately linked with the body, the violence directed to the latter inevitably affects the former, and this violence is self-imposed. In contrast to the placing of the blame for lack of spirituality on the other, be it a society or an individual, the woman narrator takes responsibility for her own physical monstrosity and for her "terrible soul," presenting the awful transformation as a necessary and inevitable task: "Slowly, with your own hand to sculpt yourself into a monster freak. To sculpt this terrible soul. Begin to decompose."[10]

Tarasova links the initial stages of the disease with her protagonist's wish to escape her own corporeality and sexuality in adolescence. When "the facts of life" become known to her she feels betrayed by her parents and her own body. The fear of physicality and sexual repression produce monstrous physical and psychological abnormalities. The identification of Tarasova's protagonist with animals (a toad and a hippopotamus) is a sign of an approaching plunge into madness, a response to what she calls the summons of blood *(zov krovi),* first experienced shortly after her suicide attempt and a stay in an insane asylum.

Tarasova's protagonist is the observer of her own death, documenting the losses—of hair, body parts, memory—in painstaking detail. God does not exist in this unjust universe, beauty is only an antonym for monstrosity, and the only reality is degradation followed by extinction. "A fat, ugly woman will howl in the mad stormy night. Her huge bulging eyes will reflect mocking smiles. . . . And I will be this woman. Shewhodoesnotrememberevil."[11]

Vasil'eva's woman character comes to terms with the idea of dying after she acknowledges her identity as her father's descendant, as a link in the familial succession, which provides for a spiritual connection between the dead and the living. Tarasova's narrator, on the other hand, rejects her family and community as a source of spiritual and physical regeneration. In an uncanny twist of ironic appropriation, Tarasova replays Astaf'ev's call for regression articulated in "Liudochka." Yet in this story no avenger emerges out of the authorially imposed regression into the primordial past, and any search for personal or social salvation appears to be hopeless. Moreover, like Astaf'ev in his earlier village prose narratives, Tarasova's protagonist is a "hater of the present," shunned by all for her abnormality, and a "lamentor of the past," since in her world personal (and by extension, collective) memory is rapidly being lost. Contrary to the overall tenor and narrative outcomes of village prose writing, however, the future of "hopes and dreams" is unattainable for Tarasova's protagonist. The place where she finally situates herself, her "motherland" *(rodina)* is not the confines of her kin *(rod)*, nor, more broadly, is it the pre-industrialized Russian village, or a "restructured" Soviet Union of the 1980s. Rather it is an insane asylum filled with nameless rejects of her society, a space where societal boundaries no longer function, where evil can happen because here "no one remembers it."

Tarasova's profoundly pessimistic story can be easily read as an allegory of exclusion and ineffectiveness experienced by the Soviet intelligentsia on the eve of its society's collapse, the anticipated closure that shapes the entire Soviet literature of the fin-de-siècle. What distinguishes this work from other narratives that link the death of characters to the disintegration of their society, is the punishment meted out by a woman author on her female character, a punishment that is as unavoidable as it is futile.

Notes

1. For a detailed discussion of the literature of the period see Deming Brown, *The Last Years of Soviet Russian Literature: Prose Fiction, 1975–1991* (Cambridge: Cambridge University Press, 1993); Edith Clowes, *Russian Experimental Fiction: Resisting Ideology after Utopia* (Princeton, N.J.: Princeton University Press, 1993); and Nadya L. Peterson, *Subversive Imaginations: Fantastic Prose and the End of Soviet Literature, 1970s–1990s* (Boulder, Colo.: Westview Press, 1997).
2. Viktor Astaf'ev, "Liudochka," and Yurii Mamleev, "Tetrad' individualista," in *New Russian Writing: Russia's Les Fleurs du Mal* (London: Penguin Books, 1996). The Russian version of the volume appeared as *Russkie tsvety zla* (Moscow: Podkova, 1997). All of the citations come from the English edition.
3. Svetlana Vasil'eva, "Otets umer," Elena Tarasova, "Ne pomniashchaia zla," in *Ne pomniashchaia zla*, ed. Larisa Vaneeva (Moscow: Moskovskii rabochii, 1990). The translation is mine.
4. Astaf'ev, "Liudochka," 60.
5. Ibid., 66.
6. Ibid., 67, 72.
7. Mamleev, "Tetrad' individualista," 113.
8. Ibid., 111.
9. Ibid.
10. Tarasova, "Ne pomniashchaia zla," 192.
11. Ibid., 214.

Violence in Modern Russian Utopia and Anti-Utopia

BORIS LANIN and ELENA VASSILEVA

Utopia occupies a special place in the history of Russian political thought and letters. Consider the great interest in social utopian ideas on the part of Russian revolutionaries, or the intense search for a metaphysical utopian unity in which the Russian Symbolists engaged. Whether sociopolitical, metaphysical, or aesthetic, Russian literary utopia typically considered social reality not an object of contemplation but rather as something to be transformed. Utopia was never intended to remain a purely literary exercise, but almost inevitably took on the role of a manual for changing the shape of human existence (the title of Nikolai Chernyshevskii's *What Is to Be Done?* is indicative). It can be said that the dreams of utopian dreamers at least partially came true with the success of the Bolsheviks, who pronounced communism (itself an idea deriving in part from Thomas More's *Utopia*) to be the final goal of the October 1917 Revolution. As this article will demonstrate, the desire to achieve the final destination of "Utopia" has also occasioned much reflection on the costs of such projected universal happiness, some of which found expression in the literary genre of the anti-utopia (or dystopia).[1] If utopian fantasy fiction has as its implied goal the realization of a visionary future, anti-utopia depicts its dark consequences. Utopian literature treats violence as the perhaps unfortunate but necessary side-effect of realizing an ideal; in anti-utopia, on the other hand, violence acquires the status of cold hard reality. The difference between the two may be summed up as follows: "Many imaginary places lie outside utopia's boundaries. To count as a utopia, an imaginary place must be an expression of desire. To count as a dystopia, it must be an expression of fear."[2]

Interest in this kind of writing did not abate during the Soviet period, and even today, when the only consistently utopian regime—that of the Communist Party of the USSR[3]—has failed politically and ceased to exercise moral power, Russian writers strangely continue their literary forays into the realm of utopian and anti-utopian fiction. Because of its focus on social reality, works by writers and journalists who try their hand at utopia and anti-utopia often provide insight into social processes, and may register—or even help prepare society for—changes in political life, regardless of the aesthetic value of their works. In this article, after a brief overview of Russian utopian fiction in the twentieth century, we will examine three strands in this writing that touch on issues of continuing concern in modern Russia. These are: the justification of political murder and genocide; the "dictatorship of the law," that is, the totalitarian impulse in "democratic" Russia; and Russia's imperial dreams (the idea of a Eurasian empire).

The modern conception of the genre of utopia in Russian literature may be traced to the beginning of the twentieth century, to prerevolutionary works by Valerii Briusov and Aleksandr Bogdanov. The Revolution, in its turn, provided new stimulus for fantastic and utopian literature.[4] The main opposition to the communists, the so-called White Guards, by 1921 found themselves defeated and ousted beyond Russia's frontiers and began to envision Russia's future in messianic and utopian terms in the spirit of "Eurasianism." They saw the historical role of Russia as that of a mediator between Western civilization and the profound insights of the Orient. The most remarkable utopia of this type produced in emigration was General Petr Krasnov's *Behind the Thistle* (1922), which predicted Russia's political isolation as well as her gradual transformation into an exotic monarchy. The country that Krasnov envisions has rid itself of all Jews, according to the author, a condition crucial to nation's future prosperity. As we shall see, this conservative scenario reverberates in some utopias of today's authors who also grapple with Russia's ethnic heterogeneity and propose rather peculiar solutions for this condition.

Literary utopia employs fiction as a vehicle for describing the perfect future society, which may be said to be the author's main goal. Such literary devices as a narrator who visits the imaginary society and who addresses a future audience serve the objective of showcasing the ideal social arrangement. Utopia's salient poetic device is description. At the core of anti-utopia lies the impulse to satirize utopia and the utopian idea. While the author of a utopia offers a recipe to cure social and spiritual ailments that will guarantee happiness for all, creators of anti-utopia usually limit themselves to showing one erring individual so as to demonstrate how the very rigidity of utopian rules and their inability to accommodate exceptions turn a utopian order into a nightmare.[5]

The twentieth century may be said to have witnessed the first incarnation of utopian dreams in Russia, and, as a by-product, the vitality of the literary anti-utopia. One of the first powerful critiques of totalitarianism, Evgenii Zamiatin's dystopian *We* (1920), was followed by Mikhail Kozyrev's *Leningrad* (1925), and Andrei Platonov's *Chevengur* (1926–29) and *The Foundation Pit* (1929–30). Zamiatin's anti-utopia may be of particular interest, since, unlike Krasnov, the author collaborated with the new Soviet regime, and his warnings about the possible excesses of the communist idea (which proved amazingly insightful) did not arise out of political opposition. Zamiatin's novel describes the Unified State, a society in which everyone has a job and a place to live, and where state arts flourish; state music flows from public loudspeakers and people listen to state poets. Children all glow with health (otherwise the state denies them the right to life) and are indoctrinated with the state's "mathematically perfect" ideology. Zamiatin, however, focuses on the problematic aspects of the Unified State: its suppression of individualism, all-pervasive surveillance (walls are made of glass), all-embracing worship of the leader ("the Benefactor"), and, ultimately, a compulsory surgical separation of body and soul performed on every citizen of the state. The protagonist of Zamiatin's novel, D-503, serves as a vehicle for expressing all the contradictions of the utopian program. D-503's rebellion starts out in a rather humble way—by writing notes addressed to the future and by falling in love. As is typical for the genre, the conflict arises at the point when the individual refuses to perform his or her prescribed role; totalitarian forms and rituals triumph over individual expressions of will. Since utopia does not recognize individualism and needs to resort to violence to suppress it, in *We*, as in the examples of anti-utopia discussed below, violence is treated as a necessary condition of the utopian future.

Scenario 1: Violence as Genocide

Before turning to the utopian agenda of the post-Soviet era, it is useful to pause on a curious instance of dissident reflection on the consequences of utopian thinking—Iulii Daniel"s *This Is Moscow Speaking* (1960-61). One of the first postwar Russian anti-utopias, this novella was banned in the Soviet Union but published abroad in 1962, with the result that its author was eventually arrested and imprisoned for five years. *This Is Moscow Speaking* opens with a radio announcement that informs the population of a newly instituted "free murder day," a day on which everyone will have the right to kill whomever they want. The narrator, Anatolii Kartsev, faces a dilemma as his mistress immediately suggests killing her husband so that they can legitimize their relationship. The decree is announced at a birthday party whose participants perceive the news as a covert attack on Jews, and Kartsev's subsequent dream recalls the Holocaust. Daniel"s novella thus suggests how the Nazis' mass extermination continued to reverberate in the USSR during the postwar anti-Semitic hysteria. In the novella, Kartsev becomes confused over the identity of his tormentors: the soldiers who had fought with Nazi Germany now appear in fascist uniforms, but with red stars on their caps. When offered the chance to take revenge on his enemies, the protagonist declines "the invitation to murder."

The novella depicts the results of "free murder day" throughout the country in a rather optimistic light. The number of murders in Russia, we are told, is relatively low, not more than a thousand that day, which suggests a lack of interest on the part of the population in participating in state-sanctioned bloodletting. Massacres do happen on the outskirts of the empire, though—between Georgians and Armenians and Armenians and Azerbaijanis, especially in Nagorno-Karabakh, already notorious for its ethnic clashes. In Central Asia "there was no interethnic feuding. Everyone was after Russians."[6] In Ukraine newly established youth detachments receive blacklists as recommended guidelines for action, but the marked individuals succeed in hiding. The Baltic republics plainly ignore the decree. Jews are not attacked, we are told, although the danger to them does not disappear. The author's astuteness in matters of Soviet nationalist politics is crowned with an appeal to Jews to resist victimization, as the author's voice becomes recognizable in that of the protagonist: "You must not allow them to torment you to death. It is your responsibility to others to be responsible for your own life."[7] Daniel"s approach to the problem of state-sponsored anti-Semitism suggests that individual moral responsibility is the only way to resist all-pervasive totalitarian politics. The only way for one to preserve one's integrity is to ignore the authorities' criminal decrees. Daniel"s anti-utopian novella thus connects the problem of interethnic relations with utopian thinking, suggesting its connection to "total solutions" like genocide, mass terror, and ethnic cleansing, the flip side of the kind of reactionary utopia outlined by Krasnov.

Scenario 2: Dictatorship of the Law

The following two scenarios in one way or another comment on what is perceived to be the most crucial political problem of today's Russia, its lawlessness. The weakness of law in the face of a popular culture that valorizes disobedience to legal institutions has inspired the idea of a so-called "dictatorship of the law." This idea has been ascribed to President Vladimir Putin, and works on this theme may thus be seen as challenges to or warnings against the growing popularity of Putin's ideological program.[8]

Oleg Divov's recent *Selective Atomizing* (1999) envisions a society whose main principle is "dictatorship of the law." Under the assumption that it is the lack of law-abiding citizens that hampers society's well-being, Russia embarks on a simple and efficient plan of eliminating those who fail to stay legally clean. Suspension of civil liberties is complemented with endowing "social security agency" operatives with a license to kill all persistent delinquents. After seven years of this policy Russia becomes a totally safe country, or rather, a totally different country, as it is now called "The Union of Slavs." Ten million of its citizens have been sacrificed for the triumph of the law. The novel is narrated by one of the social security operatives, Pavel Gusev, who envisions himself as a modern Robin Hood and, needless to say, spares no mercy on criminals. Ethnic discrimination in the Union of Slavs achieves unprecedented heights, crowned by the popular slogan "We don't buy from non-Russians." Policies toward undesirable national groups differ: gypsies, for instance, are deported to Ukraine (not so much out of a lack of means to exterminate them, as out of malice towards the Ukraine, which refused to join the Union), whereas Jews are relentlessly "atomized" (exterminated). As the narrator rushes to explain, Jews only suffer in connection with financial crimes, for example, for trying to export the country's monetary resources abroad. The very population that had been frustrated by post-perestroika lawlessness, however, eventually comes to resent the "atomizers" and the cause they represent, since the dictatorship remains even when it is carried out on behalf of the law. The political elite, a segment of the population that is particularly disgruntled by the atomizers, eventually presses for a secret decree to eliminate them.

Scenario 3: Eurasian Empire

Selective Atomizing is primarily concerned with modes of Russia's future political regime, with its vision of the Union of the Slavs, but also expresses nostalgia for the Russian imperial past. Some have interpreted Russia's geographical position in Eurasia as promising the basis for a new, higher, synthetic civilization. This brand of political thought dreams of the reunification of former imperial subjects under Russia's heading and has inspired various fantasies about Russia's renewed superpower status.

A playful engagement with geopolitics is a frequent tool in the hands of Russian utopian writers of the newest wave. Remarkable in this respect is Andrei Stoliarov's bestselling *The Lark* (*Zhavoronok*, 1999), which consciously exploits geopolitical anxieties. In this work, a certain provincial maiden named Zhanna, whose name intentionally recalls Joan of Arc, comes to Moscow and engages in the modest labor of street vending until, following "a voice from heaven," she leads an uprising for the reunification of the Crimea with Russia. Zhanna stands at the head of a popular movement that enlists many thousands as it moves toward the Ukrainian border. The national crusade is unstoppable; it does not yield to either international pressure or to underhanded plots by treacherous political elites. It takes only Zhanna's untimely death at the hand of a vengeful murderer to delay changes in the map of the world. The author, however, sees this as only a temporary obstacle, unlikely to change the final outcome of reunification with the former Russian territory of the Crimea. Curiously, critical response to the novel did not comment on the imperial claims that Stoliarov's novel makes, instead focusing on the familiar Russian chord that the writer struck, of the "profound authentic yearning of contemporary Russians for a miracle, [and] for a charismatic, spiritual leader."[9]

Another recent success in the contemporary Russian book market has been the work published by a creative tandem known under the pseudonym "Holm van Zaichik" (a well-known fantasy writer, Viacheslav Rybakov, and a journalist-orientalist, Igor Alimov, are rumored to be the collaborators). The team's first book, *The Case of a Greedy Barbarian* (2000), narrates the tale of a utopian country named "Ordus'" (an acronym made up from the Tatar word for a nomadic tribe, "Orda" ["horde," recalling the historical Golden Horde] and "Rus'," or Russia). In describing the social arrangement of this imaginary land, the authors dwell at length on one characteristic utopian feature—its penal system. Legal provisions of utopian societies often provide a guide to their ideology, and in Ordus' corporeal punishment almost never needs to be applied, since crimes are simply never committed there. However, when it is applied, consider its severity: public shaving of the head and armpits! Fines are not administered because of their unequal significance for citizens with different incomes, making one starve and having no noticeable effect on another. By similar reasoning, rich people are subject to tougher punishments based on the understanding that bad behavior is less forgivable in citizens who have had better opportunities for cultivating their manners.

Flirtation with nomadic Tatar culture here reflects the disillusionment on the part of contemporary Russian intellectuals with Western civilization and the notion that it is inadequate for a country whose past is rooted in the Eastern or "Eurasian" cultural heritage. The scenario of a Eurasian empire has become common in contemporary Russian literature. In Pavel Krusanov's popular *Angel's Bite* (*Ukus angela,* 2000) the empire called Hesperia is initially in a state of decline but is revived and restored, even if at a high cost in human life. Krusanov's narrator optimistically assures the reader that in the empire's fight against rebels, the ratio of losses is seventy-six to one in favor of the imperial soldiers. Ideological support for the success of Hesperia is provided by people like the novel's protagonist, Petr Legkostupov, who writes catchy slogans for the empire's propaganda machine. Petr's goal is to facilitate a new emperor's accession to the throne, which he succeeds in doing by writing a mystery play featuring the future tyrant as savior.

It is not the specific form of imperial rule that seems to appeal to writers, but rather such things as its evocations of grandeur, order, stable religious affiliation, and clearly designated authority. While the resurgence of the image of empire may seem unexpected in newly democratic Russia, the treatment accorded this kind of political entity in utopian literature is not at all condescending or critical. This nostalgia for a social arrangement that none of these popular writers actually lived through does not look dramatically out of place given the huge success of Vladimir Putin's emphasis on "dictatorship of the law," the slogan of a powerful political movement that supports the Russian president's new national platform.[10] Having lived through a realization of utopian ideas in its recent past, however, most of the Russian public remains quite sensitive to social and cultural utopian constructs.

Generally, while utopian writers are concerned with finding a formula for universal salvation from moral and social deficiencies, the authors of anti-utopia inevitably question the very universality of the utopian ideal by showing what "immediate happiness for all" entails for the individual, whose interests—irrational or creative—can never be fully embraced by a universal formula.

As we have shown in this article, contemporary Russian literature is very aware of the dangers of utopian thinking, however, without quite being able to give up its traditional role as an arena for political expression. It appears that the contradiction between utopian or imperial desires and anti-utopian disillusionment remains unresolved. While strong nostalgia for order produces occasional descents into fairy-tales of a Russian "golden age," an all-too-clear awareness of the dangers of universal political and national programs such as the seemingly neutral appeal for a "dictatorship of the law" turns much of this literature into forceful cautionary tales.

Notes

1. "Anti-utopia" suggests the negation of a specific "utopian" system or construct (it implies that there may exist a genuine utopia); "dystopia" suggests the impossibility of any utopia whatsoever.

2. J. Carey, ed. *The Faber Book of Utopias* (London: Faber and Faber, 1999), xi.

3. On the USSR as a failed utopia, see, for example, Mikhail Geller and Aleksandr Nekrich, *Utopia in Power: The History of the Soviet Union from 1917 to the Present,* trans. Phyllis B. Carlos (London: Hutchinson, 1986).

4. Some examples of early Russian utopias are V. Briusov's *Republic of the Southern Cross* (1907) and A. Bogdanov's *The Red Star* (1908) and *Manny, the Engineer* (1911).

5. Iu. Latynina, "Literaturnye istoki anti-utopicheskogo zhanra" (Ph.D. abstract) (Moscow, 1992), 18.

6. Iu. Mal'tsev, *Vol'naia russkaia literatura* (Frankfurt-am-Main: Posev, 1976), 85.

7. Ibid., 88.

8. "Dictatorship of the law is the only kind of dictatorship that we should aspire to." At the same meeting with the officials from the Ministry of Justice, Putin went on to say that "state power and law enforcement agencies are parts of a unified state mechanism," thereby proclaiming "law and order" to be the main guarantor of Russia's future, "no less significant in the process of reformation

than the program of economic transformation" (*Rossiiskaia gazeta,* January 1, 2000).

9. E. Ermolin, "Glazami souchastnika," *Druzhba narodov* 1 (2001): 212.

10. The name of the movement, "Idushchie vmeste," means "going together."

The Female Face of Violence

Russian Culture and Violence against Women

TERESA L. POLOWY

Contemporary Russian culture, despite more than seventy years of official Soviet rhetoric about gender equality and a new social definition of womanhood, remains patriarchal and inclined toward misogyny. Yet enduring counter-traditions in Russian culture, such as the powerful "mother myth" or the iconic image of "Rodina-Mat'" ("Motherland"), evoked so vividly during World War II, suggest that Russian culture has not always been misogynistic in the same ways or to the same extent. However in the post-Soviet period, Russian misogynistic proclivities have been apparent in a variety of symptomatic ways, for example, in a societal tolerance of gender and age discrimination against women, in the sexual abuse and harassment of women in the workplace, in the overt marketing of women as sexual objects, and in the trafficking of women for sexual exploitation. The identification and cataloguing of such contemporary misogynistic phenomena must be seen within a meaningful cultural-historical context that suggests that traditional attitudes and beliefs about women's place within patriarchal Russian culture are being transformed to support and validate new mythologies and cultural codes. In Russia, where behaviors and attitudes regarding violence against women have been inculcated over more than a millennium, it appears that the current dynamics of economic, political, and social hardships are exacerbating these beliefs and women are taking the brunt of their force. This said, it is nonetheless significant that a new feature accompanying contemporary Russian attitudes toward women is the fact that violence against women and children has come into the public forum in a more meaningful, if still limited, way through the work of nongovernmental organizations and the establishment of crisis lines, women's shelters, and increased media coverage.

It is important to realize that historically and culturally, fundamental Russian patriarchal values differ little from those of Central and Western Europe, firstly, in the allocation of power to men, and secondly, in the requirement of service from women due to their allegedly weaker moral and physical nature, which makes them susceptible to sin.[1] In Russia, in fact, the origins of such attitudes toward women have been linked to 988 AD and the Christianization of the Kievan Rus' state (tenth to the thirteenth centuries). Church texts promoted the denigration of women in Russian society and justified their subordination to men by identifying "woman" with Eve, the temptress, and with the Fall. The clear implication of the good woman/evil woman dichotomy in this literature was that "only a woman who accommodated herself entirely to Christian mores, subordinated herself to males, and devoted her life to domesticity . . . was worthy of the epithet *good*."[2] Early ecclesiastical texts that were significant to the introduction and reinforcement of misogynistic attitudes in Russia include the fourth-century Byzantine text of St. John Chrysostom, "Parable of Feminine Evil"; the eleventh-century work by Nestor, *The Life of Theodosius;* and the twelfth-century *Petition of Daniil Zatochnik.*[3]

In the medieval Muscovite period (fourteenth to seventeenth centuries), two sociocultural phenomena focus our attention on the position of women in Russian society: the sixteenth-century household manual *Domostroi* (Law of the Home) written by the monk Sylvestor, and the institution of the *terem* for elite women. The *Domostroi* is a crucial Muscovite social and cultural document that establishes domestic rules based on monastic ones: the father is the abbot who is to save the souls of his wife and children. All household duties are described and relationships defined in great detail; even the beating of one's wife, which was condoned provided that it was moderate, was described. Concurrent with the instructional *Domostroi*, proverbs about the subordination of women became widespread: "The husband is the law unto his wife" and, in an allusion to the husband as a divine figure, "The husband is the father of his wife."[4]

In addition to written Church texts, oral folklore, especially folk songs and proverbs, and secular literature written by men have been identified by observers in diverse disciplines as perpetuating an enduring misogynistic attitude in Russian culture.[5] In such male-authored oral and written texts, through various periods and with increasing sophistication, women have been portrayed as sinful, in possession of evil and magical powers, and in need of punishment. Barbara Heldt, writing about Russian fiction authored by men, asserts that "misogyny in its undiluted form constitutes a none too small and chronologically very persistent stream in Russian literature." Heldt suggests that both oral and written proverbs have been an especially productive genre for the misogynistic impulse in Russian culture due to their appealing structure and style: parallelisms, rhymes, and imaginative analogies are all found widely in Russian folk speech.[6] Two graphic examples are: "A hen is not a bird, a woman is not a person" ('Kuritsa ne ptitsa, a baba ne chelovek') and "Where Satan fails, a woman will succeed" ('Gde satana ne smozhet, tuda baba poshlet').[7] The latter proverb reflects a popular theme of Kievan literature: every woman is an Eve, willful, rebellious, and disobedient, who will lead her man astray.[8] The proverb "From our rib no good will come to us" ('Ot nashego rebra, nam ne zhdet dobra')[9] clearly states the position of both the patriarchal clergy and state (the "our" and "to us" here) toward women. This traditional notion that "woman is not a person," according to Joanna Hubbs, attests "paradoxically to their power and stubborn resistance to male authority."[10]

Feminist historians and cultural observers have recently begun to analyze this resistance and to suggest that Russian women were more actively involved in society than has been assumed; women learned to accommodate themselves and, without challenging the patriarchal status quo that gave them security, were able to take great advantage of the informal power they gained through the roles assigned to them. Nancy Shields Kollman has suggested that even the seventeenth-century *terem* tradition, in which upper-class women were segregated from men and only occasionally left their rooms to attend church, was a response to the emergence of an elite society.[11] Elite females were protected in a patriarchal society that valued purity of bloodline and arranged marriages as vital to the well-being of the aristocracy, and this afforded them power and influence within their own sphere. This included arranging their children's marriages and negotiating alliances with other families, as the need arose. Christine Worobec notes that women had control over childbearing and childrearing, influence over their children's marriages, household economic responsibilities, and honor accorded to them (and thus the entire family) in the patriarchal system. She concludes: "Women's contributions and sacrifices must finally be recognized as enabling their society to operate effectively."[12]

Two additional themes concerning the relationships between men and women have been replicated in many variations in Russian society and culture: the potent insult and humiliation of a man being likened to a woman, and the permissive cultural and social attitude toward wife-beating.[13] Culturally sanctioned violent behavior toward women has roots in the notion that men are weakened by their association with women. One of the worst insults for a Russian man is to be called a woman *(baba):* "He who gets involved with a woman, will become a woman himself."[14] This attitude was reinforced in a new way in Soviet times, according to psychologist Igor' Kon, by a general trend toward "demasculinization of man," which manifested itself as social futility among men and often led to "aggressive sexism" and sexual violence.[15] This "demasculinization" may be seen as a complex result of the Bolshevik ideological push in the 1920s for the "emancipation of women," the results of which were poorly anticipated in Soviet social planning, which did not take into account resistance posed by traditional and prevalent gender values and codes.[16]

The collapse of the Soviet Union and transition to a market economy has led to the acute deterioration of women's position, which is marked by sexual violence against women. The 1993 UN Declaration on Violence against Women states that violence against women includes "any act of gender-based violence that results in, or is likely to result in, physical, sexual, or psychological harm or suffering to women, including threats of such acts, coercion or arbitrary deprivations of liberty, whether occurring in public or private life."[17]

In today's Russia, women face overt gender and age discrimination when looking for jobs. For example, it is common for advertisements to require that female applicants be "no older than 25," "without inhibitions," or "blond with long legs."[18] Readers and viewers are daily bombarded with female flesh from print ads, billboard media, and television commercials: using sex to sell products extends even to serious journalistic pieces to which the reader's eye is drawn by women in various stages of undress. For example: a photograph accompanying an article about the European Association of Police Women, which helps train women for sensitive crisis center work, showed a scantily clad woman in black shorts and a halter top, with a long-barreled pistol extended above her head and a superimposed image of the Kremlin's tower pointing directly between her legs.[19]

To a certain extent, violence against Russian women outside the home can be observed and gauged, but it is much more difficult to quantify violence that takes place privately—in the home and within the family—and to understand how the attitude about what happens in private translates into permissive public stances about implied or implicit violence against women. A permissive social attitude toward wife-beating underlies many proverbs and jokes in Russian folk culture, for example, "Beat your wife before lunch, and before dinner too"; "The more you beat your wife, the tastier the cabbage soup will be"; "I beat whom I love. If I don't beat my wife, things will not be good."[20] In the Soviet period there was a conspicuous absence of discussion about the issue of domestic violence against women despite such troublesome social indicators as a high divorce rate, the soaring rate of alcoholism in the male population, and the pressures of the chronic housing shortage—factors that exacerbated potentially violent situations. This silence was due to the "official rhetoric of gender equality,"[21] which allowed little autonomy to publicly acknowledge or discuss the question; in other words, the issue was ignored and even suppressed. Moreover, as Tat'iana Zabelina points out, the very concept of violence in Soviet society was reduced to ideological discussions about violence between classes or between states, the result of which was "several generations of Soviet people unaccustomed to thinking about violence as a violation of the rights of the individual and unable to see the problem of violence toward children and women."[22] It is only very recently that private issues have come into the public forum in Russia due to "official acknowledgement of widespread incidence of domestic violence, combined with increasing public discourse, victims' testimonies, the efforts of women working in crisis centers, and research."[23]

Officially acknowledged statistics are shocking: only three years after the collapse of the Soviet Union, figures in the National Report for 1994 of the Russian Federation show that "14,500 women were killed by their male partners, and another 56,400 were injured out of a total of 331,815 crimes against women." This was almost three times the number of women reportedly killed by their male partners in the Soviet Union in 1991 (5,300), which in itself is a figure that had increased significantly from 1989 (1,623) and 1990 (1,914). Statistics show that women constitute 95 percent of domestic violence victims and almost all of the offenders are men.[24]

Notions of "privacy" underlie prevalent myths that have had tremendous implications for the manner in which domestic violence against women as a legal issue has been handled in Russia. Just as the proverb states "A wife is always guilty before her husband,"[25] so it is commonly accepted that a woman who is beaten by her husband is to blame and has provoked the behavior[26] or has "encouraged," "helped," and "supported" the violence.[27] The idea of "privacy" is often closely tied to that of "provocation": Johnson observes that the latter is very broadly understood and can include such disparate criteria as a woman "earning too much money, wearing the wrong clothes, being unfaithful, taunting the abuser, nagging, and complaining about bad behavior."[28] A strong cultural myth that discourages the private from entering the public sphere condemns any public talk about private family matters as "washing one's linen in public."[29] The power of this sentiment is also felt at every level of law enforcement, as the Russian police and Ministry of Internal Affairs maintain that domestic violence is a private affair and that "the right to privacy in the Russian Constitution proscribes their involvement." In actuality, however, there are limits to this inviolability.[30] Moreover there are a number of statutes in Russian criminal law that could be applied to domestic violence, but there is simply no will to do so in Russia, where the vast majority of lawmakers and law-enforcers are men.[31] "A woman's cry to the police of 'Help, he's killing me!' will usually get an unconcerned response to the effect 'So? If he kills you, then come to see us.'"[32]

Equally damaging cultural myths hold that only poor and uneducated women experience domestic violence. In fact most women calling crisis hotlines are well-educated, from higher income brackets, and the wives of businessmen.[33] Other myths place blame for the violence on extraneous factors that provide excuses for not acknowledging and dealing with the problem. For example, the idea that harsh socioeconomic conditions and phenomena are the underlying causes of domestic violence is a holdover from Soviet ideology which held that political and economic issues are of primary importance in society; social problems are secondary and remediable given the correct reforms. A report filed for *Russia Weekly* on the occasion of International Women's Day in 2001 about domestic violence in Russia contains such an explanation by an Interior Ministry spokesman: "As for domestic violence, [Mikhail] Kurkin said it was mainly the result of growing alcoholism and 'could be resolved if alcoholics were forced to get treatment.'"

However, experts on domestic violence counter this argument with the position that "domestic and sexual violence's underlying cause is an unbridled need for control. Alcoholism or difficult social conditions . . . are extra risk factors but *not a necessary condition for violence*" (emphasis added).[34] While accepting the fact that Russian abuse of alcohol is not necessary for violence to occur, one need only mentally review the theme of drunkenness in Russian oral and written cultural genres to be struck by the sheer number of occurrences of gender-related misogyny accompanied by drunkenness. Indeed, in Russian attitudes about drink is the *explicit* idea that one loses one's mind: "When drunkenness rages, reason stays quiet" and "Drink is no friend to reason," which translates into the implicit idea that one is not responsible for actions undertaken while in a drunken state: "Drink, don't be shy; drink wine, beat your wife, don't be afraid of anything!"[35] And in fact in a 1996 survey of Moscow women, over 50 percent of cases of physical abuse were triggered by the husband's excessive drinking; the proverbs and statistics suggest that alcohol may often be used as a male excuse for domestic violence, and all speak to a need for control.[36]

Women's economic dependence on their husbands and thus a shift in the balance of power within the Russian family has become a growing social and economic reality. In Russian society in the past decade, Russian women have been marginalized economically and politically. In fact, women are the first workers to be let go from their jobs. For example, in 2000 women comprised 63 percent of the unemployed and made about 50 percent less than men,[37] whereas in the Soviet era 84 percent of women held jobs and earned on average 75 percent as much as men.[38] During the late 1980s, a conservative and continuing trend toward family life—notions about the importance of male dominance, strong family ties, chastity, and stability—was noted.[39] Perhaps the class of "new Russians" provides the clearest example of the results of recent social and economic shifts. Because a stay-at-home wife is considered a status symbol, a "new Russian" husband with a handsome income may prefer that his wife leave her job and remain at home to look after him and the children, thus rendering her totally dependent on him. Larisa Babitskaia, a psychologist in a Yaroslavl women's center, describes one example of a woman married to a rich businessman who endured spousal psychological abuse: "The woman said her husband gives her the exact sum of money she needs for shopping. He counts it down to the last kopeck . . . and if she has to take [public transport], he pays out according to her exact itinerary. She didn't have a single ruble extra. And she lived like that for two years before calling us. She described [her situation] as slavery.'"[40]

Marina Pisklakova of the Women's Crisis Center in Moscow echoes this account and characterizes the calls to the center's hotline made by wives of "new Russians" as exhibiting intellectual degradation and various other forms of psychological and emotional abuse: "They sit in [their gilded cages], cared for, elegantly dressed, like pretty dolls. But they call us to let it all out."[41] Whatever a husband's motivation might be for wanting his wife at home, in post-Soviet Russia it is now more likely to be supported by deeply ingrained cultural attitudes toward women as well as the prevailing economic culture. Yelena Potapova, executive director of the nongovernmental group ANNA (Association "No to Violence") speaking about the "female face of unemployment" and low wages makes a direct connection between economic dependence and domestic violence: "This gives men a feeling of superiority and makes women feel dependent, all of which is fertile ground for violence."[42]

Also new in post-Soviet Russia is the way that domestic violence is responded to by the police and handled in the legal system: prior to 1991, the battery of women was covered under several criminal statutes such as "hooliganism," "violation of public order," "clear disrespect for society," all of which dealt with unacceptable behavior in the public sphere. Additionally, the local Party or trade union committee commonly intervened in domestic situations and sanctioned the perpetrator. Today, the state demands witnesses and evidence of severe bodily injury before it will consider a woman's battery "real." Many women's activists assert that "one of the costs of political liberalization and privatization of property has been the creation of a private sphere where men are given almost free rein to batter women."[43] Thus, it appears that the basic misogynistic impulse in Russia responds to changing factors and uses any excuse to victimize women. Violence against women, and its underlying need for control, is a constant, but increases or decreases according to political, ideological, or economic circumstances.

Women around the world have faced and continue to face misogynistic attitudes and violence in general and domestic violence in particular, yet they are different in cultural nuance. In today's Russia, in the painful throes of acquiring new freedoms unknown under Soviet rule, we acknowledge such social phenomena as "the feminization of poverty" and "the female face of domestic violence." Increasingly, the problem of gender relations in Russia is being addressed in a growing body of writing about women by women that evidences a complexity of "feminism," as several articles in this volume (Novikov, Skomp, Kolchevska) demonstrate. Because of the pervasiveness of cultural attitudes in Russia that support the abuse of women, a broad participation and bridging of "rhetorical distances"[44] at every level—from literature and the arts, to women's groups and nongovernmental organizations, to the media, to various state agencies—will be required to change the stance of individuals, the justice system, and public policy regarding violence toward women. Still and all, through work which has already begun, violence against women in Russia is finally percolating into the public consciousness and is being increasingly viewed as a problem, rather than accepted as a given.

Notes

1. Barbara Evans Clements, "Introduction: Accommodation, Resistance, Transformation," in *Russia's Women: Accommodation, Resistance, Transformation*, ed. Barbara Evans Clements, Barbara Alpern Engels, Christine D. Worobec (Berkeley: University of California Press, 1991), 3.

2. Christine D. Worobec, "Accommodation and Resistance, "in Clements, Engels, Worobec, *Russia's Women*, 19.

3. A good source for English translations of some of these texts is Serge A. Zenkovskii, *Medieval Russian Epics, Chronicles, and Tales*, ed. and trans. Serge A. Zenkovskii, rev. ed. (New York: Dutton, 1974). Additionally, see *Anthology of Old Russian Literature*, ed. A. Stender-Petersen with Stefan Congrat-Butlar, 3rd ed. (New York: Columbia University Press, 1966), for English language introductions and notes to early texts in Russian.

4. Quoted in Joanna Hubbs, *Mother Russia: The Feminine Myth in Russian Culture* (Bloomington: Indiana University Press, 1988), 173. For an annotated translation of this work, see *The Domostroi: Rules for Russian Households in the Time of Ivan the Terrible*, ed. and trans. Carolyn Johnston Pouncey (Ithaca, N.Y.: Cornell University Press, 1994).

5. For example, see Barbara Heldt, *Terrible Perfection: Women and Russian Literature* (Bloomington: Indiana University Press, 1987), 25–27; Hubbs, *Mother Russia*, 92–94; Sharon Horne, "Domestic Violence in Russia," *American Psychologist* 54:1 (1999): 58; and Clements, "Introduction," 6.

6. Heldt, *Terrible Perfection*, 25, 26.

7. Vladimir Dal', *Poslovitsy russkogo naroda* (Moscow: NNN, 1994), 221–22. All translations from Dal' are mine.

8. See Hubbs, *Mother Russia*, 93.

9. Dal', *Poslovitsy*, 222.

10. Hubbs, *Mother Russia*, 93. Writing specifically of the literature of male authors, Barbara Heldt reiterates this position: "The misogynist regards physical abuse of women as proof of their endurance and of the transience of men" (*Terrible Perfection*, 27).

11. Nancy Shields Kollman, "The Seclusion of Elite Muscovite Women," *Russian History* 10:2 (1983): 170–87. Lower-class women were not segregated from men because of their practical economic importance; nonetheless their occupation and leadership opportunities were severely limited. See Horne, "Domestic Violence," 56.

12. Worobec, "Accommodation," 20. See also the work of I. Thyret on the very important and influential role of women in religious life: Isolde Renate Thyret, *Between God and Tsar: Religious Symbolism and the Royal Women of Muscovite Russia* (DeKalb: Northern Illinois University Press, 2001).

13. Heldt identifies similar themes in her discussion of modern male writers like Zamiatin, Bely, Olesha, and Babel': "Death in domesticity, the humiliation of a man by a woman, and sexual pollution or engulfment illustrate a basic but often irresistible fear" (*Terrible Perfection*, 25).

14. Dal', *Poslovitsy*, 222.

15. Igor' Kon, *The Sexual Revolution in Russia: From the Age of the Tsars to Today* (New York: Free Press, 1995), 150–53.

16. Ibid. In Kon's view, the lack of sexual and economic freedom in the USSR was personified by the feminization of institutions and processes of socialization. Illustrative examples include such facts as almost all kindergarten and school teachers were women, every fifth child in the USSR was fatherless, and three-quarters of *komsomol* secretaries were female. See also, Eric Naiman, *Sex in Public: The Incarnation of Early Soviet Ideology* (Princeton, N.J.: Princeton University Press, 1997).

17. UNICEF, the Monee Project, Regional Monitoring Report no. 6: "Women in Transition," Eastern European/Eurasian Comparative Report for 1999 (Florence: International Child Development Center under the auspices of UNICEF [http://unicef.icdc.org]), 77.

18. Horne, "Domestic Violence," 57.

19. Clare Warmke, "Russian and American Women Battle Domestic Violence," *Off Our Backs* 27:10 (November 30, 1997): n.p.

20. Dal', *Poslovitsy*, 235. It is perhaps indicative of cultural attitudes that there is no word for "wife-beating" in Russian: the transitive and active verb "to beat" is used in its infinitive *(bit')* and imperative *(bei)* forms.

21. UNICEF, "Women in Transition," 77. Warmke tells us that until recently the word "gender" was unfamiliar to most Russians ("Russian and American Women," n.p.), while Kon asserts that even in the mid-1980s "the word 'sexism' didn't exist even in the professional sociological language" (*The Sexual Revolution*, 269).

22. Tat'iana Zabelina, "Sexual Violence towards Women," in *Gender, Generation and Identity in Contemporary Russia*, ed. Hilary Pilkington (London: Routledge, 1996), 170.

23. Horne, "Domestic Violence," 60.

24. Ibid., 55. It is useful to compare U.S. statistics in this area. According to a

1998 study, 1,350 women were killed by an intimate, and whereas the ratio of women to men killed by an intimate in the US is 2.3:1, in Russia it is 6:1. See Janet Johnson, "Privatizing Pain: The Problem of Woman Battery in Russia," *NWSA Journal* 13:3 (2001): 154.

25. Dal', *Poslovitsy*, 233.

26. See Sophie Lambroschini, "Russia: Domestic Violence Persists," *CDI Russia Weekly* 144 (9 March 2001, 14 September 2001) http://www.cdi.org/russia/144.html#; and Georgii Tselms, "War on Women," *Current Digest of the Post Soviet Press* 52:47 (2000): 17.

27. Warmke, "Russian and American Women," n.p.

28. Johnson, "Privatizing Pain," 156. This excuse for abuse is used at every level (law enforcement, courts, legislation) to "justify" the crime and absolve the perpetrator (as well as the state) of responsibility for it.

29. See Horne, "Domestic Violence," 57, and Lambroschini, "Russia: Domestic Violence," 7. This attitude directly echoes the proverb: "A husband should curse his wife, and a third person shouldn't interfere." Dal', *Poslovitsy*, 234.

30. Johnson, "Privatizing Pain," 156.

31. For example, when a women's hotline service volunteer asked an Interior Ministry representative whether a better process could be initiated to handle rape victims, who currently must "wait several days before the administrative process turns them over to a forensic doctor, by which time all of the evidence has often disappeared . . ." he smiled and answered: "'We can't set up something like that just for you!'" (Lambroschini, "Russia: Domestic Violence," 9).

32. Lora Velikanova, "Women Are Being Beaten," *Russian Social Science Review* 37:59 (1996): 23.

33. See Tselms, "War on Women," 17, and Horne, "Domestic Violence," 58.

34. Lambroschini, "Russia: Domestic Violence," 8.

35. Dal', *Poslovitsy*, 500, 499.

36. UNICEF, "Women in Transition," 82.

37. Tselms, "War on Women," 17.

38. Katherine E. Young, "Loyal Wives, Virtuous Mothers," *Russian Life Magazine* (1996): n.p. See Helena Goscilo, "Perestroika or Domostroika? The Construction of Womanhood under Glasnost," in *Dehexing Sex: Russian Womanhood during and after Perestroika* (Ann Arbor: University of Michigan Press, 1996), 17, for a discussion of the current separation of masculine and feminine areas of activity based on essentialized concepts of "the law of nature."

39. Kon, *The Sexual Revolution*, 311 n37. Currently, "demasculinization" in the domestic arena may be assumed to be less prevalent, yet such current conditions as Russia's military weakness, economic hardships, and a burgeoning gender awareness among women may be understood as "demasculinizing."

40. Lambroschini, "Russia: Domestic Violence," 8.

41. Velikanova, "Women Are Being Beaten," 5.

42. Tselms, "War on Women," 17.

43. Johnson, "Privatizing Pain," 163. Johnson notes that through this broad conception of public sphere, domestic violence made up 40 percent of "hooliganism" charges.

44. Ibid.

Angry Women's Voices

Revenge Fantasies in Nina Sadur's Stories

TATYANA NOVIKOV

Fundamental democratic changes in Russia over the last fifteen years have led to the creation of a new society. The abolition of official censorship, the rediscovery of freedom of expression, and a new liberal climate inspired vigorous developments in writing and publication that would have been unthinkable twenty years ago in the Soviet context. In those days women's writing "tended to settle for politically safe themes," excluding potentially threatening "feminocentric" topics and issues of gender, while its "docility paralleled women's tacit accommodation with their unacknowledged status as second-class citizens in a society falsely advertising itself as gender democratic."[1] In sharp contrast, recent fiction by Russian female authors—a rapidly growing body of literature—directly confronts the problem of what it means to be a woman in Russia. Writing within what is perceived as a highly gendered context, these new literary talents—among them Nina Sadur, Svetlana Vasilenko, Valeriia Narbikova, and Marina Palei—offer a complex and varied response to the multiple social, cultural, and sexual challenges that face Russian women today.

With their valorization of masculinity, traditional Russian stereotypes have reinforced patriarchal values equating the feminine with passivity, ignorance, and obedience and masculinity with aggression, intelligence, and force. Oppressive cultural attitudes produce hierarchical structures that have elevated men and denigrated women, resulting in women's low status and social marginalization. The social reality of violence against women and the abusive and dehumanizing context reflect men's chronic need to assert their authority. According to R. W. Connel, "Violence is part of a system of domination, but is at the same time a measure of its imperfection. A thoroughly legitimate hierarchy would have less need to intimidate."[2] With the nation's legacy of oppression, violence continues to cut deep. Patriarchal mythology still dominates in the Russian social climate, if only as a "mute ideal," but one that still demands female subjugation. Contemporary women's fiction exemplifies the painful process of moving out of silence by challenging its culture's most deeply rooted beliefs about women. The recurring trope of violence in their fiction reflects both the reality of gender-based suffering and women's concern with violence as a pervasive cultural disease.

As Michael Kowalewski notes, "in studying fictional violence one must explore the power of words to sicken and befoul as well as freshen and redeem."[3] For women, traditionally victims in Russian culture, literary portrayal of violence and women's subjugation to tyranny may offer emotional catharsis. Women writers are finally able to express anger and passion, to confront their frustrations instead of burying them. Embedded in many of their narratives is rage directed toward their entire culture with its conservative gender structures. Concerned with how violence in various manifestations of masculinity might be registered or overcome, these texts appeal to a large audience of women, who find in them reflections of their own bitterness and hope. Contemporary women's literature also recognizes violence among women and its potential to change women's lives. Some plots feature female violence, an extreme form of anger that authors only recently have begun to explore. The work of Nina Sadur is an outstanding example of such writing and may be said to establish her place as the leader of modern Russian "violent fiction." Sadur's short dramatic pieces are disturbing in content, intense and enigmatic, in part because the boundaries between reality and the world of the imagination of her female characters are blurred. Incorporating elements of folklore, witchcraft, and magic, these parable-like stories create a fictional world that is often incomprehensible, unpredictable, and disorienting. Further, the reality portrayed in Sadur's stories becomes refracted through the consciousness of her psychologically distant women narrators, whose gossipy and at times ironic and malicious voices are presented as those of ordinary Russian women. Recounted from the narrator's unreliable perspective, Sadur's stories become an extended exercise in interpretation.

The author's vision is that of all-encompassing violence. Countless episodes of physical and psychological aggression punctuate her texts, which focus on women's attempts to survive in a world that cruelly destroys illusions of happiness through violent reality. Sadur's female protagonists are subjected to violence and subordination, and they in turn react with the wish to retaliate. A quintessential liberating gesture for her victimized characters, female violence is frequently presented not as actual violent acts of revenge, but as fantasy or contemplation of revenge. Employing fantasy as a "narrative lever," Sadur "plays with the tension between the real and fantastic, placing both in the context of violence."[4] Through feminist revenge, real or imagined, Sadur counters the patriarchal agenda, establishing a daring poetics of violence by which she attacks inappropriate images of womanhood and overturns traditional assumptions about gender. In giving voice to the silenced, Sadur shatters these assumptions, subverting clichés about women's behavior and prescriptive social roles. Her fiction generates what we may call aesthetic counterviolence that, clashing with dominant cultural paradigms, helps her readers to break their boundaries, reclaim their vision, and ultimately alter the way in which they view their culture.

In this chapter, I will focus on some of Sadur's short stories in which violence figures most centrally and which illuminate the artistry with which she manages this literary breakthrough.[5] Sadur often figures violence as sexual harassment associated with a chauvinistic male code that defines female roles. "Rings" presents a dangerously distorted view of male-female relationships. Here masculinity is envisioned as control and power over women, and reflects the widespread Russian acceptance of a dehumanizing view of women. This story depicts the coming-of-age of its two female protagonists not so much as journeys to social and sexual maturation as their subjugation to men's private desires and interests. Both Liuba and Larisa long desperately for love but find only calculated exploitation. Tied to abusive behavior, male hostility toward women is disturbingly persistent throughout the text, most graphically described in the relationship between the seventeen-year-old, still childlike Liuba, and the story's tough-guy Sasha, an unfeeling destroyer of innocence who is unable to see women as anything other than bitches. His misogynist logic is part of the patriarchal mentality by which he lives and which thoroughly commodifies the female, reducing her to an inferior without rights or voice. Using the tactics of shame, he humiliates Liuba into submission to his sexual advances. His utter incomprehension of Liuba's emotions eliminates the possibility of communication and genuine dialogue. Instead, verbal violence establishes the story's tone from the start. Sasha is abusive in his behavior and in his language, apparently believing that the only possible relationship between men and women is that of prostitute and client; he calls Liuba "bitch," "slut," and "whore." Repeated so often, the words become as violent and as vicious as stab wounds, reducing Liuba to infantile obedience. Exemplifying his culture's deep-rooted misogyny, Sasha thinks of Liuba as a hated object, not as an object of sexual desire. She is not only objectified by her boyfriend but is self-objectified as well, as her confidence and sense of self are destroyed by the arrogant male.

Larisa's parallel relationship with the married Levan only supports the story's dismal view of manipulative and deceptive male behavior. Levan shares Sasha's singular objective of exploiting the female. He is not so much actively cruel to Larisa as coldly detached, and their relationship strangely lacks emotional content. Openly unfaithful to his wife, he shares his community's sense of male entitlement, its double standard and belief that men can betray women without being morally responsible. Since Larisa never attains the status of a human being for him, Levan believes himself empowered to use and then discard her. Larisa's own identity as victim is clear and the result is the same: her loss of self. She finally has a moment of illumination as she views Levan's wedding ring as a symbol of her own humiliation: "Two snakes, Levan and his unloved wife and a gap between them—me-unloved by anyone."[6] The ring aptly summarizes Larisa's entrapped status and the powerlessness of both women. Clearly, Levan views both his wife and his mistress as commodities and tokens to be manipulated. Larisa is forced to confront the reality and overcome her humble and passive acceptance of Levan's subject position by moving beyond the victim/victimizer worldview.

In the meantime, Liuba's discovery of a precious antique ring transforms her into a financially independent woman. Put on a state subsidy, she is informed that her "children and even her grandchildren would live off the money that the ring was worth."[7] In contrast to Levan's ring, this one serves as a metaphor of liberation, but Sadur is careful to show that Sasha feels threatened by Liuba's empowerment, which challenges the basic principle of patriarchal authority. As soon as he finds out about Liuba's newly acquired autonomy, his anger mounts and he breaks up with her after a violent scene.

The story leaves us with a hopeful image of the two girls recognizing their shared oppression and progress to a higher awareness of their identities, affirming their gender and individuality. It further confirms female friendship as a medium of empowerment and redemption. With the bond between them, Liuba and Larisa will have to draw on their strength to overcome the biases of their culture and achieve selfhood. Sadur creates a world where feminine traits of commitment and communication are valued. A pocket of security, this female world represents an alternative to male-dominated versions of authority.

The story "Wicked Girls" deals with spousal abuse. Emmie is bound to the domineering, insensitive, and ferocious Bern, who, in contrast to Emmie's markedly feminine self, has the masculine identity of an aggressor. There is an inescapable aura of danger in the opening passage that quickly establishes Bern as the dreaded enemy: "He was a beast. With the face of a beast. Because he was a German; his German mother had him in a camp . . . You couldn't like a man like that—German hair and the eyes of a beast. A wiry, harsh, wheezy man."[8] The narrator's description of the couple's first meeting refers to Bern's "limpid eyes" in which "rage flashed" and to "something of a fascist in him" that prepare us to expect his violent display of power. Bern's courtship is narrated in language that indicates that violence is an integral, natural part of his psychological make-up. As the story continues, Emmie experiences repeated physical and verbal abuse, a pattern explicitly defined when he threatens to kill her if she would try to leave him. Bern's violent temper flares in an assault on Emmie: "Then he flung himself at her and started to beat her. Emmie fell, shut up, covered her head and just lay there, but he kicks her anyway and howls in German. Until the blood flows. Until she's nearly dead. The beast."

As Bern's brutal treatment of Emmie increases in intensity, violence takes the place of communication while Sadur's wife-beating protagonist is continuously depicted as being overwhelmed by anger, unable to control his rage. He manipulates Emmie and demands her subordination. All Emmie's plans for a normal married life are defeated while Bern appropriates her pain as further evidence of his own empowerment. The frustrated and abused wife, now carrying Bern's child, chooses to lash out against her victimization. Sadur creates new and unpredictable forms of violence and endows Emmie with the strength to fight back by using a surrealistic force—a magic candy box that makes men sick. Every time Bern eats a candy, it is miraculously restored, while he suffers from headaches, becomes restless, and cries. He is obsessed with solving the mystery of the candy box: "He abandoned everything. He suffered. He became completely transparent, like a blue flame. He can't do anything. He struggles . . . He became like the flame over an alcoholic lamp, and everything in him died down."[9] In this curious way, Bern's role is reversed from that of victimizer to victim; the balance of power is changed, as Bern's well-being and even his very life are threatened. He deserves the violence that befalls him, and his vulnerability and loss of control are a mark of Emmie's triumph. Her violence is also a form of maternal protective aggression, redeemed by the imperative to survive and protect her unborn child. In a violent world, such action is to be applauded, and Emmie offers a bold challenge to the hierarchical view of marriage and to physical abuse. The story closes with acknowledgment of female power to hurt and a suggestion of women's own potential as abusive agents.

"Worm-Eaten Sonny" is a rhetorically harsh, violent monologue by a woman that reflects the unforgiving anger it describes. Exploring the ways in which women are diminished in Russian culture, the story brings to the foreground the issue of the universal male privilege that this culture approves. The sad saga of the narrator's mistreatment by abusive lovers depicts a universe of pain, where humiliation is piled upon humiliation, and male violence completely shapes female existence. In this world, where the traditional boundaries of human decency are discarded, women do not matter as people, and the dynamic of female-male relations is that of trust followed by betrayal, innocence by violation. Images of aggression fill the text: "men are traitors . . . wearing masks. . . . They gobble us up along with our innocence, our future, our bones. They corrupt us and poison us with death." Sadur encourages her readers to see men as violent strangers, "shameless before us—we're not kin to them." By making her narrator speak from the perspective of an entire exploited group, Sadur multiplies the impact of violence on the reader. The narrator analyzes all men in one sweeping gesture. They are portrayed as self-centered spiritual and emotional bullies, capable of reducing women to complete obedience and mastering them through dehumanizing violence. They are primitive and savage, vainly selfish, aggressive, vulgar, and dirty: "But in fact he's a boor. He is a goat. A marauder. A mercenary."[10] Dishonest and threatening, men use, abuse, and ultimately betray women.

The female narrator conforms to sex role expectations: she is amenable, compliant, and subservient—a stereotypical Russian woman: "I scrub and scrub, deny myself in everything, and for what? He'll only come along and gobble it all up. Or worse, he won't come at all, and then there's no reason to live . . . and no one to gobble up your paycheck." Because the heroine has internalized the patriarchal master/slave dialectic, she perpetuates the process of her objectification. At the same time, men emerge as emblems of evil beyond redemption. Egoism and moral blindness drive them to destroy women: "He stings. He tramples a woman down, poisons her, teaches her everything and then hates her for having learned all his dirty games so well. Men covet our underage daughters."[11]

However, the heroine may refuse to capitulate to abusive treatment. Sadur depicts her narrator's new affirmative self, rooted in overwhelming anger and resentment, brought to the surface by injustice and persecution. "The whole history of suffering cries out for vengeance and calls for narrative,"[12] observes Paul Ricouer, and Sadur offers her character a chance to overcome victimization by demonstrating a capacity for ferocity and aggression. Nevertheless, the narrator's abandonment of her victim status remains in the realm of fantasy. Her long-kept frustration erupts though the seams of her monologue. Man is the target of her rage and she wants to hurt him as much as possible. She fantasizes about striking back: "You need to treat him like this—a kick in the noggin and a warning—know your place, servant." Her thoughts are violently retributive; in her dreams, men "need to have their heads cut off." The author champions her violent heroine by exaggerating her fantasies to the extreme: "man has been bitten by the demon of betrayal. . . . It would have been better to bite women. So that she could corrupt man, deprive him of his innocence and future, drink him down, leave him to grow old alone. So that men would become women, and women men." In this striking reversal, the macho stereotype receives a demythifying blow as the narrator's vision transfers men into objects of dominance and oppression, displacing the conventional patriarchal hero and subverting the prevailing image of a Russian woman as passive and voiceless. Affirmation of independent subjectivity, then, comes from equally violent "masculine" behavior rather than by nurturing maternal desire. At the end, the story offers a horrific visual image of a "worm-eaten" male: "Worms have moved into man's brain, because of all his dangerous life. And they gnaw at his brain . . . and suck at his gray matter, and they make man even more brutish. And when he is lying down asleep, the worms peep out from his ears."[13] Virtually a parody of the cult of masculinity, this image indicates the failure of the male code and man's ultimate degradation.

"Siniaia ruka" (The Blue Hand) explores the motives behind women's violence against other women. In this story, the traditional male perpetrator of violence is replaced by a female tormentor who acts in a similar "male way," exercising power by brutalizing the helpless. Violence is Maria Ivanovna's dominant trait, and she unwittingly does the work of patriarchal culture. At the heart of the story is the relationship between Maria Ivanovna and Valia, her neighbor in a communal apartment. In every way Maria Ivanovna is a despicable character, small-minded, truly abusive, and vulgar, feared not only by Valia but also by her own family. A "masculine" woman, she is a tough dominant wife who controls her husband with a firm and heavy hand. Valia personifies the nonviolent woman, passive, regularly terrorized by her neighbor.

The story records numerous incidents of grotesque abuse, as when Maria Ivanovna makes her husband urinate on the bathroom floor when it is Valia's turn to clean, or her destruction of Valia's supply of potatoes in the storage room. Valia apparently accepts patriarchal constructions of her as a submissive and silent woman and is the frequent target of Maria Ivanovna's insulting comments. We are told that her neighbor "addressed Valia in an arrogant, brutish and insolent manner, waiting for Valia to talk back," trying to provoke her to "yell at the top of her lungs." But frightened and humiliated, Valia "silently pressed herself against the wall" not knowing "how to handle Maria Ivanovna" or "how to shout back." Portrayed as a victim, Valia is subjected to constant psychological torment and violation of her personal boundaries. Maria Ivanovna harasses Valia by eavesdropping when she has male company: "Maria Ivanovna started to groan in her own room, plunged into the hallway, her eyes popping out, and sat down on the communal chair—to eavesdrop, even if there was a movie showing on TV or she herself had company, she gave everything up for Valia, for her amorous sobs behind the thin dirty wall."[14] Projecting patriarchy's hatred of women onto Valia, Maria Ivanovna denies her rights as a private and sexual being, and when Valia acts in an independently sexual manner, Maria Ivanovna decides she is a "whore" and treats her accordingly. The enthusiasm with which she harasses Valia resembles sadistic sexual pleasure.

Interestingly, the question of Maria Ivanovna's own victimization is also articulated in the story; she is depicted not only as the perpetrator of violence but as the victim of external pressures that drive her to violent behavior. Echoing Bern's childhood in a prison camp, Sadur reveals her angry history of serving time in prison. Harmed if not actually destroyed by the brutal environment, she is driven by hatred for anyone who was never in jail, and assaulting Valia constitutes a safe way of rescuing her endangered sense of self. The text makes clear other roots of Maria Ivanovna's aggression: fear of advancing age, poverty, sexual frustration, and an existence saturated with boredom. Since Valia's love life is part of the overall threat to her shaky and challenged femaleness, Maria Ivanovna's animosity toward the young woman seems inevitable.

Crippled physically and emotionally as the violence intensifies, Valia is on the verge of breakdown. Cowed by the effects of Maria Ivanovna's harsh judgments and surveillance, Valia internalizes her conviction that she is a guilty, unworthy woman. Maria Ivanovna's habitual displays of anger trigger Valia's attacks of migraines, when her "hands go numb and turn pale, almost blue." Her identity as a victim reflects on her sexuality: her love life stops and "bunches of warts" grow on her left eyelid, her lip, and her chin, making Valia repellent. To shield herself from victimization, Valia withdraws into her dreams and empowers herself by imagining her enemy violated in every possible way: "Maria Ivanovna . . . is kicked in the ass, crawls in a pool of blood looking for her glasses; Maria Ivanovna is hanged in a prison yard with an alarming roll of drums in the background; her rectum falls out . . . while Maria Ivanovna is taken down, brought back to life . . . and after she opens her eyes, they make her stand up, bury her rectum and then hang her again."[15] Such fantasy subversions of Maria Ivanovna's power over her is Valia's way of self-preservation.

Maria Ivanovna's abuse is so unrelenting that one can only be glad when Valia does finally retaliate. Her violence erupts unexpectedly and is the defiant act of an outraged and determined woman. In a brief, sharply focused scene, we witness Valia murder her vicious tormentor, and the story presents this act as the successful resolution of the violence that has dominated the text. Sensing that Sadur herself has considerable sympathy for the killer, the reader justifies the murder. However, Sadur manages her art in unconventional ways. The section of the text that presents Valia's assault operates on a fantastic level. Maria Ivanovna's violent death is actually caused by witchcraft. Recalling Valia afflicted with migraine, the murder scene includes the magic image of "the blue hand," which can be seen as a surrealist force avenging the oppression.

This graphic episode is filled with the rhetoric of violence: "the hand grabbed her chubby throat and started choking her. Maria Ivanovna began to wheeze, waving her fingers trying to get away, but the hand squeezed harder and harder until funeral lights swam before her eyes."[16]

Because we do not know exactly how Valia made the miracle occur, the story's fairy-tale-like finale leaves us off balance. Other than assuming that Valia turned into a witch, we cannot account for the appearance of the blue hand, and it continues to haunt us. The story becomes even more fantastic with Valia's mysterious disappearance and the fact that her nightgown crumbles into dust at first touch. While our imaginations are left to ponder this enigmatic ending, we feel pleasure at the magic closure. The story affirms the possibility of miracles, miracles that symbolize the rejection of oppression, and that move from silence to anger to defiant action. The text depicts violence as a requirement for personal redemption and self-affirmation, and perhaps even more, as justified by the imperative to survive. Sadur's stories are striking for what they reveal about the prevailing cultural attitudes toward women in Russia and for her brave and direct presentations of violence against women.

The author deconstructs inherited ideologies, seeking liberation from violent social conventions and questioning flawed notions of masculinity. Subversive of the patriarchal ideal of an autonomous masculine subjectivity, her narratives call for change in dominant fictions of manliness. Through the trope of violence, Sadur confronts the ruthless males who people her fiction and explores perverse and cruel elements in the production of masculine subject and objectified feminine other. That Sadur's works have enjoyed such success suggests that they reveal a very profound level of anger in Russian women. The abusive heritage they document serves as incentive for strategies of female empowerment and survival. In Sadur's fictional world, the change is inevitably associated with aggression or revenge fantasies. As Amy Gottfried suggests, "the inclusion of the historically dispossessed demands a violent undoing of their equally violent exclusion."[17] Marked by female concerns of revenge, Sadur's use of aggression through fantasy, magic, and the supernatural interrogates Russian gender politics, imagining a powerful female world away from the patriarchal law. Her celebration of female violence fantasies as the source of potential new freedom is a mark of a new, affirmative feminist landscape that opens possibilities for individual and collective therapy of destructive cultural codes. Through its treatment of violence, Sadur's work focuses on the injustice and suffering that are part of contemporary Russian culture and illuminates the sources of the oppression of women. However, to what extent this represents an actual step in the direction toward women's liberation remains ambiguous, as her female revolt through violence remains a fantasy that may simply serve as a steam valve, a way to dissipate female rage. Nevertheless, an angry impulse against patriarchy, Sadur's fiction might be viewed as at least a basis for greater self-consciousness, radicalization, and more assertive action on the part of Russian women.

Notes

1. Helena Goscilo, introduction to *Present Imperfect: Stories by Russian Women*, ed. Ayesha Kagal and Natasha Perova (Boulder, Colo.: Westview Press, 1996), 1.
2. R. W. Connel, *Masculinities* (Berkeley: University of California Press, 1995), 84.
3. Michael Kowalewski, *Deadly Musings: Violence and Verbal Form in American Fiction* (Princeton, N.J.: Princeton University Press, 1993), 11.
4. Nadya L. Peterson, *Subversive Imaginations: Fantastic Prose and the End of Soviet Literature, 1970s–1990s* (Boulder, Colo.: Westview Press, 1997), 163.
5. However, these stories represent only a fraction of her writing that deals with violence. The theme of violence is explored in such major works as "Sad" (The Garden), "Iug" (The South), "Krasnyi paradiz" (The Red Paradise), "Nemets" (The German), "Zamerzli" (The Frozen), and others.
6. Nina Sadur, "Rings," in *Present Imperfect*, 139.
7. Ibid.
8. Nina Sadur, "Wicked Girls," in *Lives in Transit: Recent Russian Women's Writing*, ed. Helena Goscilo (Dana Point, Calif.: Ardis Publishers, 1995), 69.
9. Ibid., 70.
10. Nina Sadur, "Worm-Eaten Sonny," in *Lives in Transit*, 203.
11. Ibid., 203, 204.
12. Paul Ricoeur, *Time and Narrative* (Chicago: University of Chicago Press, 1985), 62.
13. Sadur, "Worm-Eaten Sonny," 203–4.
14. Nina Sadur, "Siniaia ruka," in *Glazami zhenshchiny. Daidzhest novoi russkoi literatury* (Moscow: GLAS, 1994), 86, 87.
15. Ibid., 87.
16. Ibid., 88.
17. Amy S. Gottfried, *Historical Nightmares and Imaginative Violence in American Women's Writing* (Westport, Conn.: Greenwood Press, 1998), 135.

Violence, Madness, and the Female Grotesque in Nina Sadur's *The South* and Svetlana Vasilenko's *Little Fool*

ELIZABETH SKOMP

The application of gender theory to texts by Russian women writers is a relatively recent phenomenon. While the notion of feminism remains anathema to many of these authors (as well as to the majority of Russians), gender-based readings gradually are gaining acceptance in Russia. This essay will examine Nina Sadur's *The South* (*Iug*, 1992) and Svetlana Vasilenko's *Little Fool* (*Durochka*, 1998) through a comparison of their respective female protagonists, Olia and Ganna, and the various forms of violence they experience.[1] We will employ several concepts used in recent feminist criticism, including martyrdom, the grotesque, and madness, in order to help define the ways in which these characters are stigmatized or able to come to terms with their liminal status. In contrast to many Western feminist writings, both novellas ultimately situate their protagonists within an older established Christian framework of sin, punishment, and salvation, even though the action takes place in a secular (Soviet or post-Soviet) context. The path of transgression, suffering, and redemption each protagonist takes demonstrates that hope may surface from bleak circumstances and that there is a place in society for these martyr figures.

In *The South* and *Little Fool,* both writers modify the established Russian trope of the passive female. The role of the female victim is read not exclusively in a domestic context (indeed, both Olia and Ganna remain without fixed abodes for most of their respective texts) but within a markedly religious one.[2] Violence surfaces within this religious frame and is at once more subtle and complicated than comparatively straightforward male-on-female physical abuse, as evidenced both by the wide-ranging sources of violence and the idea that the women who suffer may as a result emerge as stronger, more complete individuals. In this way, Sadur and Vasilenko employ violence as a tool for revisiting gender stereotypes.

The motifs of itinerancy and martyrdom provide a useful framework for examining violence vis-à-vis the protagonists of the key texts. In *The South,* Olia appears to be on an aimless journey that is articulated as a spiritual pilgrimage only at the close of the novella, while Ganna's development as a saint is evident from early on in *Little Fool.* Each character, largely passive, experiences suffering mixed with physical and emotional violence, and both are labeled as madwomen by those they encounter.[3] Heldt notes that "the more powerless women have been in actuality, the more powerful the myth that has arisen of their redemptive, care giving, nation-identified essence."[4] Sadur and Vasilenko follow this pattern of mythmaking, creating a contemporary variant of the downtrodden, saintly female that is so deeply entrenched in Russian culture. Olia is saved by religious pilgrims, and Ganna completes her transformation from (passive) martyr to (active) saint, becoming a healer. The rebirth and redemption Olia and Ganna experience appear to serve as a "cure" for their perceived madness.

In a world of extremes, where the excessive and hyperbolic become commonplace, those who exist outside the established social order are targets; these grotesque figures become the victims of violence and are punished for their transgressive, unacceptable behavior. Mary Russo notes that the concept of the grotesque is always subjective; it is closely tied to normalization, because what is grotesque deviates from the norm. Grotesque status thereby implies some sort of transgressive activity. However, in the texts discussed here, the characters are not complicit in their alterity or liminality. They seem unaware of and perhaps unwilling or unable to control their outsider status. In this sense, the female links naturally with the grotesque: Russo notes that "women and their bodies, certain bodies, in certain public framings, are always already transgressive—dangerous, and in danger."[5]

Grotesque femaleness and supposed transgression combine in both novellas to create putative madness in the protagonists of these texts. Lillian Feder defines "madness as a state in which unconscious processes predominate over conscious ones to the extent that they control them and determine perceptions of and responses to experience that, judged by prevailing standards of logical thought and relevant emotion, are confused and inappropriate."[6] Examining this definition, it is easy to see that liminal characters on apparently aimless journeys who fail to conform to accepted standards for female behavior might be interpreted as madwomen.[7]

Such "grotesque realism" combined with literal or figurative transformations may be said to characterize the presentation of violence in Nina Sadur's prose, in which the grotesque female surfaces as aggressor as well as victim. Sadur's novella chronicles the spiritual journey of Olia to the South in hopes of recovering from a mysterious illness. She has no particular symptoms except a feeling of melancholy, but she gradually goes mad. In an interview with Sadur, Denis Salter notes her preoccupation "with characters . . . who manage to recover from a protracted period of spiritual and emotional destruction."[8] In *The South,* Olia's transformation is seen through varying narrative perspectives: third-person narrative permits the reader to view Olia as she is seen by society, while stretches of first-person narrative reveal part of the workings of Olia's inner world. While on the beach, Olia embarks on a mental journey of memories in which she travels through much of her life, beginning with childhood. Dark and violent images often accompany these memories, such as abusing and tormenting a German schoolboy with her friend Tania and the disturbing consequences of inadvertently neglecting childhood pets. As the novella progresses, Olia appears to meet violence and suffering wherever she goes—it confronts her in recurring violent vignettes embedded in the text, including a cautionary tale told to a group of children and an encounter with women who work at a slaughterhouse and a hospital.

Typical Russian associations with the South as a special location are reflected in Sadur's novella—that of an exotic, lush, and highly romanticized setting.[9] Here, departure from one's normal surroundings presents the dual possibility of recuperation and transformation. Despite the relaxed atmosphere, Olia's behavior still seems strange to other vacationers. As Otto Boele notes, "Directly related to the image of the South as a source of light and warmth is the idea of its life-restoring powers."[10] However, the landscape in *The South* is not a wholly benign element. In winter, the sea turns wild and "gnaws" at the town. Various functions are attributed to the sea, including cleansing, killing and ritual purification. Razor-sharp mussels on the beach are a threat, as is the sun, and because Olia's skin does not tan, her comparative pallor further serves as a physical reminder of her outsider status. These female protagonists face not only human threats—they are also oppressed and attacked by their natural surroundings.

Olia's powers of language ebb and flow, thus accounting for some of the alterations in narrative perspective. Paradoxically, she laments her inability to communicate with others and her loss of language in a stretch of first-person narrative, and by the end of the novella, her descent into silence has become complete.[11] She couches her linguistic difficulties in terms of unease about communication and experiences a physical reaction to this social discomfort. As Olia descends into madness, fear also marks her relations with others, and when she encounters a man at the top of a hill, she expresses her need to "say murderous things to people." For Olia, language has tremendous cathartic power, and when she loses this ability to vent her frustrations, she alienates the people around her. With no release, "everything inside gets frozen and I want to throw up . . ." (118). She speaks of a violent trembling inside her body, and when she leaves the hill, an attack of nausea corroborates her statements.

Foucault identifies one explanation of madness as stemming from the inability to control passions or desires—in fact, the presence of these strong passions or desires provides a foundation for madness,[12] as in the case of Olia's unacceptable actions. Her transgressive behavior culminates in the attempted seduction of Kostia, her landlady's fifteen-year-old son. Hovering between childhood and manhood, Kostia is a figure of emerging sexuality. Though it is unclear whether the seduction actually takes place, Kostia's mother finds the two in bed together at dawn, and tells Olia, "I won't kill you . . . I'm being nice, I'm not even going to hit you" (134). In her mind, violence is the logical retribution for the seduction of her son. Others at the house tie Olia up and plan to take her to the police, punching her in frustration and abandoning her on the beach after they cannot untie her bonds. These scenes follow a quasi-Orthodox pattern of punishment following sin; salvation only emerges as a possibility as the text progresses and Olia sinks further into abjection and misery.

Olia's alienation and abjection are painfully obvious when she approaches a Georgian amputee on the beach and he asks her, "Which of us is worse off? What does a woman need a brain for anyway, or a voice? All she needs is legs and a face." Recognizing her incompleteness, he adds, "I'm all cut off outside . . . with you it's all inside—there's nothing there" (149). He notices that Olia wears a ring with no stone, signifying her emptiness.

At the conclusion of *The South,* Valia and Tonia, two religious pilgrims of sorts, find Olia on the beach. They call her Maria, symbolizing her spiritual conversion and newfound purity. Each of the women has experienced her own spiritual awakening after prolonged suffering, including domestic violence, abandonment, and illness. Sadur has commented that these women are "Christians who help her to understand the nature of love. She has, to that point, been a pilgrim who does not realize that she has been journeying towards a new life. This kind of unconscious journey is an eternal theme in Russian literature."[13] At the end of the text, the sea is calm, mirroring spiritual serenity and Olia's rescue. After the ailing Tonia dies on the beach, Olia finally speaks, uttering her new name in an affirmation of her salvation and symbolic rebirth. With Olia's rescue and redemption and recovered powers of speech at the conclusion of *The South,* her new life begins.

The motifs of salvation and redemption also figure prominently in *Little Fool,* Svetlana Vasilenko's weightiest literary work to date. The itinerant protagonist Ganna, a mute and a saint-martyr figure, leaves an orphanage and embarks on a journey in which she provides a promise of redemption and healing in various contexts. Though framed by scenes from the early 1960s, in which the narrator struggles to understand his deaf-mute sister Nad'ka, who is Ganna's double, the bulk of the novella takes place in the 1930s. The Christian notions and folkloric elements of the central narrative contrast starkly with the hyperbolic imagery of nuclear war presented in the frame text, highlighting some of the leitmotifs in Vasilenko's prose. As we will see, on one level the text may be read as illuminating alternatives to conventionally accepted femininity. However, it also seems plausible for the reader to interpret Ganna, Nad'ka, and their experiences as metaphors for the Soviet people confronting the threat of Stalin-era purges and, in the 1960s, what appeared to be the imminent threat of nuclear destruction. Vasilenko uses a narrative frame to situate her protagonist in both the early Soviet period and the dawning of the nuclear age, presenting the idea of a female "holy fool" in markedly different, though equally nonreligious, contexts.[14] The contrast between these two settings draws the concept of the holy fool out of a religious context and permits analysis of Ganna as a woman experiencing suffering and wonder. Embedded within the text are numerous bits of history and legend, all of which contribute to an understanding of Ganna's role.

Little Fool's title itself suggests that Ganna should be examined as a holy fool. Taking the holy fool out of a religious context, Rancour-Laferrière writes: "Psychoanalytically viewed, the holy fool was a sufferer, part of whose masochism was specifically provocative or exhibitionistic in style." He also states that the concept of the fool automatically elicits ideas of violence and punishment: for Russians, fools are, or should be, beaten often "or otherwise abused" because they "must be 'taught' by violent means."[15] This description may explain partially the treatment Ganna receives from others who do not understand her behavior, though when her healing powers are discovered, her reception changes dramatically.

Miracles and magical occurrences are integral to the text, notably Ganna's status as healer and the "miraculous" birth at the conclusion of the text. Mystical and folkloric elements contribute to an assessment of the text as magical realist, and religious ideas provide a distinct alternative to the godless Soviet state: violent events throw these contrasts into sharp relief. One massive fistfight in which a father who has become religious knocks out the teeth of his Komsomol son encapsulates the tension between religion and the state.

Violence emanates from multiple locations in the text, ranging from the landscape to family dynamics to the Stalinist terror and the NKVD (precursor of the KGB). Abjection is manifested in social rejection, Ganna's muteness, and the isolation some characters experience when demonstrating their opposition to the social order. Deviations from the norm are especially evident in the presentation of female characters, including the orphanage director Traktorina Petrovna (who identifies herself as a Communist, not a human being), a tea-room hostess called Katerina (who is shot in the heart by a jilted lover), and a drunken woman (who is shot by villagers who believe she is spreading cholera).

Scenes of Ganna's chaotic existence at an orphanage inhabited mainly by deaf-mute children segue into a description of the local marketplace, which contains a number of strikingly violent images. The poetic description of purple potatoes (like a child's disembodied violet eyes), beets dangling (like severed heads), carrots (like broken and twisted fingers), and bloody slices of meat suggest a grotesque, latent violence in the stuff of everyday life. The motif of muteness is reflected in the strangely quiet marketplace, where vendors signal prices with their fingers and nod or mouth agreement with their customers. Muteness thus serves as a marker of abjection or otherness; for much of *Little Fool,* Ganna can only utter "Ga" as a cry of pain—which is also, of course, the first syllable of her own name. In a parallel to Ganna's muteness, the priest Father Vasilii tells of the church bell's clapper (literally, *iazyk,* or tongue) having been torn out: the church has been silenced.

As in *The South,* the landscape in *Little Fool* emerges as a destructive, oppressive element. The Akhtuba River represents Ganna's relationship to the world and its relation to her: though the river thrashes and abuses her, she still tries not to disturb its water. When Ganna rides into the steppe on a camel, she is injured by a thorny bush that later protects her. She suffers and bleeds in the steppe, and salt eats at her wounds "as if her soul were burned through." The landscape shuns Ganna, then saves her when the Baskunchak Lake, formed from the tears of Tatar women, appears.

Apart from extreme sensitivity and compassion, additional characteristics distinguish Ganna from ordinary people. When snow falls on Ganna's head, it does not melt. She endures humiliation and beatings, and after she is raped, she is visited by the Virgin Mary, who calls her to heal and enables her recognition as a saint. Significantly, Ganna temporarily regains her power of speech when visited by the Virgin.

The final segment of the text marks a return to 1962 and the reappearance of Ganna's double, Nad'ka, who is mysteriously pregnant: one theory presented in the text is that she was raped by soldiers; another is that an "immaculate conception" has occurred. The grotesque nuclear imagery at the end of *Little Fool,* hyperbolic in its magnitude and proportions, suggests the ultimate threat of violence in the second half of the twentieth century. At the conclusion of the text, Nad'ka slowly levitates and gives birth to a blood-red sun (ironically, a dual symbol of salvation and the apocalypse). This image links to the sun's red glow at the conclusion of *The South,* and to wedding images of redemption and destruction.

Because Olia and Ganna are unable or at times unwilling to correct the misperceptions others formulate about them, their supposed madness enables their victimhood. Their liminal status as itinerant women results in accusations of criminal activity, abuse for failing to respond to others, beatings, and sexual violation, while the dreamlike, disjointed quality of their narrated wanderings creates further ambiguity. At the conclusion of both works, salvation rescues the heroines from true martyrdom and prompts a reconsideration of their putative madness. Even if these women do not conform to expected roles as wives and mothers, they too may secure a place of relative acceptance in society: as a convert and a healer respectively, endowed with new powers, they are poised once more at the margins of society, ready to reenter or to be reclassified as other permutations of the female grotesque. Whether Olia and Ganna achieve salvation because of or in spite of their suffering, they demonstrate resilience crucial for survival in a harsh and ever-changing world.

Notes

1. *The South (Iug)* appears in Nina Sadur, *Sad* (Vologda: Poligrafist, 1997); *Little Fool (Durochka)* appears in Svetlana Vasilenko, *Durochka* (Moscow: Vagrius, 2000). Page numbers are given immediately following textual quotations.

2. Barbara Heldt notes that some "sexual/religious symbolism [was] accepted by the Soviet reader, believer and atheist alike. In many rhetorical stances in the Soviet Union today the curse of communism is prayerfully exorcised by a sentimentalized discourse of religiosity" ("Gynoglasnost: Writing the Feminine," in *Perestroika and Soviet Women*, ed. Mary Buckley [Cambridge: Cambridge University Press, 1992], 163). Certainly this symbolism still retained currency during the years in which *The South* and *Little Fool* were written.

3. For an extended treatment of suffering in Russian culture, see Daniel Rancour-Laferriere, *The Slave Soul of Russia: Moral Masochism and the Cult of Suffering* (New York: New York University Press, 1996).

4. Heldt, "Gynoglasnost," 173.

5. Mary Russo, *The Female Grotesque: Risk, Excess, and Modernity* (New York: Routledge, 1994), 60.

6. Lillian Feder, *Madness in Literature* (Princeton, N.J.: Princeton University Press, 1980), 5; see pp. 3–34 for a survey of approaches to literary madness.

7. This focus on madness has been described as one of the hallmarks of contemporary Russian "destructive" literature. See M. Galina, "Literatura nochnogo zreniia: Malaia proza kak razrushitel' mifologicheskoi sistemy," *Voprosy literatury* 6 (1997): 3–21.

8. Denis Salter, "Under Western Eyes: Perspectives on Contemporary Russian Theater," *Theater* 25:3 (1995): 73.

9. See Susan Layton, *Russian Literature and Empire: The Conquest of the Caucasus from Pushkin to Tolstoy*, Cambridge Studies in Russian Literature (Cambridge: Cambridge University Press, 1995), which provides a survey of the portrayal of the Caucasus in Russian literature. See also Katharina Hansen Löve, *The Evolution of Space in Russian Literature: A Spatial Reading of Nineteenth and Twentieth Century Narrative Literature*, Studies in Slavic Literature and Poetics 22 (Amsterdam: Rodopi, 1994), 49–66, for an analysis of Lermontov's "Mtsyri" with respect to the South and its role in Russian literature.

10. Otto Boele, *The North in Russian Romantic Literature*, Studies in Slavic Literature and Poetics 26 (Amsterdam: Rodopi, 1996), 151.

11. Feder notes a similar paradox in Antonin Artaud's *Fragments of a Diary from Hell:* "Ironically, language—which he hated because it seemed to taunt him, ever eluding what he diagnosed as the verbally inexpressive, somatic sources of his psychic pain—was his chief vehicle for obsessively portraying this condition. Concrete, violent language was his principal means of conveying the rage and frustration of instinctual diffusion and repression" (*Madness in Literature*, 260).

12. Michel Foucault, *Madness and Civilization: A History of Insanity in the Age of Reason*, trans. Richard Howard (London: Routledge, 2001), 85.

13. Salter, "Under Western Eyes," 73.

14. The holy fool *(iurodivyi)*, an important motif in Russian culture, is an itinerant individual who behaves strangely but often recognizes and reveals larger prophetic truths about society that others are unwilling to accept. He or she is a saintly figure who is also the object of ridicule and abuse. See Ewa Thompson, *Understanding Russia: The Holy Fool in Russian Culture* (Lanham, Md.: University Press of America, 1987).

15. Rancour-Laferriere, *Slave Soul of Russia*, 21, 124.

Chechen War Memoirs and Nationalist Identity in Contemporary Russia

ANNA BRODSKY

In the last decade of the twentieth century a new expression achieved notoriety—"ethnic cleansing." This phrase was initially associated with Yugoslavia, where it referred to efforts by Serbs to displace the Muslim population through deportations and massacres. It also involved mass rapes. Russians then picked up the idea and the word *(zachistka)* to describe their incursions into Chechnya, where Russians have "cleansed" the population by (among other means) hurling grenades into occupied houses and rounding up males between the ages of twelve and sixty-five, who then disappear into notorious "filtration camps" and prisons. Both Russians and Serbs use the term as a matter of course, while for the rest of the world the word conjures up the horrors of genocide.

Scholars have been trying to come to grips with the virulent kind of nationalism that has arisen in the former Soviet Union and the Soviet bloc after the collapse of Communism. One of the most significant recent claims is that it is misleading to think of these ethnic conflicts as simply a reversion to ancient traditions and age-old ideas of blood kinship, as many have assumed. Rather, scholars like Benedict Anderson, Norman Naimark, Michael Ignatieff, and Charles Taylor stress the distinctly modern aspects of nationalism.[1] As Anderson and Naimark have observed, collective national identity has been enormously shaped and facilitated by mass communication. At the same time, technological advances have also made genocide feasible. Taylor, like Naimark, traces twentieth-century nationalism to the pressure on states to create homogeneous and easily mobilized populations. This pressure fosters patriotism and a strong identification of ethnicity with the state, but also creates an inhospitable climate for minorities.

As these remarks may suggest, many theorists see nationalism as a top-down phenomenon—a social force stirred up among the masses by elites who act as advocates and masterminds of nationalist ideology. Yet this "top-down" view of the dissemination of nationalist ideologies seems to me to be a serious weakness in current thinking about nationalism, one encouraged by the very technologies the theorists are trying to understand. For, after all, it is the elites that have traditionally had access to the press and the latest technology, but now, thanks in part to the Internet, access to the broad public has become far easier. Information can be quickly and broadly disseminated, and popular reactions more quickly registered. In this sense, web publications may throw new light on the origins of nationalism, and this suggests that it is not something simply visited on the essentially innocent masses by powerful "masterminds."

One can now, for example, go to the web to inspect book-length ruminations of Russian soldiers fighting in Chechnya. These web publications indicate that virulent nationalism often has very much a "from-the-ground-up" character. In this chapter I will take a close look at two such prowar testimonies by actual participants in Russia's incursion into Chechnya—Gennadii Troshev's *My War (Moia voina),* and Viacheslav Mironov's *I Took Part in That War (Ia byl na etoi voine).*[2] These two texts will allow us to examine the importance of grassroots nationalism and its relationship to official (elite) ideology. Both of these texts have in fact been published as books, but may be taken as representative of many similar accounts posted on web (Mironov's actually began on the Internet). My aim here is not to survey Internet accounts of the Chechen war, but to investigate the broad-based character of contemporary nationalist ideology. The two texts I have chosen support the case that post-Communist conflicts waged against national minorities fill in the identity vacuum left by the collapse of Communism, as many scholars have suggested. This brand of nationalism is markedly ahistorical and opportunistic, feeding off of any ideas that can reassure people of their strength and ascendancy.[3] In works on Chechnya, Russian soldiers emerge as personally invested in the war and deeply committed to the idea that their enemies are "scum" who ought to be wiped out. These texts also call into question the claim that nationalism is primarily fomented by ruling elites. This is not to deny that elites whip up nationalist fervor. Of course they do. But we also need to come to grips with the enthusiastic collusion of non-elites. Nationalism turns out to be a sickeningly equal-opportunity enterprise.

Troshev and Mironov both fought in the Chechen war, and one of their goals in writing is to give a personal account of the reasons for the war. The two memoirs complement each other on a number of levels. Troshev is a general, and belongs to those who benefit professionally from the military conflict. Mironov, on the other hand, is a low-ranking officer, and, as such, fodder for commanders like Troshev—a soldier compelled to risk his life daily in combat. Troshev makes the blatant emptiness of official nationalist-patriotic discourse startlingly clear, as he himself seems quite aware that his words mean nothing. He predictably characterizes the war as "a fight to maintain the Motherland's unity," as "the defense of Russia's honor and integrity." He writes, "With gratitude I will remember my military colleagues, my comrades in arms, from the [common] soldiers to the generals, who rose to defend the integrity of the New Russia in its hour of need."[4] This is the kind of official rhetoric that any general might be expected to use. The point, however, is the obvious emptiness of the rhetoric: "integrity" is essentially meaningless after the loss of several republics in the 1990s. It is mere verbiage that once upon a time meant something, when something like integrity existed and was sustained by Soviet ideology. People like Troshev and Aleksandr Mikhailov, another general of the Russian Federal Army, continue to use it, even after all substance has been drained out of it.[5]

Not only is "integrity" meaningless, but it is also impossible for Troshev to describe what "new Russia" stands for. The novelty of this "new" Russia seems to lie only in the absence of Soviet ideological rhetoric, at least Troshev does not speak of any affirmative new values that might animate or sustain post-Soviet Russia. It is even difficult for Troshev to define who the noble defenders of new Russia are. His favorite word for government troops, for example, is "federaly" (federals)—a murky term without clear ideological identity. In dramatic contrast to his blurry definition of government troops, Troshev has a rich, evocative vocabulary to describe the Chechen enemy. He describes them as "fighters" *(boeviki)*, "bandits" *(bandity)*, "Chechen extremists" *(chechenskie ekstremisty)*, "Chechen separatists" *(chechenskie separatisty)*, "members of illegal band-formations" *(chleny nelegal'nykh bandformirovanii)*, "dudaevists" (supporters of Dudaev, *dudaevtsy*), "mountain folk" *(gortsy)*, and "ghosts" *(dukhi)*, a military slang term. Curiously, the Russians have also appropriated American racist rhetoric as a way to insult Chechens. The British journalist Vanora Bennett points out that in both their literature and in common parlance Russians refer to Chechens as "blacks," "black mugs," "black asses."[6] To be sure, there has been a long tradition of stereotyping the people of the North Caucasus. In his study of literary myths and their place in the media representation of the Chechen war, Harsha Ram points out that the Romantic image of the noble savage is among the most enduring.[7] The old colonial stereotypes however stress the cultural inferiority, rather than the racial one. Unlike the traditional colonial stereotypes, the "whites" vs. "blacks" racist dichotomy asserts a previously unknown and dangerously nonnegotiable racial hierarchy. We see here the structure of scapegoating, a community forged by projecting its hatreds onto an external other. The scapegoat serves as a kind of exoskeleton, binding the community together from the outside. Certainly, this seems to be the case with the Russians, depleted of their historical identity after the collapse of the Soviet Union, and the Chechens, who are vividly and prolifically demonized.

Troshev is fully aware of the ideological vacuum surrounding the military action in Chechnya. Indeed, he refers to the present-day period in Russia as "the time of washed-out ideals,"[8] and he himself is strikingly devoid of any clear ideological base. He makes no claim, for example, that Russian troops bring law and order to the local population. Nor does he argue that the army is defending Russia's political system. He does not even see himself as a faithful servant of the government, carrying out its orders, and makes no secret of his almost personal hatred for Boris Yeltsin, the Russian president who started the Chechen debacle.

Throughout his narrative, Troshev uses Soviet-era vocabulary, but—as with the notion of Russia's "integrity"—the old words have now been entirely emptied of meaning. For another example, true to the heroic vocabulary of World War II, Troshev speaks of "liberating" Chechen towns and villages. However, he is under no illusion about the real character of these "liberations," and his own narrative makes it plain that they amount to nothing more than brutal and unprincipled destruction. Troshev writes: "After a battle, we captured the mountain Elilen; we now began cleansing the territory and the nearby villages that had been captured by the Chechen fighters. Tomorrow we will be liberating Tando." "Liberation entails three 'echelons' of federal troops," Troshev explains. "The first 'echelon' fights the Chechen units, the second conducts the 'cleansing' operation (throwing grenades into the houses), and the third 'echelon' walks through the town with large bags and collects everything of value left in the village."[9] Troshev's own detailed descriptions of actual military operations are fatal to his vacuous ideology.

What is stunning and unprecedented, however, is that Troshev seems fully aware of this yawning gap between word and reality.[10] It is obvious to him, for example, that Russians are the occupiers, a fact that might have escaped an ideologically driven Soviet general. Troshev admits repeatedly that Russian troops are on a foreign territory and fighting people in their own land. Tellingly, he advises Aslan Maskhadov, the military commander and later elected president of Chechnya, that he "will not send my [Russian] soldiers into the mountains. They don't know the mountains well, unlike your people who were born here and who grew up here. I will be sending the aircraft and will be getting you from the air." Troshev also admits that the Chechens see themselves as defenders of their homeland. Hence he makes a clear distinction between the fighters who come to Chechnya as volunteers or mercenaries and the Chechens who are forced to defend their land and their families from the Russian assault: "Unlike the Chechens, fellows from Ukraine cannot claim that they are defending their land, their families, the independence of their Republic, and the honor of the mountain people." Nevertheless, despite the cruelty and aggression of Russian troops that Troshev himself describes, he presents the Russian soldier as unequivocally good, regardless of his leaders, mission, or behavior. Without bothering to give any examples of their actions, Troshev writes about the federal soldiers' selflessness *(samootverzhennost')* and nobility *(blagorodstvo)*. Responding to the charges that Russian soldiers lived in squalid conditions, he writes that "in Chechnya, the [Russian] soldier was unwashed only on the outside—on the inside he was clean. . . . He could hold up proudly his unwashed head."[11] There is a circular logic here: the Russian soldier is good simply because he is Russian, and not Chechen. What we may conclude from Troshev's memoirs is that official words of national pride and patriotism have been drained of meaning. Troshev continues to use them even though his own narrative shows their falseness and vacuity. These words are the detritus left by a dead ideology.

When we turn to the second military memoirist, Viacheslav Mironov, we see how a nationalist agenda rushes in to fill the void left by the lapse of the old, sustaining ideology. What is fascinating about Mironov is his absolute lack of illusions: he is acidly cynical about the war. He is convinced that the incursion into Chechnya essentially serves only corrupt "Mafia" interests, and expresses contempt for the Chechens for failing to understand this. "He [a Chechen] naively believes that he is fighting for his stinking independence and does not suspect, idiot that he is, that all of us are participating in some Mafiosi squabble."[12] The war, in Mironov's view, is nothing more than a Mafia fight over oil profits. This, by the way, is not at all idiosyncratic. On the contrary, it is a widely shared view—at least, it was during the first Chechen conflict (1994–96). Many Russian soldiers told reporters at that time that they believed the war was Mafia-driven, and it seemed plain to the majority of Russians back in 1994 that the real power in Russia lay in the hands of the Mafia.[13] Mironov recognizes the unprecedented absence of ideology that informs the Chechen conflict. He is nostalgic for the time when soldiers fought for God and Tsar or Motherland and Stalin: "In the old days the soldiers yelled 'For God, the Tsar, and the Fatherland,' later 'For the Motherland and Stalin'! And what's happening now? Is it 'For the Motherland and the President,' or for 'the Motherland and Grachin'—it's disgusting."[14]

The question that such a view of the war poses, however, is why, then, would anyone agree to fight? As a reporter once wrote, after hearing what Russian soldiers thought about the war in 1994: "What sane man is going to risk having his legs torn off and his guts ripped out for the Mafia without even being paid for it?"[15] The answer, not surprisingly, is that soldiers are moved by a sense of war camaraderie; each fatality becomes a reason to commit oneself more deeply. The affective, emotional bonds between combatants thus supply a reason to fight, even when it is painfully clear that the war serves only corrupt interests. What is striking about Mironov, and what makes him so revealing, is his ability to think two contradictory thoughts at once: yes, the war is designed to line the pockets of the Mafia, but yes, the Russian soldier has a "spiritual glory" *(velichie dukha russkogo soldata)*,[16] and that "glory" is really what's at stake in the conflict. Undoubtedly, vengeance is one of the most common experiences on the battlefield, and the thirst for vengeance is one of the most pervasive motives in the mayhem of war. What singles out the Chechen conflict, on the other hand, is that it is not tethered to, or situated within, any encompassing vision of larger reasons for war. Mironov knows that he is prosecuting a cynical, unjust war waged solely for the profit motive. And so ideas of comradeship and vengeance for fallen comrades get inflated into the sole, driving force behind soldiers' willingness to fight. But how do such ideas become sufficient reason for the soldier to fight?

The first point is that, for Mironov, the spiritual glory of the Russian soldier is rigorously confined to ethnic Russians: it does not include all soldiers of the Russian Federation. Russia has ceased to be a political category and has become a purely ethnic one. Mironov likes to describe his comrades-in-arms as "Brother Slavs" *(bratishki slaviane),* a term favored by nineteenth-century Pan-Slavists, but, unlike them, Mironov uses the term to exclude all non-Russian national groups, even other Slavs! He ties his participation in the war and his patriotic statement directly to his ethnicity: he loves Russia because he is Russian and not "a gypsy, not a Jew, nor any kind of nomad." Indeed, for Mironov, being Russian is a physical property, a blood-tie. He even identifies corpses by their "Slavic" (Russian) or non-Russian look: "A couple of corpses. According to their shapes, they look like our guys—Slavs." Mironov can identify even a totally mangled and crushed body as belonging to a Russian or a Chechen: "I look down and see the remains of a 'ghost.' No less than a hundred people have already walked over him . . . There is something sticky and slippery under my feet. Was this a human being? No, this was a 'ghost.' No need for discussion."[17]

In Mironov's eyes, being a Slav also carries certain undefined moral characteristics. When a group of Russian soldiers senselessly hoard crudely counterfeited dollars from a looted bank in Groznyi, Mironov, disgusted by their behavior, denies them a place in the Slavic brotherhood: "No, these are not my brother Slavs," he exclaims.[18] Identity, then—the fighting soldier's identity—is based on racial background: the soldier fights because of his comrades, and they are comrades because they share a common blood heritage. This definition denies more complex cultural means of establishing identity and roots it instead in something essentially irrational. It is a return to the primitive. But there is something more: as Mironov's memoirs also make clear, this quest for identity is blatantly opportunistic and feeds parasitically off of any image of power it finds. Despite the alleged racial exclusivity, Mironov appropriates cultural traits and stereotypes belonging to entirely different national groups. It is as though culture were an enormous trash heap, and the identity-seeker were picking his way through it. Identity turns out to be a kind of "bricolage" (to invoke Levi-Strauss)—but a sinister and deeply unscrupulous version of it. I am tempted to speak of "identity theft"—availing oneself of the prerogatives and meaningfulness of another's identity.

To cite the most striking instance, Mironov recurrently invokes Nazi Germany—one of Soviet Russia's deadliest enemies—as the model for Russia in the war in Chechnya. This identification might seem only too appropriate, since Russians might well be seen as criminal aggressors. But Mironov does not mean to criticize the Russian effort by invoking the Nazis. To the contrary, he uses them as an image to praise Russia's own ruthless power. The destruction of Groznyi, in particular, prompts Mironov to identify himself with the Germans. "We will show them Stalingrad!" he exclaims, while observing how much the Russian troops have already destroyed and how much they are prepared to destroy. German might is appropriated to express Russian might: "Aha, we got you ugly bastards. Now we will show you Kristallnacht."[19] Mironov's identification with the Nazis goes beyond mere rhetoric. Mironov proudly trumpets the SS-type cruelties now perpetrated by the Russian military. He revels in gruesome details of torture the Russian military inflicts on captured enemy fighters—for example, taking the enamel off their teeth with a file, electrocuting them with telephone wire, or shooting off a prisoner's toes one by one.[20] To be sure, the Nazis did not have a monopoly on brutality. We need look no further than Stalin's camps. Nonetheless, the idea of unthinkably sadistic cruelty is undoubtedly linked, in the Russian imagination, to the Nazis.

Mironov also appropriates characteristically "Chechen" motives for his comrades. Russia, he writes, is fighting in Chechnya because of a blood-feud: Russia is seeking vengeance. "Here in Chechnya we do nothing but vengeance. We avenge our fallen friends or the Russians who were killed in Chechnya."[21] Mironov appropriates a traditional Chechen judicial custom—and seriously distorts it. The Chechen practice of blood vengeance was in fact highly regulated by tribal rules.[22] In other words, a Chechen practice has been warped and hijacked to explain why Russian boys are fighting Chechen "ghosts."[23] Mironov seems oddly clear about what he is doing—appropriating cultural images from the enemy for his own purposes. He writes of the Chechens: "Everybody who could bear arms or who could think more or less clearly joined the guerrillas—for the sake of revenge. Well, we too will have our revenge."[24] Mironov, then, sees that he is taking an ideological image of the Chechens and applying it to himself and his comrades.

Notably, however, vengeance is the rallying cry of people who see themselves as victims and who want to redress the wrongs they have been made to suffer. By invoking vengeance, Mironov casts the Russians in the role of those who have had to endure injustice. It is worth pointing out in this regard that a small state the size of Chechnya is overwhelmingly outclassed by Russia. Yet this enormous disparity in size and power has done nothing to inhibit myth-formation whereby Russians feel themselves threatened by their enemy to the south. Mironov uses images of both power and of powerlessness, of iron might and injured grievance. This may be unprincipled and incoherent, but not unprecedented. Germans during the Third Reich learned to see themselves as victims of a supposed Jewish conspiracy and, at the same time, as the master race. The combination was potent: an entire nation was led to participate in the murder of millions of people. Similarly, Mironov's insistence on his power joins hands with his emphasis on his own and his comrades' victimization by the Chechens. Soldiers not sent into battle during the siege of Groznyi, he writes, wept and yearned to wreak vengeance for their comrades.[25] Comradeship and vengeance are powerful tools, and serve to justify atrocities committed by Russians in Chechnya. "Atrocities" are political; they are violent deeds looked at objectively. Vengeance, however, is personal, and imbued with a compelling sense of right. As Mironov's memoirs make only too clear, personal vendetta can be inflated into the sole reason for fighting, taking over the role usually played by there being some objective reason for fighting—or at least some claim of an objective reason. When Mironov describes an imaginary conversation with a Chechen fighter, his thirst for revenge is entirely personal: "Why did you, scum, shoot at the Russians? Only wait, you bastards and bitches, we will show you no mercy now—there will be no mercy either for the old, or for children, or women."[26]

Vengeance, then, is forced to bear an enormous weight, because it has to do the work normally performed by the conviction that the war makes some larger sense. The idea that Russians are victims of Chechen aggression has come to pervade contemporary Russian culture. Vanora Bennett describes numerous conversations with ordinary Russians who see themselves as vulnerable to the Chechen aggression.[27] The same idea may be found in any number of cheap books and songs. Dmitrii Solov'ev, for example, a former soldier who posts his work on the Internet, in his autobiographical story "Slope" ("Sklon") writes of his wish, as a soldier, to have his revenge on the Chechens: "I wished to become an atomic bomb to be dropped on the center of Groznyi so that I could burn them with my hatred, burn their skin, burn their flesh and listen to their screams . . ."[28] Lev Puchkov, another former soldier, has written an action novel set in Chechnya entitled, significantly, *The Blood Avenger (Krovnik)*.[29] In it, a husband searches for his lost wife and, in the process, wages war against the entire Chechen people. Popular Russian songs about Chechnya, too, emphasize the thirst for revenge:

Rebiata, chechenskim ubliudkam
Dolzhny my teper' otomstit'
Za shturmana Sashku, za Grishku, za Pashku
Inache ne smozhem my zhit'.[30]

[Guys, we now must take our revenge on the Chechen scum. And avenge the death of Sashka the navigator, of Grishka, and Pashka; otherwise we will not be able to live.]

This is a song about a young and innocent Russian pilot killed by a Chechen anti-aircraft rocket. But the song is also quite specific about the nature of the pilot's mission: he was delivering rockets to kill "the black mugs" *(chernorozhie)* in the mountain district of Vedeno. (And, in fact, the Russian army completely destroyed this district from the air.) Once the pilot is killed, his friend vows to avenge his death:

My plavno idem na snizhen'e,
K sebe priblizhaia polia.
Privet chernorozhym, my vas
Unichtozhim raketami "vozdukh-zemlia"

[We are descending smoothly bringing the fields closer. Greetings, you black mugs, we will annihilate you with "air-to-land" rockets.]

What draws one's immediate attention is that the song lyric is very clear about the offensive nature of Russia's invasion of Chechnya, even as it sentimentally insists on the victimization of pure-blooded Russian boys by the "Checks." This is not simply a case of trashy novels and cheap sentiments. The notion of "blood revenge" has even entered the Russian judicial system as a legitimate excuse for murder. A Russian court recently acquitted a certain Colonel Budanov of charges of kidnapping, raping, sodomizing, and strangling a Chechen teenage girl. The reason for acquittal was his temporary insanity, triggered by his thirst to avenge the deaths of his comrades shot by a Chechen sniper.[31]

To conclude, Russia's genocidal war against the tiny republic of Chechnya satisfies a deep need among many people who see themselves in essentially mythic and irrational terms, as a victimized ethnic group fighting against all odds to defeat a threat to their continued existence. This mythical image is a powerfully resonant one, despite the fact that it flies in the face of historical fact. It has licensed a brutal and immoral war and seems to justify all acts of destruction or sadism, no matter how degraded. It also affords an illuminating, cautionary example of the deep and broad-based need for cultural identity and the brutality that such a need, when frustrated, can unleash.

Notes

1 Norman M. Naimark, *Fires of Hatred: Ethnic Cleansing in Twentieth-Century Europe* (Cambridge, Mass.: Harvard University Press, 2000), 3–10; Charles Taylor, "Nationalism and Modernity," in *Theorizing Nationalism,* ed. Ronald Beiner (Albany: State University of New York Press, 1999), 55–67; Benedict Anderson, *Imagined Communities: Reflections on the Origin and Spread of Nationalism* (London: Verso, 1991); Michael Ignatieff, *Blood and Belonging* (Princeton, N.J.: Princeton University Press, 1993), 91–102.

2. Gennadii Troshev, *Moia voina* (Moscow: Vagrius, 2001); Viacheslav Mironov, *Ia byl na etoi voine* (Moscow: Biblion-Russkaia Kniga, 2001). I quote from the Internet edition: The Art of War, http://artofwar.ru/m/mironow_w_n/text_0010.shtml. Accessed 10 Aug. 2007. All translations are mine.

3. Shari J. Cohen addresses the lack of shared understanding of the past and the rise of "historyless" elite in post-Communist Eastern Europe in *Politics without a Past: The Absence of History in Postcommunist Nationalism* (Durham, N.C.: Duke University Press, 1999), 7–57.

4. Troshev, *Moia voina,* 7.

5. Mikhailov also speaks of defending Russia's "integrity": "Based on its constitution, Russia strove to preserve the integrity of its territory and borders" (*Chechenskoe Koleso: General FSB svidetel'stvuet* [Moscow: KS, 2002], 91).

6. Vanora Bennet, *Crying Wolf: The Return of the War to Chechnya* (London: Pan, 2001), 10–18, 40–41, 85–86, 305, 345.

7. Harsha Ram, *Prisoners of the Caucasus: Literary Myths and Media Representations of the Chechen Conflict* (Berkeley: University of California Press, 1999), 3–20.

8. Troshev, *Moia voina,* 39.

9. Ibid., 77.

10. The Human Rights Group "Memorial" has published a number of investigations of massacres committed by Russian troops in "liberated" towns in Chechnya. See, for example, *Vsemi imeiushchimisia sredstvami . . . Operatsiia MVD RF v sele Samashki 7–8 aprelia 1995 g. Rezul'taty nezavisimogo rassledovaniia nabliudatel'noi missii pravozashchitnykh organizatsii v zone vooruzhennogo konflikta v Chechne* (Moscow: Pravozashchitnyi Tsentr "Memorial," 1995); *Zachistka. Poselok Novye Aldy, 5 fevralia 2000g. Prednamerennye prestupleniia protiv mirnogo naseleniia* (Moscow: Zven'ia, 2000). A number of foreign and Russian journalists who have visited Chechnya in recent years have described heinous crimes routinely committed by the troops against the civilian population. See El'vira Goriukhina, *Puteshestvie uchitel'nitsy na Kavkaz* (Moscow: Teksty, 2001); Ann Nevat,

Chienne de Guerre: A Woman Reporter behind the Lines of the War in Chechnya (New York: Public Affairs, 2001); Anna Politkovskaia, *The Dirty War: A Russian Reporter in Chechnya* (London: Harvill, 2001).

11. Troshev, *Moia voina*, 60, 352, 7, 134.

12. Mironov, *Ia byl na etoi voine*, 13.

13. Anatol Lieven, *Chechnya: Tombstone of Russian Power* (New Haven, Conn.: Yale University Press, 1998), 213.

14. Mironov, *Ia byl na etoi voine*, 73. In his memoirs, Mironov changed slightly the names of public figures. The name Grachin alludes to Pavel Grachev, defense minister in Boris Yeltsin's government.

15. Lieven, *Chechnya*, 203.

16. Mironov, *Ia byl na etoi voine*, 28.

17. Ibid., 73, 2, 138.

18. Ibid., 106.

19. Ibid., 72. Kristallnacht, or "The Night of Broken Glass," was a Nazi pogrom directed against Jews and conducted throughout Germany and Austria on November 9 and 10, 1938. Hundreds of synagogues were destroyed and burned, shop windows of Jewish-owned businesses were shattered and the stores were looted. In many instances, Jews were physically attacked. About thirty thousand Jews were arrested and sent to concentration camps.

20. Mironov, *Ia byl na etoi voine*, 7.

21. Ibid., 52.

22. V. O. Bobrovnikov, *Musul'mane Severnogo Kavkaza: Obychai, pravo, nasilie* (Moscow: Vostochnaia literatura, 2002), 54–60. Bobrovnikov explains that blood revenge was a custom highly regulated by the traditional judicial systems of the community. Usually a system of monetary compensation prevented murder as an act of revenge. Revenge killing aimed directly at the offender, and it was rare for the act of revenge to be transferred to another male member of the family.

23. In his book about Russian General Lev Rokhlin, Andrei Antipov writes about the notorious Chechen thirst for vengeance (*Lev Rokhlin: Zhizn' i smert' generala* [Moscow: Express, 1998], 12).

24. Mironov, *Ia byl na etoi voine*, 13.

25. Ibid., 28.

26. Ibid., 12.

27. Bennett, *Crying Wolf*, 203.

28. Dmitrii Solov'ev, "Sklon," Art of War, http://artofwar.ru/s/solowxew_d/. Accessed 10 Aug. 2007.

29. Lev Puchkov, *Krovnik* (Moscow: Eksmo Press, 1999).

30. The author is unknown. Song cited from Biblioteka Maksima Moshkova, "Pesni chechenskoi voiny," http://www.lib.ru/KSP/afgan/chechnya.txt. Accessed 10 Aug. 2007.

31. For details about the Budanov case, see Anna Politkovskaia, "Delo Budanova," *Novaia gazeta*, 23 May, 2002.

Contributors

ANNA BRODSKY is associate professor of Russian at Washington and Lee University. She has written extensively on Russian twentieth-century fiction, and especially on the literature of Russian Modernism and post-Communist Russian literature. She is the author of articles on Nabokov, Sokolov, and Petrushevskaia. Her research interests also include issues related to the war in Chechnya.

DANIEL BROWER, deceased, was professor of history at the University of California, Davis. His research interests included modern Russian history and modern world history. He is the author of *Turkestan and the Fate of the Russian Empire* (2003), *Russia's Orient: Imperial Borderlands and Peoples, 1700–1914* (with Edward Lazzerini, 1997), *The World in the Twentieth Century: From Empires to Nations* (2002), *Training the Nihilists: Education and Radicalism in Tsarist Russia* (1975), and other books.

NINA EFIMOV is associate professor of Russian at Florida State University. She is the author of *Intertekst v religioznykh i demonicheskikh motivakh V. P. Aksenova* (1993). She has written extensively about the work of Vasilii Aksenov. Her other research interests include Soviet dissident literature, contemporary women's writing, and twentieth-century Russian fiction.

ANNA GEIFMAN is professor of history at Boston University. She is the author of *Thou Shalt Kill: Revolutionary Terrorism in Russia, 1894–1917* (1993), *Entangled in Terror: The Azef Affair and the Russian Revolution* (2000), and *La Mort sera votre dieu: Du nihilisme russe au terrorisme islamiste* (2005). She is also the editor of *Russia under the Last Tsar: Opposition and Subversion, 1894–1917* (1999). She has authored a number of journal articles and book chapters on Russian political and cultural history. She is currently working on "Psychohistory of Russian Revolution," a volume addressing the psychology of political violence.

J. ARCH GETTY is professor of history at UCLA. He is the author of *Origins of the Great Purges, The Soviet Communist Party 1933–1939*, and (with Oleg Naumov) *Road to Terror: Stalin and the Self-Destruction of the Bolsheviks, 1932–1939*.

He served as editor of the first catalog of the archives of the former Soviet Communist Party, where he conducts research on the history of the Soviet Communist Party in the Stalin period.

JAMES FRANK GOODWIN is assistant professor of Russian at the University of Florida. He is writing a book on the legacy of Bakuninism in twentieth-century Russia.

CHARLES J. HALPERIN received his doctorate in history from Columbia University in 1973, under the direction of Michael Cherniavsky. He is the author of *Russia and the Golden Horde* (1985) and *The Tatar Yoke* (1985). He is currently an independent scholar, and researching a monograph on Ivan the Terrible.

BRIAN HOROWITZ is Sizeler Family Chair Professor at Tulane University and director of the Jewish studies program. In addition to many articles on Russian thinkers, he is finishing a book on the Society for the Promotion of Enlightenment among the Jews of Russia, 1863–1914.

NATASHA KOLCHEVSKA is professor of Russian and chair of the Department of Foreign Languages and Literatures at the University of New Mexico. She is the translator and editor of Sofie Kovalevskaia's *Nihilist Girl* (2002). She has also written numerous articles on Evgeniia Ginsburg and on women's autobiographical writings.

ELENA KRASNOSTCHEKOVA is professor of Russian literature at the University of Georgia, Athens. She is the author of books and articles on Russian nineteenth- and twentieth-century literature.

BORIS LANIN is Head of Literary Studies at Russian Academy of Education and professor of semiotics at State Tax Academy in Moscow. He worked as visiting professor and senior research fellow at Kennan Institute (Washington, D.C.), Hokkaido University (Japan), University of Bath (U.K.), and Central European University (Budapest). He is the author of *The Eve of Postmodernism: Russian Teaching and Studying Literature Prose in 1960–1980* (2004, with D. Gillespie), *The Prose of the Third Wave* (1997), and other books.

RONALD D. LEBLANC is professor of Russian and humanities at the University of New Hampshire and research associate at the Davis Center for Russian and Eurasian Studies at Harvard University. He is the author of *The Russianization of Gil Blas: A Study in Literary Appropriation* (1986) and numerous articles on nineteenth- and twentieth-century Russian literature. He is currently completing a book project, "Slavic Sins of the Flesh: Food, Sex, and Carnal Appetite in Nineteenth-Century Russian Fiction," which examines how a number of nineteenth-century Russian writers represent the act of eating as a trope for male sexual desire.

MARCUS C. LEVITT is associate professor of Russian at the University of Southern California. He is the author of *Russian Literary Politics and the Pushkin*

Celebration of 1880 (1989) and editor of *Early Modern Russian Writers, Late Seventeenth and Eighteenth Centuries (Dictionary of Literary Biography*, vol. 150, 1995). He has written many articles on eighteenth- and nineteenth-century Russian literature, and is currently completing a book entitled "Making Russia Visible: The Visual Dominant in Eighteenth-Century Russian Literature and Culture."

MARK LIPOVETSKY is associate professor of Russian studies and comparative literature at the University of Colorado, Boulder. He is the author of *Russian Postmodernist Fiction: Dialogue with Chaos* (1999), along with four other books and numerous articles on contemporary Russian literature and culture. He coedited (with M. Balina) *Russian Writers since 1980* (*Dictionary of Literary Biography*, vol. 285, 2004) and coauthored (with N. Leiderman) *Modern Russian Literature, 1950s–1990s* (2003, 2005). He also coedited (with M. Balina and H. Goscilo) *Politicizing Magic: An Anthology of Russian and Soviet Wondertales* (2005).

JULIAN MOSS earned his B.A. and Ph.D. in Russian language and literature from the University of Birmingham, England. He was a language tutor then lecturer in Russian in the Center for Russian and East European Studies (CREES) at Birmingham. He now works in the Academic Registrar's Office of the University of Warwick, England.

HARRIET MURAV is professor of Russian and chair of the Department of Slavic Languages and Literatures at the University of Illinois at Urbana-Champaign. She is the author of *Holy Foolishness: Dostoevsky's Novels and the Poetics of Cultural Critique* (1992), *Russia's Legal Fictions* (1998), *Identity Theft: The Jew in Imperial Russia and the Case of Avraam Uri Kovner* (2003), and has received a Guggenheim Fellowship for her current project on Soviet Yiddish and Russian-Jewish literature of the twentieth century.

TATYANA NOVIKOV is professor of Russian and Ralph Wardle Chair in the Arts and Sciences at the University of Nebraska, Omaha. She is the author of numerous articles on Russian Symbolist poetry, contemporary Russian women's fiction, Russian satirical writing, and the utopian/anti-utopian literary tradition.

VICTOR PEPPARD is professor of Russian at the University of South Florida, Tampa. He has written extensively about Russian literature and the history of Russian and Soviet sport. He is the author of *The Poetics of Yury Olesha* (1989) and *Playing Politics: Soviet Sport Diplomacy to 1992* (with James Riordan, 1993). Currently he is chair of World Languages, College of Arts and Sciences, University of South Florida.

MAUREEN PERRIE is emeritus professor of Russian history in the Centre for Russian and East European Studies, University of Birmingham, England. Her books include *The Agrarian Policy of the Russian Socialist-Revolutionary Party* (1976), *The Image of Ivan the Terrible in Russian Folklore* (1987), *Pretenders and Popular Monarchism in Early Modern Russia* (1995), *The Cult of Ivan the Terrible in Stalin's Russia* (2001), and (with Andrei Pavlov) *Ivan the Terrible* (2003). She has edited the first (pre-Petrine) volume of the three-volume *Cambridge History of Russia* (2006). From 2001 to 2004 she was president of the British Association for Slavonic and East European Studies.

NADYA PETERSON is an associate professor of Russian literature at Hunter College of the City University of New York. Her professional interests include Russian women writers, Russian literature of the Soviet period, Chekhov, and Russian education.

KEVIN M. F. PLATT is associate professor and chair of the Department of Slavic Languages and Literatures at the University of Pennsylvania. He is the author of *History in a Grotesque Key: Russian Literature and the Idea of Revolution* (1997) as well as articles on Russian history and literature. He is currently completing a manuscript entitled "Ivan, Peter, Russia: Nation (A Cultural Historiography)."

TERESA L. POLOWY is associate professor of Russian and head of the Department of Russian and Slavic Studies at the University of Arizona in Tucson. She is the author of *The Novellas of Valentin Rasputin: Genre, Language, and Style* (1989) as well as articles on contemporary Russian women's writing, twentieth-century Russian literature, cultural studies, and the problem of alcoholism in Russian literature.

DAVID POWELSTOCK is assistant professor of Russian and East European literatures and chair of the Program in Russian and East European Studies at Brandeis University. He is the author of *Becoming Mikhail Lermontov: The Ironies of Romantic Individualism in Nicholas I's Russia* (2005) as well as articles on Lermontov, Pushkin, Bakhtin, and Olesha. He has also translated poetry and prose from the Czech and Russian.

ELIZABETH SKOMP is visiting assistant professor of Russian at Sewanee, the University of the South. Her research interests include contemporary Russian women's writing and the motif of motherhood in contemporary Russian fiction.

LUDMILLA A. TRIGOS received her Ph.D. in Russian literature from Columbia University. She has taught at Barnard College and Columbia, New York, and Drew universities. She is currently an independent scholar and is completing her book, "Ardent Dreamers in the Land of Eternal Frost: The Decembrist Myth in Russian Culture."

ELENA VASSILEVA is a doctoral candidate at the University of Southern California. Her research interests include Soviet cinema, film theory, gender studies, nationalism, and postcolonial theory.

ILYA VINITSKY is assistant professor of Russian literature at the University of Pennsylvania. His research interests include Russian and European

Romanticism and eighteenth- and nineteenth-century Russian intellectual culture. He is the author of *The Pleasures of Melancholy* (1997; in Russian) and *The Interpreter's House: Vasily Zhukovsky's Historical Imagination* (2006; in Russian).

Index

www.ingramcontent.com/pod-product-compliance
Lightning Source LLC
Chambersburg PA
CBHW070639310726
48982CB00001B/340
* 9 7 8 0 2 9 9 2 2 4 3 0 1 *